Dictatorship in History and T...

BONAPARTISM, CAESARISM, AND TOTALITA...

This book is unusual in bringing together the work of historians and political theorists under one cover to consider the subject of nineteenth- and twentieth-century dictatorships. A distinguished group of authors examine the complex relationship among nineteenth-century democracy, nationalism, and authoritarianism, paying special attention to the careers of Napoleon I and III and of Bismarck. An important contribution of the book is consideration not only of the momentous episodes of coup d'état, revolution, and imperial foundation that the Napoleonic era heralded, but also the contested political language with which these events were described and assessed. Political thinkers were faced with a battery of new terms – "Bonapartism," "Caesarism," and "Imperialism" among them – with which to make sense of their era.

In addition to documenting the political history of a revolutionary age, the book examines a series of thinkers – Tocqueville, Marx, Max Weber, Antonio Gramsci, Carl Schmitt, and Hannah Arendt – who articulated and helped to reshape our sense of the political.

Peter Baehr is Professor of Political Sociology at Lingnan University. His books include *Founders, Classics, Canons* (2002) and *Caesar and the Fading of the Roman World* (1998). He is the editor of *The Portable Hannah Arendt* (2000) and co-editor, with Gordon Wells, of *The Protestant Ethic and the "Spirit" of Capitalism and Other Writings* (2002) and *Max Weber* (1995).

Melvin Richter is Professor Emeritus of Political Science at the City University of New York, Graduate Center, and Hunter College. He is the author of *The History of Political and Social Concepts* (1995), the editor of *The Political Theory of Montesquieu* (Cambridge, 1977), and co-editor, with Hartmut Lehmann, of *The Meaning of Historical Terms and Concepts* (1996).

PUBLICATIONS OF THE GERMAN HISTORICAL INSTITUTE
WASHINGTON, D.C.

Edited by Christof Mauch
with the assistance of David Lazar

The German Historical Institute is a center for advanced study and research whose purpose is to provide a permanent basis for scholarly cooperation among historians from the Federal Republic of Germany and the United States. The Institute conducts, promotes, and supports research into both American and German political, social, economic, and cultural history; into transatlantic migration, especially in the nineteenth and twentieth centuries; and into the history of international relations, with special emphasis on the roles played by the United States and Germany.

Recent books in the series

Norbert Finzsch and Dietmar Schirmer, editors, *Identity and Intolerance: Nationalism, Racism, and Xenophobia in Germany and the United States*

Susan Strasser, Charles McGovern, and Matthias Judt, editors, *Getting and Spending: European and American Consumer Societies in the Twentieth Century*

Carole Fink, Philipp Gassert, and Detlef Junker, editors, *1968: The World Transformed*

Roger Chickering and Stig Förster, editors, *Great War, Total War: Combat and Mobilization on the Western Front*

Manfred F. Boemeke, Gerald D. Feldman, and Elisabeth Glaser, editors, *The Treaty of Versailles: A Reassessment After 75 Years*

Manfred Berg and Martin H. Geyer, editors, *Two Cultures of Rights: The Quest for Inclusion and Participation in Modern America and Germany*

Manfred F. Boemeke, Roger Chickering, and Stig Förster, editors, *Anticipating Total War: The German and American Experiences, 1871–1914*

Roger Chickering and Stig Förster, editors, *The Shadows of Total War: Europe, East Asia, and the United States, 1919–1939*

Elisabeth Glaser and Hermann Wellenreuther, editors, *Bridging the Atlantic: The Question of American Exceptionalism in Perspective*

Dictatorship in History and Theory

BONAPARTISM, CAESARISM, AND TOTALITARIANISM

Edited by
PETER BAEHR
Lingnan University, Hong Kong

MELVIN RICHTER
City University of New York

GERMAN HISTORICAL INSTITUTE
Washington, D.C.
and

PUBLISHED BY THE PRESS SYNDICATE OF THE UNIVERSITY OF CAMBRIDGE
The Pitt Building, Trumpington Street, Cambridge, United Kingdom

CAMBRIDGE UNIVERSITY PRESS
The Edinburgh Building, Cambridge CB2 2RU, UK
40 West 20th Street, New York, NY 10011-4211, USA
477 Williamstown Road, Port Melbourne, VIC 3207, Australia
Ruiz de Alarcón 13, 28014 Madrid, Spain
Dock House, The Waterfront, Cape Town 8001, South Africa

http://www.cambridge.org

© German Historical Institute 2004

This book is in copyright. Subject to statutory exception
and to the provisions of relevant collective licensing agreements,
no reproduction of any part may take place without
the written permission of Cambridge University Press.

First published 2004

Printed in the United States of America

Typeface Bembo 10/13 pt.   *System* LaTeX 2_ε [TB]

A catalog record for this book is available from the British Library.

Library of Congress Cataloging in Publication Data

Dictatorship in history and theory : Bonapartism, Caesarism, and totalitarianism / edited by
Peter Baehr, Melvin Richter.
p. cm.
Some articles previously presented at the Hunter College conference, 1999.
Includes bibliographical references and index.
ISBN 0-521-82563-6 (hc) – ISBN 0-521-53270-1 (pbk.)
1. Dictatorship – History.   2. Dictatorship – Europe – History.   3. Authoritarianism – History.
4. Authoritarianism – Europe – History.   I. Baehr, P. R. (Peter R.)   II. Richter, Melvin, 1921–
JC495.D483   2004
321.9–dc21   2003051238

ISBN 0 521 82563 6 hardback
ISBN 0 521 53270 1 paperback

Contents

Contributors		page ix
Preface		xi
	Introduction *Peter Baehr and Melvin Richter*	1

PART I. BONAPARTISM TO ITS CONTEMPORARIES

1	From Consulate to Empire: Impetus and Resistance *Isser Woloch*	29
2	The Bonapartes and Germany *T. C. W. Blanning*	53
3	Prussian Conservatives and the Problem of Bonapartism *David E. Barclay*	67
4	Tocqueville and French Nineteenth-Century Conceptualizations of the Two Bonapartes and Their Empires *Melvin Richter*	83
5	Marx's *Eighteenth Brumaire of Louis Bonaparte*: Democracy, Dictatorship, and the Politics of Class Struggle *Terrell Carver*	103
6	Bonapartism as the Progenitor of Democracy: The Paradoxical Case of the French Second Empire *Sudhir Hazareesingh*	129

PART II. BONAPARTISM, CAESARISM, TOTALITARIANISM:
TWENTIETH-CENTURY EXPERIENCES AND REFLECTIONS

7	Max Weber and the Avatars of Caesarism *Peter Baehr*	155
8	The Concept of Caesarism in Gramsci *Benedetto Fontana*	175

9	From Constitutional Technique to Caesarist Ploy: Carl Schmitt on Dictatorship, Liberalism, and Emergency Powers *John P. McCormick*	197
10	Bonapartist and Gaullist Heroic Leadership: Comparing Crisis Appeals to an Impersonated People *Jack Hayward*	221
11	The Leader and the Masses: Hannah Arendt on Totalitarianism and Dictatorship *Margaret Canovan*	241

PART III. ANCIENT RESONANCES

12	Dictatorship in Rome *Claude Nicolet*	263
13	From the Historical Caesar to the Spectre of Caesarism: The Imperial Administrator as Internal Threat *Arthur M. Eckstein*	279
Index		299

Contributors

Peter Baehr, Professor of Political Sociology, Lingnan University, Hong Kong

David E. Barclay, Margaret and Roger Scholten Professor of International Studies, Department of History, Kalamazoo College, Michigan

T. C. W. Blanning, Professor of Modern European History, Cambridge University

Margaret Canovan, Professor of Political Thought, University of Keele, Keele

Terrell Carver, Professor of Political Theory, University of Bristol, Bristol

Arthur M. Eckstein, Professor of History, University of Maryland, College Park

Benedetto Fontana, Assistant Professor of Political Science, Baruch College, CUNY, New York

Jack Hayward, Emeritus Professor, Oxford University; Research Professor, Hull University

Sudhir Hazareesingh, Tutor in Politics, Balliol College, Oxford

John P. McCormick, Associate Professor of Political Science, University of Chicago, Chicago

Claude Nicolet, Professeur honoraire à la Sorbonne et à l'École pratique des hautes études, Paris

Melvin Richter, Emeritus Professor of Political Science, City University of New York, Graduate Center, and Hunter College

Isser Woloch, Moore Collegiate Professor of History, Columbia University, New York

Preface

Between April 9 and April 11, 1999, Hunter College of the City University of New York hosted a conference to mark the bicentenary of Napoleon Bonaparte's coup d'état. Organized by Melvin Richter, with help from Isser Woloch and Peter Baehr, and generously co-sponsored by the German Historical Institute, Washington, D.C., the event constituted the International Meeting of the Conference for the Study of Political Thought.

With the exception of the contributions by Margaret Canovan, Terrell Carver, Sudhir Hazareesingh, and Claude Nicolet, the chapters of this book comprise amended versions of papers delivered at the Hunter College conference. The organizers owe a great debt of gratitude to Detlef Junker, then the director of the GHI, and to the staff of the GHI, especially Raimund Lammersdorf, without whom the meeting would never have taken place. Thanks are also due to those who participated in the conference, usually in the roles of chair or commentator, but whose remarks do not appear in this volume: Andrew Arato, Jean Cohen, David Kettler, Jerzy Linderski, J. G. A. Pocock, Martyn Thompson, Charles Tilly, Cheryl Welch, Wolfgang Wippermann, Wulf Wülfing, Bernard Yack, and Zwi Yavetz.

This book is dedicated, in memoriam, to the greatly missed François Furet (1927–1997).

Introduction

PETER BAEHR AND MELVIN RICHTER

I

This book was occasioned by a conference noting the bicentenary of Napoleon Bonaparte's coup d'état of the Eighteenth Brumaire (November 9), 1799. At that time no one could have imagined that this nearly botched seizure of power would put an end to the First Republic, lead to the Consulate and First Empire, and thus alter the course of European and world history.[1] Often taken to be the squalid end to the great revolution begun in 1789, this first coup of Napoleon Bonaparte's served as the precedent for a second in December 1851 by his nephew, Louis Napoleon. Then another Bonaparte terminated another great revolution, that of 1848, by replacing the Second Republic with his own empire.

What was the significance of these ostensibly repetitive sequences: a major revolution against a relatively mild monarchy, overthrow by force of the successor republican government, and the creation of an empire much more repressive than the monarchy prior to its republican predecessor? After 1851, many acute analysts of European politics concurred in the judgment that, taken together, these events constituted a qualitatively new phenomenon, a type of rule at once growing out of the French revolutions and a reaction against them.

Such a government could be said, varying with the allegiance of the analyst, to presuppose not only the preeminence of the military, but also manhood suffrage, centralized bureaucracy, conscription, appeals for sacrifice in the name of the nation, mobilization for conquest abroad. Or else this regime could be described sometimes as serving the purposes of

---

1 Previous accounts of the coup and its aftermath have been superseded by the first chapter of Isser Woloch's *Napoleon and his Collaborators* (New York, 2001), 3–35.

counterrevolution, sometimes as rule by a dominating class and church. On both the right and left, connections were alleged between "dictatorship" and democracy, defined either generically (by its liberal or reactionary opponents) or in its bourgeois form (as by Marx). Elaborate theories were evolved to explain how powerful leaders could claim to be democratic at the same time that they interdicted popular participation in government. Appealing to "the masses" by manipulating opinion and the use of censorship, such rulers could claim democratic legitimacy because of their success in plebiscites. At the same time, they dominated "the masses" through a centralized state with police, military, and administrative controls at a level never before attained. Such characteristics could be made to fit into the diagnoses made by Marx and Engels in terms of class struggle and the exploitation of the proletariat by the bourgeoisie.

The implications of this putatively new type of government for future politics, for the state, society, and economy were to preoccupy practicing politicians as well as political and social theorists for the rest of the nineteenth century and well into the twentieth. Even those who believed that the two Bonapartes and their empires had created a uniquely modern post-revolutionary and post-democratic type of regime could not agree on what it should be called. Among the names most frequently given to it were "Bonapartism," "Napoleonism," "Imperialism," and "dictatorship," now greatly expanded from previous formulations limited to Roman republican emergency rule of limited duration.[2]

Against this view that a novel form of rule had been created by the two Bonapartes out of the French revolutions of 1789 and 1848, there arose another perspective that insisted upon the resemblances of the governments produced by these episodes to the regime Julius Caesar or, alternatively, Augustus had created out of the Roman Republic at its close. Those who argued such a view might either condemn or approve what they chose to call "Caesarism." Some of its supporters regarded it as the only possible authoritative response in their time to revolution, anarchy, and the crisis produced by the breakdown of both monarchical and republican institutions after 1789 and 1848. Others treated this phenomenon as a warning, as proof that democracy and the principles of the French Revolution – by

---

2 Careful treatments of the histories of all these terms as political and social concepts occur in the entries for "*Cäsarismus, Napoleonismus, Bonapartismus, Führer, Chef, Imperialismus*" by Dieter Groh and "*Diktatur*" by Ernst Nolte in *Geschichtliche Grundbegriffe*, eds. Otto Brunner, Werner Conze, and Reinhart Koselleck (9 vols.; Stuttgart, 1972–95), I, 726–71, 900–24. For brief histories in English of Bonapartism, Caesarism, and dictatorship, see the entries by Peter Baehr in *The Blackwell Dictionary of Twentieth-Century Social Thought*, eds. W. Outhwaite and T. Bottomore (Oxford, 1993).

giving power and legitimacy to the will of the masses – led ineluctably to Caesarism.³

With this verdict, Marx in part agreed, but for the most part dissented. Using a rhetorical formula that was to become famous, he denied the identity between the first and second Napoleons, their coups, and their empires. Yet he conceded that each Bonaparte in his time had achieved an extraordinary degree of control over France through further centralizing the French state. When Marx placed both empires within his general interpretation of history as class struggle, he explained bureaucratic centralization as the means indispensable to the French bourgeoisie in first breaking the power of the feudal aristocracy, and then establishing and maintaining bourgeois domination.

A number of the essays in this volume treat the history of these two coups, the contested descriptions and analyses of the empires they produced, and the no less disputed conceptualizations of them as a distinctive type of regime. During the second half of the nineteenth century, each version of these regime types played a prominent but very different part in the arguments employed in European political and social theories and ideologies. In an unstable context, where, as in France, revolution, counterrevolution, restoration, and imperial foundation occurred more than once, these regime types became what Reinhart Koselleck has called basic political concepts (*Grundbegriffe*):

As distinguished from concepts in general, a basic concept ... is an inescapable, irreplaceable part of the political and social vocabulary. ... Basic concepts ... become indispensable to any formulation of the most urgent issues of a given time. [T]hey are always both controversial and contested.⁴

What a regime was called and how it was characterized could not be matters of indifference to political actors, whether incumbents or contenders for power. Nor could their agents and intellectual supporters neglect counterarguments and alternative hostile descriptions. To establish convincing reasons for supporting any regime necessitated disestablishing the claim of its rivals; a positive position required negating that of its opponents. Persuasion entailed dissuasion; dissuasion, in turn, entailed denying, neutralizing, redefining, or redescribing competing regime types and principles. In such a situation,

---

3 See Peter Baehr, *Caesar and the Fading of the Roman World* (New Brunswick, NJ, 1998) for the nineteenth- and twentieth-century usages of the concept of Caesarism.
4 Reinhart Koselleck, "Response to Comments," in *The Meaning of Historical Terms and Concepts. New Studies on Begriffsgeschichte*, eds. Hartmut Lehmann and Melvin Richter (Washington, D.C., 1996), 64. For the context of this statement, which is a reply to J. G. A. Pocock, see Melvin Richter, "Opening a Dialogue and Recognizing an Achievement," *Archiv für Begriffsgeschichte*, 39 (1996), 19–26.

political theorists had to master more than the one set of terms they themselves preferred – for they could not ignore the audiences they addressed. Unless polemicists took notice of those concepts favored by their opponents, they could not successfully attack them and succeed in convincing their publics of the superiority of their own positions.[5]

Thus the title of this book is not meant to suggest that any of these competing regime forms – Bonapartism, Caesarism, and dictatorship – can be, or have ever been, uncontroversially used. Such contestation was no less true of names and concepts characterizing fascist and communist rule in the twentieth century than of the two Bonapartes and their regimes in the nineteenth. The present volume underlines the fundamental disagreements separating those who have described, sought to conceptualize, explain, and evaluate two of the most critical periods of the past two centuries. Several chapters stress the use of regime types in political argument, thus shifting attention away from the adequacy of such terms as descriptions of actual cases or examples.

In the 1920s and 1930s, the concepts of Bonapartism, Caesarism, and dictatorship were once again applied as regime types. At first, these were the names given to governments created by fascist movements that had overthrown representative democracies and replaced them with regimes more ideological and repressive than anything experienced in France during the nineteenth century. Although dictatorship came to be used more often than any other term to characterize such twentieth-century creations, its adequacy as an empirical classification was frequently called into question. This was because dictatorship was frequently, although not invariably, used as a positive self-characterization by fascist regimes. To be sure, much depended upon their ideologies. Hitler rejected the title of dictator in part because of its contemporary use by Marxist regimes and parties to justify the "dictatorship of the proletariat." He claimed, in contrast, to be the *Führer* of his racially pure people, a concept of leadership he alleged to be unique to organic Germanic thought. Hitler saw dictatorship, democracy, and the worldwide Jewish conspiracy (*Diktatur, Demokratie, Judentum*) everywhere.[6] All were inseparably linked and condemned in Nazi ideology. After World War II, the concept of totalitarianism, applied to both Nazi Germany and the Soviet Union, became similarly contested on both empirical and theoretical grounds. Because even the mention of totalitarianism has become so

---

5 This analysis is developed in Melvin Richter, "Toward a Concept of Political Illegitimacy," *Political Theory*, 10 (1982), 185–214.
6 Hitler, Speech of March 7, 1936, cited by Nolte, "*Diktatur*" in *Geschichtliche Grundbegriffe*, I, 922.

controverted, a recent book devoted to a sophisticated treatment of Stalinism and Nazism calls both regimes dictatorships. The editors of that book – Ian Kershaw and Moshe Lewin – apparently were searching for a neutral comparative term less controversial than "totalitarianism."[7]

The present volume, by contrast, is devoted in good measure precisely to the relentless controversy over political categories, controversy made urgent to both theorists and actors of the day by alarming (or at least surprising) contemporary political developments. Disputes about the nature, impact, and reception of the sequences connected with Napoleon and Louis Bonaparte assumed center stage. Both regimes provoked their share of admiration and hatred, of emulation and repulsion, or, in the case of Prussia, emulation out of repulsion. Both stamped France with administrative structures that long seemed indestructible. And both furnished images – heroic and demonic alike – of a regime type employed by subsequent political thinkers as a template against which political realities of their own time were to be measured.

But first of all the template itself had to be worked out, a task as unstable as its subject was protean. Practicing politicians such as Bismarck, theorists such as Tocqueville, Proudhon, Marx and Engels, Bagehot, Lorenz von Stein, Donoso Cortes, Jacob Burckhardt, and Max Weber – all sought to analyze, explain, and explore the implications for the future of this novel form of rule, at once post-revolutionary and post-democratic. In the second half of the nineteenth century and well into the twentieth, several issues separated those choosing one or another conceptualization of the Bonapartist or Caesarist phenomenon.

The first question was whether that phenomenon was distinctively French or whether it could occur elsewhere in Europe or the world. Some of the most detailed and most valuable modern historical studies of Bonapartism simply evade this historiographical question, even though it assumed major importance at the time. Frédéric Bluche, for instance, in both his brief and more extensive books, treats the subject from a purely French point of view.[8] Louis Bergeron's excellent volume not only shares Bluche's historical exceptionalism, or view of Bonapartism as a French *Sonderweg*, but passes judgment on the relation of the First Empire to the French revolution by his choice of title, *L'épisode napoléonien*.[9] Explanations in terms of national character, although seldom flattering, provide still another way of restricting

---

7 *Stalinism and Nazism: Dictatorships in Comparison*, eds. Ian Kershaw and Moshe Lewin (Cambridge, 1997).
8 Frédéric Bluche, *Le bonapartisme* (Paris, 1981) and *Le bonapartisme (1800–1850)* (Paris, 1980).
9 Louis Bergeron, *L'épisode napoléonien* (Paris, 1972).

this type of regime to France. In a passage combining his theory of national character with his dim view of democracy, Chateaubriand wrote:

[T]he French are instinctively attracted by power; they have no love for liberty; equality alone is their idol. Now equality and tyranny have secret connections. In these two respects, Napoleon had his fountain-head in the hearts of the French, militarily inclined toward power, democratically enamoured of a dead level. Mounting the throne, he seated the common people beside him; a proletarian king, he humiliated the kings and nobles.[10]

Second, was it feasible or credible to insert the two Bonapartist reigns into previous regime classifications, such as those of Aristotle, Polybius, or Montesquieu? Alternatively, was a new concept other than tyranny or despotism needed to designate the features of what many regarded as a distinctively modern phenomenon? Often this type of disagreement was phrased in terms of what Dieter Groh has called "the great parallel" between the termination of the Revolution and the history of how the Roman Republic came to its end at the hands of Julius Caesar or else of Augustus, who engineered the transition to the Principate. In the second German edition of *The Eighteenth Brumaire*, Marx attacked this kind of thematic juxtaposition and the term Caesarism associated with it. (See Terrell Carver's chapter in this volume.)

A third question concerns how much weight to attach to the military origins and character of the first Bonaparte, his and his nephew's use of the army in their respective seizures of power, and the pursuit of an aggressive foreign policy of conquest in the name of national glory. Here again, there is wide disagreement. Some historians of the First Empire insist that it was an unequivocally civil rather than a military dictatorship. Their argument has an authoritative precedent since it was Napoleon Bonaparte himself who, in 1802, claimed that: "I govern not as a general, but because the nation believes that I possess the civilian qualities needed to govern."[11] On the other hand, it has been held that the First Empire was dominated by military values, that mobilization and conscription were its administrative priorities, and that its key features, not least in foreign policy, must be understood in that light. Again, Louis Napoleon pursued what many have regarded as an aggressiveness counterproductive to both his personal and French national interests.

---

10 François-René Chateaubriand, *Mémoires d'outre-tombe*, eds. Maurice Levaillant and Georges Moulinier (2 vols.; Paris, 1951), I, 1004; *The Memoirs of Chateaubriand*, ed. and trans. Robert Baldick (Harmondsworth, 1965), 329.
11 Cited in Bluche, *Le bonapartisme*, 8.

Fourth, in what relationship did the two Bonapartes stand to the French Revolution? Did they terminate it? Or was there some significant sense in which they preserved its basic achievements while putting an end to the disorder it provoked, and to the dangers posed by extremists urging the reign of virtue and permanent revolution? Did the two empires retain the revolutionary preference for equality over liberty? Did they secure the new interests created by the revolution? Was the source of such legitimacy as they attained in fact the general will of the citizens, as they claimed, or did the Bonapartes create and manipulate opinion by the skillful use to an unprecedented degree of propaganda and police surveillance?

Fifth, what sort of domination was exercised by this type of government? Did its control over political and social life go beyond that of the ancien regime or of revolutionary governments, including the Committee of Public Safety? Such a position was argued by Benjamin Constant and by Mme. De Staël about the First Empire and by Karl Marx about the Second. Was Bonapartism a type of rule that was illegitimate because of its monopoly of all state powers? Because of its refusal to allow citizens to take a part in decisions involving them? Because of the denial of freedom of association, of freedom of speech and the press, of genuine representation rather than by a fictitious ceding of popular sovereignty? Or was the state as it functioned during the two empires nothing but an instrument of class domination? Alternatively, did the French state, because of exceptional circumstances, ever achieve the autonomy sometimes attributed to it by Marx?

Sixth, did the differences between the two Napoleons, and their regimes, outweigh the similarities? Marx certainly thought so, and his view finds support from modern students of the Second Empire such as Alain Plessis, Theodore Zeldin, and Sudhir Hazareesingh, even if typically they adduce reasons different from the ones Marx himself gave.[12]

II

The contributors to this volume have sought to provide answers to these enduring questions. Isser Woloch's essay, for instance, sheds important new light on how Napoleon Bonaparte's "usurpation"[13] actually took place: not

---

12 Theodore Zeldin, *France 1848–1945. Politics and Anger* (Oxford, 1979); Alain Plessis, *The Rise and Fall of the Second Empire* (Cambridge, 1987); Sudhir Hazareesingh, *From Subject to Citizen* (Princeton, 1998).

13 Benjamin Constant, "The Spirit of Conquest and Usurpation and their Relation to European Civilization" (1814) in *Benjamin Constant. Political Writings*, ed. and trans. Biancamaria Fontana (Cambridge, 1988), 45–167.

in terms of the Eighteenth Brumaire coup, about which much is known, but as the step-by-step process that elevated Napoleon from First Consul to Consul for Life and thence to Emperor in 1804. Bonapartism is thus not simply a coup d'état, but a transformation from republic to hereditary empire, "monarchy in a new key" as Woloch felicitously calls it. Self-aggrandizement was undoubtedly one of the driving forces of this transformation, since Napoleon increasingly resented the restraints that the Consulate's institutions placed on his power. But without a justification for creating a monarchy (toward which the consulship for life was the expedient transitional stage), and without allies to support his imperial pretensions, Napoleon's ambition would doubtless have been stymied. The justification was left largely to Napoleon's apologists in the Tribunate, such as Jard-Panvillier, who argued that the Revolution had not originally intended to destroy monarchy; only the Bourbons' treachery had produced that outcome. The time had arrived to renew the institution, with Napoleon as its founding monarch, a task made even more necessary by Bourbon-English plots to create turmoil in France. Only a hereditary emperor would have the authority to confound such machinations and definitively seal, and thereby protect, the Revolution's accomplishments.

Those old revolutionaries in the Council of State and the Tribunate who opposed the transformation to monarchy were in the minority. Outmaneuvered, men like Berlier and Boulay chose to support the new order rather than break all ties to it once the Empire was a fait accompli. They did so with a relatively good conscience, convinced that while their objections had been honorable, it was now necessary to rally round their chief and to support the nation's will. Napoleon had once more prevailed over dissenters. His allies included ministers such as Talleyrand, Roederer, and Regnaud, pliant tribunes and senators, and the army, menacingly orchestrated in the spring of 1804 by Napoleon's formidable chief-of-staff, Alexandre Berthier.

As we know, Napoleon's dynastic hopes were short lived: "The Desolator Desolate!/The Victor Overthrown!/The Arbiter of others' fate/A Suppliant for his own!"[14] Having prosecuted a series of military campaigns across Europe, he was himself overwhelmed on the battlefield, just as his nephew would be at Sedan. And central to both defeats was Prussia, arguably the fiercest and most unforgiving of Napoleon's foes. The depredations Prussia suffered during the war of 1806–7, during the occupation that followed, and in 1811–12, when it became Napoleon's launching pad for the invasion

---

14 Lord Byron, "Ode to Napoleon Buonaparte" (1814) IV: 37–40 in *Lord Byron. Selected Poems*, eds. and preface by Susan J. Wolfson and Peter J. Manning (London, 1996), 308–14, at 309.

of Russia, are all well documented by Tim Blanning in his contribution to this volume.

"As an exercise in counterproductivity," Blanning points out, "Napoleon's treatment of Prussia had few equals." Prussia's humiliation and near implosion were the catalysts for the Reform Movement of 1806–19, to which King Frederick William III lent his support and authority. The result was a program of "offensive modernization" that reinvigorated the Prussian army, mobilized a popular militia, and extended to Prussian society those legal rights and civil liberties now required by all modern states seeking to galvanize the patriotic allegiance of their citizens. To be sure, Prussian reformers like Freiherr vom Stein and his circle were also influenced by Kantian moral philosophy and the political economy of Adam Smith. Nonetheless, it was hatred of Napoleon more than anything else that propelled the Prussian state into action. With the victory in 1815 over France, Prussia acquired three new regions – the Aachen-Cologne-Krefeld triangle, the Saarland, and the Ruhr – which made possible its subsequent industrialization, economic power, and military might.

Under Napoleon III, a counterproductive French foreign and military policy once again enabled Prussia to gain at its rival's expense. France's aggression in the Crimea (1854–6) and intervention in Italy in 1859 not only activated another round of Prussian military reform, but drove a wedge between itself and a potential ally – Russia. With Austria increasingly marginalized and Russia embittered by the neutralization of the Black Sea and Napoleon III's support of Polish nationalism, France had become dangerously isolated. When war with Prussia broke out in 1870, masterminded by Napoleon III's nemesis, Otto von Bismarck, defeat was almost instantaneous.

Tim Blanning's chapter ends with a question that has exercised the minds of many historians and political theorists: to what extent was Bismarck himself a Bonapartist figure? Blanning considers the parallels to be superficial. While Napoleon I was a general, Bismarck was not a military man, and unlike both Bonapartes he was ultimately dependent on his sovereign – not the sovereign people but the Prussian king. In addition, Bismarck was a Realpolitiker who, though restrained by pessimism, looked steadily into the future, not an adventurist with mercurial, fantastic goals. Blanning, as an historian, thus assesses him as a great statesman. But what about the judgment of Bismarck's German contemporaries, both in regard to Bonapartism and to Bismarck himself?

David Barclay's chapter seeks to answer this question by focusing on the changing fortunes and manifestations of Prussian conservatism. Like

Blanning, Barclay notes how hatred of Napoleon Bonaparte provoked the Prussian monarchy into revitalizing itself. But Barclay's theme is not the Prussian reform movement or the paradoxes of French foreign policy, but the decomposition of Prussian conservatism in the face of "Bonapartist" developments at home.

Prussian conservatism was always a heterogeneous, fluid phenomenon, composed of various strands and preferences: romantic, aristocratic, bureaucratic, Christian, *ständisch*. Of particular interest to Barclay is the High Conservative faction spearheaded by Leopold and Ludwig von Gerlach. The Gerlach brothers, and like-minded individuals such as Friedrich Julius Stahl and Hermann Wagener, were, Barclay explains, "fervent advocates of a divinely ordained, patrimonial, *ständisch*, that is, decentralized and organic-corporative, monarchy." This led them to oppose just as assiduously "contract theory, parliamentary institutions, or the incendiary, 'mechanistic,' universalist principles of 1789."

Such High Conservatives were not, however, sycophantic apologists of monarchy. Where monarchy degenerated into "absolutism," they repudiated it absolutely. They initially believed that their monarch, Frederick William IV, entertained values and objectives similar to their own, and, before the revolutions of 1848, they were probably correct to do so. But 1848, when the Prussian throne seemed to be threatened, was the annus mirabilis for Frederick William. From then until his death in 1861, he pursued a modernization strategy of his own. In time, even the Gerlachs came to see the opportunities afforded by constitutions and parliaments to those who could exploit, rather than simply deplore, them. Nonetheless, other initiatives of Frederick William after 1848, or rather of his two key advisors – Otto von Manteuffel (Interior Minister and, later, Minister President) and Carl Ludwig von Hinckeldey (Berlin's chief of police) – persuaded the High Conservatives that absolutism was once more a danger in Prussia. The manipulation of public opinion, the growth of a spy and intelligence network from which no group – the High Conservatives included – could feel safe, the Haussmannesque rebuilding of Berlin, led them to invoke the stigma of Bonapartism. Their sense of alarm and disenchantment was further aggravated by Bismarck's political trajectory from conservative "man of principle" to Realpolitiker, willing to traffic with Napoleon III whenever it appeared to be in the Prussian state's interest to do so. For the Gerlach brothers and their supporters, authority, morality, and the interests of the state were simply indivisible. That Bismarck now thought otherwise, and acted accordingly, proved to them that he had adopted the hated Bonapartism.

The willingness of nineteenth-century political actors to think in terms of such abstract categories as Bonapartism, Caesarism, and Imperialism was immeasurably fortified by the ascent to power of Louis Bonaparte. For after Louis Bonaparte launched his own coup in December 1851 – his own Eighteenth Brumaire, as Marx quipped – and established another post-democratic and post-revolutionary regime claiming to ensure social order and popular sovereignty, many acute observers concluded that European politics was exposed to a pathological syndrome rather than something contingent, fortuitous, or purely French. Accordingly, political thinkers intensified their attempts both to discern the future direction and shape of European politics and to reinterpret the recent past.

The more they envisaged Bonapartism as an evolutionary or structural principle, the less plausible became heroic, individualistic interpretations of modern history like that of Heinrich Heine, who insisted that Napoleon Bonaparte "could have become a Washington of Europe" if his ambition had not led him astray.[15] Increasingly, such views were considered facile and as focusing on epiphenomena, ignoring root causes, and reversing Constant's insistence that Napoleon exemplified a new tendency: "usurpation." Constant had conjoined that argument with the hopeful prognosis that a commercial, liberal, and pacific society would soon make extinct the Napoleons of this world. Later thinkers tended to share Constant's structural approach, while abandoning both his preferred category of usurpation and his optimism.

Among the greatest of such thinkers was Alexis de Tocqueville. Although Tocqueville was no determinist or prophet of doom, he was deeply alarmed at the career of the two Napoleonic empires: perplexed, as Melvin Richter remarks, "that from the two French Revolutions of 1789 and 1848 . . . had emerged not emancipation, but a regime considerably more repressive than the monarchies that had been overthrown." How was one conceptually to characterize this new kind of regime? Tocqueville struggled for most of his adult life to find a conclusive answer. Of one thing, however, he became increasingly certain: that orthodox descriptions of the First and Second Empires were hopelessly anachronistic. True, both Empires were products of French history; they had extended and intensified the practice of

---

15 Heinrich Heine, "French Painters" (1831), trans. David Ward in *Paintings on the Move*, ed. Susanne Zantop (Lincoln and London, 1989), 150. Five years earlier, in "Ideas: The Book of Le Grand" Heine had compared Napoleon with Christ and St. Helena to the Holy Sepulchre. "Strange!" Heine observed, "the Emperor's three greatest antagonists have all met a terrible fate: Londonderry [Lord Castlereagh] cut his throat, Louis XVIII rotted on his throne, and Professor Saalfeld is still a professor at Göttingen," in Heinrich Heine, *Selected Prose*, ed. and trans. Ritchie Robertson (London, 1993), 91–143, at 115.

centralization that absolutist monarchs had begun. To that extent there was continuity with France's past. Tocqueville also fell back heuristically on the concept of "despotism," while wavering over the Roman analogy. Nonetheless, the thrust of his analysis pointed repeatedly to the post-republican, post-revolutionary, and post-democratic novelty of the states over which Napoleon I and III presided.

The political culture and attitudes of France, Tocqueville believed, revealed the depth to which the nation's *moeurs* had been corrupted. The Consulate and First Empires were the vital precedents for the Second; incrementally, Frenchmen had become ever more habituated to violence in politics and to the normality of state indifference to minority rights. Increasingly the French, drawn to the cult of the omnipotent leader, felt contempt for representative government. They accepted restrictions on the press, on the right to free assembly, and on local government. Coupled with administrative centralization and legal structures that impeded deliberative action in common, the First and Second Empires had worked to eviscerate the practice of democratic citizenship. Napoleonic rule not only encouraged a general opportunistic subservience. It also induced a kind of schizophrenia among its chief agents in which personal probity and scrupulousness could coexist with slavish obedience to orders, whatever the cost or consequence.

Richter also examines Tocqueville's rich, though equivocating, appraisal of the Bonapartes, especially Napoleon I, as political innovators. In some contexts, Tocqueville grants the importance of Napoleon I's abilities and skills, the qualities that enabled him to fine-tune the engine of repression with unrivaled mastery and precision. In other contexts, however, the emphasis is very different as Napoleonic rule is assimilated to structural tendencies – centralization, mobilization, repression – deeply, though not indelibly, embedded within the French body politic.

At the time of his death in 1859, his great work on the Revolution and Napoleon unfinished, Tocqueville was more convinced than ever that analogies with Rome in its period of decline were untenable. France retained the capacity to become a free and great nation. In 1859, Louis Bonaparte still appeared to be unassailable, having garnered the support of the church and the propertied classes. Yet, Tocqueville predicted that the Second Empire would fall through defeat in an unnecessary battle brought on by the same aggressive strategy that had brought down the First. While the military legacy, the legend of Bonapartist glory, might have helped bring Louis Napoleon to power, he was also doomed to be the victim of the illusions inherited from his uncle.

The capacity for historical illusion was a favorite target and topos of Karl Marx. We are apt to think of Marx's materialist interpretation of history and politics as finding its archetypal expression in the "Preface to a Contribution to the Critique of Political Economy" (1859). Terrell Carver, in his reading of Marx's *The Eighteenth Brumaire of Louis Napoleon*, cautions against such a simplistic interpretation. Rather than emphasizing those passages that seem to foreshadow more abstract and high-level generalizations found in later works of Marx and Engels, Carver examines the text of *The Eighteenth Brumaire* to reveal "the untidy categories" of Marx's narrative. Carver proposes to read Marx's *Eighteenth Brumaire* not as a defective version of the 1859 "Preface," but the "Preface" as an oversimplification of his *Eighteenth Brumaire*. Such an interpretation emphasizes what Marx might have been expected to dismiss as mere ideology and superstructure: "Tradition from the dead generations weighs like a nightmare on the brain of the living."[16] "Through historical tradition it has come to pass that the French peasantry believed in a miracle, that a man by the name of Napoleon would bring them back their former glory."[17] This recalls Tocqueville's prediction that the Second Empire would fall because of the belief dear to Louis Napoleon: that his position as Emperor depended upon his public image as a reincarnation of his all-conquering uncle, almost always supreme, in Chateaubriand's words, in "that game which was always being won, yet went on being played."[18] Marx also saw the predominance of the army as crucial to both empires:

The army was the *point d'honneur* for the smallholding peasantry; it transformed them into heroes, defended their new position from outside threats, glorifying their recently acquired nationality, plundering and revolutionising the world. The dazzling uniform was its own national dress, war its poetry, the smallholding its fatherland and patriotism was the ideal form of their sense of property.[19]

As Carver emphasizes, Marx, in *The Eighteenth Brumaire*, did not abandon his "guiding thread," that is, his economic interpretation of politics. Rather, he produced several highly stimulating variants of that theory, which he applied to the coup and then to the state of Louis Napoleon. In Carver's view, Marx's *Eighteenth Brumaire* should be appreciated for the contextual richness and complexity of his narrative, the paradoxes and irony of his style, rather than criticized for its logical incompatibility with his later work.

16 Karl Marx, *The Eighteenth Brumaire* in *Later Political Writings*, ed. and trans. Terrell Carver (Cambridge, 1996), 32.
17 Marx, *Eighteenth Brumaire*, 117–18.   18 Chateaubriand, *Mémoires*, I, 869; *Memoirs*, 24.
19 Marx, *Eighteenth Brumaire*, 122.

Marx's analysis of class interest in *The Eighteenth Brumaire* is more complex, open-ended, aware of contradictions and reversals, and psychologically individualist than is usually admitted by those holding a more schematic view of his theory.

The three principal applications of Marx's general theory of history as class struggle to the French case come from his analysis of the conflicts arising from the nature of capital in mid-century France. This derived from differences in the interests of those groups controlling respectively landowning, finance, and industrial capital. With the political economy of France thus framed, Marx underlines: (1) the opportunity for Louis Napoleon created by the fact that the bourgeoisie had lost, and the working class had not yet acquired the ability to rule the nation; (2) the fact that the bourgeoisie preferred at this time not to rule itself, but to conceal its interests by having its political work done for it first by the Second Republic and then by Louis Napoleon; (3) the exceptional autonomy achieved by the centralized state, thus eluding its more usual function as an instrument of the dominant class.

Yet Sudhir Hazareesingh suggests in Chapter 6 that the Second Empire produced much more ambiguous consequences than Tocqueville might have predicted and than Marx, writing through the entire period of Louis Bonaparte's ascendancy, understood at the time. Hazareesingh does not deny the obvious: that Napoleon III sought to control France during the Second Empire and marginalize its enemies, with repressive means where necessary. His argument is rather that the Second Empire was a social order with deep contradictions and oscillations. That complexity is often obscured by two assumptions: first, that an "essence" of Bonapartism can be identified, and, second, that the French Napoleonic tradition was guided not by a set of ideas of any sophistication, but simply by commitments to glory and expansion.

Hazareesingh dismisses both assumptions as simplistic. To begin with, Bonapartism is a chameleon.[20] "The flamboyant but despotic First Empire was radically different from the 'popular' and proto-republican Bonapartism which emerged in the 1820s and 1830s. The Bonapartism of the young Louis-Napoleon in the 1840s was in turn different from the 'official' Bonapartism of the Second Empire." In addition, there are "notable political variations as between the authoritarian years of Napoleon III's rule and the later 'liberal Empire.'" As for the visceral "Imperialism" of Louis Bonaparte, it, too, is a simplification that underestimates the political

---

20 On the internal complexity of Bonapartism, see also Zeldin, *France*, 140–205, and Plessis, *Rise and Fall*.

concepts that guided the regime. On Hazareesingh's account, the orthodox republican interpretation of the Second Empire has glossed over its contribution to mass democracy and to the institutions of its successor, the Third Republic.

To support this argument, Hazareesingh focuses on the practice of territorial democracy that unfolded during the Second Empire. Its evolution began in the most unlikely way. The territorial system of the Second Empire was both highly centralized and hierarchical, with each unit (commune, canton, and department) supposedly contributing to the "order, discipline and rationality" of the whole. All levels of administration were, however, subject to state orchestration from above. Following the reorganization of local government in July 1852 and May 1855, mayors and assistant mayors were appointed by the state. So, too, were the departmental prefects whose powers enabled them to override the decisions of municipal councils, suspend them if necessary, and dismiss mayors. Political representation was subjected to strict administrative control. Paternalism, anti-factionalism, and technocracy were the trinity around which citizenship was to be organized.

The regime's commitment to mass democracy as a principle of legitimation increasingly collided, however, with its equally strong desire to impose state fiat on the nation as a whole. As Hazareesingh notes, bureaucratic formalism provoked frustration and resentment. Appointed mayors who failed to garner the support of their municipal councils faced obstruction and contempt, leading a number of these magistrates to seek election, with the regime's guarded approval, so the better to secure cooperation and compliance. Yet once elected, mayors were no longer the sole agents of the imperial state. During the 1860s, prefectural control over local politics weakened as it became increasingly challenged by mayors, General Councillors, and elected representatives in the Corps Législatif. As electoral politics became ever more agitated, the regime responded through a decentralist strategy of its own, designed to transform social discontent into government capital and, in particular, to rebuild credibility among the rural populace so to play it off against growing urban hostility. The paradoxical result was "creeping (or incremental) democratization."

Hazareesingh concludes that there was no radical rupture between the Second Empire and Third Republic. Instead, he considers the republican regimes of the 1870s and beyond as attempts to reconcile the "conflicting imperatives" that the Second Empire had thrown so dramatically into relief: "depoliticization and the practice of universal suffrage, administrative omniscience and citizen involvement in local life, the maintenance of social order and the preservation of the Revolutionary heritage of civil equality, the cultivation of a traditional and deferential polity and the modernization of political life."

III

During the twentieth century, the emergence of new regimes prompted advocates, critics, and analysts to coin a correspondingly new terminology to describe them. "Fascism," "Nazism," "Stalinism," "Maoism," and "totalitarianism" were added to the older lexicon of Bonapartism, Caesarism, and Imperialism. This last term had originally been coined to describe the expansionist policies of the Bonapartes, particularly Napoleon III. After his fall, it took on new meaning as it now came to be applied to the latest mode of international capitalist accumulation. Until roughly the Second World War, the newer and older vocabularies coexisted. Political thinkers and actors alike drew on past experiences and models to interpret current realities. In the process, however, the concepts of Bonapartism and Caesarism were subject to remarkable adaptation. We get a vivid sense of this inventiveness in Gramsci's analysis of modern Caesarism, to which we shall return, or Trotsky's urgent attempts in the 1930s to distinguish "preventive Bonapartism" (Giolitti, Brüning-Schleicher, Doumergue) from "Bonapartism of fascist origin" (Mussolini and Hitler) and both of these from the "senile Bonapartism" represented by Marshal Pétain.[21]

Still, even before the emergence of the new twentieth-century "dictatorships," the language of Caesarism and Bonapartism had been stretched far beyond its original referents. The pioneer was Max Weber. Typically remembered for his work on charismatic domination, Weber's analysis of Caesarism, in contrast, is still not widely known. But, as Peter Baehr maintains, neither concept can be adequately comprehended without identifying the relationship between them. Caesarism, Weber argued, was inevitable under conditions of modern "democracy" because the entry of the "masses" into political life put a premium on plebiscitary leadership and party organization. The real question was not whether Caesarism could be avoided, but which form of Caesarism should be adopted. Historical conditions in Germany had produced a particularly destructive variety of the modern Caesarist phenomenon. The German mutation combined an impotent parliament with an irresponsible monarchy. There was no

---

21 See "German Bonapartism" (1932), "Bonapartism and Fascism" (1934), and "Bonapartism, Fascism, and War" (1940) in Leon Trotsky, *The Struggle Against Fascism in Europe*, ed. Ernest Mandel (London, 1975), 325–31, 451–8, 459–68.

recognition of the distinction between bureaucratic and political modes of behavior. The result was incompetence and drift, which was bad enough in domestic politics. Worse still, it also led to the international isolation of Germany.

Weber found an alternative in Britain, where Caesarism of a decidedly different sort held sway, and he campaigned tirelessly for it during the First World War. Caesarist figures like Gladstone and Lloyd George had immense power to lead the nation, but were nonetheless constrained by the working parliament where they had received their political educations. As a leader of the masses, the British Caesarist leader had immense authority over parliament and over his own party. The reigning British monarch understood that matters of foreign and military policy should no longer be decided by kings. At the same time, an unpopular leader could be ejected from parliament following a general election, and irresponsible policies could be subjected to the scrutiny of parliamentary committees and the press.

Weber developed this theory of Caesarism in his journalistic writings and political speeches. Aiming for an informed and engaged public, he simultaneously drew on the vernacular of the day and subverted it. Weber, extrapolating from the French experience, applied the concept of Caesarism not only to Germany but to Britain and the United States as well; he distinguished between positive and negative varieties of Caesarism; and he showed how it could be compatible with the institutions of parliament and monarchy. Each of these approaches to Caesarism, especially the second and third, was unusual. And they were made utterly unique by a related development in Weber's work: the migration of fundamental elements of Caesarism into the concept of "charisma" he developed for his comparative studies. Supposedly a scientific notion, charisma concealed and naturalized many of Weber's most controversial, partisan views about the relationship between leaders and masses.

Although Weber lived to see Germany's wartime defeat, communist insurrection, and violent antirevolutionary measures by the Freikorps and other rightist organizations, it was left to his younger contemporaries Carl Schmitt and Antonio Gramsci to address the political crisis of the interwar years. Whereas Weber had sought to combine liberalism and German nationalism, Carl Schmitt believed that project to be incoherent. Further, while Weber had discussed modern dictatorship only in passing, Schmitt was resolved to reinvestigate the applicability of the institution for modern times. His starting point, John McCormick observes, was the dire situation in which the Weimar Republic found itself in the early 1920s. On the one side stood its implacable foes: the radical right and, even more saliently for Schmitt, the Marxist revolutionaries who sought to establish a Bolshevik "dictatorship of the proletariat." On the other were the liberal supporters of the Republic whose antipathy toward the institution of dictatorship was not only historically misinformed, Schmitt claimed, but also jeopardized the political system that guaranteed their very existence. Eliding dictatorship with Caesarism and Bonapartism, liberals were bereft of an important resource with which to confront their enemies and save the Republic.

As a response to the Weimar political impasse, Schmitt offered a defense of a variety of dictatorship based on the Roman precedent, an emergency mode or rule that would suspend legality in order to protect society at large and, once the danger was over, restore the status quo ante. Such a "commissarial" dictatorship stood in contrast to the "sovereign," Jacobin-inspired dictatorship appropriated by Marxist revolutionaries who sought to found an entirely new social and political order with unlimited powers for those who ruled.

When Schmitt first began to formulate his ideas on dictatorship, his principal concern was to rescue the concept from theoretical obfuscation and the institution from illegitimate use and calumny. Properly understood, Schmitt seemed to be saying, Caesarism, Bonapartism, and Bolshevism could all be countered in periods of modern emergency by resort to "commissarial" dictatorship. Yet, as John McCormick shows, Schmitt's argument became ever more extreme. From appearing to defend the idea and practice of commissarial dictatorship, Schmitt gradually abandoned it, substituting right-wing Caesarism for its leftist incarnation. By the time Schmitt joined the National Socialist party in May 1933, the unchecked "plebiscitary legitimacy" of the leader of the Reich had replaced the "statutory legality" of constitutional instruments and assemblies. The constitution that commissarial dictatorships were supposed to restore had become an irrelevancy.

Schmitt's metamorphosis was conditioned not only by the economic and political crises of the Weimar Republic, but also by how he interpreted modern liberalism. Convinced of liberalism's intellectual feebleness in times of extremity and its inability to oversee fundamental political change, he looked elsewhere for solutions. McCormick counters Schmitt's defeatism by invoking Bruce Ackerman's theory of constitutional politics, which attempts to show the resilience, dynamism, and participatory resources of the American Republic and, by extension, liberalism's transformative capacities. Still, it is striking how much the sterility and weakness of liberalism – perceived or otherwise – dominated radical thinking about Bonapartism and Caesarism in the interwar years. A conspicuous example is to be found in the analysis of one of Schmitt's Marxist adversaries, Antonio Gramsci, the subject of Benedetto Fontana's chapter.

Gramsci's theory of Caesarism is one of the least explored dimensions of his thought and, as Fontana demonstrates, one of the most complex. The theory emerged as part of Gramsci's attempt in the *Prison Notebooks* (1929–36) to account for the triumph of Italian Fascism and its precondition, the collapse of the revolutionary left and of liberalism. In his account, liberalism's travails were given explanatory pride of place. Gramsci argued that, in contrast to the experiences of Britain and France, Italian liberalism never developed a "hegemonic" relationship to the subordinate classes – that is, never managed to mobilize that degree of consent required for a class to govern with moral and political authority. The Italian ruling class and its allies had become mired in a particularistic and factional "economic-corporate" phase of development. Thus they were ill-equipped to mobilize the support of the masses to resolve structural crises. It is true that, as a Marxist, Gramsci saw the impending collapse of any modern state as an opportunity for revolution and the dismantling of bourgeois institutions. The problem was that a revolutionary conjuncture could also serve as the occasion for Caesarism.

Though Gramsci gave the concept of Caesarism different articulations, distinguishing, for instance, among qualitative and quantitative, progressive and reactionary modalities, the weight of his argument falls on the combination of domination, dictatorship, and police power that a Caesarist solution typically brings to a social-political crisis.

According to Gramsci, Caesarism emerges out of the decomposition of a ruling bloc faced with a militant challenge to its position and privileges. At some point, one particularly disquieted element in this bloc concludes, usually after conflicts with its previous allies, that the opposition of the subordinate classes is too strong to vanquish. In consequence, the breakaway element "invites" an extraneous force to intervene and resolve the crisis. The result is the subordination of all classes, temporarily at least, to this external force. Italian Fascism, on Gramsci's account, represented the solution chosen by an exhausted ruling bloc. Fascism "was the logical and natural evolution of the liberal state" or, more precisely, of a liberal state that since the Risorgimento had failed to become authoritative and to project successfully its class interest as the common good.

We have seen that from Weber to Schmitt and Gramsci the concept of Caesarism remained influential in political discussion. From 1945 onward, however, it gradually fell, with a few exceptions, into desuetude though the partner notion of Bonapartism continued to have resonance in France. For many political thinkers, the era of Fascism, Nazism, and Bolshevism had exploded familiar categories of thought. But how was the recent past to be depicted?

Few writers, Margaret Canovan explains, gave more thought to this question than Hannah Arendt. She perceived that the concepts of Bonapartism, Caesarism, and even of dictatorship itself were completely inadequate for understanding the enormities perpetrated in Europe before and during World War II. Moreover, though the Axis had been defeated, the world was still threatened by Stalinism, a regime with disturbing parallels to National Socialism. The concept Arendt deployed to describe both systems was "totalitarianism." She assiduously sought to avoid the simplifications the Cold War brought to the discussion of this notion.[22] Arendt confined the term to the twin regimes of Hitler and Stalin and emphasized their unprecedented character. (She described the post–Stalin Soviet Union as a one-party dictatorship; of Maoism she knew little.) She also defined totalitarianism in a way markedly different from most of her contemporaries.

Totalitarianism, Arendt argued, was a system of domination quintessentially typified by "motion" rather than by *Gleichschaltung* (synchronization), by unceasing turbulence rather than by a centralized, all-controlling state. To confuse totalitarianism with dictatorship or to see it as a type of dictatorship was to miss a fundamental distinction. Once consolidated, dictatorships typically become routinized and predictable, domesticating and detaching themselves from the movements that were their original social basis. Totalitarian regimes, in contrast, rise to power on a movement and, once installed, employ motion as their constitutive "principle" of domination. The mercurial will of the leader whose next decision could nullify all previous ones; ideologies of race or history to whose inexorable "laws" human beings are constantly sacrificed; the police institutions and death camps whose only purposes are to transform citizens into foes, plural individuals into an identical species and then corpses: All these features characterize a regime-type of permanent revolution and transgression. Indeed, it is the grotesque futility and destructiveness of totalitarian systems, their attack on every norm that might anchor human life in something stable, that makes them so resistant to methodical analysis.

Warning against the use of inappropriate categories, Arendt argued that the totalitarian leader was less a charismatic figure in the Weberian sense

---

22 See Abbott Gleason, *Totalitarianism: The Inner History of the Cold War* (New York, 1995); and William David Jones, *The Lost Debate. German Socialist Intellectuals and Totalitarianism* (Urbana and Chicago, 1999), 173–220.

than a figure of extreme vacuity whose fanatical zeal and all-encompassing ideology were deeply attractive to those whose "world" had fractured around them. Included in what she called the "masses" were people of all classes, or rather of none since class allegiances themselves had disintegrated under the impact of war, the implosion of nations, and expulsion of whole populations. The masses were the prime targets for totalitarian mobilization. They were made up of all those individuals characterized by social isolation and "weird disregard for ordinary utilitarian self-interest that comes from the experience of being entirely expendable."

Arendt's analysis, then, was concerned principally to delineate a new phenomenon for which a new category and subcategories were required. The point was not that previous kinds of tyranny could never be recapitulated, but that it was folly to conflate such modes with those so violently brought into existence in the 1930s and 1940s. Whether Bonapartist regimes could ever reassert themselves was not a question in which she was particularly interested. However, it was precisely this issue that once again assumed prominence in the land of Bonapartism's birth.

The precipitating events were Charles de Gaulle's rise to power in May 1958 to deal with the crisis in North Africa; the referendum soon after that gave him unusually extensive powers as prime minister of the Fourth Republic; and his election as the first president of the Fifth Republic in December 1958. De Gaulle's military background ("The General"), his habit of using referenda to endorse and validate his authority, and his peremptory, autocratic manner, all made the polemical analogy with Bonapartism irresistible, particularly among leftist critics of the regime.

Nonetheless, the parallel was not confined to detractors of de Gaulle. It also quickly became, Jack Hayward observes, a staple of discussion among academic analysts such as René Rémond. Gaullism and Bonapartism, Rémond declared, had a number of features in common: "control of the media of mass communications; reassuring property owners and business accompanied by 'social concerns'; Saint-Simonian technocratic reformism; an assertive foreign and military policy, and an authoritarian, monocratic political regime, supported by a centralized administrative elite, notably through the partisan activities of the prefects."

For Hayward, however, the parallels tell us relatively little. For one thing, many previous republican administrations had evinced characteristics similar to those now being attributed to Gaullism/Bonapartism. For another, the political career of de Gaulle, which Hayward prefers to describe as a "heroic" rather than a "charismatic" or "crisis" form of leadership, displays qualities markedly at variance with the two nineteenth-century Napoleonic regimes.

De Gaulle presided over the loss of French colonies, not their creation. He was defeated not in war, but through "suicide by plebiscite" in 1969. This proved his willingness to accept the precedence of a free, popular vote over his own authority. In this way, de Gaulle facilitated the transition from heroic rule to the more humdrum politics of Georges Pompidou. Most of all, however, de Gaulle created something unique for French politics: a system that, by combining a directly elected president and parliament, synthesized the republican and Bonapartist legacies. "As a heroic leader," Hayward concludes, de Gaulle was "able to survive his role as a crisis leader to become the founding father of an enduring regime combining assured republican authority and relative constitutional stability with dirigiste economic modernization." Whatever else this matrix of elements and achievements might be called, it would be singularly inaccurate to deem it "Bonapartist."

IV

Much of the perplexity and ambiguity that has accompanied the modern discussion of Caesarism and its cognate terms was also experienced in ancient times, according to Claude Nicolet and Arthur Eckstein. Consider more closely the idea and institution of dictatorship, which from at least the seventeenth century has been understood in two opposed ways: as a legal or "regular" office that enables a magistrate to be invested temporarily with great emergency powers to resolve a crisis and uphold the constitutional order; and as a type of rule that overthrows the legal order and replaces it by capricious, violent tyranny. Such a strange juxtaposition would appear to be semantically incoherent. Yet, as Nicolet argues, the roots of this equivocation are to be found in the history of the Roman Republic itself.

Because the classical sources on which historians rely are a mixture of folklore and records of actual events, the practice of dictatorship between 501 and 202 B.C.E. is actually a good deal more obscure than we are often inclined to suppose. With that caveat, however, the following features are discernible. The dictator was legally nominated by one or both consuls (rather than being plebiscitarily acclaimed); he was invested with exceptional powers for a short period of time, usually six months; and although supreme, he had no authority to abolish other magistracies. In short, this kind of dictatorship was limited and, ostensibly at least, designed to secure the common good. By contrast, the "revival" of dictatorship by Sulla and Julius Caesar after more than a century of disuse offers a very different political scenario. Under these warlords, constitutional restraints lost their leverage, the leader's dominion became unlimited, the army became his client, and the Senate succumbed to the violent rule of a single man.

But is this stark antinomy between the two kinds and two phases of dictatorship as straightforward as it seems? Nicolet agrees that the Sullan dictatorship is a watershed in the history of the Roman Republic. From there it is but a short step to Caesar and to the Augustan Principate that followed. He also notes that the majority of dictators appointed between 501 and 202 and usually classified as constitutional were engaged in military campaigns against foreign powers or in attempts at domestic conciliation, rather than in sanguinary repressions of sedition. Nevertheless, Nicolet maintains there were precedents for Sulla's style of rule, notably the intervention of the people in electing or endorsing the dictator. The Republican dictator increasingly came to resemble the "providential man" later associated with Caesarism. True, this term was unknown at the time, though Caesar was anathematized by his enemies as a *popularis* (the Roman word for the Greek *dēmagagōs*) candidate. But Nicolet believes that later appropriation of the term Caesarism to denote the primacy of military conquest, military leadership, and plebiscitarian representation is an altogether appropriate application of the original model.

So, with a somewhat different emphasis, does Arthur Eckstein, who, in the concluding chapter of this book, examines both the social psychology of the imperial administrator and the fear that his rule has recurrently provoked in those who have experienced or observed its excesses and depredations. Eckstein's thesis is that "the experience of governing a large province on one's own, the experience of exercising sole responsibility over large regions and great numbers of people, the experience of independence and power and control, the taste for it (and in some cases the great wealth that could be derived from it), all this sometimes created what one might call an 'imperial counterculture' to the law-ruled state at the center."

The classic exemplar of this counterculture is Julius Caesar, whose long campaign in Gaul, virtually unrestrained by the normative and juridical constraints of the metropolis, made the thought of returning to senatorial life humdrum and repellant. Moreover, irregularities in Caesar's command in Gaul made it appear that only through the help of Pompey could his safety be guaranteed in Rome. Pompey doubtless could have guaranteed Caesar's liberty, but in so doing he would have turned Caesar from demigod to dependent. That would have been an intolerable position for a man who had enjoyed absolute power for nine years in Gaul. Rather than submit to these unwelcome constraints, Caesar chose to make war on his own city. After a republican conspiracy shorted his career as dictator for life, Caesar became the archetype of the imperial "administrator" who – personally ambitious, contemptuous of regular governance and routinized accountability, habituated to rule by edict rather than law, and often seduced by wealth beyond imagination – threatened to overrun the central state.

In Caesar's case, the fear was understandable. Those metropolitans who warned of impending disaster were vindicated, often posthumously. But in other instances, Eckstein continues, alarm has often been exaggerated. During the eighteenth and nineteenth centuries, the British Empire witnessed more than once the rule of imperial administrators – Warren Hastings and Sir Richard Wellesley serve as examples – who seemed the very incarnations of Caesarism but who in fact were forced to accept discipline imposed by the metropolitan center or, after their return home, were left to vegetate in an oblivion they bitterly resented.

In twentieth-century America, General Douglas MacArthur provoked another such imperial scare. Before he was relieved from his Far East command by President Harry Truman in April 1951, MacArthur had not only directly disobeyed presidential orders on a number of occasions; he had also ruled defeated Japan as a virtual second monarch and made national policy by extending military protection to Chiang Kai-shek against the People's Republic of China. Back home, rumors and nervous jokes circulated that MacArthur was prepared to countenance a coup d'état on his return. That the "American Caesar" failed to do so is, to be sure, attributable to MacArthur's own belated sense of limits. It was also, however, the result of a republican constitution whose founders, steeped in the classical tradition, took care to incorporate a series of institutional arrangements designed to preempt the "specter of Caesarism into the civil arm of government."

V

This volume notes, then, the bicentenary of the Eighteenth Brumaire by considering its consequences, direct and remote, for the subsequent history of France, Germany, and Europe. Not least among these effects were those basic contested concepts initially registering the diverse meanings given to the two sequences connected with Napoleon and Louis Bonaparte. Some chapters treat the ways that major theorists such as Tocqueville and Marx conceptualized these two sets of events and, by treating them as either the same phenomenon, or as drastically different, took positions that became crucial to nineteenth-century theories of politics and history. Other chapters examine such issues as the sustained historical analogies with classical Rome that were such a striking feature of nineteenth-century political argument; the alleged parallels between Bismarck and Louis Napoleon; and, in the twentieth century, the supposed Bonapartism of Charles de Gaulle. A third group of chapters considers the complex interactions among these concepts, first coined in the nineteenth century, and political thought and action in the twentieth.

In concluding these introductory remarks, it is worth touching on some of the pivotal questions and issues that this volume throws into relief. When, why, and how do certain concepts cease to be inescapable parts of the political vocabulary, and drop out of discourse? Concepts once nearly synonymous lose their connections; sometimes concepts previously differentiated become conflated. It can happen that even when the meaning of a concept remains relatively stable, its antonyms may change. The attention of cultural and intellectual historians has hitherto been focused on the successful introduction of new modes of thought. The processes involved in the eclipse or transformation of concepts once crucial to political and social discourse now deserve sustained consideration. This is but one of the areas for investigation suggested by this book.

Another is the question of how the relative salience of Bonapartism, Caesarism, and dictatorship altered drastically as memories of the two Bonapartes receded, and their relevance became increasingly obscure. During the stormy periods that preceded and followed World War I, these concepts had to be adapted to new developments in the politics, societies, and economies of Europe. Significantly, the term dictatorship was used during only two periods of the nineteenth century to designate a modern regime: first, referring to France, between 1789 and 1815; and second, briefly after 1852, to denote the Second Empire. In the 1920s and 1930s, liberal opponents of the Italian Fascist and Nazi regimes adopted dictatorship as their term of choice to designate what they were fighting against. What it meant in this context was a highly oppressive and arbitrary form of rule, established by force or intimidation, enabling a person or group to monopolize political power without any constitutional limits, thus destroying representative government, political rights, and any organized opposition.[23] While such a characterization might seem to establish an overwhelmingly negative meaning for dictatorship, the situation was complicated by the use of the term by the Soviet Union and Third International. After 1917, and

---

23 This definition combines the summaries of these theories provided by Nolte, "*Diktatur*," *Geschichtliche Grundbegriffe*, I, 922–3, and Baehr, "Dictatorship," in *The Blackwell Dictionary of Twentieth-Century Social Thought*, 198.

particularly during the 1920s, Lenin's interpretation of "the dictatorship of the proletariat" remained crucial to the Soviet Union's official congratulatory self-description. In 1919, the International affirmed Lenin's reduction of political alternatives in the modern world to "Bourgeois democracy or proletarian dictatorship!" thereby lending "dictatorship" a strongly positive connotation. But, in 1933, the International converted the meaning of dictatorship into a stridently pejorative term meant to discredit Fascism in Italy and Nazism in Germany: "Fascism is the openly terroristic dictatorship of the most reactionary, chauvinist, and imperialist elements of finance capital." Still, as mentioned previously, Hitler refused to call himself a dictator, insisting that "Führer" was the only title that did justice to his leadership of the racially pure Germanic community (*Volksgemeinschaft*).

Meanwhile, well into the 1940s, in liberal, constitutional states, dictatorship continued to be used as the polar opposite of democracy in countless books, as well as in political discourse.[24] After 1945, dictatorship gradually was replaced by or conflated with totalitarianism, as in the title of Friedrich and Brezinski's *Totalitarian Dictatorship and Autocracy* (1956). Margaret Canovan points out in her chapter that Hannah Arendt derided all previous uses of dictatorship to designate the systems she herself defined as totalitarian. Even so, beginning with the 1960s, and accelerating with the end of the Cold War, there was mounting opposition both from various political camps and from academic analysts to classifying the Third Reich and the Soviet Union together. Well before 1989, the extended, liberal sense of dictatorship had largely supplanted totalitarianism in academic comparisons of the Nazi and Soviet regimes, although not in general political discourse. Thus the career of dictatorship continues, while that of Bonapartism and Caesarism has virtually ceased.

---

24 For a long list of book titles using the opposition between dictatorship and democracy in English and French, as well as in Italian, and in German (often written by political exiles), see Nolte, "*Diktatur*," *Geschichtliche Grundbegriffe*, I, 923, note 45.

PART I

Bonapartism to Its Contemporaries

1

From Consulate to Empire

Impetus and Resistance

ISSER WOLOCH

As a regime type, at least in its first two French incarnations, Bonapartism is synonymous with the seizure of power in a coup d'état (there is no Bonapartism without a Brumaire) and with the formation of an hereditary empire, monarchy in a new key. In this chapter, I focus on the second of these defining characteristics. I am particularly interested in the roles of certain individuals and small groups of Bonaparte's collaborators in advancing or resisting the transition from Consulate to Empire.[1] An hereditary empire, which had many enthusiasts in the ranks of Bonaparte's servitors, was actually a rather awkward notion, given Napoleon's utter disdain for any likely heir. The chapter traces the process by which the hereditary empire came into being; the "manufacture of consent" through public opinion (with particular attention to the military); and the allotted roles and unanticipated resistance in key institutions of the regime (the Council of State, the Tribunate, and the Senate). Throughout I will underscore the effort to legitimize the Empire by its ostensible linkage to the basic gains of the Revolution.

A FIRST STEP: CONSUL FOR LIFE

On March 25, 1802, Joseph Bonaparte and Lord Cornwallis concluded their arduous negotiations and signed the Treaty of Amiens, which ended a decade of European war. Public enthusiasm in France for Bonaparte was never higher: The first consul had achieved peace and international

---

[1] This chapter is drawn from my book, *Napoleon and his Collaborators: The Making of a Dictatorship* (New York/London, 2001), in which I study the former revolutionaries who helped put General Bonaparte into power and who continued to serve him despite his drift toward dictatorship, as well as the rare cases of dissent or disengagement. I am particularly interested in their contributions to Napoleon's regime and the benefits (psychological and material) they received in return, and in their strategies to defend the public interest (as they saw it) while maximizing their own self-interest.

preponderance through military victory, the restoration of traditional Catholic religious practice, and the repatriation of most émigrés. All this occurred without jeopardizing civil equality, the abolition of seigneurialism, or the transfer of the *biens nationaux*. Bonaparte seemed to be sustaining the most tangible interests created by the Revolution while soothing its most aggrieved victims.

In an exultant mood, the first consul chafed at the restraints on his initiative from the Consulate's web of institutions, the residue of Sieyès' "metaphysical" concern for the balance of powers. Several important collaborators reinforced his belief that France now required a return to monarchical forms. Constitutional monarchy, in this view, was the veritable form, the original intent, of the Revolution of 1789. As Bonaparte explained to his Minister of Interior Jean-Antoine Chaptal, the Revolution had stirred the people and taught them to understand their rights, but "the fall of the monarchy was merely a consequence of the difficulties that were encountered; it was not at all the intention of the revolutionaries."[2] As Bonaparte increasingly concentrated authority in his own hands (behind the watchwords of order, stability, and efficiency) he could be seen as progressing back toward the early Revolution's lost point of equilibrium, with the added attraction that he would owe his crown not to his birth but to his personal merit. Those inclined to resist this drift with talk about public liberty Bonaparte stigmatized as "ideologues."[3]

After the Treaty of Amiens, the Tribunate and Senate vied to proclaim the nation's gratitude to the first consul. The president of the Tribunate moved that "the Tribunate express its desire that a reward worthy of the Nation's gratitude be presented to General Bonaparte." However, what form this should take remained unclear. Financial rewards or symbolic gestures would not constitute a sufficient response, given Bonaparte's personality. A vote of confidence extending his mandate seemed more promising, but how far should this be carried? To Antoine Thibaudeau, an *exconventionnel* and member of the Council of State whose revealing account of these months is unsurpassed, the Tribunate's vague gesture merely hinted at the intrigue afoot. To his uneasy friend Josephine he warned: "schemes are ripening in the dark. . . . the more power Bonaparte grasps, the wider does the breach become between him and his best supporters, the Men of the

---

2 Jean-Antoine Chaptal, *Mes Souvenirs sur Napoléon* (Paris, 1893), 308–9.
3 Antoine C. Thibaudeau, *Bonaparte and the Consulate* (London, 1908), 217, 221. The French version of this invaluable memoir was published in 1827 under the title *Mémoires sur le Consulat 1801–1804, par un ancien conseiller d'état*. [All references that follow are to the English translation.]

Revolution. They will submit, no doubt; but they will no longer be attached to him."[4]

Certain collaborators, on the other hand, assuredly wished to see Bonaparte's power enhanced: notably brother Lucien, foreign minister Talleyrand, and Roederer and Regnaud, two former members of the National Assembly and original participants in the Brumaire cabal, presently leading members of the Council of State. With perhaps less zeal, second and third consuls Cambacérès and Lebrun were in their camp as well. Yet Bonaparte, sensitive to timing and public sentiment, would not publicly endorse the preferred option: designation as consul for life. Therefore, he left his supporters in the Senate, where the initiative evidently lay, somewhat in the dark.

This confusion led Bonaparte's slavishly devoted follower Lacépède, *rapporteur* of the Senate's committee, to misplay the hand. Since the constitution empowered the Senate to designate a consul for a ten-year term, Lacépède proposed that the nation's gratitude be expressed by extending the first consul's tenure here and now for an additional ten years. Another senator then proposed, as an amendment, Bonaparte's appointment for life, the response that the general actually desired. Senators Lanjuinais and Garat spoke in opposition; then a senator requested a vote on the two alternatives. President Tronchet, however, would only entertain the first proposition, and the Senate duly voted sixty to one for a prolongation of Bonaparte's term of office for an additional ten-year term, the lone dissenter being Lanjuinais, the redoubtable Breton legal scholar and liberal veteran of several revolutionary assemblies.[5]

Tronchet's maneuver slowed down the juggernaut only briefly. Since Bonaparte considered a ten-year renewal meaningless, he now launched a devious stratagem to secure the consulship for life. Responding evasively and with feigned modesty to the Senate, he declared: "I was invested with the supreme Magistracy by the vote of the people, and I cannot feel myself assured of their continued confidence in me until the act that prolongs my term of office shall have been ratified by the whole nation."[6] He then instructed Cambacérès to convene the Council of State for an act of political alchemy, to convert the Senate's proposal for a ten-year extension into a plebiscite on a life consulship.

Thibaudeau again provides light where the public record is obscure. Cambacérès convened the Council: "the questions before us are how, when,

---

4 Ibid., 219–21.
5 Ibid., 222–3; Jean Thiry, *Le Sénat de Napoléon* (Paris, 1949), 96–7.
6 Thibaudeau, *Bonaparte*, 224.

and in what terms the necessary vote shall be put to the nation?" Roederer and others maintained that the vote of the nation could not be restricted merely to the ten years fixed by the Senate: "the Senate confined itself to ten years, under the impression that it had no authority to do more; but the people's authority is unbounded, and the question to be submitted to it must be whether or not the First Consul shall be elected for life."[7] Then someone added to the mix the right of Bonaparte to name his successor, for which Roederer and Lucien had been agitating for months. When the Council finally took its vote, the members present voted yes, except for five who pointedly abstained.[8]

Cambacérès named a committee to draft a formal opinion (*avis*) from the Council of State, which it produced in short order. However, sometime between that evening and the next morning when the Council's *avis* was made public, the right of Bonaparte to name his successor disappeared from the proposition to be submitted for a plebiscite. Bonaparte considered this power to be awkward and unnecessary at the present time, and declined to accept that "duty." Thus, Bonaparte countermanded the official enactments of both the Senate (which had bypassed a life consulship in favor of a ten-year extension) and his Council of State (whose *avis* he altered to his liking). Behind the facade of the Senate and Council of State, Bonaparte himself effectively framed the brief proposition to be voted on by the French people: "Shall Napoleon Bonaparte be named first consul for life?"[9]

This turn of events distressed certain "men of the Revolution" in Bonaparte's service, but not enough for them to desert the first consul's camp. For Counselor of State Théophile Berlier, an *exconventionnel* and dedicated republican and one of the abstainers, the discomfort level was substantial, as he recalled in his memoirs: "It was painful for me to feel that we were drifting from the goal of consolidating our republican institutions. But the name [republic] still remained, and the reality could still bring a recovery of some of its rights," he maintained.[10]

After the plebiscite and the subsequent *senatus-consulte* revising the constitution, Bonaparte patiently reassured Thibaudeau that the new arrangements assured the stability and durability of the Consulate and placed the first consul on a level with foreign sovereigns, a consideration of paramount importance in Bonaparte's view. To Thibaudeau's comment that "the

---

7 Ibid., 225.   8 Ibid., 226.
9 Ibid., 226–8.
10 Théophile Berlier, *Précis de la Vie Politique de Théophile Berlier écrit par lui même et adressé à ses enfans...* (Dijon, 1838), 88; also *Boulay de la Meurthe, 1761–1840* [Mémoires publies par sa famille] (Paris, 1868), 158–9.

impression of the Revolution is still too fresh and this transition too abrupt," Bonaparte replied with his standard refrain: "For the Men of the Revolution I am the best guarantee," a mantra that liberals such as Boulay, Berlier, and Thibaudeau evidently internalized and from which they would never free themselves.[11] The more so since Bonaparte's steps toward monarchy were spaced apart, gradual, and embedded in avowals of fidelity to the Revolution's underlying achievements, garnished with the reminder that the general himself owed his career to the Revolution, although in truth that notion held little meaning for him by this time.

As he also told Thibaudeau, "the plebiscite [of 1802] has the advantage of legalizing my extension of office and placing it on the highest possible basis."[12] This was to be the first veritable plebiscite in French history. Though reminiscent of the three referenda in which citizens had approved the Jacobin constitution of 1793, the directorial constitution of 1795, and the post-Brumaire constitution of the Consulate in 1800, the coming vote concerned only Bonaparte's title and personal power. Constitutional modification would come in due course through an act of the Senate without consulting the citizens.

Back in 1800, with eligibility to vote approximating universal male suffrage, about 1.6 million citizens had turned out to endorse the Constitution of the Year VIII. However, wishing to bolster the Consulate's image with a stronger mandate than the 2 million votes recorded for the Jacobin constitution of 1793, the government falsified the results of the referendum by announcing 3.1 million "Yes" votes. Minister of Interior Lucien Bonaparte supervised the conflation of cantonal returns into spurious departmental totals unsusceptible to verification, which added 900,000 fictitious "Yes" votes, and also created around 500,000 military votes out of thin air.[13]

In 1802, by contrast, the announced result of about 3.6 million "Yes" votes was essentially honest and accurate. The wait-and-see attitude that many French citizens prudently adopted in 1800 (the *attentisme* that had become a habit after so many abrupt political changes) seems to have yielded to genuine acceptance. As historian Claude Langlois suggests, however, the falsification of 1800 inhibited the regime's public relations in 1802, since the number of verifiable "Yes" votes had actually doubled rather than increasing by a mere 20 percent over the (falsified) official results of the previous vote![14]

---

11 Thibaudeau, *Bonaparte*, 232–3.   12 Ibid., 233.
13 Claude Langlois, "Le Plébiscite de l'An VIII, ou le coup d'état du 18 pluviôse an VIII," *Annales historiques de la Révolution française* (1972), 43–65, 231–46, 391–415.
14 Claude Langlois, "Napoléon Bonaparte Plébiscité?" in *L'Election du Chef de l'Etat en France, de Hugues Capet à Nos Jours* (Paris, 1988), 81–93.

Of course voter turnout was actively promoted by local prefects in 1802 under prodding from Paris, as it could not be in 1800. Parisian officials insisted "that the voting registers be opened and available to everyone; . . . that no one neglects to express his view in the belief that it is superfluous." Official concern did not center on the prospect of "No" votes; in 1802 they numbered only 8,374. Rather, it was the extent of abstention and its implication of passive opposition that kept the government on edge. The results were reassuring and reflected an impressive advance in popular acceptance of Bonaparte's power, with the turnout of "Yes" votes actually surpassing an absolute majority of eligible voters.[15] "Men of the revolution" such as Thibaudeau and Berlier had to be impressed by this resounding quasi-democratic rite and could embrace it as a further rationale for going with the tide.

A SUCCESSOR TO BONAPARTE?

When Bonaparte excluded from the plebiscite on the life consulship the clause specifying his power to name a successor, he was rebuffing those *brumairians* who fretted incessantly, perhaps with good reason, that if Bonaparte suddenly died their entire political edifice would crumble. The Italian campaign of 1800 had sorely tested their nerves already. After the first consul disappeared over the Alps and closed with the enemy, days went by without any word from the front. Rumors of French defeat and of Bonaparte's death in battle swirled around Paris until Bonaparte cleared the air with his *bulletin* about the great victory at Marengo, in reality a near disaster, save for Desaix's heroic intervention, which had indeed led to *his* death on the battlefield.

Even without such dramatic reminders as the close call at Marengo or the royalist bomb attack of December 1800, which barely missed annihilating the first consul, the question of a successor continued to haunt his collaborators. Bonaparte himself, on the other hand, could not bear to think seriously about the succession, despite the threat of assassination plots and exposure in combat. Before 1804, he pushed aside the issue in various ways. In more candid moments Bonaparte maintained that at present no one could succeed him.

When forced by his interlocutors to discuss this, he threw up another obstacle: Suppose he did have the right to name his successor or to nominate

---

15 Roederer Papers: *Archives Nationales* (hereafter *A. N.*) 29 AP 75: circular by Roederer to prefects, 25 floréal X; *A. N.* AF IV 1432, dossier 3: Execution de l'arrêté du 20 floréal X; Rapport au Consuls, 8 thermidor X.

one to the Senate, whom could he choose? Second Consul Cambacérès, for all his loyalty, sagacity, and manifest competence, would not do, and no one ever suggested otherwise. The Bonaparte brothers (Joseph, Louis, and Lucien) even less so. Napoleon believed that his brothers owed their standing entirely to himself and had earned no consideration whatever on their own merits, despite Lucien's crucial role in Brumaire and Joseph's personal appeal and proven diplomatic talents. Napoleon could be goaded into idle speculation about other possible successors in the pre-Empire days, but only to prove how silly the whole matter seemed. Although he once told Roederer that Carnot "is perhaps worth more than another," he had long since removed Carnot from the hub of power, and probably agreed with Roederer that "the French nation will never believe itself free and honorable under a member of the Committee of Public Safety." Bonaparte also allowed that General Jean-Victor Moreau, his one-time rival, deserved consideration, only to dismiss him with this *mot*: "Si Moreau était un autre homme!" Besides, "he has no friends at all." "My natural heir is the French people," he told Roederer somewhat enigmatically. "Heredity has never been instituted by a law... it has always been established by fact... the French at this moment can only be governed by me." With such narcissistic evasions Bonaparte temporarily stymied Roederer, Talleyrand, Lucien and others seeking to fix the Brumaire settlement with the cement of an hereditary succession.[16]

Bonaparte's personal desire to take the title and powers of a king necessarily forced the succession question onto the agenda as well. With Bonaparte already consul for life, the wish to solve the succession problem in the clearest and most traditional fashion by heredity indeed provided a plausible justification for the creation of a new dynasty. But even if the linkage between imperial power and hereditary succession seemed entirely logical, it remained problematic from Napoleon's perspective.

One can almost sympathize with him as he assessed his family situation and saw a mare's nest of complications rather than an obvious solution to anything. Napoleon had no natural sons and would not have any while he remained married to Josephine, whom he unwaveringly embraced at this time. Since he had no confidence in any of his brothers, that left the option of adopting an heir, although the adoption route too had its pitfalls. Joseph, the eldest brother, had no sons as yet, and while brother Louis did, they were too young at this time to offer any certainty. The great paradox in all

---

16 Thibaudeau, 255, 257; Pierre-Louis Roederer, *Mémoires sur la Révolution, le Consulat et l'Empire*, ed. O. Aubry (Paris, 1942), 126–7, 203–11.

this is obvious: Napoleon's lack of a son coupled with his commitment to Josephine ran up against his disdain for or exasperation with the rest of his family (brothers, sisters, and their spouses), whose pretensions he resented, especially when they came at Josephine's expense. The most blatant offense to her interests was of course the advice constantly pressed on him that he should divorce her immediately and remarry a fertile European princess, advice which Napoleon adamantly rejected at this juncture as he affirmed his loyalty to Josephine.[17]

Notwithstanding such contradictions, Bonaparte's determination to acquire the cachet and powers of a monarch meshed with his collaborators' obsession with the succession issue and their concomitant desire to return to monarchical government. France would become an empire under a new dynasty, with the imperial dignity hereditary in the Bonaparte family. The specter of a first consul assassinated in yet another royalist plot mounted by the irreconcilable *chouan* chief Georges Cadoudal provided the pretext to consummate this scenario. Where gratitude to the first consul had touched off the maneuvering that ended in the life consulship, it was the imminent danger to him from this latest counterrevolutionary conspiracy that became the catalyst for establishing the Empire.[18] The process reflected a consensus, enthusiastic or grudging, within the Napoleonic elite; some remarkable notes of dissent from the same quarters; a panoply of rationalizations that are not without interest; and an intimidating mobilization of military opinion that gave this event its particular flavor.

THE LAST STAND OF THE OLD REVOLUTIONARIES

The Council of State had no tangible role to play in the turn to empire, but Bonaparte sought to build momentum among those valued and respected collaborators in the preliminary maneuvering. Second Consul Cambacérès, who usually held the chair in Bonaparte's absence, informed the Council that the first consul wished them to discuss this matter without the usual formalities and with complete candor. Not only would Bonaparte absent himself, but Cambacérès and Council secretary Locré would withdraw as well to give them maximal freedom.

Most members could not have known that Cambacérès himself did not really favor the transition, fearful that "the active inclination of the first

---

17 Roederer, *Mémoires*, 208; Owen Connelly, *The Gentle Bonaparte: a Biography of Joseph, Napoleon's Elder Brother* (New York, 1968), 50–5.
18 See Jean-Paul Bertaud, *Bonaparte etle Duc d'Enghien* (Paris, 1972), part 2.

consul, which was sometimes contained by republican forms, would no longer have any restraint as soon as we will have returned to monarchy."[19] However, if Cambacérès did not take the lead in promoting the hereditary empire he certainly did nothing publicly to oppose the tide, least of all by attempting to influence the Council of State. His withdrawal from the room in any case left the initiative to Regnaud de St. Jean d'Angély, a former member of the National Assembly of 1789, one of Bonaparte's collaborators since the first Italian campaign of 1797 (when Regnaud edited the general's house newspaper), and at the time president of the interior section of the Council.

A proposal fashioned by Regnaud and the four presidents of the Council's other sections emphatically linked the move to an hereditary empire with a reaffirmation of the Revolution's basic gains:

[T]he stability and effectiveness of hereditary power and the rights of the nation that will have voted for it must be inseparably guaranteed in the same act.... [These rights consist of] individual liberty, religious freedom, the inviolability of property, the irrevocability of the sale of the *biens nationaux*, the political equality which opens all positions to all citizens, the civil equality which assures that all citizens are judged according to the same laws, and the approval of those laws and of the levels of annual taxation by a national representation.[20]

This was the sugar coating or (as far as individual liberty was concerned) the illusion that would be used in the Senate and the Tribunate as well, and it provoked no argument. The real question before the Council was: "Is it desirable to base the Government of France on the hereditary principle?" According to Thibaudeau's credible account, Regnaud echoed Bonaparte in arguing that it was indeed "the only hope of preserving France from the disorders that an elective Government must bring upon the country. It was equally necessary, he said, to the success of our foreign relations." A prolonged silence followed, finally broken by Berlier, arguably the staunchest republican in the Council. His intervention never reached the public at the time but it has long been part of the historical record. As transcribed by Thibaudeau:

Berlier said: "If the hereditary system is now to be adopted, not a trace will remain of that Republic for whose establishment and preservation France has sacrificed untold treasure and human lives. I do not myself believe that the French people are prepared to renounce what remains of an advantage so dearly purchased. The

---

19 Cambacérès Papers: *A. N.* 286 AP 3: dossier 32, Ms carnet of 1818.
20 "Projet... pour l'établissement de l'Empire proposé au Conseil d'état par les présidents des sections en 1804," in Pelet de la Lozère, *Opinions de Napoléon... [au] Conseil d'Etat* (Paris, 1833), 302–5.

arguments deduced from our foreign relations do not seem to me to apply at all to a State the head of which has a life tenure in his office. . . ." Berlier had not, in fact, been in favor of the Consulate for life, but in the present state of affairs he was content to entrench himself behind that measure to ward off further changes. He laid special stress upon the false position in which an hereditary and monarchical system would place all those who had contributed in any degree to the success of the Revolution; a large and important class who were now to be used in reconstructing, amid the jeering contempt of their enemies, the very edifice which they had demolished. This reflection was met by Regnaud, who said: "Have no fear on that point. The man who governs France has an arm strong enough to protect one party from triumphing over another. He is himself the child of the Revolution."[21]

After Berlier's intervention a debate began around the question of whether, when all seemed to be going so well, this was an opportune time for such a change. As Thibaudeau summarized the argument (which reflected his own view): "At the present moment the world at large will see in it ambition rather than patriotism. It is both ill timed and premature. To these considerations the partisans of the hereditary system replied that a period of calm was the best possible time to prepare for the storm and to give France the best constitution possible." Within its narrow terms, the debate became highly animated and required four sittings, after the Council finished its ordinary business, to wind down. Finally twenty members endorsed the adoption of hereditary rule, while seven voted for postponement.[22]

More significantly, the seven dissenters refused to sign the address drawn up by Regnaud, claiming that they had been expressly invited to offer their individual opinions. If the majority signed Regnaud's address, the minority would draft a counter address, which might leak and embarrass the government. When Bonaparte heard of this impasse, he asked that each member individually submit his opinion to him in writing. As with Cambacérès, he showed no resentment against the members who opposed his plan since they had played by his rules, had kept their arguments in-house, and no doubt framed their reservations tactfully.

Decades later, when Berlier composed a political memoir of limited circulation intended for his descendants, he referred his readers to Thibaudeau's previously published account of that debate in the Council of State. But Berlier lingered with pride over his act of opposition. He assumed that resistance in the Council would be fruitless, he recalled, "but it was impossible for me not to render this last homage to the Republic that I had loved so

---

21 Thibaudeau, *Bonaparte*, 311–14.
22 See also Pelet, *Opinions*, 54–60. The seven who voted for postponement included Berenger, Berlier, Boulay de la Meurthe, Dauchy, Réal, and Treilhard; the identity of the seventh is not known.

much, that I had served with such good faith in the midst of so many vexations, and whose disappearance down to its very name I could not witness without experiencing the most painful feeling."[23]

All the more necessary, then, to explain his continued collaboration with Napoleon after the Empire became a fait accompli. Berlier's exact words give us the most explicit glimpse into the sentiments of a once-ardent republican in the service of Emperor Napoleon I:

The empire having been decreed and consecrated by the national will [in a plebiscite], it was of course necessary that I submit to it. And it was a consolation to me to think that I had done everything that my conscience prescribed to defend in legal fashion the remnant of republican government. On the other hand, looking around me I saw a host of good citizens who, initially partisans of the republic but now fatigued by the oscillations suffered for several years, ended up being persuaded that in the heart of an old and monarchical Europe, the best France could reasonably hope for definitively was a representative government under a new dynasty, whose power would be limited by liberal institutions. [Personally Bonaparte still retained Berlier's confidence] . . . His ambition satisfied by his arrival at the acme of constitutional power, victor abroad, he would make it his principal concern to govern the interior in a liberal fashion. Finally, at bottom the man was a child of the Revolution, who could not forget his origin and who (offering every guarantee to the legal interests born of the revolution) also presented a sure support for patriots concerned about order. There was in this view plenty of plausible grounds for hope. And I was prevailed on to consider it a duty dictated by liberalism not to abandon positions from which patriots could still render service to the state and to liberty.[24]

In addition, Berlier acknowledged that personal considerations helped keep him in the Napoleonic fold, and the historian must be grateful for such candor. "I was without any patrimonial fortune," he noted, and while he now enjoyed an annual income of 25,000 francs as a counselor of state, recently supplemented by 15,000 francs and free lodging as president of the *Conseil des Prises* (the commission that dealt with maritime seizures), he had commanded such income for only a short time and had not as yet amassed the capital necessary to support his family. Nor was the prospect of returning to the practice of law at the age of 45 appealing. Berlier felt both too old and too young for that: "It was a very advanced age for resuming pleading as a barrister, yet perhaps not sufficient to secure a comfortable existence in the simple work of a practice (*travail du cabinet*), which is ordinarily fruitful only for older legal consultants."[25] The pressure of family responsibility,

---

23 Berlier, *Précis*, 92–5. 24 Ibid.
25 Ibid., 95.

the lack of an agreeable alternative, a lingering confidence in Napoleon's commitment to the revolutionary legacy, and above all his habituation to public service prevailed over Berlier's mortally wounded republican sensibility.

With a lesser degree of angst, the same was true of Boulay de la Meurthe. During the Council's debate on the imperial option, Boulay supported Berlier's attempt to at least postpone the transition. His spare memoir is regrettably vague about the dissenting opinion that he finally submitted to Bonaparte (although like Berlier he mentions with pride that he retained a copy of that opinion in his personal papers): "it was motivated by the political situation of the country and the state of the parties." In addition, he offered the advice that if hereditary power was adopted, Bonaparte "should have the right to derogate from the order of succession that will be established within his family, and to choose his immediate successor." Once the Empire was in place, Boulay, like Berlier, rallied without reservation and readily rationalized his commitment: "that this political system can be reconciled with the principles proclaimed in 1789, and that [Boulay] regarded Napoleon as the man most capable of consolidating and terminating the Revolution."[26]

A 'DEBATE' IN THE TRIBUNATE

With its public sessions and unfettered speeches, the Tribunate was the Consulate's most independent institution. If a government proposal provoked opposition in the Council of State or the Senate, it usually remained within the four walls of its chamber, but a dissident address in the Tribunate might incite a ripple of public interest in the informal communications networks that no government censorship could suppress. The Consulate had devalued oratory, deeming it an invitation to demagoguery, but oratorical prowess remained central to the job description of the one hundred tribunes. True, in 1802 the most contentious tribunes had been purged by the Senate at Bonaparte's behest during the prescribed renewal of one-fifth of the Tribunate's members, but it remained the least predictable forum in the French state.

To Bonaparte, of course, the distinction between private and public meant everything. Accustomed to obedience in the chain of command and to military notions of honor, he could tolerate dissent expressed privately but could not abide public criticism. After 1802, however, even if tribunes still

---

26 *Boulay de la Meurthe*, 162–5.

raised objections to particular sections of proposed laws, the government reasonably assumed that on broad political issues the Tribunate would be as tractable as the Senate or the Council of State, perhaps more so since many tribunes were eager for advancement. Unleashing the oratory of the Tribunate therefore seemed a useful way to lay the imperial option formally before the public. While hardly anyone would hear the speeches, they could read them in the *Moniteur* or other journals.

Tribune Jean-François Curée, an *exconventionnel* and president of the Tribunate back in 1801, was tapped for the honor, and on April 28 he moved that "Napoleon Bonaparte, currently first consul, be declared emperor of the French and that the imperial dignity be declared hereditary in his family." Although the Tribunate had no power to enact this proposal, weeks of intrigue at last came to a head. Curée's colleagues crowded around the rostrum to support the motion as the president drew up a list of speakers. In a sea of solemn rhetoric, these "men of the revolution" (for the most part) would publicly herald the transition from an elective republic of sorts to an hereditary empire – to monarchy in a new key.

Beneath references to history and political theory, gratefulness to Napoleon dominated the discourse. The speakers invested this individual of extraordinary achievement with all the hopes and fears they had attached before 1800 to abstractions like the nation, the principles of 1789, or the Republic. In that respect, the Napoleonic Empire seems a logical culmination of Brumaire, when this psychological transposition, this escape from freedom, began.

An unscripted and discordant note, however, marred this marathon of adulation, when one tribune rose to oppose Curée's motion. Ultimately his speech had no effect on the outcome; if anything, it was invoked by Napoleonic loyalists to illustrate the hollow notion that French public life remained free. For the moment, the speech by Lazare Carnot, arguably the most renowned member of the Tribunate, exploded around his colleagues. Unlike Berlier's stand in the Council of State, news of Carnot's address spread quickly, although police informers claimed that it had little impact. Carnot later noted: "I received letters of congratulation from all over, I was personally astonished at the prodigious success of this speech in a city accustomed for so long to bending without resistance to all the wishes of the master."[27]

---

27 Alphonse Aulard (ed.), *Paris sous le Consulat: recueil de documents* (1909), IV: 769–70; M.-A. Cornet, *Souvenirs Sénatoriaux* (Paris, 1824), 27. But Cf. Marcel Reinhard, *Le Grand Carnot, II: L'Organisateur de la victoire* (Paris, 1952), 273.

A central figure in two regimes that preceded the Consulate, Carnot was the leading military strategist on the Committee of Public Safety in 1793–4 and a founding member of the Directory who was ousted in the Fructidor coup in 1797 and forced into hiding. Historians in the republican tradition have always celebrated Carnot as "the organizer of victory" in the Year II, and Bonaparte, too, respected the former military engineer. After Brumaire, the first consul repatriated Carnot from exile and appointed him war minister; Carnot held that post until Bonaparte, having soured on him, effectively provoked his resignation. After a brief return to private life, Carnot learned that the Senate had named him to a vacancy in the Tribunate in March 1802. Carnot stubbornly maintained his independence in that body and offered an escalating resistance to Napoleon's ambitions. First he had opposed the Legion of Honor. Then he had ruined the Tribunate's unanimous endorsement of the life consulate by recording a "No" vote in its official register.[28]

Carnot's speech in 1804 conveyed no great articulation of republican ideology but simply a series of honest, critical observations. Carnot stated: "I am very far from wishing to attenuate the praise given to the First Consul." As a direct beneficiary of the Eighteenth Brumaire, Carnot acknowledged the need for a temporary concentration of authority at that time to rescue the Republic from "the edge of an abyss." The very success of Brumaire now offered the opportunity "to establish liberty on solid foundations." The United States, he pointed out, was an example of a stable and prospering republic. In today's favorable circumstances, he added in his most striking phrase, "it is less difficult to form a republic without anarchy than a monarchy without despotism."[29]

Carnot saluted Bonaparte's accomplishments in advancing liberty such as the civil code, but asked: "would it be the proper recompense for him to offer him the sacrifice of that same liberty?" Bonaparte had a unique opportunity "to resolve the great problem of public liberty," but in effect turned his back on it. The whole monarchical model offended Carnot: "nothing has yet been invented to temper supreme power other than what has been called intermediary corps or privileged bodies. Is it therefore of a new nobility that one wishes to speak?" Having declared: "I will vote against the reestablishment of monarchy," Carnot concluded that if it was adopted by the French people he would give the Empire his adherence: "I have always made it my credo to submit to existing laws."[30]

[28] Reinhard, *Carnot*, 271–2.   [29] Ibid.
[30] Ibid.

The tribunes waiting to speak after Carnot fell over themselves to undo the damage and rebut this affront to the new consensus. Several attacked the messenger as well as his message. Carnot, they declared, was hardly the man to criticize his colleagues' political acumen. Tribune Carrion-Nisas, playwright and former classmate of Bonaparte's at the military academy, attacked bluntly: Carnot's first experience of democratic leadership on the Committee of Public Safety placed him among the *proscripteurs*, exclaimed the tribune, while during his second leadership stint, as a member of the Directory, Carnot was himself proscribed, to be rescued only by the Consulate. Lawyer Jean Albisson concluded (completely missing Carnot's sense of himself and the judgment of posterity), "I cannot contain my astonishment at having heard the apologia for an elective and temporary magistracy coming from a mouth that ought to have been sufficiently abashed by the mere recollection of the Year II or the Year V."[31]

Having disposed of Carnot, the tribunes justified the monarcho-imperial option against his aspersions. The learned financial specialist A.-H. Arnould invoked Jean Bodin on the superiority of hereditary over elective monarchy, and argued that the guarantee of liberty endured in the legislature's power over taxation. Carrion-Nisas replied bombastically to Carnot's warnings against despotism: "What! Do we not have law and a social compact? Eh! Who is speaking here of putting a man above the laws?" Unlike a king, the new emperor will not be the owner of the country. "He is the chief of the French, by their wish; his domain is moral and no legal servitude can arise from such a system." Carnot had complained that a return to monarchy would not be consensual because the press was not free to debate it; Carrion-Nisas candidly invoked Bonaparte's standard justification for muzzling the press: "Everyone knows how that liberty is fatal, how it promptly degenerates into license."[32]

Louis Costas, formerly a scientist on Bonaparte's Egyptian expedition, rejected Carnot's appeal to the example of the United States. No great power threatened to invade or foment upheaval in the geographically isolated United States. "The Americans have no need at all to defend themselves against the constantly reviving attempts of a family expelled from the throne." In France, only a fixed order of succession would put an end to the Bourbon's pretensions, he argued, as it had to those of the Stuarts in

---

31 All the speeches are reproduced in the *Moniteur*, 11–15 floréal XII. See also Roederer, "Observations sur le discours du Cit. Carnot contre l'heredité," *Journal de Paris*, 12–14 Mai 1804, and other clippings in Roederer Papers, *A. N.* 29 AP 78.
32 *Moniteur*, 11–15 floréal.

England. In a different vein, tribune Carret declared: "We are thwarting the avaricious and always bloody intrigues of elective regimes; we are precluding even the possibility of factions and the springing up of party chiefs."[33]

But we have not yet arrived at the major theme in the tribunes' apologia for the elevation of Bonaparte to hereditary emperor. This was the argument from original revolutionary intent, previously introduced in Regnaud's abortive proposal to the Council of State, where he argued that "the Revolution had not been started by the nation, in 1789, against the heredity of the supreme magistracy . . . heredity ought [now] to be established in conformity with the principles developed at the beginning of the Revolution."[34]

This reference to original revolutionary intent became a litany in the Tribunate's discourse. Tribune Jard-Panvillier, one of the "perpetuals" of the revolutionary assemblies, explained. When the nation enjoyed its maximal freedom in 1789–90, before things began to go wrong, it chose to have a unified and hereditary executive power. By their conduct, the Bourbons forfeited their right to that role and forced the nation into a democratic government which in turn produced "scourges and anarchy." Under Bonaparte's "government of One," France recovered its unity and tranquility as well as glory abroad. However, Bourbon-English plots still threatened to cause turmoil comparable to that caused by elections in the past. An hereditary emperor would definitively end that threat, return France to the path envisaged in 1789, and "preserve the advantages of the Revolution by the choice of a dynasty equally interested in maintaining them."[35]

Costas, rejecting Carnot's claim that only public functionaries were advocating the imperial title, maintained that the whole nation had expressed this kind of preference at the start of the Revolution, and that the likely plebiscite to come would represent public opinion more faithfully than "the deliberations of those tumultuous assemblies, where one voted under the knife of parties." Albisson, too, emphasized the original design of 1789: "The Revolution attached heredity to the executive power . . . that was one of the fundamental principles with which the Revolution began, and with which it was destined to be consummated." The goal of Eighteenth Brumaire, "to terminate the Revolution by fixing it to the principles with which it began," was therefore about to be realized at last.[36]

---

33 Ibid.
34 Pelet, *Opinions*, 302–4.
35 *Moniteur*, 11–15 floréal XII.
36 *Moniteur*, 15 floréal. The reliance of most tribunes on original intent in 1789 as a rationale for a return to "monarchy" in 1804 ought to give pause. It suggests that in the National Assembly's initial formulation of revolutionary ideology – the only one that mattered by now – an hereditary executive did indeed loom large as one cornerstone for stability in the new regime. It should not be so lightly

THE ARMY AND THE COMING OF THE EMPIRE

When they overthrew the Directory, the Brumaire plotters placed military units in the Paris region under General Bonaparte's command. Actively involved in the raucous showdown at Saint Cloud on 19 Brumaire, and deployed conspicuously in the capital as well, the troops played only a supporting role in a parliamentary coup; the army did not impose its will on a helpless civilian government. Now, in the passage from Consulate to Empire, the ultimate defining act for the Napoleonic regime, the army's role was at once less evident yet arguably even more significant.

In the spring of 1804, the officer corps and the troops they commanded set up an insistent clamor for the designation of Napoleon Bonaparte as emperor. Had Napoleon encountered serious resistance to his scheme, the threat of the army's manifest displeasure might well have been invoked to sweep it aside. In the event, Napoleon did not have to play that card. The petitions that poured into Paris from the military make the proclamation of the Empire seem an irresistible proposition. It is difficult to reconstruct with exactitude how this campaign of pen and ink was orchestrated, but a few markers survive in the archives.

Just after the minister of justice issued his preliminary report on the Cadoudal-Pichegru plot to assassinate Bonaparte, War Minister Alexandre Berthier (Bonaparte's inseparable chief-of-staff) swung into action. Berthier ordered commanding officers to read the minister's report to their assembled troops, and many understood that the appropriate response would be a mass petition expressing outrage at the plot and devotion to Bonaparte. Commanders of two large military encampments established for a cross-channel invasion were especially zealous. Their petitions of "homage, veneration, and devotion" contained over 21,000 signatures![37]

Since Bonaparte had not yet publicly revealed his imperial plans, this first effort to mobilize military opinion remained decidedly vague in thrust. Soon, however, the campaign of military petitions was harnessed to Curée's motion in the Tribunate for vesting Napoleon with the hereditary imperial title. As the 69th line regiment now put it: "The heredity and unity of the

---

dismissed as it is in François Furet's account, which holds that even in 1789, the sheer radicalism of the National Assembly's break with the past made France "a republic in everything but name," with the king relegated to inconsequentiality from the start. [François Furet and Ran Halévi, "L'Année 1789," *Annales E.S.C.*, 1989.] A more traditional historiographical view of 1789–90 as a compromise with the old order that fell far short of democracy and republicanism seems to find support in this unlikely setting, in this revalorization of original intent in 1804.

37 *A. N.* BB II 851A: Letters from generals Bourcier, Junot, and Soult to Berthier, 28–30 pluviôse XII.

executive power appear to us as the only satisfactory means to assure France its tranquillity and well being."

The drumbeat of military petitioning for an imperial crown came in part spontaneously but in the main from the top down through the chain of command. Officers were made to understand by their superiors that they must board this convoy and bring their subordinates along. For example, in several military divisions (the 2nd and 5th in Eastern France), divisional generals circulated model petitions for the convenience of local commanders.[38]

Berthier used a meeting of the general staff, commanders in the Paris region, and visiting commanders from other divisions to put the crème de la crème of the officer corps on record in one intimidating petition. This constituted an unprecedented intervention in the affairs of state at the highest levels of the army. Although it shares the language of base flattery common to other civilian and military petitions, this document is noteworthy because it articulates a distinct Bonapartist position quite different from the speeches in the Tribunate and essentially independent of any connection with the revolutionary experience. The array of military leaders who signed Berthier's petition assured Bonaparte that,

> You owe it to the France that has chosen you for its chief, and that regards you as its second founder, indeed you owe it to yourself, to assure for your handiwork the same immortality as for your name. Shall the fruit of so much effort and so many triumphs be surrendered to the caprices of blind chance? . . . Let this glorious heritage remain in perpetuity in your family. The moment has come when the Nation, proud of its chief, must invest him with an éclat that will reflect back upon itself. It is time that it confer on him a title more proportionate to his exploits, to the extent of the French empire, to the rank which he holds in Europe. . . . The title of Emperor that Charlemagne carried, does it not belong by right to the man who recalls it to our eyes as a legislator and warrior?[39]

Berthier's petition effectively leaves behind the dialogue over the revolutionary legacy and looks forward to a generically new order, an imperial Bonapartist order with special meaning for the glory of the armed forces.

The military petitions demanding in one voice the elevation of Bonaparte to an hereditary imperial title actually reflected three visions. The petition circulated by Berthier among the general officers and their aides, with its emphasis on military glory, effected a paradigm shift and evoked a post-revolutionary future founded on the unique talents and achievements of Napoleon Bonaparte. A second, more familiar, view welcomed the Empire

---

38 *A. N.* BB II 850B.
39 *A. N.* BB II 850A: Adresse présenté au Premier Consul, 22 floréal XII.

as a reconfiguration of the Consulate that would thwart the counterrevolution definitively and guarantee the future of liberty and equality. "Which is the family that can offer us a greater guarantee for the maintenance of public liberty and equality?" asked the Toulouse garrison. Or as the garrison in Tarbes declared with undue optimism: "The French people, having become your subjects, will not for all that lose their rights to liberty and to equality, which you yourself have cemented." A third variant, as in petitions circulated by Divisional General Dupont, anticipated the Empire as the final burial of the Revolution's legacy of anarchic disruption.[40] We can see at once the advantage of this ambiguity in creating a broad base of acceptance for the Empire. As in Brumaire, Frenchmen still saw in Bonaparte what they hoped to see. Now the degree of wishful thinking is more obvious, and Berthier's petition stands as the most accurate omen of what the future would hold. It also best conveys the sheer insistence on the imperial option emanating from the officer corps.

THE SENATE RESPONDS

Napoleon's soaring ambition thus set in motion a wave of responses. While members of the Council of State argued heatedly over the imperial option behind closed doors, the tribunes drowned Carnot's remarkable public dissent in a chorus of enthusiasm, especially by linking Napoleon's imperial status with the Revolution's original intent to incorporate hereditary monarchy. Army units across the country meanwhile generated a mass of petitions so intimidating that they made the transition to empire seem irresistible. This in turn influenced the response of the Senate, which alone could formally proclaim the change.

The Senate had itself initiated the movement toward hereditary government in an address to the first consul on March 27 that vaguely espoused the desirability of making Bonaparte's achievement permanent. By early May, the Senate was more than ready to endorse the imperial transition explicitly proposed by Curée, with the added urgency of precluding any military démarche that might preempt civil authority altogether. In its official address, the Senate would add to its many justifications of an imperial dynasty the startling observation that "it alone can curb the dangerous rivalries in a country covered with numerous armies commanded by great captains."[41]

---

40 *A. N.* BB II B; *A. N.* BB II 851A.
41 *Moniteur* No. 226, 16 floréal XII: "Réponse du Sénat, 14 floréal." For the Senate's role in general see Thiry, *Le Sénat de Napoléon*, 125–30.

In the Senate, Roederer, an active proponent of the imperial crown, proposed a bold addendum. Bonaparte had long since wearied of Roederer's pedantic zeal and had promoted him to the Senate in 1802 to get him out from underfoot in the Council of State, where he had initially seemed indispensable, but the Senator remained a tireless advocate for his theories of government. Roederer's voluminous, prolix manuscripts, published by his son in the 1850s, contain several memos from this campaign with his own particular inflection. "Around imperial heredity there must be a grand dignity that should be at the same time a great hereditary magistracy," he argued. "Without that precaution, the supreme prerogative will lack support and guarantee." As a magistrate on the Parlement of Metz before the Revolution, Roederer was perhaps nostalgic for such tenured "intermediary corps," which Montesquieu had famously extolled as bulwarks of liberty against despotism – exactly the kind of hereditary bodies abolished by the National Assembly in 1789 and derided by Carnot in his speech to the Tribunate.[42]

In an undated letter from the Year XII to Joseph Bonaparte, Roederer pressed these ideas on his friend. "All is not completed with heredity and imperiality. It is necessary to establish new families around a new dynasty." Think twenty-five years ahead, he urged, when most of young Napoleon's original supporters will be gone and he will be surrounded by potential enemies. The interests of the next generation must be anticipated. No matter how generous the emoluments and perquisites for those now in favor, their children might find themselves without patrimony or profession, but "with the memories and habits of a lavish lifestyle." As potential supporters par excellence of the new government in the future, the sons of today's senators need access and wealth. It would be best to "create hereditary seats in the Senate, which will thereby become a corps homogeneous with [imperial] power."[43]

Would this notion fly? In the notes Roederer used to prepare for the Senate's deliberation on the hereditary empire, he jotted the following headings:

- appeal to unconstitutionality
- judgment on a resolution by the Corps Législatif
- a jury for crimes of state
- policing of the book trade

---

42 Antoine M. Roederer (ed.), *Oeuvres du Comte P. L. Roederer* (Paris, 1854), III: 508–10.
43 Ibid., III: 507–8.

- guarantee against arbitrary arrests
- guarantee for the Senate: senatorial heredity[44]

Some of these points addressed potential objections to be overcome in the pending debate (that the change was unconstitutional or that the Corps Législatif had to be consulted), but more importantly other points laid down elements for the Senate's quid pro quo. While fully prepared to bless this momentous transition, the Senate hoped to extract a few concessions and guarantees, sops to its presumed status as the guarantor of liberty. During the runup to the Empire, as we have seen, certain counselors of state, tribunes, and army units represented the transition to empire as entirely consistent with the maintenance of public liberty. The Senate's official response, delivered by François de Neufchâteau, adopted that line and tried to give it some substance.[45]

François's address described the essence of the imperial transition accurately enough: "This glorious repose we will owe to an hereditary Government of one man, elevated above all others, invested with a great power, surrounded with éclat." He projected utter confidence that this new government would "defend public liberty, maintain equality, and dip its banners before the expression of the sovereign will of the people." Imperial power would be vested in a family "whose destiny is inseparable from that of the Revolution," and who will therefore protect the purchasers of national properties, which the counterrevolution would like to wrest from them; the emperor would guarantee the safety of all Frenchmen "who have remained faithful to the sovereignty of the People" and even defend those who, misled during the Revolution's political torments [i.e., Jacobins or royalists], have since sought indulgence. Finally, the new regime ought to render futile

---

44 Roederer Papers: *A. N.* 29 AP 78: Ms. Notes.
45 François had impeccable credentials as a liberal and revolutionary public servant. Poet, playwright, and man of letters during the old regime; departmental administrator elected to the Legislative Assembly of 1791; a deputy to the Convention who declined to take his seat and was arrested during the terror; a member of the Directory after Fructidor. His most important public service came as Minister of Interior from June 1798 to June 1799, where he promoted statistical surveys, modern agronomy, industrial development, and public education – what one scholar has described as an Enlightenment project for a commercial republic. (See James Livesey, "An Agent of Enlightenment in the French Revolution: François de Neufchâteau," Harvard Ph.D. dissertation, 1994.) François accepted the "revolutionary legacy" vision of the imperial transition, and for his energy in advancing it Bonaparte remained grateful. When the new order gave the emperor power to name the Senate's president, his first choice was François de Neufchâteau. Two years later, when his second term expired, Napoleon sent him a personal note of thanks, without the use of titles or flowery salutations but with a simple candor, "for your zeal in service to the *patrie* and for your devotion to my person. Do not doubt my eagerness to give you always the proof of my affection" [*A. N.* 27 AP 14, fol. 1: à St. Cloud, 19 May 1806].

any plots in behalf of the Bourbons, those upholders of "a throne uniquely composed of feudal trophies."[46]

François's final peroration turned into a liberal epiphany, a wish list of core liberal values: "Liberty and equality must be sacred; the social compact cannot be violated; the sovereignty of the people will never be ignored... with the independence of the great [institutional] authorities assured; the free and enlightened vote of taxes; the security of properties; the liberty of individuals, of the press, of elections; and the inviolability of constitutional laws."[47]

Napoleon, who publicly vaunted his dedication to "the triumph of equality and public liberty," readily agreed to proposals advocated by Roederer and his colleagues that confirmed the Senate's symbolic role as guardian of liberal values. Under its organic law establishing the Empire, the Senate would appoint two standing committees. One, misleadingly called La commission sénatoriale de la liberté de la presse, was to assure that no abuses occurred in the government's censorship of books. This committee proved a dead letter from the start, in part because the regime's efforts at regulating and censoring the written word focused on newspapers and periodicals, a domain from which the commission was expressly excluded. The second committee, La commission sénatoriale de la liberté inviduelle, on the other hand, quickly established its presence as a watchdog over the regime's extensive practice of extra-legal detention, not only of political dissidents and royalist plotters but of other "dangerous" persons, social misfits, and even certain indicted felons acquitted at trial. In effect, this committee became the repository or last vestige of the Senate's self-image as a liberal institution.[48] For the present, these provisions of the organic law establishing the Empire were meant as a balm of good conscience for senators who were "men of the Revolution" like François, although they did not suffice for the handful of Senators who are believed to have cast the Senate's three recorded "No" votes or to have abstained.[49]

In the rush to closure, however, the Senate also launched a trial balloon in an entirely different spirit, the spirit of Roederer's program for an hereditary oligarchy to surround the new dynasty. Might not the Senate be made an

---

46 *Moniteur*, No. 226, 16 floréal XII.   47 Ibid.
48 The problem of preventive detention and the role of the senatorial committee on individual liberty is discussed in my book, *Napoleon and his Collaborators*, chap. 7.
49 These are assumed to include Lambrechts, Garat, Sieyès, Volney, and Grégoire – the lone senator to speak out repeatedly against the transition – as well as the ailing Lanjuinais, who was not able to join his dissenting colleagues. Thiry, *Sénat*, 140, who cites Henri Grégoire, *Mémoires*, 439–41.

hereditary body alongside the Bonaparte family? Gingerly hoping to ride Napoleon's coattails to hereditary status for itself, the Senate provoked a firm and contemptuous rebuff from Napoleon. Which is not to say that the emperor entirely rejected Roederer's logic. On the contrary, he would later implement it on his own terms. Once ensconced on the imperial throne, Napoleon recognized that an emperor required a nobility to validate and refract his own eminence; that permanence and heredity had their place in a new socio-political infrastructure. In 1808, Napoleon created an hereditary imperial nobility from across the spectrum of his collaborators, including all leading generals and veteran servitors from the Council of State and the Senate, but he never sanctioned an hereditary body like the House of Lords.[50]

An imperial nobility would have been entirely consistent with Berthier's vision of the Bonapartist future, but for the moment it was François's "revolutionary legacy" version that framed the upcoming plebiscite on the hereditary succession, the last act of the sovereign people until 1815. The official results of the 1804 plebiscite were almost identical to the vote in 1802, with 3,572,000 votes cast (of which a mere 8,272 were "No"). If we look behind the raw total, however, we find some interesting nuances in the all-important turnout that perhaps reflect the residual civic consciousness of French citizens. For this was not in fact a robotic repetition of the previous vote.

In the first place, "France" was more extensive than in 1802, since the annexation of Italian territory had created several new departments that increased the total voting population. Second, concerted efforts had raised the turnout in a handful of departments, notably the Dyle in Belgium (from 21,000 to 74,000 in round numbers); the Seine (from 70,000 to 121,000); and the Seine Inférieure (from 46,000 to 64,000). However, against those few higher totals, thirty-nine departments in almost all sections of France proper (Brittany, the East, the Center, the Southwest, and Languedoc) saw turnout fall in 1804 by 25–40, even 50 percent from the impressive departmental totals of 1802; there were at least 10,000 or more commonly 20,000 fewer votes cast in each of these departments than in 1802.[51]

The explanation is a matter of speculation. Perhaps turnout was affected by the resumption of war, or resentment by sentimental royalists against

---

50 Thiry, *Sénat*, 135–6; Pelet, *Opinions*, 61–3.   51 A. N. AF IV 1432, fol. 3.

the murder of the Duke d'Enghien, or by chagrin among republicans at the demise of the Republic; perhaps it reflected a spreading cynicism and indifference. We can conclude only that the support of popular opinion on which Bonaparte claimed to rely for his legitimacy, canvassed in his preferred form of a plebiscite, was eroding at the margins rather than growing with the transition to Empire.

2

The Bonapartes and Germany

T. C. W. BLANNING

Of all the images to adorn the covers of histories of the nineteenth century, the most ubiquitous must surely be Anton von Werner's depiction of the proclamation of the German Empire on January 18, 1871, in the Hall of Mirrors of the Palace of Versailles. Surrounded by the German princes, the new Emperor William I looks down impassively from the dais at the cheering throng of gorgeously uniformed officers, headed by the two main architects of victory, Prince Otto von Bismarck and Field Marshal Helmuth von Moltke. Conspicuous by his absence was the sensitive young King Ludwig II of Bavaria, for whom the thought of his detested Hohenzollern uncle desecrating the palace of the Sun King he venerated was too much to bear. His refusal to attend the celebrations is a salutary reminder that not all Germans were triumphalist in 1871. Ludwig's own prime minister, Baron von der Pfordten, wrote in his diary, "seventy-eight years ago the French killed their king; today the Bavarian deputies have placed their king and country under the military domination of Prussia. *Finis Bavariae!*"[1] Well might they lament the apotheosis of the King of Prussia, for Bavaria had always flourished when French power was at its zenith. It had been Napoleon I who had turned the Wittelsbach electorate into a kingdom and had given it no fewer than eighty-three extra territories when he destroyed the Holy Roman Empire.[2]

This juxtaposition of triumphalist Prussia and despondent Bavaria was not inevitable or even natural. On the contrary, it was France and Prussia which seemed to be natural allies. During the first two of the three Silesian wars which won great-power status for Frederick the Great between 1740

---

1 Quoted in Ludwig Hüttl, *Ludwig II. König von Bayern* (Munich, 1986), 190.
2 Walter Demel, *Der bayerische Staatsabsolutismus 1806/8–1817. Staats- und gesellschaftspolitische Motivationen und Hintergründe der Reformära in der ersten Phase des Königreichs Bayern* (Munich, 1983), 59. This figure does not include smaller Free Imperial Cities or the territories of the Imperial Knights.

and 1763, they were on the same side. It was only the greed and folly of Louis XV and his advisers, together with a good slice of bad luck, which brought the *renversement des alliances* of 1756. The French Revolution put matters back on track by ending the ill-starred Austrian connection; as the Brissotin orator Vergniaud told the National Assembly on January 18, 1792, "We can see that the abrogation of this treaty [of May 1, 1756] is a revolution as necessary in foreign affairs, both for Europe and for France, as the destruction of the Bastille has been for our internal regeneration. (*Bravo! Bravo! Enthusiastic applause from the Assembly and from the public galleries.*)"[3] During the first years of the Revolution, an alliance between Prussia and France was given serious consideration by both parties. In 1790, Frederick William II sent an unofficial envoy, the banker Ephraim, to Paris to test the water. As late as 1791, the minister of war, Narbonne, was trying to enlist the Duke of Brunswick as the commander-in-chief of the Revolution's army. This was the very man who was to command the Prussian army which invaded France in the summer of 1792, lending his name to the infamous "Brunswick Manifesto" in the bargain.[4] At the heart of these attempts at rapprochement lay more than the practical if potent bonding agent of "my enemy's enemy is my friend," the enemy in question being of course Austria. There was also a strong sense of ideological affinity. Time and again radical orators in the National Assembly went out of their way to praise enlightened Prussia and the "immortal glory" (Rühl) of Frederick the Great, the "*roi-philosophe*" (Isnard), who had given his people "wise laws, modest taxation, sound finances, and prompt, impartial and cheap justice" (Hérault de Séchelles).[5]

So it was a great surprise to the Revolutionaries when Prussia joined Austria in the war of 1792. Like so many subsequent historians of the period, they had failed to appreciate that the Prussians were much more interested in Eastern Europe than in the West. It was to secure territory in Poland, especially the long-coveted city of Danzig, that they sank their differences with the Austrians. Once that booty had been secured by the second partition of Poland in 1793, they began to withdraw from the war. The peace treaty signed in April 1795 at Basle was, as the Prussian negotiator Hardenberg claimed, "advantageous, secure and honorable" for both sides,

---

3 *Archives Parlementaires de 1787 à 1860: Recueil complet des débats législatifs et politiques des chambres françaises*, 127 vols. (Paris, 1879–1913), 37: 492.
4 Kurt Holzapfel, "Intervention oder Koexistenz: Preussens Stellung zu Frankreich 1789–92," *Zeitschrift für Geschichtswissenschaft*, 25, 7 (1977): 787–802; Albert Sorel, *L'Europe et la Révolution française*, 8 vols. (Paris, 1885–1905), 2: 334.
5 *Archives Parlementaires*, 35: 398, 36: 614, 37: 89.

which was why it kept the peace between Prussia and France for the next eleven years. Prussia abandoned her alliance with Austria, withdrew from the war, and agreed that France should occupy the left bank of the Rhine until a final peace was concluded with the Holy Roman Empire. In return, France guaranteed compensation on the right bank and allowed the Prussians to gather together the states of northern Germany in a neutrality zone, thus greatly enhancing their political influence. Most important of all, peace in the west meant that they would keep their gains in Poland. In short, the Prussians achieved their main war aims and left the war as victors over their two *Erbfeinde*, the Habsburg Monarchy and Poland.

It is important to bear in mind relations between Revolutionary France and Prussia if we are to understand just how different was Napoleon's policy. In this regard, as in so many others, he most emphatically was *not* the "heir" or "executor" of the French Revolution. Amicable relations between France and Prussia could have been sustained indefinitely, so long as northern Germany was recognized as a legitimate zone of interest for Prussia. It was only when Napoleon's vaulting ambition, fed by his easy victories over Russia and Austria in 1805, turned his attention northward and eastward that this harmony was ruptured. Even then, the crushing defeats he inflicted on the Prussians at Jena and Auerstedt need not have led to any permanent disruption. It was the excessive brutality with which he treated the vanquished which turned a tradition of mutual assistance into its very opposite.

This brutality was of two kinds. The first was the despoliation inflicted by the French armies. Since 1792, they had brought to the territories they conquered a degree of sustained devastation not seen since the worst years of the Thirty Years War.[6] Prussia's fate after the war of 1806–7, however, was especially horrendous. By their own account, during the two years of their occupation the French extracted through requisitions and levies around 1,400,000,000 francs, or more than sixteen times the annual revenue of the Prussian state, to which must be added an immeasurable amount of freelance work by individual soldiers.[7] In East Prussia, the worst affected province, villages were razed, farms burned, and cattle stocks virtually eliminated, falling to between 2% and 5% of pre-war levels; in Berlin, approximately 75% of newborn children did not survive; the rate of suicide increased sharply; and

---

6 I have examined and illustrated this phenomenon in some detail in my book *The French Revolution in Germany. Occupation and Resistance in the Rhineland, 1792–1802* (Oxford, 1983); see especially chap. 3, "Military Exploitation."
7 Rudolf Ibbeken, *Preussen 1807–1813. Staat und Volk als Idee und in Wirklichkeit* (Berlin, 1970), 92.

so on.[8] As if that were not enough, Napoleon's armies returned in 1811–12, when Prussia became the main base of operations for the invasion of Russia. By all accounts, they were even more rapacious than four years earlier; when the Grand Army eventually marched off on its doomed expedition, it left virtually nothing portable or edible behind.[9] The other kind of brutality was political. By the treaty of Tilsit, Prussia lost almost half its territory. It was also subjected to enormous reparations, was obliged to support an army of occupation until they were paid, and was restricted in future to an army of 40,000. Moreover, Napoleon went out of his way to humiliate the wretched Frederick William III, making it clear that he was only allowing Prussia to survive at all as a favor to his new satrap, the Russian Tsar Alexander I.[10] In short, Prussia was demoted to third-rate status.

As an exercise in counterproductivity, Napoleon's treatment of Prussia has few equals. In normal circumstances, King Frederick William III, slow of thought and even slower to make a decision, was the last person to allow a radical reform of his state. Yet such was the deadly peril in which he now found himself that even he could see that he had no alternative. In 1806, Napoleon had dethroned the Bourbon dynasty in Naples and had made his brother Joseph king. In 1807, Napoleon created thrones for two other siblings, the kingdom of the Netherlands for Louis and the kingdom of Westphalia for Jérôme. In 1808, he deposed the Bourbons of Spain and transferred Joseph from Naples. By now running low on brothers (he disliked and mistrusted little Lucien), he made his brother-in-law Joachim Murat king of Naples in Joseph's place. Against this backdrop, no European monarch could feel secure. So Frederick William found himself sacking the old guard, appointing or promoting reformers, and agreeing to their proposals.

The "Prussian Reform Movement" that followed has generated an enormous amount of literature, much of it of distinction. There is neither the need nor the space to review its course here. Suffice it to say that between 1806 and 1819 (when it can be said that the movement finally ran out of steam) both the institutions and the ethos of the Prussian state were transformed. It was a program of "offensive modernization" designed first and foremost to rescue Prussia from its current state of impotence and

---

8 Ibid., 94–5; Bernd von Münchow-Pohl, *Zwischen Reform und Krieg. Untersuchungen zur Bewusstseinslage in Preussen 1809–1812* (Göttingen, 1987), 56.
9 Ibbeken, *Preussen 1807–1813*, 344.
10 The French Foreign Office composed a memorandum shortly after the battle of Jena envisaging dethroning the Hohenzollern dynasty altogether and giving Silesia to Jérôme Bonaparte; Thomas Stamm-Kuhlmann, *König in Preussens grosser Zeit. Friedrich Wilhelm III. der Melancholiker auf dem Thron* (Berlin, 1992), 256–7.

humiliation, to maximize its resources, both human and material, and to make it ready for the day of retribution.[11] During the past generation, there has been a tendency to talk down its achievements, to emphasize its failings, and to compare it unfavorably with reforming initiatives undertaken at the same time in the other German states. Yet when every qualification has been noted, the obstinate fact remains that the Prussia which took the field against Napoleon with such devastating effect between 1813 and 1815 was as dynamic and vigorous as the Prussia of 1806 had been feeble and hesitant. It was summed up ruefully by Napoleon himself after his first and bloody encounter with the New Model Prussian Army at Lützen on May 2, 1813: "These animals have learnt something."[12]

Indeed they had. They had learned from the French Revolution that now neither an army nor a state could be run mechanically as if it were a machine. All the various members of both, from field-marshal to private soldier, from king to meanest subject, had to be involved. In the future, every legitimate regime would need to embrace the new concept of a society of citizens supported by legal equality and civil liberties. As Hardenberg argued in his celebrated "Riga Memorandum" of 1807, these principles had acquired such general recognition that the state which refused to accept them could choose only between having them imposed by force and extinction.[13] Combined with the overwhelming military force unleashed by the Revolution and raised to even greater intensity by Napoleon, the cogency of this central axiom carried all before it.

Yet the Prussian reformers were never imitators of the Revolution, in the sense of adopting policies first promulgated in Paris. Everything they did, whether it was the emancipation of the peasants or the introduction of municipal self-government or whatever, had its roots in long-standing native experience and reform projects. Even the stress on self-determination owed more to Kantian moral philosophy than to the Declaration of the Rights of Man and the Citizen.[14] When reading almost anything written by the Prussian reformers, especially Freiherr vom Stein and his group, one cannot help but be struck by the Kantian influence. In December 1807, for example, Stein wrote to Hardenberg from East Prussia about his projected reforms in words taken almost directly from Kant's celebrated essay *What is*

---

11 I borrow this helpful phrase from Brendan Simms, *The Struggle for Mastery in Germany, 1779–1850* (Basingstoke, 1998), which contains an excellent concise account of the reforms.
12 Quoted in David Chandler, *The Campaigns of Napoleon* (London, 1966), 887.
13 Thomas Nipperdey, *Deutsche Geschichte 1800–1866. Bürgerwelt und starker Staat* (Munich, 1983), 32–3.
14 Ibid., 34.

Enlightenment?: "We need to get the nation used to taking care of its own affairs and to emerge from that state of immaturity in which governments try to keep mankind."[15] His near namesake Altenstein added in equally Kantian terms that the overall purpose of the reform program was the destruction of a system in which individuals were not regarded as ends in themselves but as means to the ends of others.[16] Among other things, this strongly moral emphasis resulted in a remarkably ambitious, and remarkably successful, policy of educational reform. This was a regime which, despite its financial straits, charged no less a figure than Wilhelm von Humboldt to found a new university at Berlin, whose first professor of philosophy was Fichte and whose second was Hegel. These examples could be multiplied at will. And because it is so important to stress the native origins of the Prussian Reform Movement, I shall conclude these observations by invoking the support of no less authorities than Leopold von Ranke and Friedrich Meinecke, both of whom stressed the influence of Kant.[17]

If there were a second intellectual force at work in this refoundation of the Prussian state, it was not Rousseau or Sieyès but Adam Smith:[18] Stein's personal copy of *The Wealth of Nations* was well-worn and copiously annotated.[19] In Reinhart Koselleck's challenging formulation: The Prussian reformers self-consciously adopted Adam Smith as a weapon against Napoleon, that is to say, they accepted the challenge of the industrial revolution to help them deal with the French Revolution and to avoid their own version of it.[20] The Prussian Reform Movement could go so deep so fast and leave such a lasting impression just because it was not a foreign import but was rather an intensification of native traditions.[21]

This is not to underestimate the impact of Napoleon. Without his eruption into Prussian affairs in 1806, it is extremely improbable that the

---

15 Quoted in Walther Hubatsch, "Der Reichsfreiherr Karl vom Stein und Immanuel Kant," in Otto Büsch and Wolfgang Neugebauer (eds.), *Moderne Preussische Geschichte*, 3 vols. (Berlin and New York, 1981), 3: 1335.
16 Reinhart Koselleck, *Preussen zwischen Reform und Revolution. Allgemeines Landrecht, Verwaltung und soziale Bewegung von 1791 bis 1848*, 3rd ed. (Berlin, 1981), 154.
17 Leopold von Ranke, *Preussische Geschichte*, ed. Hans-Joachim Schoeps (Munich, 1981), 357; Friedrich Meinecke, *The Age of German Liberation, 1795–1815*, ed. Peter Paret (Berkeley, Los Angeles, and London, 1977), 100.
18 Ilya Mieck, "Vom Merkantilismus zum Liberalismus," in Büsch and Neugebauer (eds.), *Moderne Preußische Geschichte*, 2: 996.
19 Meinecke, *The Age of German Liberation, 1795–1815*, 57. On the influence of Adam Smith, see also Nipperdey, *Deutsche Geschichte*, 34.
20 Koselleck, *Preussen zwischen Reform und Revolution*, 14.
21 "The reformers put into practice the military ideas of the French Revolution and developed them further, not only to counter the outside threat, but because the seeds of their innovations were already present in Prussian soil"; Peter Paret, *Yorck and the Era of Prussian Reform, 1807–1815* (Princeton, 1966), 244.

reformers would have been able to take control. Many a far-sighted Prussian, notably Scharnhorst, had spotted long ago what was needed to counter the threat from Revolutionary France. They had seen how the largest army in the history of Europe had been mobilized and charged with a demonic energy, but the side effects had been so disagreeable, including: the execution of the king and queen, the abolition of the nobility, and the expropriation of the church. The game did not seem worth the candle. It was only when Napoleon's galloping megalomania put Prussia's very existence at stake that even the greatest risk had to be taken. Something very similar happened in Russia following the invasion of 1812 when the Tsar made the hazardous decision to arm the serfs.[22]

In Prussia, where the formation of a popular militia (*Landwehr* and *Landsturm*) was a fundamental plank in the military reforms, no risk was involved. Scholars such as Rudolf Ibbeken and Bernd von Münchow-Pohl who have examined the popular mood after 1806, and in particular the mobilization of 1813, are agreed that there was a significant amount of popular participation. Proportionally, the Prussians were able to mobilize a higher percentage of their population than any other combatant – approximately 280,000 or around 11% of the male population – but lost a smaller percentage through desertion. Both figures testify to the enthusiasm with which even the conscripts went about their work. Nor was the popular slogan "the King called, and all came running" entirely without foundation: After meticulous work in the archives, Ibbeken was able to show that 27,763 volunteers enlisted in the Prussian army in 1813–14.[23] The motivation of most of them must remain a mystery. Did the reform movement restore such credibility to the Prussian system that citizens flocked to defend it in its hour of need? We shall never know for certain. Ibbeken speculated that the introduction of "freedom of trades" (*Gewerbefreiheit*) did indeed make an impact, as was shown by the disproportionately high number of volunteers drawn from the urban artisan group. This has been doubted by Münchow-Pohl, who points out that the brisk wind of competition was the last thing the artisans wanted.[24] However, both are agreed that the main combustant feeding the flames of Prussian patriotism was simply hatred of the French and a desire for revenge for the humiliations and depredations inflicted in 1807–8 and again in 1812.[25]

---

22 L. G. Beskrovny (ed.), *Narodnoe opelchenie v otechestvennoy voyne 1812 goda. Sbornik dokumentov* (Moscow, 1962), 4–7.
23 Ibbeken, *Preussen 1807–1813*, 405.
24 Ibbeken, *Preussen 1807–1813*, 406; Münchow-Pohl, *Zwischen Reform und Krieg*, 6, 408.
25 Ibid., 46, 396, 426–7.

From this combination of reform from above, and vengeance from below, there sprang a political myth of great and enduring power: the myth of a war of liberation (*Befreiungskrieg*) to free Prussia, and with it Germany, from the Napoleonic yoke. Of course it was a war which militarily was won by the regular armies of the old regime, but historians such as A. J. P. Taylor miss the point when they dismiss with derision the popular element.[26] The belief that "the King called and all came running" and that even those who could not fight in person "gave gold for iron" had a germ of truth which could only grow with the passage of time. Iron became the favored metaphor for the Prussian war effort's grim austerity, in self-conscious contrast to what had become the sybaritic luxury of Napoleon and his entourage. It was best expressed in Arndt's poem of 1813 "in praise of iron." It is significant that the cult of iron was promoted, if not initiated, by the state, for it was Frederick William III who took the decision to found the order of the Iron Cross in 1813, sketching out the original design for the medal himself, then having it worked up into the finished article by no less an artist than Karl Friedrich Schinkel. Schinkel also designed the first war memorial for the War of Liberation, the monument on the Kreuzberg in Berlin, made of iron and topped by an iron cross.[27] To commemorate the Prussian army's triumphal entry into Paris in 1814, an iron cross was also added to the Quadriga above the Brandenburg Gate when it was returned from Paris.[28]

For a king with a reputation for being slow-burning, Frederick William III showed himself to be remarkably adept at organizing public opinion. Whether consciously or not, he made skillful use of Queen Luise both in life and in death, employing her beauty and charisma to surround his throne with that combination of glamour and accessibility for which all royal families strive but which very few achieve. The story of her defiant courage in the face of Napoleon's contemptuous and boorish behavior at Tilsit in 1807 established her as a fragrant symbol of Prussian resistance. Her return to Berlin with the King in 1809 for the first time since the disasters of 1807 was more like a victory parade, while her sudden death the following year unleashed a popular frenzy of grief and completed her canonization as the "Prussian Madonna" or the "Prussian *mater dolorosa*."[29] If Frederick William did not begin the cult, he certainly encouraged it, building monuments and

---

26 A. J. P. Taylor, *The Course of German History* (London, 1961), 39. He wrongly supposes that there were only 10,000 volunteers.
27 Andreas Dörner, *Politischer Mythos und symbolische Politik. Sinnstiftung durch symbolische Formen am Beispiel des Hermannmythos* (Opladen, 1995), 177 n. 95.
28 Ibid., 185 n. 105.
29 Münchow-Pohl, *Zwischen Reform und Krieg*, 207–8.

setting a personal example of veneration by treating the handkerchief with which she wiped away the beads of perspiration in her final agony as a holy relic.[30]

Napoleon's other main service to the Prussian state was to reverse its natural Francophilia. The hatred which welled up in the wake of the French occupation was as intense as it was widespread. The liberal nationalist Ernst Moritz Arndt was not speaking only for himself when he wrote: "In the name of my God and of my people, I hate all the French without exception... I teach this hatred to my son... All my life long I shall labor to make contempt and hatred for the [French] people strike the deepest possible roots in the hearts of Germans."[31] If that *cri de coeur* seems pathological, it was nothing compared with Heinrich von Kleist's literary hymn of hate, *Herman's Battle* [*Die Hermannsschlacht*], which purported to deal with the events surrounding the defeat of Varus's legions by Herman the German in the Teutoburger Forest in A.D. 9 but which was obviously a call to arms against Napoleon. Among many other atrocities depicted, perhaps the most stomach-churning is the scene in which Herman has the body of a young virgin, who has been gang-raped by the Romans, dismembered, and her body parts dispatched to the various German tribes as an encouragement to join the revolt.[32] Prussian soldiers were notoriously the most bloodthirsty during the victorious campaigns of 1813–15. For example, senior officers regretted that Paris had not offered resistance, thus depriving them of the excuse to put the city to the torch and the sword.[33]

Driven by hatred and a fierce determination to efface the memories of 1806, the Prussians also proved to be the most effective of the allied armies. Despite their truncated territory, they made such a contribution to the allied cause that they were in a strong bargaining position when the time came to divide the spoils of war. Frustrated in their desire for all of Saxony, they had to settle for a greatly expanded position in the west, taking most of the left bank of the Rhine and Westphalia. Developments over the next half-century were to show just how fortunate they had been, for they acquired three regions with enormous economic potential: the Aachen-Cologne-Krefeld triangle, the Saarland, and the Ruhr.[34] Together with the northern

---

30 Stamm-Kuhlmann, *König in Preussens grosser Zeit*, 322, 356.
31 Quoted in Hans-Ulrich Wehler, *Deutsche Gesellschaftsgeschichte*, vol. I: *Vom Feudalismus des Alten Reiches bis zur defensiven Modernisierung der Reformära 1700–1815* (Munich, 1987), 523.
32 Dörner, *Politischer Mythos und symbolische Politik*, 165–7.
33 See the letter from Graf Gustav von Schlabrendorff to Caroline von Wolzogen, Paris, July 22, 1815: Caroline von Wolzogen, *Literarischer Nachlass der Frau Caroline von Wolzogen*, 2 vols. (Leipzig, 1848–9), 2: 98.
34 Wehler, *Deutsche Gesellschaftsgeschichte*, 2: 634.

half of Saxony, these acquisitions set Prussia on the road to becoming the dominant economic force on the European continent.

This was yet another inadvertent Napoleonic contribution to Prussia's conquest of Germany, but it was to be left to his nephew to complete the task. After 1815, Prussia voluntarily took a back seat in international affairs, leaving Austria to dominate the new German Confederation. It was not until 1848 that the carapace of legitimacy erected by the Congress of Vienna began to crack. The decisive moment came in December 1848 when Louis Napoleon Bonaparte won the presidential election of the new French Republic by a landslide. For the first time since 1815, a major power was headed by a revisionist. Moreover, Napoleon III, as he styled himself after his coup of 1852, announced that his foreign policy would be determined by what he claimed to have been his uncle's "great idea," a Europe of national "agglomerations" formed according to the "principle of nationalities" under the guiding patronage of France.[35]

Driven by the charismatic leader's necessary quest for visible achievement, the new Emperor was soon involved in war. Yet ironically his apparent victory in the Crimean War (1854–6), sealed by a peace signed in his capital, was to benefit the only great power not to have been involved in the crisis, Prussia. The most obvious loser was Austria, whose policy of neutrality offended both sides in the conflict. Particularly hostile were the Russians, who had expected active support following the help they had given the Austrians to master their Hungarian insurgents in 1849 and to ward off Prussia's premature bid for mastery in Germany in 1850. Alexander II was quick to take revenge, by giving Napoleon III the green light to intervene in Italy in 1859 to exclude the Austrians from Lombardy.[36] That episode inflicted a deep wound on both Austrian prestige and Austrian finances. It also prompted William of Prussia (regent for his deranged brother from 1858, king from 1861) to embark on a program of military reform, precipitating a prolonged political crisis which brought Bismarck to power in 1862.

With the advantage of hindsight, we can see that Napoleon III had been prompted by the nature of his power (the charisma of his name) and the nature of his ideology (the principle of nationalities) to impose a fatal handicap on his policy. For he had both weakened Russia and made cooperation with it impossible. Defeat in the Crimean War had come as a terrible shock to a power which had liked to think it was invulnerable. No sooner did peace

---

35 Robert Tombs, *France 1814–1914* (London, 1996), 84.
36 W. E. Mosse, *The European Powers and the German Question, 1848–71. With Special Reference to England and Russia* (Cambridge, 1958), 83.

return than Alexander II began the Herculean task of setting his house in order. The emancipation of the serfs in 1861 was only the most spectacular of a raft of radical reforms. Consequently Russian energies, and Russian finance, were directed at domestic targets. As the foreign minister, Prince Gorchakov, told his ambassador in Paris at the end of 1863: "At the present time all our efforts are directed towards keeping Russia out of foreign affairs."[37] So the army was actually being reduced, just as the situation in Germany came to the boil – from 805,000 men in 1866 to 726,000 in 1869.[38] Yet reforming was a slow business, especially when it came to creating a modern transport system. In the mid-1860s, there was still only one railway line leading to the west, so only if a war in and about Germany were a protracted war of attrition could the Russians hope to make their influence felt. In the event, all three of Bismarck's wars were to be decided within a matter of weeks.

By that time, Russian territorial ambitions had switched to softer targets in Central Asia. The capture of the fortress of Suzak in July 1863 marked the beginning of the conquest of the Khanate of Kokand; Alma Ata fell in May 1864, Chimkent in September, and Tashkent the following summer. The Russian historian who knew this period best, Narochnitskaya, was emphatic that it was this Asian diversion which obliged the Russians to abandon their traditional policy of keeping Schleswig and Holstein in Danish hands.[39] So, Prussian hegemony in northern Germany was established by default. Moreover, it was a diversion which continued: In the spring of 1866 the Russian army began an invasion of the Bukhara Khanate, forming a new *gubernium*, Turkestan, for the new territories in 1867.[40] Probably more important was another kind of diversion – and one much less welcome to the Russians – namely the rising in Poland which began in January 1863 and was not finally crushed until April 1864. As the only railway line from Russia to the west ran through Warsaw, the chances of a Russian intervention in Germany was ruled out for the foreseeable future.

The Polish issue also served to keep France and Russia apart. As the two peripheral powers, they should have entertained a common desire to keep the center of Europe soft. If the two emperors, Napoleon III and Alexander II, had cooperated, they could almost certainly have frustrated Prussian expansion. The experiences of both countries in the twentieth

---

37 Quoted in L. I. Narochnitskaya, *Rossiya i voyny prussii v 60-kh godakh XIX v. za obeninenie germanii "sverkhu"* (Moscow, 1960), 19.
38 L. M. Shneerson, *Franko-prusskaya Voyna i Rossiya. Iz istorii russko-prusskikh i russko-frantsuzkikh otnoshenii v 1867–1871 gg.* (Minsk, 1976), 9.
39 Narochnitskaya, *Rossiya i voyny prussii*, 31.   40 Ibid., 79.

century suggest that they would have been sensible to do so. Yet they were kept apart by Napoleon III's nationalist rhetoric, which obliged him to make gestures in support of the Poles, and by the Russians' belief that he personified revolution. Bismarck, on the other hand, was the last person to be trapped by mere words. His response to the Polish rising was to send General von Alvensleben off to St. Petersburg to offer all possible assistance in suppressing it. If this initiative did not achieve everything he had hoped, it did have the effect of making a rapprochement between France and Russia impossible.[41] The Polish question continued to bedevil relations between France and Russia: When Alexander II visited Paris in the summer of 1867 for the World Exhibition, he was fired at by a Pole, who turned his subsequent trial into a platform for denouncing Russian atrocities in his homeland. When he escaped the gallows, the Russians chose to believe that he had been rescued by the government and were correspondingly incensed.[42]

The other issue that kept the peripheral powers apart was the Peace of Paris of 1856. Of all its provisions, those most resented by the vanquished were the clauses that ordered the indefinite neutralization of the Black Sea. This was more than a symbolic humiliation; the Russians also believed that vital interests were at stake. Since their conquest of the northern shoreline at the end of the eighteenth century, their whole economy had been tilting round toward the south. By the 1860s, 62% of all Russian grain exports were passing through Black Sea ports.[43] From then on, revocation of the offending articles was at the top of the diplomatic agenda. Yet Napoleon III could not allow the abrogation of any part of the treaty which represented his first great triumph and bore the name of his capital. Nor, for that matter, could the British, ever anxious about routes to India, or the Austrians, equally worried about Russian expansion in the Danubian principalities. Only Prussia cared nothing about the Black Sea, and Bismarck was quick to play this negative but powerful card in his hand. His reward was a statement by Alexander II on July 16, 1870, that if Austria-Hungary tried to enter the war, then Russia would mobilize 300,000 to stop her and, if necessary, invade Galicia.[44] An Austrian declaration of neutrality followed on July 20, allowing von Moltke to move three army corps standing on the Bavarian frontier to the battle-grounds of Alsace, where they arrived in time to make an important and

---

41 Lothar Gall, *Bismarck: der weisse Revolutionär* (Frankfurt am Main, 1980), 274.
42 L. I. Narochnitskaya, "Vneshnyaya politika Rossii posle Parizhskogo mira," in B. A. Rybakov (ed.), *Istoriya SSSR*, vol. 5 (Moscow, 1968), 237.
43 Shneerson, *Franko-prusskaya Voyna i Rossiya*, 11.
44 Ibid., 108.

perhaps decisive contribution.[45] On September 2, the decisive battle of the war was fought at Sedan, ending in total defeat for the French and the surrender of their emperor. If the Prussians were more merciful than the British had been to his uncle, it was because Napoleon III cut such a pathetic figure. He was allowed to go into exile in England, where he died two years later.

One final question needs to be addressed: To what extent did the new German Empire's creator, Bismarck, borrow his style from the Bonapartes? There are certain similarities: All three used nationalism to defeat liberalism and all made direct appeals to the public, but this does not take us very far. Lothar Gall is surely right to argue that Bismarck was quite a different kind of political animal, not least in the fact that he was no autocrat and was always dependent on his King. Bismarck owed power to his uncanny ability to manipulate the balance between old and new that characterized both Prussia and Germany and was wholly lacking in France, where the old regime had been swept away in 1789. As Gall argues, it was for this reason that Bismarck could never found a political party in his support, for that would have tilted the delicate balance decisively in favor of popular sovereignty and against prescription.[46] Nor did Bismarck want any part of the *va banque* recklessness born of limitless aims which was the essence of the Bonapartist ethos, the secret of both its success and its failure. Bismarck's model was Frederick the Great, ruthless in his aggression when the opportunity arose but controlled by a sense of his state's weakness and a pessimistic view of history.[47]

In his painting of the proclamation of the German Empire, Anton von Werner places Bismarck in the leading group of officers as they hail their new emperor. Resplendent in his white uniform, he looks every inch the military man. Yet Bismarck had never served as a regular officer in the Prussian army, his dubious entitlement to military trappings stemming from an honorary command of a militia regiment. It is this perhaps which distinguishes him so sharply from the Bonapartes, especially the first. His legitimacy stemmed from his service to the Prussian state and the Hohenzollern dynasty, his overriding principle was the primacy of politics in a true Clausewitzian spirit. Throughout his wars he watched the military like a hawk, and when they threatened to subordinate the conduct of policy to military interests, he swooped, invoking the authority of his king to put them back in their

---

45 Michael Howard, *The Franco-Prussian War. The German Invasion of France, 1870–1871* (London, 1961), 120.
46 Gall, *Bismarck*, 182.
47 Walter Bussmann, "Otto von Bismarck. Geschichte, Staat, Politik," in Büsch and Neugebauer (eds.), *Moderne Preussische Geschichte*, 3: 1550.

place. That led to some titanic struggles with von Moltke and the rest of the generals, but he always won. Even the manner of his final losing battle points up the difference: While he was dismissed from office by a new emperor, the two Napoleons were dislodged by military defeat. Robert Tombs is surely right to argue that the Bonapartist combination of "active authority and passive democracy" in an oxymoronic republican monarchy has proved the best solution to the problems of post-revolutionary France. But it was not for export.[48]

48 Tombs, *France, 1814–1914*, 489.

3

Prussian Conservatives and the Problem of Bonapartism

DAVID E. BARCLAY

At first glance, the response of Prussian conservatives to the regimes of the two Bonapartes and to the phenomenon of Bonapartism, however defined, seems fairly obvious. All we have to do is dredge up some of the more colorful invective that Prussian conservatives used in their commentary on Napoleon I and Napoleon III. Thus Frederick William IV, King of Prussia from 1840 to 1861 and one of the central figures in the history of nineteenth-century German conservatism, was unsparing in his rather imaginative polemics, referring to Napoleon I at various times as "Satan," the "Prince of Darkness" (*Fürst der Finsternis*), the "*Höllenkaiser*," "*Schinder*," "Nöppel," "Nöppel-Racker," "Schnapspoleon," and the "bird of prey" (*Raubvogel*), to mention just a few.[1] In 1855, Frederick William's closest political advisor, his Adjutant General Leopold von Gerlach (1790–1861), warned of what he called "the dangerous and great power of Bonapartism, this child of the vile marriage of absolutism and liberalism."[2] Similarly, his younger brother, Ernst Ludwig von Gerlach (1795–1877), one of the leaders of the so-called *Kreuzzeitung* party in the post-1848 Prussian parliament, wrote in 1853, several months after the official proclamation of the Second Empire, that it "is good that we have eluded the Charybdis of revolution... but now we are falling into the Scylla of Bonapartism."[3] For these conservatives,

---

1 Frank-Lothar Kroll, *Friedrich Wilhelm IV. und das Staatsdenken der deutschen Romantik* (Berlin, 1990), 161.
2 Leopold von Gerlach, *Denkwürdigkeiten aus dem Leben Leopold von Gerlachs, Generals der Infanterie und General-Adjutanten König Friedrich Wilhelms IV*, ed. Agnes von Gerlach, 2 vols. (Berlin, 1891–2), 2: 323.
3 Ernst Ludwig von Gerlach to Leopold von Gerlach, February 3, 1853, Gerlach-Archiv am Institut für politische Wissenschaft der Friedrich-Alexander-Universität Erlangen-Nürnberg, Erlangen (hereafter: GA), Abschriften des Nachlasses Leopold von Gerlach (hereafter: NL Leopold von Gerlach), 23: 14. Cf. Hans-Christof Kraus, *Ernst Ludwig von Gerlach: Politisches Denken und Handeln eines preussischen Altkonservativen*, 2 vols. (Göttingen, 1994), 2: 586–7.

all of whom were adherents of what historians generally call "High Conservatism" or *Altkonservatismus*, the Bonapartes represented especially fiendish incarnations of the godless principles of what the Crown Prince Frederick William, the future king, described in 1832 as "the revolution, that monster, which first saw the light of the world forty years ago, and which, were I apocalyptically inclined, I would immediately compare to the Beast *par excellence*."[4]

If things were as straightforward as these quotations suggest, the issue of Prussian conservatives and their assessment of the Bonapartes and of Bonapartism would be quite simple. However, they are much more complicated, as the High Conservatives themselves understood. In a commentary written in early December 1851 on Louis Napoleon Bonaparte's coup, Ludwig von Gerlach warned that "Bonapartist appetites [*Gelüste*]" were stirring among many conservatives.[5] In fact, as I shall attempt to show, a consideration of conservative responses to Bonapartism can help us understand not only the complexities and contradictions of conservative political thought and political action in Prussia after 1800, but can also contribute to an updated typology of nineteenth-century German conservatism in general.

These remarks will focus on two major themes. The first part will look in some detail at the High Conservatives between roughly 1813–14 and 1848: that is, during the Restoration and *Vormärz* periods, when they were probably the most intellectually interesting, though not necessarily the most politically influential, group of conservatives in Prussia. Then the remainder of the chapter will consider the evolution of conservative responses to the phenomenon of Bonapartism during the decade after 1848, that is, during the so-called decade of reaction after 1848. I shall argue that conservative responses to the Second Empire and to Bonapartism were highly complex, both in theory and in political practice, and that Ludwig von Gerlach was quite right to be worried about "Bonapartist appetites." For reasons of space, this part of the chapter will be limited to the relatively little-understood 1850s and will exclude the old discussion and controversies about Bismarck and Bonapartism after the 1860s.

Recent research suggests that between roughly 1807 and 1848 one can distinguish among three – and this is crucial to emphasize – often fluid and overlapping strands of conservative thinking and political action in Prussia: (1) the nostalgic, backward-looking, particularistic, and aristocratic

---

4 Frederick William (IV) to Prince Johann of Saxony, May 31, 1832, in Johann Georg, Herzog zu Sachsen, ed., *Briefwechsel zwischen König Johann von Sachsen und den Königen Friedrich Wilhelm IV. und Wilhelm I. von Preussen* (Leipzig, 1911), 127.
5 Quoted in Kraus, *Gerlach*, 2: 587.

opposition (*Adelsopposition*) of a Friedrich August Ludwig von der Marwitz; (2) what Barbara Vogel and Lothar Dittmer have called *Beamtenkonservatismus* (bureaucratic conservatism) that, although hostile to demands for modern forms of political participation and representation, embraced a few reformist ideas and also tried to make itself attractive to prominent members of emerging bourgeois publics; (3) the group that is of particular interest to us, the *Alt-* or *Hochkonservativen*.[6]

The "High Conservatives" were bound together not only by similar backgrounds, family connections, and shared politics but also, and perhaps above all, by common generational experiences. Most of them were born between 1785 and 1795, most were opponents of Hardenberg's reforms in Prussia, most had served in the wars of liberation against Napoleon (in many ways the decisive experience of their lives), and most had experienced a highly personal religious transformation in the context of the post-1815 "Awakening" (*Erweckungsbewegung*) in many parts of Germany. The real leaders of this group, which after 1823 found itself increasingly in opposition to the policies of the *Beamtenkonservativen* and the "Metternicheans" in the government of Frederick William III, were Leopold and Ludwig von Gerlach, who were joined by people like Carl von Voss-Buch, Joseph Maria von Radowitz (until about 1840), Carl Ernst Jarcke, to a certain extent Friedrich Julius Stahl, and, after 1848, Marcus Niebuhr, Heinrich Leo, and Hermann Wagener. Influenced by Friedrich Karl von Savigny's historical

---

6 David E. Barclay, "Die Gegner der Reformpolitik Hardenbergs," in Thomas Stamm-Kuhlmann, ed., *"Freier Gebrauch der Kräfte." Eine Bestandsaufnahme der Hardenberg-Forschung* (Munich, 2001), 217–29. Among recent studies, see Barbara Vogel, "Beamtenkonservatismus. Sozial- und verfassungsgeschichtliche Voraussetzungen der Parteien in Preussen im frühen 19. Jahrhundert," in Dirk Stegmann, Bernd-Jürgen Wendt, and Peter-Christian Witt, eds., *Deutscher Konservatismus im 19. und 20. Jahrhundert. Festschrift für Fritz Fischer zum 75. Geburtstag und zum 50. Doktorjubiläum* (Bonn, 1983), 1–31; Thomas Nipperdey, *Deutsche Geschichte 1800–1866. Bürgerwelt und starker Staat* (Munich, 1983), 313–19; Panajotis Kondylis, *Konservativismus. Geschichtlicher Gehalt und Untergang* (Stuttgart, 1986); Robert M. Berdahl, *The Politics of the Prussian Nobility: The Development of a Conservative Ideology, 1770–1848* (Princeton, 1988); Wolfram Siemann, *Vom Staatenbund zum Nationalstaat. Deutschland 1806–1871* (Munich, 1995), 68–71 and passim; Christopher M. Clark, "The Politics of Revival: Politics, Aristocrats, and the State Church in Early Nineteenth-Century Prussia," in Larry Eugene Jones and James Retallack, eds., *Between Reform, Reaction, and Resistance: Studies in the History of German Conservatism from 1789 to 1945* (Providence and Oxford, 1993), 31–60; Matthew Levinger, *Enlightened Nationalism: The Transformation of Prussian Political Culture, 1808–1848* (New York, 2000), 163–89. Lothar Dittmer, *Beamtenkonservativismus und Modernisierung. Untersuchungen zur Vorgeschichte der Konservativen Partei in Preussen 1810–1848/49* (Stuttgart, 1992); Eric Dorn Brose, *The Politics of Technological Change in Prussia: Out of the Shadow of Antiquity, 1809–1848* (Princeton, 1993); Kraus, *Gerlach*; Hermann Beck, *The Origins of the Authoritarian Welfare State in Prussia: Conservatives, Bureaucracy, and the Social Question, 1815–70* (Ann Arbor, 1995); Axel Schildt, *Konservatismus in Deutschland. Von den Anfängen im 18. Jahrhundert bis zur Gegenwart* (Munich, 1998), 42–62; Bernd Heidenreich, ed., *Politische Theorien des 19. Jahrhunderts*, vol. 1, *Konservatismus* (Wiesbaden, 1999).

school of law and more significantly by Carl Ludwig von Haller's *Restauration der Staatswissenschaft* (1816–22), the High Conservatives were fervent advocates of a divinely ordained, patrimonial, *ständisch* – that is, decentralized and organic-corporative – monarchy based on historically sanctioned estates (*Stände*), rather than on contract theory, parliamentary institutions, or the incendiary, "mechanistic," universalistic principles of 1789. They aspired to create a Christian state that could serve as an antidote to mechanistic rationalism and to what Ludwig von Gerlach liked to call "pantheism," by which he meant an historical relativism that rejected Christian universalism. At the same time, they were not simply old-fashioned nostalgists or aristocratic mossbacks. Indeed, they early on appreciated the utility of modern forms of propaganda, publicity, and political organization. A number of them were involved in the 1830s with the well-known *Berliner Politisches Wochenblatt*, which included on its masthead Joseph de Maistre's well-known remark that the aim of conservatives should be not so much to engage in *contre-révolution* as to undertake the *contraire de la révolution*; and it was Ludwig von Gerlach who in the early summer of 1848 created the *Kreuzzeitung*, Prussia's first truly modern political newspaper, celebrated and feared for its polemical edge and its scabrous style. To paraphrase Henry Kissinger's famous remark, they were conservatives in a revolutionary age, a fact of which they were constantly aware and which they themselves reiterated over and over again. They were ideologues in the twentieth-century sense of that term, or, to put it in German and a bit more accurately, *Prinzipienreiter*, people who were consciously engaged in what would today be called "ideological struggle." For example, someone like Ludwig von Gerlach could never really associate himself uncritically with those Junkers who adopted conservative politics simply to advance what he denounced as "egoistic" group interests.

Much of this will be quite familiar to many readers. Robert Berdahl wrote about it a few years ago, I have dealt with it in my own work on Frederick William IV and the Prussian monarchy, and several other writers, most notably Hans-Christof Kraus and Frank-Lothar Kroll, have also discussed it at some length. However, what needs to be emphasized here in the context of the Bonapartes and Bonapartism is the resolute opposition of the High Conservatives to all forms of what they regularly denounced as "bureaucratic absolutism." By no means identical with Bonapartism, they noted, absolutism had long been an especially pernicious expression of the revolutionary spirit of the modern age. In fact, the High Conservatives believed, it antedated the French Revolution and continued, according to the Gerlachs and their friends, to pose a real danger to historically established rights, freedoms, and liberties as well as to divinely sanctioned monarchical authority. Absolutism in all its guises, whether bureaucratic or royal, had to be repudiated. For example, despite their deep-seated legitimism, the Gerlachs and their fellow High Conservatives were never uncritical Russophiles, for in their view the empire of the Tsars was the very embodiment of autocracy and military despotism, an empire that over the course of its history had crushed locally based and historically derived group rights. Similarly, they were stern critics of Chancellor Karl August von Hardenberg's reforms before 1819 and of what they regarded as the bureaucratic rigidity of the Prussian government itself during the last two decades of the reign of Frederick William III; and they were especially unhappy with the policies of the King's intimate friend Prince Wittgenstein, who of course was one of Metternich's close allies. Absolutism was synonymous with policies of "mechanistic" centralization, with the elimination of tradition and historically conditioned distinctiveness. As Ludwig von Gerlach repeatedly said, the principal features of any centralized bureaucratic apparatus were "arbitrariness, absolutism, and a lack of character"; bureaucratic absolutism inevitably led to "revolution" and to "Bonapartism."[7] Thus absolutism, the equally evil twin of 1789, was by its very nature revolutionary. Although not a Prussian, a conservative Bavarian jurist with the unlikely name of George P. Phillips could have been speaking for the High Conservatives when he wrote in June 1848: "I fear the unity [*Einheit*] of a dictatorship, and at the same time I fear the weakness of unity. I fear and hate the unity of a dictatorship because it threatens freedom. God forbid that in our Fatherland people will start calling in the streets for a dictator, crying out: 'A dictator! A dictator! An empire for a dictator!'"[8]

To the High Conservatives, Bonaparte had been peculiarly evil, for he represented the distilled essence of centralized despotism, revolutionary leveling, and the destruction of historically sanctioned institutions. To make things worse, he had posed as a dynastic monarch, aping and then overshadowing older, legitimate dynasties, even as he tried to destroy them. However, the Bonapartes would always remain usurpers, just as Bonapartism itself would always remain revolutionary; and any kind of political or intellectual accommodation with a Bonaparte was anathema to the High Conservatives. Like his royal master Frederick William IV, Leopold von Gerlach had been indelibly stamped by his experiences between 1806 and 1815, and a half

---

7 Kraus, *Gerlach*, 1: 305.
8 Quoted in Hans-Christof Kraus, "Revolution – Gegenrevolution – Gegenteil der Revolution. Die Bewegung von 1848 und ihre Gegner," in Patrick Bahners and Gerd Roellecke, eds., *1848 – Die Erfahrung der Freiheit* (Heidelberg, 1998), 128.

century later he still regarded any Bonaparte, whether uncle or nephew, as "the Revolution incarnate" and "our natural enemy."[9] The two Napoleons were bound to the revolution, Gerlach believed; as he explained to Otto von Bismarck in May 1857, "My political principle is and remains the struggle against revolution. You will not persuade Bonaparte that he is not on the side of revolution."[10] By "revolution," of course, Gerlach understood, as I have already indicated, popular sovereignty, the elimination of historic rights and liberties, leveling democracy, the denial of religion and divine authority, and aggressive wars of conquest. It is thus not surprising that Frederick William IV loathed both Napoleons with particular intensity; and it is Frederick William who is, in a real sense, the focal point of these remarks.

In 1855, Leopold von Gerlach wrote that since 1827 he had regarded Frederick William as the true leader of "my party."[11] Throughout the decade of the 1830s, many of the leading High Conservatives were associated with him in what was called the "Crown Prince's Circle," and after his accession to the throne in 1840 they came to play an important, though never dominant, role at the court and in the Prussian state. Frederick William IV can rightly be regarded as the most historically significant German monarch in the century between the death of Frederick II in 1786 and the accession of William II in 1888. Blessed with exceptional intelligence, a highly developed aesthetic sensibility, and genuine artistic ability (especially in architecture), Frederick William was far more than the "Romantic on the throne" of David Friedrich Strauss's influential pamphlet, or the mercurial, dreamy, dithering, slightly ridiculous reactionary of the late nineteenth century "Borussian," *kleindeutsch* historians' caricature à la Heinrich von Sybel or Heinrich von Treitschke. Rather, Frederick William devoted his entire adult life to what I call his "monarchical project," a sustained and, for the most part, conscious attempt to create in Prussia an example of de Maistre's *contraire de la révolution*. It was, in many respects, a full-blown and quite modern ideological project, an attempt to create a *ständisch*, Christian, monarchical, anticonstitutional alternative to what had been coming out of France. In the last *Vormärz* years, Frederick William devoted most of his energy to an attempt to make his project real, culminating with the United Diet of 1847, which he described to his skeptical brother Prince Carl as "the first active response

---

9 Leopold von Gerlach to Bismarck, June 5, 1857, in Horst Kohl, ed., *Briefe des Generals Leopold von Gerlach an Otto von Bismarck* (Stuttgart, 1912), 218, 219.
10 Leopold von Gerlach to Bismarck, May 6, 1857, in Kohl, *Briefe des Generals*, 211–12.
11 Leopold von Gerlach, diary, October 13, 1855, GA, NL Leopold von Gerlach, 12: 127.

by a conservative power to the principles of popular representation, which have laid hold of so many states and ruined them since the French Revolution."[12]

In doing all of this, Frederick William availed himself of techniques of governance, methods of persuasion, and structures of representation that in odd ways were mirror images of the revolutionary and Napoleonic France that he so loathed. He was the first Prussian monarch to deliver public speeches to his civilian subjects, and everyone agreed that he was very good at it. The architectural projects of his mature years were specifically designed to convey unmistakable monarchist and legitimist messages. Before 1848, he was particularly effective at orchestrating grand public festivals with himself at their center, most notably the great festivals of public homage at Königsberg and Berlin in 1840 and the festival to launch the completion of Cologne Cathedral (*Dombaufest*) in 1842. On these and other occasions, Frederick William liked to invoke an image of a Prussia and a Germany renewed by what he called "truly German corporative institutions" (*ächtteutsche ständische Einrichtungen*) rooted in history, tradition, and, especially, the values of the Middle Ages. At the same time, the King of Prussia, in sharp contrast to most of the High Conservatives, was not at all immune to the cause of German unity. Where the High Conservative critique of Bonapartism extended to its supposed endorsement of the "national principle," Frederick William attempted throughout his reign to come up with a conservative alternative to "revolutionary" ideas of the nation, beginning with his endorsement of a revived Empire and culminating with his support for the abortive Prussian Union project of Joseph Maria von Radowitz in 1849–50, a proposal that would have called for a Prussian-dominated "narrow" union of German states and a looser, "broader" union that would have included the Habsburg Monarchy.

In short, for all of his supposedly retrograde views, Frederick William IV was in many ways a quintessential product of the nineteenth century, and his monarchical project represents almost the ideal type of that "invention of tradition" which historians were talking about so much a few years ago.[13] In fact, as a number of critics then and now rightly noted, Prussia had always represented the very opposite of Frederick William's vision. It had always been a "rough state based on reason" (*rauher Vernunftsstaat*), to use Sebastian

---

12 Frederick William IV to Prince Carl, March 19, 1847, Geheimes Staatsarchiv Preussischer Kulturbesitz Berlin (hereafter GStA), Brandenburg-Preussisches Hausarchiv (hereafter: BPH), Rep. 50 J Nr. 986, Bl. 25.
13 See, for example, Eric Hobsbawm and Terence Ranger, eds., *The Invention of Tradition* (Cambridge, 1981), as well as various subsequent studies.

Haffner's felicitous formulation.[14] Indeed, Count Friedrich Wilhelm von Brandenburg, the King's own uncle and minister president from 1848 to 1850, once chided him for failing to understand Prussia's real traditions: "Its real life principle was its opposition to the *ständisch* principle. A centralized military and bureaucratic state. That was its signature. That is black-white [the colors of Prussia–DEB]."[15]

For a variety of reasons, Frederick William was determined to proceed with his project. In this enterprise, he was at once haunted and driven by the nightmare of revolution, the *monstrum horrendum ingens*, as he called it in 1848.[16] Therefore, revolution meant France. It meant Bonaparte, who would always be nothing more than a usurper. (It should be noted that Frederick William IV, with his literally mystical notions of monarchy "through the Grace of God," was more consistently legitimist than most of the High Conservatives. Thus he also regarded the Orleanists as deplorable usurpers, and in 1848 he argued that Louis-Philippe's fall from power was the logical result of the circumstances that had brought him to power in the first place.) Frederick William's antipathy toward the first Napoleon was both personal and ideological, and his hostility extended to post-1789 France in general. It was said that he bitterly remembered the time he met Napoleon at Tilsit, in 1807, on the occasion of his father's humiliation, and that during this meeting the French Emperor, who was always known for his personal coarseness, grabbed the twelve-year-old boy by the chin and shook him as he greeted him. It was also sometimes said that Frederick William blamed Napoleon personally for the suffering and the early death of his mother, Queen Luise, at the age of only thirty-four in 1810. He liked to call Paris a "cesspool" or a *Sünden-Pfuhl*, while the French in general were "a disgusting people" (*ein ekliges Volk*). As late as the mid-1850s, reported one of his aides-de-camp rather delicately, the King was almost invariably a pleasant and charming conversationalist, "except that things boiled over in him whenever he got around to the Napoleonic period, and in talking about Napoleon I he used strong expressions that were otherwise alien to him."[17]

Of course, this was the monarch who faced his own worst nightmare when the long feared revolution finally came to Prussia in March 1848.

---

14 Sebastian Haffner, *Preussen ohne Legende* (Hamburg, n.d. [1979]).
15 Friedrich Wilhelm Graf von Brandenburg to Frederick William IV, September 4, 1850, GStA, BPH, Rep. 50 J Nr. 212, Bl. 74.
16 Frederick William IV to Graf Carl von der Groeben, August 30,1848, GStA, Rep. 92 Graf Carl von der Groeben B Nr. 4^e 1848, Bl. 13^v.
17 Friedrich von Bismarck-Bohlen, "Aufzeichnungen aus meinem Leben als Flügeladjutant Seiner Majestät König Friedrich Wilhelm IV," manuscript (1880), GStA, BPH, Rep. 50 F 1 Nr. 6, Bl. 10.

The king who believed in the renewal (or invention) of medieval, corporative institutions and of a regenerated Christianity now presided over Prussia's transition to a form of constitutionalism and parliamentarism. Although he kept his throne, and though Prussia's traditional elites were able to regain the political initiative in the autumn of 1848, the result was not a victory for Frederick William's cause or for his monarchical project, but rather, as Günther Grünthal has written, a compromise, symbolized by the imposed (*oktroyierte*) constitutional draft of December 1848, which was revised in 1849 and to which Frederick William took an oath in February 1850. The decade of reaction after 1848 thus did not represent a reversion to any kind of *Vormärz* status quo, but something quite new. The High Conservatives adapted adroitly to the new constitutional and parliamentary age. Though Leopold von Gerlach, the King's Adjutant General, bemoaned these developments and remained deeply pessimistic throughout the 1850s, both he and his more vigorous brother Ludwig recognized that constitutions and parliaments could be turned to the conservatives' advantage. Ludwig von Gerlach, who, together with Friedrich Julius Stahl, led the so-called *Kreuzzeitung* party in the Prussian parliament, became convinced that this institution could serve as a check on the bureaucratic absolutism that he so loathed. Indeed, by 1853 he was warning that among the many bad features of Bonapartism was not only its hostility to established religion but also its tendency to suppress parliaments![18] This did not represent a late conversion on his part. In fact, the High Conservatives had never rejected all forms of constitutionalism; it depended on what kind of constitution one was talking about. Back in 1832, for example, Leopold von Gerlach had written that existing German constitutions could not be rejected out of hand: ". . . some are simply there, others in a sense have legitimized themselves. They are not simply advancing toward Jacobinism, but instead are retreating from it. One has to limit constitutions by cleansing them of lies and nonsense; but then one has to approach what is left without any kind of *reservations mentales*, which in my view are utterly inappropriate."[19] In other words, constitutions could be used for counterrevolutionary purposes, which is certainly what the *Kreuzzeitung* party had in mind.

It is also what Frederick William IV had in mind after 1848. Determined to salvage as much as he could of his monarchical project, he wanted above all – as he put it in 1853 to his Austrian nephew, the young Emperor Francis

---

18 Ernst Ludwig von Gerlach to Leopold von Gerlach, February 3, 1853, GA, NL Leopold von Gerlach, 23: 14.
19 Kraus, *Gerlach*, 1: 259.

Joseph – to do what was necessary within the bounds of his oath, to kill the "French-modern constitution."[20] He never succeeded in doing this, but in his efforts to do so and in his style of governance he opened the door to those conservatives who were afflicted with the "Bonapartist appetites" that Ludwig von Gerlach had warned against. Frederick William had in fact never been and never would be a consistent High Conservative. (Indeed, as we have already indicated, these kinds of categories were in any case rather slippery and elusive.) Although he was far more consistent in the pursuit of his monarchical project than many historians have recognized, the project itself did contain a number of inconsistencies – a fact which the High Conservatives themselves recognized in their often fierce criticism of the monarch. For example, Frederick William was never able to reconcile his support for historically ordained group rights and liberties with his own high-flown, exalted notions of monarchy and monarchical authority. The Gerlachs, especially the stern Ludwig, in turn regularly denounced the King for his unwillingness to recognize his own limits and his own sinfulness. As a good Hallerian patrimonialist, Ludwig von Gerlach regularly liked to remind everyone who would listen that "I too am a king" (*Ich bin auch ein König*), as indeed was every *paterfamilias*. The divine authority and the historical authority which were the sources of royal power also limited and circumscribed it: the king, the Gerlachs complained, often forgot this fact after 1848. In their view, the King himself was too often open to absolutist inclinations, or more correctly, to the advice of absolutist advisors, by which they meant two people above all: Otto von Manteuffel and Carl Ludwig von Hinckeldey.[21]

Indeed, throughout the decade after 1848, Frederick William liked to keep his political options open by surrounding himself with advisors who represented a variety of opinions and a number of competing points of view. As a result, he was able to maneuver among them to his own advantage with the ultimate aim of neutralizing the constitution and maximizing the authority and power of the crown. Some of his confidants in those years were simply bizarre (not to mention unqualified), like the school director Carl Wilhelm Saegert. However, others like Manteuffel and Hinckeldey suggested the new directions in which post-1848 Prussian conservatism was moving, and they were not directions that the High Conservatives liked.

20 Frederick William IV to Francis Joseph, September 28–9, 1853, GStA, BPH, Rep. 50 J Nr. 939, Bl. 59ᵛ–60.
21 Much of the material in the following two paragraphs is derived from my book *Frederick William IV and the Prussian Monarchy, 1840–1861* (Oxford, 1995), 240–4, 264–5.

Otto von Manteuffel (1805–82), interior minister from 1848 to 1850 and minister president of Prussia from 1850 to 1858, is one of the most interesting and least appreciated figures in modern German history. He also defies easy classification, for he does not clearly fit the category of the *Beamtenkonservativen*, despite the fact that he devoted his entire adult life to state service. Nor was he ever more than a tactical ally of the High Conservatives, with whom he was often involved in interminable disputes throughout the 1850s. Günther Grünthal has written that, in some ways, Manteuffel anticipated Bismarck's style of governance after 1862.[22] Certainly there was a great deal about that style which led Manteuffel's conservative enemies to grumble, he was himself a "Bonapartist."[23] He liked to manipulate public opinion, he created a Central Press Office to coordinate his efforts to influence or bribe journalists, and he made lavish use of intelligence agents to spy on his enemies, including the Gerlachs and other High Conservatives. Moreover, as if to confirm his "Bonapartist" reputation among his enemies, the minister president also tried to come up with an intellectual justification for his regime, turning, among other things, to the avowedly Bonapartist views of Constantin Frantz. However, at the same time, the minister president rejected Frantz's more radical ideas, especially his support for a "Caesarist," plebiscitary state. Manteuffel's own view of Germany's social condition was more strongly influenced by the conservative writer Wilhelm Heinrich Riehl, whose analysis of civil society, *Die bürgerliche Gesellschaft*, appeared in 1851. In this influential study, Riehl asserted that four groups now dominated German society: the peasantry and the aristocracy, or the "powers of conservation," on the one hand, and, on the other, the "powers of movement" in the *Bürgertum* and the still largely artisanal "fourth estate." Manteuffel was convinced that a conservative, monarchical government had to recognize and deal with those fundamental divisions. Ignoring them or pretending that they could not or should not exist would be foolish and even catastrophic. Similarly, a modern conservative government could no longer afford to cater to one social group while ignoring (or repressing) all the others. To minimize the threat of revolution and to isolate the potentially revolutionary underclass, a stable monarchy necessarily depended upon the cooperative efforts of peasantry, aristocracy, and an autonomous *Bürgertum*. Government itself should attempt to stand above conflicts among the various "bodies" (*Körperschaften*) of society; indeed, it should serve as a kind of

---

22 Günther Grünthal, "Im Schatten Bismarcks – Der preussische Ministerpräsident Otto Freiherr von Manteuffel," in Hans-Christof Kraus, ed., *Konservative Politiker in Deutschland. Eine Auswahl biographischer Porträts aus zwei Jahrhunderten* (Berlin, 1995), 127–8.
23 Ibid., 128.

impartial social referee or political mediator. A political system of this sort, Manteuffel insisted, would balance *ständisch* and constitutional structures and would most effectively help to maintain a stable monarchical order. Now it might be suggested that these ideas possibly contain Bonapartist elements; but on the whole, the evidence of his eight years as minister president suggests that Manteuffel was not so much a Bonapartist as a statist neo-absolutist, which is not quite the same thing. Indeed, Manteuffel himself looked more to Frederick II than to Napoleon as a role model. (It is interesting to note in this connection that Ludwig von Gerlach disliked the "godless" cynic Frederick, even opposing the erection in 1851 of the famous statue of that monarch on Unter den Linden in Berlin.)

Carl Ludwig von Hinckeldey (1805–56), another of Frederick William's advisors after 1848, might more accurately be called a "crypto-Bonapartist"; certainly the maledictions of the High Conservatives suggest that they thought he was. Like Manteuffel, Hinckeldey was a career bureaucrat whose pre-1848 record was so outstanding that Frederick William IV named him police president of Berlin at the time of the counterrevolution in November 1848.[24] Hinckeldey was able to leverage his position as Berlin police chief to become what Karl August Varnhagen von Ense called Prussia's unofficial "second king." In fact, Hinckeldey was one of the most creative and astute conservative officials in nineteenth-century Prussia, and his resemblance to his Parisian contemporary, Baron Haussmann, is quite remarkable. He enjoyed a meteoric career after 1848 and quickly gained the King's complete confidence as his principal advisor on security matters. Hinckeldey was often quite indifferent to bureaucratic norms and procedures, especially that painstaking sense of order and "legality" (*Rechtsstaatlichkeit*) which was so characteristic of the civil service. He was more than willing to bend the law in his zeal to crush "subversion" and harass opponents of the government, even though he sometimes found himself in competition with Manteuffel. At the same time, Hinckeldey envisaged a vastly expanded role for positive state action as part of a conservative strategy to mobilize popular support for the monarchical cause. Thus he created a modern political police force, organized surveillance of political opponents of all stripes, and regularly confiscated newspapers that had offended him, especially the *Kreuzzeitung*. At

---

24 Although, in contrast to Baron Haussmann, Hinckeldey is little-known in this country, several biographical essays have appeared over the years: Berthold Schulze, "Polizeipräsident Carl von Hinckeldey," *Jahrbuch für die Geschichte Mittel- und Ostdeutschlands* 4 (1955): 81–108; Heinrich von Sybel's posthumous "Carl Ludwig von Hinckeldey 1852 bis 1856," *Historische Zeitschrift* 189 (1959), 108–23; Wolfram Siemann, *"Deutschlands Ruhe, Sicherheit und Ordnung." Die Anfänge der politischen Polizei 1806–1866* (Tübingen, 1985), 342–55; Barclay, *Frederick William IV*, 240–4, 274–5.

the same time, he introduced a number of modernizing reforms to Berlin itself that, like Haussmann's simultaneous rebuilding of Paris, transformed the face of the city and paved the way for its explosive growth after the 1860s. He created a system of public baths for the poor, established a regular fire department for the first time, updated the municipal street cleaning system, and promoted the construction of a new waterworks. His efforts helped to ensure a steady supply of cheap but healthy food to the city, and he used his police force to plant trees on public streets. He was also responsible for introducing the familiar public notice columns (*Litfasssäulen*) that visitors to Berlin can still see today. By undertaking all these projects, Hinckeldey became a hero to the Berlin bourgeoisie, who also appreciated his personal sobriety and incorruptibility, his modest lifestyle, and his commitment to what we would now call "family values." With his mixture of rough authoritarianism, populism, and welfare paternalism, with his emphasis on the extension of state power and his simultaneous support for modern forms of economic activity, Hinckeldey does indeed represent an early form of Prussian crypto-Bonapartism. Certainly his conservative enemies thought so, and they could scarcely hide their glee when a well-born aristocrat shot and killed him in a duel in 1856.

The examples of Manteuffel, Hinckeldey, and even the King himself led the High Conservatives to the gloomy conclusion that, despite their own political successes, post-1848 Prussia was succumbing to a creeping Bonapartism. It was especially painful to them to observe their fellow conservatives succumb to revolutionary amorality, despotism, bureaucratic excess, and lack of principle. However, perhaps the most worrisome example of apostasy, from their point of view, was the Gerlachs' erstwhile protégé, Otto von Bismarck.[25] This familiar story, which Henry Kissinger has recently retold, concerns Bismarck's shift from High Conservative *Prinzipienpolitik* to a *Realpolitik* based on amoral calculations of state interest. As Prussian representative to the Diet of the German Confederation in Frankfurt am Main, Bismarck increasingly chafed under the dominance of Austria in that organization. Moreover, by 1856, the year in which the Crimean War had come to an end, he had reached the conclusion that, if it were in Prussia's state interest to treat with Napoleon III, it should not hesitate to do so.

---

25 Henry Kissinger, *Diplomacy* (New York, 1994), 120–36. On the Gerlach-Bismarck exchange and the evolution of the latter's views, see Lothar Gall, *Bismarck: The White Revolutionary*, trans. J. A. Underwood, 2 vols. (London, 1986), 1: 131–40; Ernst Engelberg, *Bismarck. Urpreusse und Reichsgründer* (Berlin, 1985), 409–50; Otto Pflanze, *Bismarck and the Development of Germany*, vol. 1, *The Period of Unification, 1815–1871*, 2nd ed. (Princeton, 1990), 92–97; Frank-Lothar Kroll, "Bismarck und Friedrich Wilhelm IV," in Jost Dülffer, Bernd Martin, and Günter Wollstein, eds., *Deutschland in Europa. Gedenkschrift für Andreas Hillgruber* (Frankfurt am Main and Berlin, 1990), 205–28, esp. 221–2.

Throughout the so-called Oriental crisis and the subsequent Crimean conflict, Frederick William IV had pursued a policy of strict neutrality; he was supported in this by the *Kreuzzeitung* party and, more opportunistically, by Manteuffel, who in contrast to the Gerlachs certainly had no objection to dealing with a Bonaparte. However, by the end of the war Bismarck had decided that the Bonapartist regime posed a greater threat to Austria than to Prussia, and that Prussia should thus not be afraid of dealing with the Second Empire. Fear of ideological contamination and of the spread of revolution should take a back seat to the advancement of Prussian state interests. In any case, Bismarck was under no illusions about France's actual capacity for revolutionary expansion in the 1850s and 1860s; the world had changed since 1806, and the nephew was not the uncle. Such ideas were, of course, anathema to Leopold von Gerlach, who with his brother Ludwig had helped launch Bismarck's political career in 1847–8. The growing gap within the ranks of the Prussian conservatives – and the political and intellectual isolation of the older generation of High Conservatives – became increasingly evident in the remarkable exchange of letters between Leopold and Bismarck that began in 1856 and ended in 1860. Gerlach insisted in this correspondence that his "political principle is and remains the struggle against the revolution. You will not persuade Bonaparte that he is not on the side of revolution." Bismarck countered these arguments by asserting that Prussia would have to deal with France "without regard to its current ruler, purely as a piece, an unavoidable piece in the chess game of politics, a game in which it is my duty to serve only *my* king and *my* country."[26]

Bismarck, of course, had the last word. Leopold von Gerlach died in January 1861, only a few days after Frederick William IV. Ludwig von Gerlach lived on until 1877, railing against virtually all of Bismarck's policies (especially the war with Austria), denouncing him as a Caesarist, and, in the 1870s, actually joining the Catholic Center party, which he believed represented the only effective opposition to Bismarck's godlessness and amorality.

So what conclusions can we reach from all this? First, it seems to me that a consideration of Prussian conservatives' responses to, evaluation of, and, to a certain extent, adoption of Bonapartist outlooks and strategies tells us more about the evolution of conservative thinking and conservative action than it does about Bonapartism itself. For the first half of the century, Prussian conservatives generally tended to regard Napoleon as a

---

26 Leopold von Gerlach to Bismarck, May 6, 1857, and Bismarck to Gerlach, May 2, 1857, quoted in Gall, *Bismarck*, 1: 130, 133.

peculiarly diabolical character and his system, with its mixture of despotic and plebiscitary elements, as the logical, perhaps inevitable end result of bureaucratic absolutism and of revolution. However, after 1848, conservatives began to rethink the nature and purpose of state action, even as they were beginning to reevaluate Prussia's European role after the breakdown of the Vienna system. In doing so, they began to adopt certain measures and practices that the High Conservatives deplored but could not reverse. Second, the example of shifting conservative responses to Bonapartism reminds us just how difficult it is to come up with typologies of German conservatism. Many distinguished scholars have tried to do so, from Karl Mannheim and Sigmund Neumann to Ernst Rudolf Huber, Klaus Epstein, and Hans-Ulrich Wehler.[27] Although we can learn a great deal from their efforts, nineteenth-century conservatism remains a phenomenon that is at once protean and slippery, and one which tends to elude classification.

---

27 Karl Mannheim, *Konservatismus. Ein Beitrag zur Soziologie des Wissens*, ed. David Kettler, Volker Meja, and Nico Stehr (Frankfurt am Main, 1984); David Kettler, Volker Meja, and Nico Stehr, "Karl Mannheim and Conservatism: The Ancestry of Historical Thinking," *American Sociological Review* 49, no. 1 (February 1984): 71–85; Sigmund Neumann, *Die Stufen des preussischen Konservatismus. Ein Beitrag zum Staats- und Gesellschaftsbild Deutschlands im 19. Jahrhundert* (Berlin, 1930); Klaus Epstein, *The Genesis of German Conservatism* (Princeton, 1966); Ernst Rudolf Huber, *Deutsche Verfassungsgeschichte seit 1789*, vol. 2, *Der Kampf um Einheit und Freiheit 1830 bis 1850*, 3rd ed. (Stuttgart, 1988), 331–45; Hans-Ulrich Wehler, *Deutsche Gesellschaftsgeschichte*, vol. 2, *Von der Reformära bis zur industriellen und politischen "Deutschen Doppelrevolution" 1815–1845/49* (Munich, 1987), 440–57.

4

Tocqueville and French Nineteenth-Century Conceptualizations of the Two Bonapartes and Their Empires

MELVIN RICHTER

I

Much has been written about Tocqueville's concept of liberty. But how did he conceptualize the types of regime most threatening to liberty in societies of the sort (*état social démocratique*) he declared inevitable? While some important answers have been offered, they are limited to *De la Démocratie en Amérique*, which tends to be treated as though there were no subsequent developments in Tocqueville's concept of democratic or administrative despotism. Nor has there been critical analysis of the ambiguities, shifts, and varied applications of this concept, as Tocqueville used it throughout his life. For despite his cogent criticisms of "despotism" and "tyranny" as classifications of modern regimes, Tocqueville nevertheless retained these terms when he dealt with those regimes systematically denying political liberty. To understand the concept as employed in Tocqueville's thought, his formulations of it must be located both within his texts and considered in relation to his experience within the three decades of his career as political theorist, politician, and historian. Tocqueville never stopped analyzing how the regimes founded first by Napoleon and then Louis Bonaparte were related to those concepts which dominated his thought: democracy, revolution, centralization, liberty, and equality.

After many vacillations, Tocqueville diagnosed the two Bonapartes, their coups d'etat, and their empires as distinctively modern, as post-revolutionary and post-democratic. He emphasized the unacknowledged paradox that from the two French Revolutions of 1789 and 1848, the greatest hitherto known, had emerged not emancipation, but a regime considerably more repressive than the monarchies that had been overthrown. As Tocqueville wrote, "out of the very entrails of a nation which had just overthrown its monarchy, there appeared suddenly a power at once more extensive, and more minute in its application, a power more absolute than any ever exercised by a French king."[1] Although this judgment in *L'Ancien Régime* ostensibly was leveled against the Convention, the Committee of Public Safety, and above all, the First Empire of Napoleon Bonaparte, no French reader in 1856 could have missed the tacit parallelism with Louis Napoleon and the Second Empire.

Both Bonapartes executed military coups that overthrew republican governments, themselves created after great revolutions. They used plebiscites based on universal manhood suffrage to register ostensible popular approval, first of their use of violence, and then of the empires they founded. Thus, both empires and emperors were post-democratic, claiming that their regimes were legitimate because the people had delegated to them the supreme power to rule directly in the general interest of the nation. This pseudodemocratic argument held that by such an exercise of popular sovereignty after the use of force, the people withdrew approval for the parliaments they had previously chosen to represent them. Hence, it was argued, voters could and did confer political power upon the man who had overthrown the representative institutions of the republic. The two Bonapartes' empires were also post-revolutionary. Their founders further justified them by reference to their own stances vis-à-vis the great revolutions that prepared their way. Both Bonapartes reassured the beneficiaries of the Revolution that, on the one side, they had nothing to fear from the nobility or the Church, and, on the other, that the Empires protected them from radicals or extremists, whether Jacobins. Sans-culottes, or socialists.

From this diagnosis, however, Tocqueville did not conclude that either revolution or democracy in France necessarily entailed such a repressive regime, or if it were established, guaranteed its indefinite continuation. Tocqueville rejected any such historical determinism. His point was rather that a democratic revolution was subject to certain dangers, which could be mitigated or obviated, but only if the electorate were alerted to these perils and their representatives took decisions calculated to avoid them. As will be seen, Tocqueville rejected the view that France was irremediably decadent or doomed.[2]

---

1 Alexis de Tocqueville, *L'Ancien Régime et la Révolution, Oeuvres complètes*, II, 1: 248. Henceforth, this edition (Paris, 1951) will be designated as *OC*. The Pléiade edition of Tocqueville (Paris, 1991) will be designated as *OCP*. The older edition of the *Oeuvres complètes*, edited by Gustave de Beaumont, 9 vols. (Paris, 1864–6) will be designated as *OCB*. There are two critical editions of *De la Démocratie en Amérique*; one edited by Jean-Claude Lamberti and James Schleifer in *OCP*, II; the other by Eduardo Nolla, 2 vols. (Paris, 1990).

2 "I have long been convinced that the soil of French society cannot at present provide a solid or permanent foundation for [any type] of government. [Yet] I do not believe that all is over, nor, on the

Tocqueville's analyses of the two Napoleonic regimes also have an intrinsic value. Had he lived to complete his projected volume on Napoleon Bonaparte and his empire, Tocqueville would in all probability have contributed as much to their analysis and evaluation as did his *L'Ancien Régime* to the study of the French Revolution. When examined within the context of Tocqueville's career as a political theorist and actor, the two Bonapartes and their empires turn out to have been among Tocqueville's most durable concerns. This is not to say that on these subjects Tocqueville never altered his views. Indeed, references to the Bonapartes can and should serve as one marker for tracing both the alterations and consistencies in Tocqueville's thought. While maintaining his repertoire of themes and concepts, Tocqueville's use of them varied greatly, depending upon the theoretical problems which at any particular point most concerned him. Perhaps even more important was his judgment at any given time of the relationship of his analysis to the French political situation. He wrote not only as a theorist, but to attain his goals as a political actor.

II

Bonaparte's success in appropriating the first French Revolution was initially attributed to his unique combination of charisma with exceptional military and administrative abilities. Little thought was given to the question of whether Bonaparte had invented a new type of regime which, after his passing from the scene, could be institutionalized and used by lesser mortals.

After the Bourbon Restoration was overthrown in 1830, its successor, the July Monarchy, itself fell in 1848. This second great revolution was at first French, but became European in scope. Its initial product, the Second Republic, was ended by Louis Napoleon's coup d'état. Following his uncle's precedent, Louis Napoleon claimed that both the forcible seizure of power and the establishment of the Second Empire had been legitimized by a plebiscite based on his restoration of universal manhood suffrage. Since the nephew's abilities had been rated as far below those of his indubitably exceptionally gifted uncle, the question was at once raised about the meaning of this significant repetition of a pattern once assumed to be unique.

other hand, that all is lost. I consider my country as a sick man, whom we cannot, it is true, hope to cure all at once, but whose illness, at least for the moment, may be greatly alleviated, whose existence may be made extremely prosperous. This sickness may thus lead to great things." This translation is adapted from *Correspondence and Conversations of Alexis de Tocqueville with Nassau William Senior, 1834–59*, ed. M. C. M. Simpson, 2 vols. (New York, 1968), I: 89–90.

Why had Louis Napoleon succeeded in producing for the second time an undesired and unanticipated outcome of a great European revolution begun in Paris? Rather than being attributed to a unique individual, the recurrence of Bonapartism now had to be conceptualized and explained. Tocqueville's diagnosis differed fundamentally from other theorists'. Tocqueville's problematic – his comparative diagnosis of democracy in France, America, and Great Britain; his theory of revolution; his stress on the continuity between the centralization of pre- and post-revolutionary France – all pushed him to formulate in his own distinctive set of terms his inquiry into these imperial regimes.

It was only after Louis Napoleon's coup that many political theorists and actors came to believe that a qualitatively new form of government had appeared in the wake of revolution and democratization. Novel but contested terms were proposed to conceptualize this type of regime. Even the names of the "isms" meant to designate it provoked controversy. Contemporaries had to choose among such neologisms as "Bonapartism," "Caesarism," "Napoleonism," and "Imperialism." Quite discrepant meanings and implications came to be connected with these rival political and social concepts. To treat both empires under the same rubric, to class them together as the same phenomenon, and give them the name of Napoleonism or Bonapartism is already to go some way toward treating them as a modern French rather than as a European or Western form of regime. To call the phenomenon Caesarism or Imperialism is already to posit a pattern of significant recurrences under modern conditions of ancient political experiences dating back to the termination of the Roman Republic and the creation of the Principate. This is to give up the concept of a distinctively modern post-revolutionary and post-democratic type of regime such as Tocqueville believed had been established by the two Bonapartes.

Such concepts or regime types provide evaluative redescriptions of rule by an individual who, after seizing power by force from elected constitutional and representative governments, then establishes an authoritarian, highly centralized, and nonrepresentative regime refusing previous civil liberties in the name of a legitimacy claimed to be democratic. Thereafter, popular participation in the political process is considered by those holding power to have been permanently waived by the electorate.

In the second half of the nineteenth century and well into the twentieth, theoretical speculations about the regime called Bonapartism and/or Caesarism constituted an integral part of political discourse throughout Europe. Disputes about the characteristics, functions, and worth of such a regime were almost as prominent in nineteenth-century discussion of politics as "absolute monarchy" had been in the seventeenth and eighteenth centuries and debates about "totalitarianism" in the twentieth century.

Concepts such as Bonapartism and Caesarism tended to be used pejoratively as denoting illegitimate forms of domination by theorists of diverse views: royalist, reactionary, conservative, republican, liberal, and anarchist. However, there were many others who used Bonapartism and Caesarism in positive senses to characterize that mode of rule or type of leader that, in their view, alone could resolve what they saw as the political and social dilemmas of the century. Among them was Auguste Romieu, who in 1850 wrote *L'ere des Césars*. He predicted that since liberalism was impotent and monarchical legitimism dead, the rule of force by the military would succeed indecisive parliaments. Other positive characterizations of such regimes claimed that they represented the triumph of the will over mere reason; of heroic and idealistic national purpose over selfish group or personal interests, as well as the recognition by the masses that they need to be led by exceptional leaders or elites. Did such formulations feed currents of twentieth-century fascist thought and even Leninism and Stalinism?

III

Rather than attempting to present here the diverse forms and uses to which the concepts of Bonapartism and Caesarism have been put, I shall first list the principal issues separating different conceptualizations of the two Empires, of the way they were established, and of those who led them. This grid of differences will then be used to raise questions about Tocqueville's formulation and uses of the concept. For he has been identified, and rightly so, as having been the first to develop a political sociology of this phenomenon.[3] Equally significant is the fact that Tocqueville intended, but did not live to complete the final two volumes of his *L'Ancien Régime et la Révolution*: the second on the Revolution itself; the third on Napoleon Bonaparte and his Empire. It was here that Tocqueville proposed to assess the ultimate effects

---

3 Dieter Groh, "Cäsarismus," in *Geschichtliche Grundbegriffe*, ed. Otto Brunner, Werner Conze, and Reinhart Koselleck, 9 vols. (1972–97), 1: 726–71, in particular 745–8. See also Heinz Gollwitzer, "The Caesarism of Napoleon III as seen by public opinion in Germany," tr. Gordon C. Wells, *Economy and Society* XVI, 357–404, and above all Peter Baehr, *Caesar and the Fading of the Roman World. A Study in Republicanism and Caesarism* (New Brunswick, 1998).

on French political culture and institutions of the sixty years of revolution which twice produced "imperial despotisms."[4]

What was at issue in the competing conceptualizations of the two Empires? Let me state them briefly, indicating Tocqueville's own (sometimes fluctuating) position on each:

1. Was the pattern followed by the two Bonapartes distinctively French or could it occur elsewhere in Europe or the world? Tocqueville held that however different the institutions and characters of European nations, this type of regime would not be confined to France.

2. Could the two reigns of the Bonapartes be fitted into previous regime classifications, such as those of Aristotle, Polybius, and Montesquieu? Or, as Constant thought, was a new concept needed to designate the unique features of this post-revolutionary phenomenon occurring in a modern commercial society?

Often this type of disagreement was phrased by those who thought in terms of what has been called "the great parallel" between the history of how the Roman Republic came to its end at the hands of Julius Caesar or Augustus, who engineered the transition to the principate. In the second German edition of his *Eighteenth Brumaire*, Marx attacked this analysis and the term Caesarism associated with it because of the differences he attributed to class struggle under the two modes of production, ancient and modern bourgeois. "[T]heir political products... can have no more in common than the Archbishop of Canterbury has with the High Priest Samuel."

On this subject, Tocqueville's position was ambiguous. While admitting that the concepts of tyranny and despotism were inadequate to characterize unfree regimes in the democratic society he saw developing, Tocqueville refused to coin and name any concept designating a new type of regime, whether generically democratic, revolutionary, or growing as did that of the two Bonapartes, from the two combined. He continued to use old concepts qualified by adjectives such as *despotisme impérial*.[5]

3. How significant were the military origins of the Bonapartes, the use of the army to seize power? Were these civil or military regimes? Napoleon Bonaparte had claimed that: "I govern not as a general, but because the nation believes I possess the civilian qualities needed for governing." On the other hand, it has been held that the First Empire was dominated by military values, and that its key features and priorities, particularly its foreign

---

4 See Melvin Richter, "Tocqueville, Napoleon, and Bonapartism," in *Reconsidering Tocqueville's DEMOCRACY IN AMERICA*, ed S. E. Eisenstadt (New Brunswick, 1988), 110–45.
5 *OC*, III, 466.

policy of unlimited expansion, must be understood in that light. Auguste Romieu, Konstantin Frantz, and Donoso Cortes all held that in the wake of the French Revolution, only the military stood between the collapse into anarchy of state and society. Tocqueville thought that the Eighteenth Brumaire had been "almost as much a civil as a military revolution." The coup of December 2, 1851, in his view, marked a new phase. "Every previous revolution had been made by a political party. This is the first time that the army has seized France, bound and gagged her, and laid her at the feet of its ruler."[6] The Second Empire was military and Napoleonic, which enabled it to find a solid support in the army, the new aristocracy of democratic society, and to re-establish the traditions of imperial despotism (*despotisme Impérial*).[7]

4. What was the relationship between the two Bonapartes and the French Revolution? Did they terminate or perpetuate it? To what extent did they preserve its basic achievements? Tocqueville saw both empires as based on the revolution.[8]

5. What degree of domination was exercised by the two Bonapartist empires? Was their power absolute, more repressive than that exercised by the ancien régime, the revolutionary Convention and the Terror? Tocqueville thought that this was true of the Second Empire.[9] What were its prospects for the future? Here Tocqueville distinguished between the short and long term. He thought that while the Second Empire would last for a time, it could not do so indefinitely. The positive qualities of the French, as well as their defects and even their vices, would make the perpetuation of absolute power impossible.[10]

---

6 *Correspondence and Conversations*, II, 3–4.
7 "Indépendamment de l'origine révolutionnaire, il a l'origine militaire et napoléonienne, ce qui lui permet d'abord de trouver dans l'armée, indépendamment même de la nation, un appui solide, une sorte d'aristocratie, et secondement d'user tous les procédés du gouvernement militaire et de rétablir toutes les traditions du despotisme impérial." *OC*, III, 466.
8 Tocqueville described the Second Empire as: "révolutionnaire dans ses origine et ses traditions, de telle façon qu'il n'alarme aucun des grands intérêts que la Révolution a créés; il ne fait craindre ni le retour de l'ancien régime, ni la prépondérance des nobles, ni la domination du clergé; il satisfait, en un mot, à tous les instincts nouveaux, sauf celui de la liberté, et s'en appuyant sur tous ces instincts qu'il peut parvenir à comprimer le dernier." *OC*, III, t. 3, 466.
9 "[L]e gouvernement me semble mieux placé qu'aucun autre... pour exercer le puvoir absolu..." Tocqueville, *OC*, III, t. 3, 466.
10 "Je ne suis pas de ceux qui disent avec assurance que la longue et terrible révolution à laquelle nous assistons depuis soixante ans aboutira necessairement et partout à la liberté. Je dis, au contraire, qu'elle pourrait bien finir par mener partout au despotisme. Mais ces temps sont encore loin de nous, s'ils doivent jamais venir. Je tiens l'établissement du pouvoir absolu impossible aujourd'hui. Il y a dans nos qualités, dans nos défauts, dans nos vices mêmes quelque chose qui s'y oppose encore invinciblement. Nos habitudes luttent avec avantage contre lui, alor même qu'il se trouve momentanément aidé par nos idées. L'esprit général du temps, en un mot, résiste et en aura raison, malgré les cironstances accidentelles et passagères qui le servent." *OC*, III, t. 3, 466.

IV

Highly charged condemnations of Napoleon Bonaparte, perhaps influenced by Chateaubriand, appear in Tocqueville's travel notes when he came to the United States:

> Bonaparte's mind was at once broad in scope and rational. He was perfectly aware of the advantages of civil liberty, towards which he was always liberal and generous. But at the same time, Bonaparte was the greatest enemy of political liberty, which put obstacles in the way of his program. Bonaparte felt towards liberty that carefully considered hatred peculiar to his genius, which was at once ambitious and dominating.[11]

Again in his travel notes, Tocqueville coupled Danton with Bonaparte as examples of different types of revolutionaries contemptuous of freedom:

> When Danton had the throats cut of those unfortunates whose only crime was that of not thinking as he did, was that liberty? When later Robespierre sent Danton to be guillotined because he dared to become his rival, no doubt that was justice, but was it liberty? ... When Bonaparte then a consul substituted the tyranny of a single person (*la tyrannie d'un seul*) for the tyranny of factions, was that liberty?[12]

Two points made in this entry recur in the *Démocratie*. The first was Tocqueville's conflation of the Terror and Napoleon Bonaparte as constituting a distinctively French style of despotism born of the Revolution. In his conclusion to the 1835 *Démocratie*, Tocqueville repeated the phrase "the tyranny of a single person" (*la tyrannie d'un seul*) when defining the choice confronting modern egalitarian societies:

> But I think that if democratic institutions are not introduced gradually among us [in France], and if all citizens are not provided with those ideas and sentiments that first prepare them for liberty and then allow them to apply such ideas and sentiments, there will be no independence for anyone, not the bourgeois, not the nobility, not the poor, not the rich, but an equal tyranny for all. And I foresee that if in time we do not succeed in establishing the peaceful rule of the greatest number, we shall end up sooner or later under the unlimited power of a single person.[13]

---

11 *OCP*, I, 190–1. Twenty years later, after the establishment of the Second Empire, Tocqueville repeated the same judgment in his account of how, during his Consulate, Napoleon Bonaparte had abolished the Academy of Moral and Political Sciences. Tocqueville now added a comment on Bonaparte's relationship to the Revolution as well as to political liberty:

> The revolution continued its course, but liberty soon was the loser. For "revolution" and "liberty" are two words between which historians must strictly distinguish. The First Consul, who in his own way personified and continued the French Revolution, was nevertheless among the greatest enemies ever known of human liberty. *OC*, XVI, 234, note 6a.

12 *OCP*, I, 191. 13 *OC*, I, i, 330.

It was at this time (January 1835) that, in a letter to Kergorglay, Tocqueville identified the reign of Napoleon Bonaparte as a modern example of such a regime:

> If an absolute government were ever established in a country as democratic in its state of society (*état social*) and as demoralized as France, there would be no conceivable limits upon tyranny. Under Bonaparte we have already seen one excellent specimen of such a regime.[14]

With few signs that a second Empire could be established, Tocqueville chose not to name the Empire and Napoleon Bonaparte when, in the 1835 *Démocratie*, he warned his French readers on the greatest dangers to liberty. Instead he stated the alternatives as the choice between either a democracy with internal checks and rights for all, or the tyranny of the Caesars. This historical comparison, we now know from the critical edition, was immediately contested by his brother and father in their comments on the manuscript.[15] Together with Tocqueville's dismay at his first direct experience of political life in France, this exchange led him to a series of analyses first testing, then qualifying, and finally rejecting the applicability of the Roman parallel, Tocqueville's closest approximation to the concept of Caesarism.

The new critical editions have identified in the draft manuscript of the *Démocratie* a specific acknowledgment by Tocqueville that he had changed his mind about his striking assertion at the end of the 1835 volumes that if rights were not given to all, the only alternative was rule by a single person. He contrasted what he would now say in his famous chapter in the 1840 *Démocratie* on "What Type of Despotism Democratic Nations have to Fear" (part IV, chapter 6) with his rejected conclusion to the 1835 volumes: "This picture is both true and original; that given in the first volume is exaggerated, commonplace, trite, and false. The version presented here gives the full originality and profoundity of my idea. What I wrote in my first work was trite and superficial."[16]

What were the reasons for this reversal? In another note to himself, dated on his arrival in Paris (April 1837), Tocqueville wrote that everything he saw and heard led him to a reevaluation of French political life. It was now most menaced not by an omnipotent tyrant, but by the materialism,

---

14 Tocqueville to Kergorlay, January 1835, *OC*, XIII, t. 1, 373.
15 In a letter to Kergorlay, January 1835, he identified Tiberius and Claudius as the Caesars he had in mind. *OC*, XIII, t. 1, 373. The passages in the 1835 *Démocratie* occur in chapter 9, *OCP* II, 365; Nolla, I, 224, where the comments of his brother and father are given in notes d and g.
16 *OCP*, II, 837, 1177; Nolla, II, 264n.

individualism, and political apathy of the society as a whole, soldiers as well as civilians.

On October 30, 1836, Louis Napoleon failed ignominiously in the coup he attempted in Strasbourg. Tocqueville wrote to his friend Kergorlay:

> No doubt reports of that scuffle have already reached you. It has long been evident that the greatest dangers will come from the army... the same reasons that cause a democratic people to wish for peace and tranquillity also cause a democratic army to wish for war and trouble. Both originate in the same desire to improve one's status and in the same uncertainty of being able to do so...
>
> The actual coup was absurd, and was put down very easily. But the tranquillity and immobility of the people were appalling. For this immobility originated not in disgust with the present government but in profound indifference towards every form of government. Commerce and industry prosper; that suffices. Their passion for well-being is so imbecilic that they fear even to think about the causes that produce or maintain it.[17]

When Tocqueville returned to his chapter, "What Type of Despotism Democratic Nations have to Fear," he wrote to himself:

> If I wish to impress my readers by my picture of administrative despotism, I must not omit *what we see before our eyes* [Tocqueville's emphasis]. A tyranny of the Caesars was a scarecrow which could frighten no one. [See note 16.]

In this chapter, Tocqueville remarked that he had not changed his opinion that a democratic society creates conditions that could easily lead to political despotism. Now he revised his estimate of the forms that tyranny and degradation would assume in a democratic age.

Once again, Tocqueville turned to comparison when making his point. He now argued that if total domination were ever established in a modern egalitarian society, it would both differ from and far exceed the degree of control ever achieved in that period of Roman history when the power of the Caesars was at its height. That power was at once immense and unchecked; but it was a tyranny that was used against a relatively small part of the population and limited to relatively few objectives. Ordinarily the private lives of individuals lay beyond its reach. Thus, tyrannical power in antiquity was violent in its mode of exercise, but limited in the number of those it affected; the details of both social and individual life were for the most part unregulated. This last point had been made in De l'esprit de conquête et de l'usurpation (1813) by Benjamin Constant, who saw the novel threat of the First Empire as being directed for the first time against the minds of its subjects. As for administration, this was carried on differently in each

---

17 OC, XIII, t. 1, 416–17.

province. All peoples subject to Roman rule were allowed to preserve their customs and *moeurs*. It could not and did not occur to anyone, including the ruler, to seek to administer everything from above, to subject all subjects to the same uniform laws, to destroy all the intermediary powers that stood between the citizen and the political authority.

Thus in returning to the comparison he had made in the 1835 *Démocratie* between the power of the Roman emperors and the unlimited power of a single ruler in a democratic age, Tocqueville now drew different conclusions. He minimized the extent of even the greatest power achieved in Rome in order to show how much greater would be that enjoyed by the person or persons who held unlimited power in a modern democratic society. For such power would exceed any ever attained in imperial Rome. A modern democratic society would possess a centralized administration capable of making its will prevail throughout its empire; it could codify and make uniform its legislation; it could penetrate and regulate in detail both private and social life.

Such a democratic tyranny of the moderns, Tocqueville conjectured, although exercising greater power than that attained in antiquity, would be mild [*doux*] rather than violent, as at Rome. It would degrade but not torment those it ruled. As Tocqueville had argued earlier, in a democratic age when men are approximately equal in their power, wealth, and even in their desires, their *moeurs* become more humane and mild.[18] Even those who rise to power have their desires limited by the type of society in which they live. Such rulers are apt to prefer the role of paternalistic guardian (*tuteur*) to that of tyrant. Democratic governments may become violent and cruel in exceptional periods of revolutionary effervescence or external dangers. However, crises and revolutions will become increasingly rare. Yet in a democratic age, it will be easier for rulers to concentrate all powers in their own hands and to penetrate more deeply and more regularly into the private lives and even the minds of individuals.

This comparison of modern society and government with that of Imperial Rome was meant to emphasize not similarities but contrasts, particularly in the extent of their respective power and the severity with which it was exercised. In the late 1830s, Tocqueville was finishing the *Démocratie*. As the first decade of the July Monarchy came to an end, his greatest fears centered on the political weaknesses of French society. He was not to return to the overt comparison of modern France and ancient Rome until his final decade, when he had to deal with Louis Napoleon and the Second Empire.

18 *OC*, I, ii, part III, ch. 1.

V

The success of the *Démocratie* made possible Tocqueville's election in 1842 to the Académie française. Obliged by its protocol to deliver a eulogy of his predecessor's life and work, his address had to center on Jean-Gérard Lacuée, whom Napoleon Bonaparte had made Comte de Cessac for his indispensable services. A junior army officer prior to the Revolution, Cessac joined its army, where he rose to the rank of general. In 1791, he was briefly President of the Legislative Assembly. Under the Empire, he became minister of war administration and director general of conscription. In that position, he carried through what Isser Woloch has called the most surprising triumph of the new Napoleonic regime, the successful establishment of conscription.[19]

Since Cessac had written so little, Tocqueville, at the suggestion of his aged mentor, Royer-Collard, turned his eulogy into a philosophical judgment of the Empire. Royer remembered how before his death Cessac had spoken of his bad conscience, which did not concern the fate of those conscripted. He could not forget how badly he had treated his mistresses. Cessac also told how he had become enormously wealthy because of Napoleon Bonaparte's many gifts to him for his performance as a military bureaucrat. Yet, Cessac went on, "I did nothing extraordinary. He needed 400,000 men for his army every year. I provided them."[20] Cessac's conscience was not at all troubled by the memory of the young men he had furnished for slaughter in battle. This man, Tocqueville noted, had belonged to a peculiar class, the first citizens of absolute power: upright, personally honest, but carrying out every order of their master, no matter what they saw, heard, or felt about its consequences.

In this 1842 address, Tocqueville applied arguments he had made in the *Démocratie* to the analysis of the First Empire as a system. Above all, he made the most sustained assessment of Napoleon he had written up to this point. Only after 1850 did Tocqueville analyze Bonaparte and the Empire at comparable length. When he did so, he followed the scheme developed in 1842.

Questions previously raised in both parts of the *Démocratie* about the potential political dangers of democratic society recurred in Tocqueville's treatment of the First Empire. Napoleon Bonaparte and his new regime were treated as a specimen, as one possible outcome of the more general

---

19 Isser Woloch, *The New Regime. Transformations of the French Civic Order, 1789–1820s* (New York, 1994), 424.
20 *OC*, XVI, 252, n. 3.

syndrome or pathology caused by the failure to circumvent or mitigate individualism, materialism, governmental centralization, the preference of equality to liberty, the dangers created by the military, and, above all, general acceptance of the theory of unlimited popular sovereignty. In the *Démocratie*, Tocqueville identified the dangers of a government which exploited rather than counteracted the worst instincts of a democratic society.

Just a few years after completing the *Démocratie*, Tocqueville had been drawn by his election to the Academie française into an intensive consideration of Napoleon Bonaparte and the First Empire. Because he was discussing a regime in the past, Tocqueville employed that mode of historical explanation developed in his chapter in the 1840 *Démocratie* on "Some Characteristics of Historians in Democratic Times" (part I, chapter 20). Tocqueville repeated his distinction between general causes and those he called secondary or accidental. When dealing with Napoleon Bonaparte, the point of his inquiry was to ask how many of the effects produced by Napoleon are attributable to his own exceptional abilities, and how many to opportunities provided by his period, nation, and the French Revolution. Tocqueville emphasized the revolutionary mobilization of France against its external enemies, but did not minimize the leadership of Napoleon:

> Although the Empire's achievements were surprising, it was not itself the real source of this grandeur. It owed its éclat to accidents rather than to any intrinsic merits of its own. The Revolution had brought France to its feet; Napoleon ordered it to march. The Revolution had amassed enormous and unprecedented forces; these he organized and utilized. He produced prodigies, but in an age of prodigies. The person who founded and maintained this Empire was the most extraordinary phenomenon to appear for many centuries. Napoleon was as great as a man without virtue can be.[21]

Tocqueville's verdict derived from his analysis of the dangers to liberty from a leader who uses pseudodemocratic theories to legitimate the seizure and exercise of power in a democratic society. Such an abuse of democratic theory is explicitly attributed to Napoleon, who had not been identified by name in the 1835 text. There Tocqueville had written about the strange discovery by modern demagogues that there can be legitimate tyrannies, provided only that they are exercised in the people's name. The unlimited popular sovereignty claimed by Napoleon Bonaparte is again Tocqueville's target when addressing the Académie française:

> Once the powers of directing and administering the nation were no longer considered the privileges of certain men or families, such powers began to appear as the

---

21 *OC*, XVI, 263.

product and agent of the will of all [*la volonté de tous*]. It was then generally recognized that this will ought to be subject to no other limits than those it imposed upon itself. After the destruction of classes, corporations, and castes, this will appeared to be the necessary and natural heir of all secondary powers. Nothing was left so great that it was inaccessible; nothing so small that it could not be reached. The ideas of centralization and popular sovereignty were born on the same day. Although these ideas originated in [demands for] liberty, they could easily lead to servitude. Those unlimited powers that had been rightly refused to a king now were conceded to an individual ostensibly representing the nation's sovereignty. Thus Napoleon could say, without much offending public opinion, that he had the right of command over everything because he alone spoke in the name of the people.[22]

From what point of view did Tocqueville criticize the First Empire? He returned to his 1835 formula of granting rights to all and encouraging public participation in order to counter the dangers to liberty endemic to egalitarian society, as he defined it:

The diffusion of knowledge [*des lumières*] and the division of property has made each of us independent and isolated from the rest. Only interest in public affairs can temporarily unite our minds, and on occasion, our wills. But absolute power would deprive us of this unique setting for deliberating together and acting in common. It chooses to enclose us in that narrow individualism, to which we are already over inclined.[23]

Second, Tocqueville provided his own diagnosis of the blow dealt to liberty in France by Napoleon. By recreating and perfecting the centralized state machinery, Napoleon had come closer to total domination of French society than anyone before him. Perceiving the unprecedented opportunities for such domination that had been created by a democratic revolution, he exploited the possibilities offered by an individualistic, materialist, and egalitarian society.

These passages are among Tocqueville's most important contributions to the study of the Bonapartes' empires, which he characterized as a type of political system. Tocqueville provided a model of a new form of total domination based on an unprecedented reorganization of government and society. Its power, which eclipsed anything sought by absolute monarchs was, he argued, illegitimate:

The emperor without difficulty executed an extraordinary project. At one stroke and on a single plan, he rebuilt the entire fabric of society. He did so in order to make it accommodate absolute power without strain.... This permitted Napoleon to construct a despotism far more rational and skillfully articulated than any previously attempted. After having promulgated with the same unitary spirit all those laws

---

22 Ibid., 262.   23 Ibid., 266.

regulating the relations of citizens with one another and to the state, he was able to create at a single stroke all the powers charged with executing those laws. Thus he could structure all of them so as to constitute a great but simple machine of government. Napoleon alone was its motor... The formidable unity of the system, the powerful logic that linked all its parts, left no refuge for liberty.[24]

Finally, Tocqueville gave his reasons for believing that, in the long run, France could not and would not acquiesce permanently in regimes denying it political liberty. Later he would reject the judgment that in the Bonapartes' empires France had found governments appropriate to its passions and needs. He went even further when he refused to accept the excuses of those who had not resisted absolute power:

In societies with religious faith, or little knowledge, absolute power often constrains men without degrading them. This is because such power is acknowledged as legitimate... In our time, this cannot be the case. The eighteenth century and the French Revolution have not left us any moral or honorable ways of submitting to despotism... Thus when men submit to its laws, they can only despise it and themselves.[25]

In words calculated to deflate what we might now call Napoleon Bonaparte's charisma, Tocqueville wrote:

His singular genius justified and in a sense legitimated [*legitimait*] the extreme dependence of his contemporaries in their own eyes. The hero concealed the despot. It seemed plausible that in obeying him, submission was rendered not to his power, but to the man. Yet after Napoleon ceased to light up and animate the new world he had created, nothing was left of him except his despotism.[26]

The balance sheet of the First Empire, in Tocqueville's view, showed a series of unprecedented disasters for France. Napoleon had used his genius to restore and to perfect despotism, thus defeating the generous purposes of the Revolution at its inception. As for the project of conquering Europe, this had led to no ordinary defeat in battle, but to the ignominious occupation of France by its foreign enemies. However extraordinary Napoleon's abilities, he ruined himself and the nation. No one else had been in a position to dislodge him from power. This only he could do, and in fact he destroyed himself. Napoleon's most durable achievement had proved permanently harmful to France, for he had perfected the machinery of administrative centralization continued by all successor regimes.

---

24 Ibid., 264–5. 25 Ibid., 265–6.
26 Ibid., 264.

VI

After the coup d'etat that overthrew the Second Republic, Tocqueville turned to writing his three-volume project. In his 1853 notes, there is an explicit identification of Napoleon and the Empire with "unlimited despotism." Would Tocqueville have developed a theory of plebiscitary dictatorship? He explicitly linked the two empires as embodying "the idea conceived by Napoleon and even more completely realized by his nephew."[27] In sketching for himself what model he ought to use for the First Empire, he returned to themes prominent in the *Démocratie* and his French Academy inaugural:

> When I arrive at the Empire, analyze carefully this fabric: the despotism of a single person raising himself upon a democratic base; the combination best suited for producing the most unlimited despotism, the one best supported by the appearance of originating in right [*droit*] and sacred interest, that is, of the greatest number; and at the same time, the least responsible. How extraordinary [such lack of responsibility] is in a government that pretends to have derived its original mandate from popular election. What is nevertheless true about this claim.[28]

Tocqueville continued to denounce the Bonapartes' seizures of power by coup d'état and their efforts after the fact to legitimate such rule by plebiscite. Tocqueville's notes of the 1850s are explicit, dismissing scornfully such rationalizations as those concocted by Troplong, one of the prominent jurists who rallied to Louis Napoleon.[29] Thus, the use of Caesarist arguments by defenders of the Second Empire led Tocqueville to attack First Empire rationalizations of the Eighteenth Brumaire, when Napoleon seized power:

> Produce examples to show how jurists [*legistes*] create a theory and a philosophy [to justify] power in fact created by violence and force. Ever since the spread of Roman law, tyrants in all European nations have found it easier to recruit jurists than hangmen, although under despots both types flourish. Even the most mediocre usurper has his legal expert to prove that violence is law; tyranny, order; servitude, progress.[30]

This bitter indictment of the Bonapartes as engaging in the cynical manipulation of masses by reversing the meaning of words recalls George Orwell's *1984*. Tocqueville's most explicit indictment of this aspect of Bonapartism occurred in the single paragraph about the first emperor and Empire in his

---

27 *OC*, II, 2, 319.
28 *OC*, II, 2, 319. This point had been developed in far greater detail by Tocqueville in his letter to F. Lieber, August 4, 1852, *OC*, VII, 143–5.
29 *OC*, II, ii, 319; Tocqueville to J. J. Ampere, December 27, 1855, *OC*, XI, 305.
30 *OC*, II, ii, 319.

introduction to *L'Ancien Regime*. Such a charge of the reversal of meaning indicates how fraudulent Tocqueville found Bonapartist versions of democratic theory.[31]

Here again Tocqueville proposes a comparison between Roman and French history. This time he is equally interested in both similarities and differences:

> To use in the chapter dealing with the inception of the Empire. The differences and resemblances between those revolutions, which in [ancient] Rome and in [modern] France, passed from liberty to despotism . . . Exploitation of democratic passions and theories in both cases. The same procedure: to govern in the name of the people but without the people; to provide citizens with a political representation based upon number, but to administer them nevertheless by the use of the most educated [*classes éclairées*]; to satisfy the lowest classes [*les basses classes*] by pretending to recognize them, and by abolishing all the intermediate orders that had humiliated them, thus satisfying the feelings of envy and their desire for equality in its grossest form, where everyone is reduced to the same level of servitude; to satisfy the highest classes by ensuring them material order, the undisturbed enjoyment of their goods, well-being and enrichment through either their industry or through obtaining official positions.[32]

As for the legal basis of imperial rule, Tocqueville viewed Roman public law as an instrument of absolute rule that imposed the spirit of servitude in all relationships between sovereign and subject. When Ulpian and Gaius held that the wish of the ruler has the force of law, this referred to the transfer by the Senate of every right of the people to the prince.[33] Tocqueville identified this with the key argument of Bonapartism: the people had freely given all its power and rights to the Emperor. Even the success of absolutism in France was attributed by Tocqueville to royal sponsorship of the Roman law. Only the English had refused it; only the English had retained their independence and liberty.[34]

This use of Roman analogies in his 1853 notes recalls those passages of the *Démocratie*, in which Tocqueville warned that modern society might fall into the hands of a Tiberius. Later, in a letter of 1854, Tocqueville wrote that administrative centralization in Europe was on the rise, that the trend was not toward modern liberty, but ancient despotism. He characterized centralization as the modernized form of the Roman Empire. In the same letter, he applied to the Roman Empire, to Byzantium, and to China the

---

31 *OC*, II, i, 72. For an extended treatment of this topos, see James Boyd White, *When Words Lose Their Meaning* (Chicago, 1984).
32 *OC*, II, ii, 320.   33 Ibid., 322.
34 Tocqueville to Alexis Stoffels, January 4, 1856, *OCB*, VI, 468.

analysis he had made in the 1840 *Démocratie* of "administrative despotism."[35] The trend toward centralization will produce the same effects in Europe as in those other societies: "a race, very civilized and at the same time, degraded; troops of intelligent men, but never energetic and productive nations." Thus, Roman history was used for a time by Tocqueville to present admonitory lessons to Frenchmen once again subjected to imperial rule.

Apologists of the Second Empire followed the lead of Louis Napoleon, who wrote a book on Julius Caesar, in seeking to vindicate his regime. Their attempts to legitimate the regime were phrased for the most part as tendentious theories of Caesarism. As a result of them, Tocqueville began to abandon his earlier interest in making his own analysis of French politics dependent upon analogies to Roman history. The Second Empire apologists stressed the need for a redeeming Caesar and an Augustus, who had to seize power in order to restore order and reform a society fallen into anarchy and corruption. By 1856, Tocqueville rejected such comparisons between contemporary France and late Republican Rome as intrinsically misleading and playing into the hands of Louis Napoleon and his apologists.[36] Tocqueville believed that those who, like Gobineau, held France to be irretrievably decadent, were in the Imperial camp. Tocqueville had elected to continue his own treatment of modern French history. Fully engaged in this enterprise, he was in no position to follow his friend J. J. Ampere in writing on Roman history in order to refute Imperial propaganda.

In one of his last analyses of France, Tocqueville again rejected any comparison to Roman history:

I am not among those who tell us that our nation is decrepit and corrupted, destined forever to live in servitude. Those who fear and those who hope that this is our situation; those who show us the vices of the Roman Empire, and those who are pleased to believe that we are going to reproduce these vices on a small scale, all such people I believe to live in books alone and not in the reality of their time. Our nation is not decrepit, but fatigued and frightened by anarchy. Although our concept of liberty is not as lofty and healthy as it should be, we deserve better than our current fate. For we are not yet ready for the establishment of a despotism that will be definitive and regular.[37]

Or, as Tocqueville wrote to Freslon, "I find defective [*inexactes*] all the comparisons that are being made between our society and that of Rome

---

35 Tocqueville to his nephew, Hubert de Tocqueville, March 25, 1854, *OCB*, VII, 322–3.
36 Tocqueville to Henry Reeve, April 16, 1856, *OC*, V, 1, 167; Tocqueville to Ampere, January 17, 1856, *OC*, XI, 305.
37 Tocqueville to Beaumont, February 27, 1858, *OC*, VIII, 3, 543–4.

in decline. Most of our nation are neither corrupt, nor fearful [*craintive*], nor in a state of subjection like the Roman mob [*canaille*]."[38]

CONCLUSION

Let me sketch the overall view of Napoleon held by Tocqueville. In Tocqueville's view, the French Revolution had left an ambiguous heritage, two traditions of democracy. One tradition was compatible with citizens ruling themselves while enjoying liberty, the rule of law, and individual rights; the other was not. Characteristic of this second type of French democracy was rule in the name of the people by individuals, groups, or parties openly contemptuous of any limitations on popular sovereignty, the ostensible source of the power they exercised. Prominent among the significant contributions to the Revolution's illiberal legacy were those Tocqueville attributed in large part to Napoleon Bonaparte: the perfection of a centralized administrative machinery; and the codification of a civil law that encouraged individualist self-enrichment, but sharply limited freedom of the press and of association as well as the autonomy of local governments. This went along with the launching of theoretical justifications and actual precedents for seizing power by force from constitutional governments; the invention of plebiscitary dictatorship as a pseudodemocratic alternative to regularly elected representative governments; and among those who regarded themselves as revolutionary, the creation of a tradition of disregard for individual rights and constitutional government.

All these aspects of rule by the two Bonapartes reinforced tendencies developed earlier in what Tocqueville considered the most violent and least defensible periods of the revolution. As a result of the series of revolutions it had undergone – in which Tocqueville included the Eighteenth Brumaire, 1799, and December 2, 1851, the Consulate, and the First and Second Empires – France now had a distinctive set of post-revolutionary political *moeurs* (operative practices or political culture). All too many Frenchmen accepted the assumptions that violence is normal and acceptable in politics, that the state may as a matter of course set aside individual or group rights whenever they are alleged to conflict with the general or national interest; that strong leadership is incompatible with representative institutions. Napoleon had instilled the taste for decisive action and leadership; he had perfected the centralized administration requisite for executing national policy without genuine consultation of the citizens. At the same time, he

---

38 Tocqueville to Pierre Freslon, January 12, 1858, *OCB*, VII, 481.

availed himself of and further developed means for conducting the national mobilization and propaganda developed during the wars of the Revolution. Thus, to these existing post-revolutionary political *moeurs*, Napoleon added the Empire's bureaucratic and legal structures, which effectively excluded citizens and their representatives from deliberating together and from making decisions on any level. Once in power, all successor regimes not only used but expanded the machinery put into place by the first Emperor. The Second Empire followed the precedents as well as the theory of the First.

To sum up, although Tocqueville confined his analysis of the two Bonapartes' empires to France, he did so in terms applicable to democratic theory and administrative practice everywhere. As for the novelty of this, Tocqueville wavered. Sometimes he viewed it as did Constant, as different from any regime previously known because of its post-democratic and post-revolutionary quality; sometimes Tocqueville thought that there were valid historical analogues such as the Caesars after the destruction of the Roman Republic. The military quality of Bonapartism Tocqueville located in its undefined and reckless goals in regard to foreign policy, and in its appeals to the ambitious soldiers of a democratic army.

Tocqueville saw both the Bonapartes as presenting themselves as bastions of order while simultaneously reassuring those who had profited from the Revolution that its settlement would not be reversed. The first Bonaparte defined himself as a bastion against the Jacobins; his nephew, against the socialists. Observing the acceptance in many quarters of the Second Empire despite the loss of political freedoms, Tocqueville could see how exaggerated were the fears of socialism and how they were driven by the appeal to materialism made by the regime. Tocqueville was no less repelled by the church's rallying to the Empire. His views of the political functions of religion, so favorable in the *Démocratie*, were very much altered by the end of his life when he condemned the French church's support of Napoleon III. It is intriguing to speculate what other changes he would have made in his theory had he lived to complete his work.

5

Marx's Eighteenth Brumaire of Louis Bonaparte

Democracy, Dictatorship, and the Politics of Class Struggle

TERRELL CARVER

> The history of all society up to now is the history of class struggles.
> Karl Marx and Friedrich Engels, *The Communist Manifesto*[1]

Would Louis Bonaparte be much remembered now if it weren't for Karl Marx? Of those who might recognize the name (but almost certainly not the image) of Napoleon III, Emperor of the French, how many would correctly identify him as M. Louis Bonaparte, democratically elected President of the Second Republic (1848–51)? The "June Days" of the Revolution of 1848 and the workers' cooperatives of republican Paris have been memorialized by socialist historians, of whom Marx was the first (in *The Class Struggles in France*,[2] the little-read precursor of *The Eighteenth Brumaire of Louis Bonaparte*). Indeed, even the memorialization of M. (le Président) Louis Bonaparte in Marx's *Eighteenth Brumaire* has been rather neglected, and the circumstances of his coup d'état hardly ever analyzed historically and theoretically. The moment of Louis Bonaparte's democratic presidency has been lost in the obscurity of the short-lived Second Republic, and the moment of his military dictatorship (from December 2, 1851) has been merged into his rather forgettable Second Empire (which began a year later) and lasted remarkably until 1870. Before examining Marx's *Eighteenth Brumaire* for what it has to say to us about democracy, dictatorship, and class struggle, it will be necessary to examine very closely the way the text has been framed by "all the dead generations" of commentary.[3] This will entail a discussion of the text as history, the text as Marxism, and the text as English prose.

---

1 Karl Marx, *Later Political Writings*, ed. and trans. Terrell Carver (Cambridge, 1996), 1.
2 Karl Marx, *The Class Struggles in France*, in Karl Marx and Frederick Engels, *Collected Works*, vol. 10 (London, 1978), 45–145.
3 Karl Marx, *The Eighteenth Brumaire of Louis Bonaparte*, in *Later Political Writings*, 32.

Marxists have framed the text as history (rather than theory), but historians on the whole have not been very impressed with it, rather understandably not rating Marx as one of the "pros." Actually the *Eighteenth Brumaire* was high-quality political journalism, more like docu-drama or "instant history" as we know it.[4] In terms of theory, Marxists have regarded the *Eighteenth Brumaire* as problematic rather than classic. This is specifically with regard to the base-superstructure model of society, as outlined in Marx's 1859 "Preface" to *A Contribution to the Critique of Political Economy* and the vast subsequent literature on the materialist interpretation of history.[5] As a final blow, the English translation by Daniel de Leon (1898) is the worst of the classic early translations of Marx, producing muddle, inaccuracy, and wodges of a language that is neither English nor German.[6] Because the work is so unintelligible in translation, English readers have rightly found much of what is supposed to be mere detail in Marx's text irrelevant to the Marxism that interests them. Hence they tend to focus on passages in the *Eighteenth Brumaire* that seem to accord with other texts by Marx (and/or Engels) that are better known (and better translated), especially when those texts deal with what are apparently more abstract issues and higher-level generalizations.

In this chapter, I shall be considering these questions as I go along, in order to refresh the whole question of Marx and Bonapartism. Framing the work with a new contextual account, I examine it politically, drawing out what Marx had to say about the relationship between democracy, dictatorship, and class struggle. Marx's view of democracy was highly substantive rather than abstractly procedural, and his account of class politics was far from crudely reductionist. A refreshed reading of the *Eighteenth Brumaire* reveals that Marx was a pioneer analyst of the politics of representation and a first-rank theorist of contingency. Balanced against that, his account reveals a structural dependence between the class content of representative democracy and an impetus to dictatorship that does not come from a "great" and/or "evil" personality. Rather against the grain of most historiography,

---

[4] Or at least that was true until Hayden White recast history as narrative and so reversed the terms of engagement, promoting Marx to the top ranks. See Hayden White, *Metahistory: The Historical Imagination in Nineteenth Century Europe* (Baltimore, 1973). Theodore Zeldin rather respectfully credits Marx with journalism and a "heuristic" intent, and notably leans toward Marx's analysis in considering the "June Days" of 1848 and the relationship between Louis Bonaparte and the class interests of French industrialists, as well as French peasants; *France 1848–1945* (Oxford, 1973), 130, 131, 471, 473, 504.
[5] Karl Marx, "Preface" (1859) to *A Contribution to the Critique of Political Economy*, in *Later Political Writings*, 158–62. See G. A. Cohen, *Karl Marx's Interpretation of History: A Defence* (Oxford, 1978).
[6] Terrell Carver, "Translating Marx," *Alternatives* 22:2 (1997), 191–204, and later in this chapter; Maximilien Rubel, *Bibliographie des oeuvres de Karl Marx* (Paris, 1956), 91.

Marx's theory of dictatorship does not depend on a dictator, his theory of Bonapartism does not depend on a Bonaparte, and his theory of Caesarism is one of resurrection and parody. In the *Eighteenth Brumaire*, it is the class politics of representative democracy that delivers a deadly dictatorship to the living republic and a mock empire to the farcical Bonaparte. As Marx put it: "Men and events appear as Schlemihls in reverse, as shadows that have lost their bodies. The revolution has paralysed its own proponents and has endowed only its enemies with passion and violence."[7]

Marx's contribution to the theory of Bonapartism is really a contribution to the theory of democracy, but it is not a contribution that many democrats are willing to entertain. Living in a post-Hayekian world in which markets and democracy are said to be indissolubly linked (through a logic of information flows based on mutually reinforcing freedoms), few democrats today are anxious to examine the radically inegalitarian world that Marx portrays in the antidemocratic struggles that took place within the Second Republic.[8] This is a world of big capital and vested interests, with little enthusiasm for allocating power to the wider, poorer sections of society. Marx argued that "the party of order" paved the way for Louis Bonaparte's coup of December 2, 1851, and scornfully detailed the extent to which the party of order fooled themselves into believing that Louis Bonaparte was really the fool he seemed to be. The irony of history is more in evidence in this text than the workings of any dialectic, but more pertinently, Marx identified a dynamic within "free market" liberal democracy that is ever-present. This dynamic is a predictable relationship between capitalist wealth, authoritarian institutions, and the capacity of some politicians to fool most of the people at least some of the time, including themselves. Marx traces out a delusionary politics and focuses on collective as well as individual self-delusions. Those who lived through the "Thatcher Years" in the United Kingdom will surely find some similarities.

MARX AND HISTORY

Marx's work has been treated by professional historians as politically suspect at best and dismissed as propaganda at worst. Had he been an eyewitness to at least some of the important events (like Thucydides), his account would be an important primary source. Also, his docu-dramatic reconstructions would then be respected (again, rather like Thucydides).[9] However, Marx

---

7 Marx, *Eighteenth Brumaire*, in *Later Political Writings*, 53–4.
8 F. A. Hayek, *The Constitution of Liberty* (London, 1960).
9 Thucydides, *The Peloponnesian War*, trans. Rex Warner (Harmondsworth, 1977), 46–8.

spent only March 1848 in Paris, having been expelled from Belgium for belonging to a democratic association which had sent a message of support to the French revolutionaries. He was welcomed into France by a friend who was a member of the republican provisional government, which had been formed at the end of February just after the overthrow of Louis Philippe, King of the French:

Brave and loyal Marx,
The soil of the French Republic is a place of refuge for all friends of freedom. Tyranny has banished you, free France opens her doors to you and all those who fight for the holy cause, the fraternal cause of all peoples. Every officer of the French Government must interpret his mission in this sense. *Salut et Fraternité*.
        Ferdinand Flocon
        Member of the Provisional Government[10]

Marx's credentials as a political democrat and as a democratic theorist need some clarification. In the 1830s and 1840s, democracy was by definition a revolutionary movement, and perforce, advocating it under authoritarian regimes was illegal or at least quite risky. Following the post-Napoleonic settlements of the Congress of Vienna in 1815, such liberal regimes as there were in Europe slipped back into nonconstitutional rule under restored monarchies. Democratic politics was really about establishing constitutional governments through which representative institutions could share power with sections of society at least somewhat wider than a royal family and their courtiers, advised, of course, by bureaucratic minions. Marx's revolutionary communism was securely positioned in the 1840s within the framework of middle-class coalitional politics, where he could get at it, which was not anywhere in Germany, then divided into states and state-lets. None of those entities was constitutional in the sense of offering government accountable to the people through free and fair elections.

Marx's early career as an economic and political liberalizer on the *Rheinische Zeitung* was only possible through a brief respite in Prussian royal censorship, and it ended in 1843 when the paper was disbanded. He then entered a world of émigré politics amongst German workers and intellectuals in Paris and Brussels, and rather more remotely in London and other European centers. This was mainly a politics of representing them on "correspondence committees" allied to the radical press and politer forms of semi-legal struggle. As a communist, he positioned himself on the far left, specifically as a gadfly to force economic issues of class inequality onto the political agenda and to ensure the participation of (male) workers in the

---

10 Quoted in David McLellan, *Karl Marx: His Life and Thought* (London, 1973), 190; see also 189–94.

political process, whether that of violence and force of arms, or (where possible) that of electoral politics and representative institutions. The final section of the *Communist Manifesto* (written December 1847/January 1848 and published in February before any overtly revolutionary events) makes this clear, giving a useful rundown on how coalition strategies were expected to differ country-by-country:

> They [communists] struggle for the attainment of the immediate aims and interests of the working class, but within the current movement they also represent the future. In France the communists ally themselves to the social-democratic party... In Switzerland they support the radicals... In Poland the communists assist the party which works for an agrarian revolution... In Germany the communist party struggles in common with the bourgeoisie against absolute monarchy.[11]

Marx was thus acutely sensitive to the need for coalition politics to make democratization successful, and all his life he was against Blanquism, the strategy of the coup masterminded by the small band of conspirators.[12] He had no problems with armed struggle as such, however, but his model was that of calling the population to arms in the French revolutionary tradition ("*Aux armes, citoyens!*" as it says in "The Marseillaise"). How purely democratic his coalition politics was as a matter of practice rather than of goal-driven practicality, is a matter of debate, as it is bound to be the case with anyone involved in actual politics.

Marx was neither the theorist nor the practitioner of the vanguardist party, and his hands were never very dirty. Possibly this was a fault, but it is not a reason for discounting his commitment to representative and responsible government by and for the people. In the longer term, he expected the people to coincide with the working class, and the bourgeoisie and other reactionary classes to be dissolved in order to make exploitation disappear. That is what made him a communist. That vision is not in itself undemocratic, nor were the methods that he advocated any less democratic than those used by more conventional liberals to establish and secure constitutional forms of government. There has been a good deal of violence, terrorism, armed struggle, civil war, and worse in the history of the foundation and defense of democratic regimes. By definition, none of them emerged through democratic processes, and the closer any struggle comes to force of arms, the less democratic it is bound to become. Probably

---

11 Marx and Engels, *Communist Manifesto*, in Marx, *Later Political Writings*, 29.
12 See Shlomo Avineri, *The Social and Political Thought of Karl Marx* (Cambridge, 1968); and Michael Levin, *Marx, Engels and Liberal Democracy* (Basingstoke, 1989).

Marx's methods as an activist were more democratic than average (during the revolutionary events of 1848 the Communist Party was dissolved as unnecessary, given the politics of popular insurrection). And probably he was more unsuccessful than average because of this commitment to popular participation in democratic decision-making.

MARX AND MARXISM

Read in this light, the complicated political narrative and complex analytical categories of the *Eighteenth Brumaire* begin to make sense. Marx was fascinated by the interaction of economic interest with political tradition, and the interaction of both of those with individual psychology, strategic maneuvers, and collective decision-making. This kind of reading then begins to open up the question of what the basic categories of Marxism are, taking that to mean the fundamentals of Marx's approach to social theory and political analysis. The Marxist tradition has been built up from the categories of the 1859 Preface: relations of production, material productive forces, economic structure of society, "real basis," legal and political superstructure, social consciousness, mode of production, social being, and property relations.[13] Engels glossed this in a book review at the time in terms of higher order concepts, again familiar foundational categories for Marxism as it subsequently developed: materialism, metaphysics, dialectic, interaction, contradiction, reflection.[14]

It is possible now to read Marx forward through the *Eighteenth Brumaire* of 1852 to the 1859 Preface and thus to see the 1859 Preface as a rather gross oversimplification of the *Eighteenth Brumaire*. The *Eighteenth Brumaire*, however, is usually seen as an untidy version of the 1859 Preface, and therefore rather out of line with Marxism and thus with Marx himself. Indeed, my forward-looking, antiteleological reading of Marx can be performed *within* the *Eighteenth Brumaire* itself, as the text contains not merely the untidy categories that comprise Marx's brilliantly engaged and engaging narrative, but also a contextualized version of those very simplifications that later appeared as a "guiding thread" in the 1859 Preface. It is from those simplifications that the doctrinal puzzles of the materialist interpretation of history were famously constructed, but the 1859 Preface itself contextualizes them only biographically, not politically.[15] Thus the *Eighteenth Brumaire* could be read,

---

13 Marx, "Preface" (1859), in *Later Political Writings*, 159–60.
14 Terrell Carver, *Engels* (Oxford, 1981), 40.
15 The phrase "materialist interpretation of history" derives from Engels; see Carver, *Engels*, 38–40.

against the Marxist tradition, as a foundational classic, rather than as an embarrassing and largely unintelligible compendium of anomalies. Moreover if we do this, the notion of what a Marxist tradition is supposed to look like then alters materially. Is it supposed to look like a set of rather abstract generalizations that define a research agenda, set puzzles for historians and social scientists, and provide a stimulus for empirical analysis and testing? Or is it supposed to look more like a way of analyzing politics — specifically the class politics of modern democracy — from which a few generalizations emerge, albeit locally and tentatively? This chapter argues for the latter, not just to rearrange anyone's idea of Marxism, but rather to re-establish the link generally between Marx's work and the potential for class politics, even within the supposed stabilities of representative democracy.

From the Marxist perspective, there are a number of famous aporia within the *Eighteenth Brumaire*, notably the opening lines on history repeating itself, the well-known quotation that "men make their own history" but not "just as they please," the comments on the peasantry being like a "sack of potatoes," the composition and role of the lumpenproletariat, the "independent" state that has brought society "into submission," and state power that appears suspended in mid-air but isn't.[16] From the perspective of the *Eighteenth Brumaire*, however, these are not aporia at all, that is, problematic ideas and views that must somehow be reconciled with the supposed truths of the 1859 Preface. To do that they would have to be shown to be consistent with the guiding thread that Marx elaborated there, which is actually very confused and confusing.[17] Rather, these supposed aporia could well be comments that Marx made in the *Eighteenth Brumaire*, precisely because he thought that they were truthful, and truthful with respect to his analytical perspective on class politics within the fragilities of revolutionary democracy. That perspective was rooted in the view that class struggles make history, and that class as a social phenomenon is rooted in the technologies and relationships of material production. However, the urge within Marxism to reduce Marx to a set of propositions, or indeed to a method (as Engels and Georg Lukács notably attempted)[18] ought to be resisted, and I shall argue that Marx makes more sense about democracy and dictatorship when he is let off that kind of leash. As a work of instant history, docu-drama, and immediate political intervention (or attempted intervention, anyway), the

---

16 Marx, *Eighteenth Brumaire*, in *Later Political Writings*, 32, 116–17, 120–1.
17 See Terrell Carver, *Marx's Social Theory* (Oxford, 1982).
18 See Carver, *Engels*, 38–40; Georg Lukács, "What is Orthodox Marxism?" in *History and Class Consciousness: Studies in Marxist Dialectics*, trans. Rodney Livingstone (London, 1971), 1–26; and Terence Ball and James Farr (eds.), *After Marx* (Cambridge, 1984), chaps. 10–12.

Eighteenth Brumaire is the premier place to find Marx at his moment of high *theoretical* engagement.

In the 1859 Preface, Marx claims that a legal and political superstructure rises from the economic structure of society because the mode of production of material life conditions political life, yet he never claims that the relationship between the state and the economic structure of society is all that simple, and certainly not determined/determining.[19] Previously in the *Eighteenth Brumaire* he had already argued – and indeed he repeated this argument in his later Preface to a new edition of the *Eighteenth Brumaire* in 1869 – that only under Louis Bonaparte "does the state *seem* to have achieved independence with respect to society and to have brought it into submission."[20] In the *Eighteenth Brumaire*, Marx constructed a lengthy history of the French state, an analysis of the *apparent* situation under Louis Bonaparte, and an explanation of the *real* situation at the level of economic conditions and class politics.

At the opening of the *Eighteenth Brumaire*, Marx waxed lyrical about "the eighteenth Brumaire of the genius," that is, the first Napoleon Bonaparte "with his roundtable of military marshals." For Marx, the "high tragedy" of history the first time round was the French Revolution, with its drive to democratize in terms of political power and social status (if not in terms of an egalitarian economy), and its descent via revolutionary defense and revolutionary conquest into military dictatorship. This happened when the first Napoleon undertook his coup against the Directory (18 Brumaire VIII = November 9, 1799), and the dictatorial regime was subsequently ratified by the plebiscites of May 10, 1802 (Bonaparte as First Consul) and May 15, 1804 (Bonaparte as Emperor).

Assessing the (First) Empire as an historical episode, Marx, as always, aimed to integrate a political account with an economic one. The economic account is fairly simple – the advance of commercial society creating and benefiting the class-fractions of the bourgeoisie – at the immediate or eventual expense of other classes in society, namely feudal aristocrats and peasants, as well as the new urban proletariat. The main political development is the advance of the French bureaucratic state:

But under the absolute monarchy, during the first revolution, under Napoleon, bureaucracy was only the means of preparing the class rule of the bourgeoisie.

---

[19] Note that even in the classic translation "determines" appears in only one passage of the "guiding thread"; this is a poor and highly misleading translation of *bestimmt*. Cf. my alternative translation in *Later Political Writings*, 159–60.

[20] Marx, *Eighteenth Brumaire*, in *Later Political Writings*, 116; emphasis added.

Under the restoration, under Louis Philippe, under the parliamentary republic, it was the instrument of the ruling class, however much it also strove for power in its own right.[21]

Later, in an 1870 draft of *The Civil War in France*, Marx revisited this, writing of a "parasitical [excrescence upon] civil society, pretending to be its ideal counterpart," something that "grew to its full development under the sway of the first Bonaparte." Under "the first Bonaparte it served not only to subjugate the revolution and annihilate all popular liberties, it was an instrument of the French revolution to strike abroad." The "state parasite," Marx continued, received "only its last development during the second Empire." While it may have "apparently" been the final victory of governmental power over society, and "to the uninitiated" it certainly "appeared" as an autocracy over society and "pretending" to be superior to it, nonetheless for Marx the real situation was different.[22]

As Marx had said in the *Eighteenth Brumaire*, the French peasantry had elected Louis Bonaparte President of the Republic, but the antidemocratic maneuvers that enabled him to mount his coup d'état and then to create the Second Empire were performed by the bourgeois party of order. What Marx expected was that economic development – the impoverishment of both proletariat and peasantry – would produce a political alliance against which even the large-scale corruption of Napoleon III would be powerless, and against which the bourgeoisie would have insufficient forces. This political alliance would be between the proletariat and the peasantry.

> The aspirations of the Proletariat, the material basis of its movement, is labor organized on a grand scale... On the other hand, the labor of the peasant is insulated, and the means of production are parcelled, dispersed. On these economical differences rests superconstructed a whole world of different social and political views... [P]easant proprietorship itself has become nominal, leaving to the peasant the delusion of proprietorship... What separates the peasant from the proletarian is, therefore, no longer his real interest, but his delusive prejudice.[23]

The conclusion Marx draws here is not that state power has triumphed over the economic strength of the bourgeoisie – quite the opposite – but that in the regime of the second Bonaparte a final episode in the class war is being played out, namely the delivery of the peasantry at last into the arms of the proletariat. Louis Bonaparte's parody of the (First)

---

21 Ibid., 116
22 Karl Marx, "First Draft of *The Civil War in France*," in Karl Marx and Frederick Engels, *Collected Works*, vol. 22 (London, 1986), 484–5.
23 Ibid., 494–5.

Empire[24] (note that Marx spotted this delivery before it actually took place) was the site in which the interests of the bourgeoisie and peasantry, which Marx saw as coincident under the first Napoleon, would come apart. After the first Brumaire, "the parcelling out of land and soil complemented free competition and the beginnings of large-scale industry in the cities." "Even the preferment of the peasant class," Marx continued, "was in the interest of the new bourgeois order."[25] After Louis Bonaparte's "second Brumaire," Marx noted that "the state is not suspended in mid-air," meaning that Bonaparte's machine, by double-crossing the bourgeoisie, destroying democracy, and establishing military rule, had not set itself free from the powers invested in class society. It did represent a class, Marx said, "indeed the most numerous class in French society," the small-holding peasants.[26] This has famously caused uproar amongst Marxists, who are anxious to preserve the apparently unrelenting forward progression and tight linkage between the economic and the political that the guiding thread seemed to imply. The Second Empire, as foretold by Marx in the *Eighteenth Brumaire*, seems to represent a regression to feudalism, and a bizarre linkage between an otherwise modern state and a backward and antiproletarian class, barely in contact with the modern world of industrial technology and commercial finance.

The *Eighteenth Brumaire*, as ever, is much more interesting than that. It is not generally appreciated that Marx added that Louis Bonaparte "felt that it was his vocation to safeguard 'bourgeois order'" and that "the strength of the bourgeois order is in the middle classes." Rather unsurprisingly, Marx wrote that Bonaparte "protects its material power" precisely because he "would like to appear as the patriarchal benefactor of all classes" but "cannot give to one without taking from another."[27] Louis Bonaparte's battle against the bourgeoisie was merely apparent – they made the money he needed. His appeal to the peasantry as an invocation of Napoleonic ideals actually represented only "hallucinations of its death struggle, words transformed into phrases, ideas into spectres, befitting dress into preposterous costumes."[28] The peasantry would find that it could not live Napoleonic illusions, and rather presciently (with respect to some "peasant countries" at least) Marx concluded that "*the proletarian revolution will obtain the chorus without which its solo becomes a swan song.*"[29] The reason for this was economic

---

24 Marx, *Eighteenth Brumaire*, in *Later Political Writings*, 123.
25 Ibid.,120.   26 Ibid., 116; emphasis in original.
27 Ibid., 124–5. One of the most hilarious yet trenchant paragraphs in Marx is on p. 125, detailing Louis Bonaparte's financial shenanigans.
28 Ibid., 123–4.   29 Ibid., 123; emphasis in original.

development predicated on the ever-penetrating commercial relations of bourgeois society:

> But in the course of the nineteenth century the place of feudal orders was taken by urban usurers, the place of feudal obligation attached to the land by the mortgage, and the place of aristocratic landed property by bourgeois capital. The smallholding of the peasant is only a means for capitalists to draw profit, interest and rent from the soil, leaving to the farmer himself how to extract his wages. The mortgage interest weighing on French soil imposes on the French peasantry an interest burden equal to the annual interest on the whole of the British national debt. In this slavery to capital, as it inevitably develops, small-scale landed property transforms the bulk of the French nation into a nation of troglodytes.[30]

Rather than conclude with the Marxist tradition that, after all, the economic structure is ultimately "determining" for "the legal and political superstructure," and that the *Eighteenth Brumaire* confirms this, I would argue instead that the strength of Marx's historical and analytical account is precisely the political acuteness that allowed him to focus on the way that democratic politics incorporates certain flexibilities and outright contradictions. These attempt to disguise the class politics *that liberal democracy itself denies* when its institutions presume that all citizens are economic equals, or that economic inequalities are not crucial in their lives, or indeed that economic inequalities are necessary, good, and productive.[31] Historians may or may not be convinced by Marx's sweeping generalizations about the condition of the peasantry and the nature of the state, but in political theory terms, it could well be added to Marx's credit – and this is rather against the Marxist tradition – that his framework evidently encouraged him to see an apparently victorious dictator in terms that were not just comic, but diagnostic:

> The contradictory tasks that face this man explain the contradictions of his government, the confused poking about to try to win over and then to humiliate now this, now that class, turning them all equally against himself; and his uncertainty in practice forms a highly comic contrast to the peremptory and categorical style of governmental decrees, a style obediently copied from the uncle [Napoleon]. So the speed and recklessness of these contradictions is supposed to imitate the complicated doings and quick-wittedness of the Emperor [Napoleon].[32]

In theoretical terms, Marx locates dictatorship as a structural and ever-present possibility within representative ("bourgeois") democracy, precisely because of the way that he separates out the complex class-relations *within*

---

30 Ibid., 120.
31 This, of course, was the burden of Marx's critique of liberal democracy in *On the Jewish Question* (1844), in Karl Marx and Frederick Engels, *Collected Works*, vol. 3 (1975), 146–74.
32 Marx, *Eighteenth Brumaire*, in *Later Political Writings*, 124.

the bourgeoisie, and precisely because of the way that he traces the interaction of personal and collective "spin" within mass electoral politics, most particularly a hallucinatory politics of delusions. If the *Eighteenth Brumaire* is read through the lens of traditional Marxism, this analysis of democracy and dictatorship almost disappears, precisely because the fit between representative democracy and bourgeois class interest is presumed at the expense of fine-grained political analysis, and precisely because class action and class interest are presumed to have primacy over the "individual in history." In the context of democratic politics, it should come as no surprise that for Marx the individual in history is not a hero in the classical mode, such as Caesar or Napoleon, but rather an image, an empty signifier, a cypher who wins elections.

In the *Eighteenth Brumaire*, Marx himself passes quite naturally from a journalistic and conceptually untidy array of concepts into a version of the guiding thread and then back out again into his analytical narrative – *all in the same paragraph*. Not only does he see no inconsistency, he explicitly denies that there might be any, and further, he fails to privilege the abstractions over the untidy terms that he employs throughout the text. His discourse in the *Eighteenth Brumaire* vividly conveys the situation as he saw it politically and sends a perlocutionary message of revolutionary engagement to his German-speaking, émigré audience. This is quite important for understanding Marx's view of dictatorship in relation to democracy and for getting the precise sense in which some aspects of class politics lean far closer to authoritarianism than the apparently sharp binary line dictatorship/democracy usually suggests. Note that for Marx class politics is not always working-class politics, as, indeed, by definition in terms of class struggle, it couldn't be. Marx was deeply interested in the classes and class-fractions that exercised ownership over, and got their wealth from, the means of production.[33]

The long paragraph in question (in the central section III of the *Eighteenth Brumaire*) deals with "the two great factions of the party of order" – legitimists and Orléanists. Marx poses the question as to what binds these two factions to their respective royal pretenders: was it royalist symbols ("lily and tricolor") or "royalist faith at all"? Unsurprisingly he suggests that their differences, their factionalism, was explained by "their material conditions of existence, two different kinds of property... the rivalry between capital and landed property." Thus the "legitimate monarchy [1816–1830] was merely the political expression of the hereditary rule of the feudal lords, and the July

---

33 The *Communist Manifesto* famously details the power and achievements of the bourgeoisie in order to set the context for the proletarian side of class struggle; in Marx, *Later Political Writings*, 1–12.

monarchy [1830–1848] was likewise merely the political expression for the usurping rule of bourgeois parvenus." Or in other words, the legitimist and Orléanist factions within the "party of order" were expressions of the opposition between "large propertied interests" and "high finance, large-scale industry, large commercial interests, i.e. capital." Interestingly Marx goes on to say: "That at the same time old memories, personal antipathies, hopes and fears, prejudices and delusions, sympathies and antipathies, convictions, articles of faith and principles bound them to one or the other royal house, whoever denied this?"[34]

At that point in the text, the now familiar guiding thread appears, though in this context "the different forms of property, the social conditions of existence" and "an entire superstructure of different and peculiarly formed sentiments, delusions, modes of thought and outlooks on life" look of more equal importance, and less like an implied reduction of the one ("superstructure") to the other ("social conditions of existence").[35] The political contextualization of these apparent abstractions and historical generalizations within the *Eighteenth Brumaire* is striking and promotes a rather different, less reductive, and less schematic reading than the one developed within the Marxist, and particularly analytical Marxist, tradition.

Marx continues this balanced approach, suggesting that the "whole class creates and forms" these sentiments, delusions, and so on, "from the material foundations on up and from the corresponding social relations," turning next to the "single individual, to whom they are transmitted through tradition and upbringing." The individual "can imagine that they form the real motives and starting-point for his actions," and Marx then reverts within this single paragraph to his comments on Orléanists and legitimists, each faction seeking "to convince itself and the other that loyalty to their two royal houses separated them." "Facts," Marx says, "later proved that it was rather their divided interests which forbade their unification," and "in historical conflicts" one must "distinguish between the fine words and aspirations of the parties and their real organization and their real interests." Marx's simplification of this point to a contrast between "image" and "reality," wrenched from a philosophical or methodological context in Marxism, and viewed in this political context, now looks much less reductionist, precisely because "image" – particularly in the events recounted in the *Eighteenth Brumaire* – is such an important factor in politics generally and so essential to understanding the way that events unfolded.[36] In the Second Republic,

---

34 Marx, *Eighteenth Brumaire*, in *Later Political Writings*, 56.
35 Ibid.   36 Ibid.

democratization was undone *in and through democratic institutions*, and the state was handed over to Louis Bonaparte as democracy collapsed. Marx's account of this transition from democracy to dictatorship actually turns on an astonishing view about the self-image of key politicians and groups in a class context, and a flight in political engagement from the facts of class interest and class oppression.

On the one hand, Marx took a very hard-headed, economistic line on the legitimist–Orleanist split in the bourgeoisie between the groups that paradoxically functioned in alignment together as the party of order: "If each side wanted to carry out the *restoration* of its own royal house in opposition to the other, then this signified nothing but the desire of each of the *two great interests* into which the bourgeoisie had split – landed property and capital – to restore its own supremacy and to subordinate the other."[37]

"On that basis he tracked their political project of exercising a more unrestricted and sterner dominion over the other classes of society than they had been able to do under the restoration or the July monarchy, as was possible in a parliamentary republic, for only under that form could the two great divisions of the French bourgeoisie unite and make the rule of their class the order of the day"[38]

On the other hand, Marx then drew back from explaining their political tactics within these republican institutions in straightforward class terms. The party of order, he noted, "insulted the republic and expressed aversion to it." This was not because of "royalist recollections," but rather "from the instinct that the republican form made their political dominion complete and stripped it of all alien appearances." Thus "without the crown for cover, without being able to distract the interests of the nation with their secondary quarrels amongst themselves and with royalty," they gave in to weakness and recoiled "from the pure conditions of their own class rule." They hankered after "the incomplete, undeveloped" forms of dominion – i.e. dictatorship – which they construed at that point as less dangerous than ruling directly themselves. Rather than follow the logic of class-rule, the party of order, as Marx portrayed it, was trapped in a politics of self-images. The two factions had opposing self-images as dual lines of monarchy; they had another but singular self-image as good republicans, defending the National Assembly against Louis Bonaparte's presidential executive; and they had yet another singular self-image as devious republicans, rejecting the naked class rule that republican government offered them and longing instead to rule through an authoritarian intermediary. That intermediary turned out, in the

37 Ibid., 57.   38 Ibid.

end — contrary to their desires and as a direct result of their machinations — to be Louis Bonaparte.

Louis Bonaparte did not take France on horseback, as his uncle was famously said to have done; he got it by winning an election on December 10, 1848, for a fixed term of four years in office, with no possibility of immediate re-election. He then waited while politicians and political interests used democratic institutions to wind down democracy. The law of May 31, 1850, passed by the National Assembly, reduced the electorate by about a third. In the *Eighteenth Brumaire*, Marx gives the details:

> The parliamentary majority knew the weakness of its adversary [the social democrats or *montagne*]. Bonaparte had left it the job of organizing an attack and taking responsibility for it; seventeen grandees worked out a new electoral law ... a bill to abolish universal manhood suffrage, to impose a three-year condition of residence on the electors, and finally in the case of workers to make proof of residence depend on certification by their employer ... The electoral law was followed by a new press law completely eliminating the revolutionary newspapers ... The law of 31 May 1850 was the *coup d'état* of the bourgeoisie.[39]

These antidemocratic measures were only later openly opposed by Bonaparte as President of the Republic (from October 10, 1851), as a way of stealing a march on the National Assembly by returning to the universal male suffrage that had elected him president. Undoubtedly this helped him to win his "Bonapartist" plebiscites, held on December 20, 1851 (confirming his decree that gave him a ten-year term as president) and on November 21, 1852 (sanctioning the "Prince-President" in his restoration of the empire).[40]

The point to note here, because it is the point that Marx noted, is that it was parliamentary politicians in the Second Republic, acting lawfully but antidemocratically, who engineered the demise of democracy. They did this by restricting the suffrage to protect the economic and political interests of their class, and in doing so they removed the full legitimacy of popular sovereignty from their regime. They assumed the resulting parliamentary dictatorship would provide orderly rule in their interests and that Louis Bonaparte would function as a mere tool. While it is true that Louis Bonaparte outmaneuvered these parliamentary antidemocrats, it is also true that they made authoritarian rule look necessary and respectable. Louis Bonaparte took it away from them unheroically, or in Marx's terms,

---

39 Ibid., 74–5, 106.
40 For the historical detail see Philip Thody, *French Caesarism from Napoleon I to Charles de Gaulle* (Basingstoke, 1989), chap. 2 and 161 n. 9.

"the second time as low farce," "the eighteenth Brumaire of the fool."[41] Bonaparte practiced what the party of order had preached. As Marx said: "Bonaparte noted well all this invective [of 1848–1849] against the power of the legislature, learnt it by heart, and showed the parliamentary royalists on 2 December 1851 that he understood it. He quoted their own catchphrases back to them."[42] And then again with sarcasm: "Thus the *party of order* itself... denounced the parliamentary regime. And it protests when 2 December 1851 banishes the *parliamentary regime* from France! We wish it a pleasant journey."[43]

In the *Eighteenth Brumaire*, Marx was not schematically arguing that modern technology and capitalist relations of production lead (inevitably) to representative ("bourgeois") democracy and thence to proletarian revolution, as the Marxist paradigm would suggest – notwithstanding any genuflections (from Engels) toward "determination in the last instance" or "dialectical interaction."[44] Rather, Marx's own analytical apparatus in the *Eighteenth Brumaire* was far more complex, far more indeterminate, far more celebratory of contradictions and reversals, and far more psychologically individualist than Marxist schemata are wont to allow. This means that high-flown delusions (such as those that Marx detects in the party of order *as a coalition*), anachronistic illusions (such as Marx detects in the peasantry *as voters*), and low-grade dissembling (such as Marx detects in Louis Bonaparte *as a person*) constitute major factors in the far from straightforward and predictable ways that class struggles make history. It is not that Marx contradicts his guiding thread, or that his guiding thread poses difficulties for his analysis of politics. Rather it is that Marx's guiding thread only arises in a complex nonreductionist account of political events, including the interplay of personalities and proclivities in the widest sense. This is precisely because the "superstructure" is the way that "the social conditions of existence"[45] are interpreted by the "men [who] make their own history"[46] as a "history of class struggles."[47]

MARX AND ENGLISH PROSE

If Marx had had a simplistic theory of history, the *Eighteenth Brumaire* would not have been written in such colorful language, with such extravagant

---

41 Marx, *Eighteenth Brumaire*, in *Later Political Writings*, 31–2.
42 Ibid., 50.   43 Ibid., 51–2; emphasis in original.
44 Carver, *Engels*, chaps. 6–7.
45 Marx, *Eighteenth Brumaire*, in *Later Political Writings*, 56.
46 Ibid., 32.
47 Marx, *Manifesto of the Communist Party*, in *Later Political Writings*, 1.

metaphor, and on such levels of irony. The narrative in the *Eighteenth Brumaire* is itself an intricate interlocking mechanism of quite precisely formulated thoughts. The thoughts of the *Eighteenth Brumaire* are *in the language* and inseparable from it; the language is not just perfervid style or literary talent. These thoughts involve both complexities of detail in terms of personalities and events, and multiple levels of irony in the authorial voice. Because of that, any little slip in the way that Marx's thoughts are made to fit together starts to make it even more difficult for the reader to follow along, deriving meaning from the narrative. In that way a semantic fog creeps in – highly ironic in virtue of the fact that Brumaire was the month of fogs in the French revolutionary calendar. A few examples[48] will illustrate how this process begins – that is, just where the standard translation typically slips out of focus – but I stress that the effect throughout a reading of the *Eighteenth Brumaire* is cumulative, and I rely on readers' extrapolating onward in order to imagine the full effect. I imagine that amongst English-speaking readers of this chapter there are at least a few who have finished the *Eighteenth Brumaire* wondering, "Just where did I lose the thread?"

Sometimes the standard English translation is merely fuzzy and needs sharpening to catch Marx's venom. Compare de Leon's literal and insipid text: "Thus, so long as the *name* of freedom was respected and only its actual realization prevented, of course in a legal way, the constitutional existence of freedom remained intact, inviolate, however mortal the blows dealt to its existence *in actual life*."[49] With the sting in the tail as retranslated: "Hence so long as freedom is *nominally* respected and only its actual exercise is hindered, in a very legal way you understand, then the constitutional existence of freedom remains undamaged, untouched, however much its *commonplace* existence is murdered."[50]

At times in the traditional version one is left wondering what at all is going on:

Thereby they [republican constitutionalists] merely made the impotent attempt still to exercise, when only a parliamentary minority, as which they already saw themselves prophetically in their mind's eye, a power which at the present moment, when

---

48 These examples are adapted from Carver, "Translating Marx," 200–202.
49 Karl Marx, *The Eighteenth Brumaire of Louis Bonaparte*, in Karl Marx and Frederick Engels, *Collected Works*, vol. 11 (London, 1979), 115. The German text reads: "So lange also der *Name* der Freiheit respektiert und nur die wirkliche Ausführung derselben verhindert wurde, auf gesetzlichem Wege versteht sich, blieb das konstitutionelle Dasein der Freiheit unversehrt, unangetastet, mochte ihr *gemeines* Dasein noch so sehr todtgeschlagen sein." Karl Marx and Friedrich Engels, *Marx-Engels Gesamtausgabe*, Abt. I, Bd.11 (Berlin, 1985), 109–10.
50 Marx, *Eighteenth Brumaire*, in *Later Political Writings*, 43.

they commanded a parliamentary majority and all the resources of governmental authority, was slipping daily more and more from their feeble hands.[51]

Sorting this out was not too difficult: "At a time when they [republican constitutionalists] controlled a parliamentary majority and all the resources of governmental authority, they saw themselves prophetically as a parliamentary minority, and made only an impotent attempt to exercise a power, which was day by day slipping from their feeble grasp."[52]

My overall point here is that after even two or three such passages, in as many pages, the intricacy of Marx's thought is blurred and the reader frustrated. Marx is scathing about the naïveté of the National Assembly, damning about Louis Bonaparte's character, and clear about the would-be dictator's craftiness. Virtually all of these vital shades of judgment and their relation to the thrust of the narrative are lost in the first passage below, and (I hope) captured in the second, in which I straighten out the syntax, but also update the language somewhat from the quaintness (e.g., "rascally") and obscurity (e.g., "reviews") of the late 1890s.

The traditional text:

Bonaparte, who precisely because he was a Bohemian, a princely lumpenproletarian, had the advantage over a rascally bourgeois in that he could conduct a dirty struggle, now saw, after the Assembly had itself guided him with its own hand across the slippery ground of the military banquets, the reviews, the Society of December 10, and finally, the *Code pénal*, that the moment had come when he could pass from an apparent defensive to the offensive.[53]

The re-translation:

Because he was such a bohemian, and such a prince of thieves, Bonaparte had the advantage over bourgeois grafters of fighting dirty; once the National Assembly itself had escorted him over the treacherous terrain of regimental dinners, army

---

51 Marx, *Eighteenth Brumaire*, in *Collected Works*, vol. 11, 117. The German text reads: "Sie machten damit nur den ohnmächtigen Versuch, noch als parlamentarische Minorität, als welche sie sich schon prophetisch im Geiste erblickten, eine Macht auszuüben, die in diesem Augenblicke, wo sie über die parlamentarische Majorität verfügten und über alle Mittel der Regierungsgewalt, täglich mehr ihren schwachen Händen entschlüpfte." Karl Marx and Friedrich Engels, *Marx-Engels Gesamtausgabe*, Abt. I, Bd.11 (Berlin, 1985), 111–12.
52 Marx, *Eighteenth Brumaire*, in *Later Political Writings*, 45.
53 Marx, *Eighteenth Brumaire*, in *Collected Works*, vol. 11, 157. The German text reads: "Bonaparte, der eben als Bohémien, als prinzlicher Lumpenproletarier den Vorzug vor dem schuftigen Bourgeois hatte, dass er den Kampf gemein führen konnte, sah nun, nachdem die Versammlung selbst ihn über den schlüpfrigen Boden der Militärbanquets, der Revuen, der Gesellschaft vom 10. Dezember und endlich des Code pénal mit eigner Hand hinübergeleitet hatte, den Augenblick gekommen, wo er aus der scheinbaren defensive in die Offensive übergehen konnte." Karl Marx and Friedrich Engels, *Marx-Engels Gesamtausgabe*, Abt. I, Bd.11 (Berlin, 1985), 151.

reviews, the Society of 10 December and finally the criminal law, he saw that the moment had come to go openly on the offensive.[54]

Thus it is only by working from the text of the *Eighteenth Brumaire* in its first edition of 1852 (before its subsequent framing as a rather wayward classic of Marxism) that Marx's supposed work of history can be assessed as a contribution to democratic theory. Following Melvin Richter's method of taking antinomies together in analysis,[55] I have considered dictatorship in this theoretical context, and I now draw my conclusions about Marx and Bonapartism.

CONCLUSIONS

Marx's most extended account of the realities and practicalities of democratic politics and its decline into dictatorship and Bonapartism is undoubtedly the *Eighteenth Brumaire*. This work is more than prescient; it is potentially defining for our view of dictatorship today. This is because since Marx's time we necessarily see dictatorship as something that happens within democracies, rather than the reverse as was originally the case. Democracy in Marx's day was a movement against authoritarian, nonconstitutional states in which power was held by an individual with a family in the background, or sometimes by families or associates foregrounding individuals. Either way, democracy was a revolutionary doctrine and practice directed at widening the circles of power, regularizing the rule of law, subjecting rulers to the laws they make, and enforcing the accountability of rulers to the ruled. Once democracy was established, however, the situation reversed: Dictatorship became a kind of revolutionary activity to expunge, or at least severely curtail, democratic practice. Sometimes, of course, this can be a blow that arrives from the outside, usually through foreign intervention or conquest. More often, though, dictatorship arrives from within, and the coup is one that occurs with the support, or indeed the connivance, of politicians who were themselves supposed to be parliamentary democrats. Typically these forces are identified as "far right" or "reactionary" or, as in the *Eighteenth Brumaire*, royalist in an extra-constitutional sense.

Theories that modern democracies legitimated by popular sovereignty and universal suffrage have some supposed inherent tendency toward military

---

54 Marx, *Eighteenth Brumaire*, in *Later Political Writings*, 86.
55 See Melvin Richter, "Toward a Concept of Political Illegitimacy: Bonapartist Dictatorship and Democratic Legitimacy," *Political Theory* 10:2 (1982), 185; and Peter Baehr, "Accounting for Caesarism: Introduction to Gollwitzer," *Economy and Society* 16:3 (1987), 347.

rule and plebiscitary dictatorship (as opposed to "moderate" republican regimes) were not Marx's concern in the *Eighteenth Brumaire*.[56] Rather, Marx supported radical popular sovereignty extended from the usual political spheres into the economic realms of consumption and production, both in terms of control of resources and in terms of decision-making practices. His support for "bourgeois" democracy as a revolutionary anti-authoritarian movement was fervent but qualified by his perspective on class politics in commercial societies. While he has things to contribute to discussions of Caesarism and/or Bonapartism, his historical and theoretical premises about democracy are rather different from most of those involved in these debates. The historian Philip Thody, for instance, has little problem with the way that General Cavaignac "put the working class in their place in June 1848," and also concludes that the coup d'état of December 2, 1851, took place "with remarkably little support from civilian politicians."[57] Marx's perspective on the inclusiveness of democracy both in terms of people and issues, and on the exclusiveness of wealthy and privileged parliamentary politicians, is markedly different, and a better explanation for the success of Louis Bonaparte's coup. Parliamentary democrats made it easy for him by reneging on the democratic idea of universal (male) suffrage and by gearing the state to the politics of their class.

Marx's analysis has the advantage of delving further into the economic interests of these antidemocratic forces than is often the case in contemporary media reporting. This goes back to his fundamental vocation within the democratic movement, which, in opposition to the view that democracy leaves economic matters to the "free market," was to get economic issues accepted at the top of the agenda for democratic movements and elected governments. He made this work both ways: He pushed to get the economically deprived masses involved in political struggle, and he wrote about what the economically privileged actually did in contemporary politics when they had power. To do the latter he did more than merely trace out their economic interests in terms of class and class-fractions; he also explored the vagaries of their collective mind-sets and individual minds, using an untidy vocabulary of concepts and a repertoire of intuitions.

That is why issues of translation are so important in English; Marx's prose is vivid and his narrative highly complex. If the translation creates muddle, then we don't know what he is saying, and the text fragments into echoes

---

56 These theories are surveyed in Richter, "Toward a Concept of Political Illegitimacy," 185–214, esp. 192, 196; see also Baehr, "Accounting for Caesarism," 341–56.
57 Thody, *French Caesarism*, 49, 153.

of passages that occur elsewhere with more apparent clarity. This is what has happened in the relationship between the *Eighteenth Brumaire* and the 1859 Preface. The *Eighteenth Brumaire* has functioned as a troubling adjunct to the explication of the materialist interpretation of history, as it has been conceived in the Marxist tradition. Partly because the 1859 Preface is not itself a political narrative, partly because of Engels's originary re-presentation of Marx as a man with a method, and partly because of Engels's investment in reductionism as the basis of science, it has become almost impossible to read the *Eighteenth Brumaire* as a work of political intervention that itself explains how Marx's simplifications should be read. In my contextual and political reading, the base–superstructure formulation within the *Eighteenth Brumaire* looks more even-handed then reductionist, less prediction-minded than diagnostic, less dully scientific than politically inspirational. Indeed I have argued that insofar as class interests have to be conceptualized within what Marx has brilliantly termed "different and peculiarly formed sentiments, delusions, modes of thought and outlooks on life," the "superstructure" is actually *more* important in predicting and explaining political events than are "the social conditions of existence" that he associates with economic activity. The latter are not erased in my reading, but rather *interpreted* within the terms of "old memories, personal antipathies, hopes and fears, prejudices and delusions, sympathies and antipathies, convictions, articles of faith and principles," as it says in the *Eighteenth Brumaire*.[58] These are the untidy categories through which the proto-"guiding thread" we find there makes sense. Far from assuming in economic terms that "men" are "somewhat rational,"[59] Marx presumes in political terms that they are determinedly delusional.

This may seem a long way from a consideration of "Marx on dictatorship and democracy," but actually it is not. Marx on these subjects already exists in published texts, and for English-language readers, these occur in translation. However, Marx also exists in a well-established Marxist context, and most accounts of his views presume that the succession of historical stages determined by economic and technological development necessarily underlies his theory of democracy and dictatorship. On this traditional view, his theory of democracy and dictatorship could and should be read off the materialist interpretation of history, or at the very least any theory of democracy and dictatorship with Marx's name attached would have to sit very squarely with the guiding thread understood in a scientific and

---

58 Marx, *Eighteenth Brumaire*, in *Later Political Writings*, 56.
59 Cohen, *Karl Marx's Interpretation of History*, 152.

foundational sense. The history of commentary on the *Eighteenth Brumaire* has been procrustean, making this text fit that expectation, or bacchanalian, celebrating the fact that it doesn't.

The virtue of contextualizing Marx's simplifications politically within the *Eighteenth Brumaire* (as he wrote it), and therefore of taking the fine detail of his narrative extremely seriously, is that it illuminates the class dynamics of democracy. It does this not merely by stripping away romantic delusions, say of royalism, but by tracing the devious strategies employed by monied interests in rendering democracy impotent with respect to the interests of the poor and powerless, and yet appearing to defend democracy as if these monied interests had the interests of poorer people at heart. As Marx tells the tale, the party of order wanted a strong executive to work on their behalf to defend their ownership of the means of production as a sacred form of private property, and to defend their antidemocratic program of limiting the franchise and securing elite rule. Louis Bonaparte outmaneuvered them by appealing over their heads to baser emotions (e.g., his foreign adventures, such as the expedition to Rome) and to higher ones (e.g., his appeal for the restoration of universal manhood suffrage, *which the National Assembly itself had curtailed*). Marx had no difficulty in linking Louis Bonaparte to a very inactive class indeed – the peasantry. After all, they only needed to vote, and with that there is a lesson. While there are no dictatorial coups without demagoguery, these characteristically do not take place without subversion from within, and Marx put his finger on just the right place to look – a conjunction between rich and powerful economic interests and influential and determined parliamentary politicians.

In Marx's view, Caesarism is passé in the modern world, that is, a literal re-enactment of the coup mounted by Julius Caesar against the Roman republic, or in the legendary rendering, the work of one man who makes a fateful decision (*Alea jacta est* or "The die is cast," in an illocutionary remark). It is finished because of the complications of class politics in the modern commercial age, and because of the complexities of the political structure of representative democracies. Writing in his preface to the 1869 edition of the *Eighteenth Brumaire*, Marx rehearsed the methodological issues involved and drew an uncompromisingly scornful conclusion. First, he ticked off Victor Hugo for portraying Louis Bonaparte's coup as "a bolt from the blue" and "a violent act of a single individual," thus inadvertently making "Napoleon the Little" (the title of his book)[60] into a great individual with powers of initiative unparalleled in world history. Second,

---

60 Victor Hugo, *Napoléon le petit* (London, 1852).

he ticked off Pierre-Joseph Proudhon (an old sparring partner)[61] for portraying the coup as the outcome of an "objective" process of historical development, thus inadvertently excusing Louis Bonaparte from any possible criticism. In one of his rare methodological pronouncements, Marx commented that by contrast he had demonstrated "how the *class struggle in France* created circumstances and relations that made it possible for a grotesque mediocrity to play a hero's part." My point in this chapter has been to draw attention to how the "circumstances and relationship" in *bourgeois* class politics prepared the way for dictatorship *within democratic institutions* and, in passing, to note how little *proletarian* politics occupied Marx in this work.

On the subject of Caesarism, Marx was characteristically withering in 1869 for a very predictable reason:

> Lastly, I hope that my work will contribute towards eliminating the school-taught phrase now current, particularly in Germany, of so-called *Caesarism*. In this superficial historical analogy the main point is forgotten, namely, that in ancient Rome the class struggle took place only within a privileged minority, between the free rich and the free poor, while the great productive mass of the population, the slaves, formed the purely passive pedestal for these combatants . . . With so complete a difference between the material, economic conditions of the ancient and the modern class struggles, the political figures produced by them can likewise have no more in common with one another than the Archbishop of Canterbury has with the High Priest Samuel.[62]

Julius Caesar defied the republican aristocracy of the Roman Senate by crossing the River Rubicon with his army, and he then destroyed the Republic with the aid of the plebs. But he faced neither the mass (though far from universal) electorate that Napoleon had created for his plebiscites, nor the intermingling of rival royalisms and devious democrats with finance and industrial capital that prepared the way for Louis Bonaparte.[63] Rather in the *Eighteenth Brumaire* Marx alludes to the way that the French revolutionaries *invoked* the heroes of classical times, Caesar among them, producing a political resurrection of the dead as they carried out the heroic deeds of the

---

61 Pierre-Joseph Proudhon, *La Révolution social démontrée par le coup d'état du 2 décembre* (Paris, 1852). Marx's *Misère de la philosophie* [*The Poverty of Philosophy*] (Brussels and Paris, 1847) was a reply to Proudhon's *Philosophie de la misère* (Paris, 1846).
62 Karl Marx, "Preface" (1869) to *The Eighteenth Brumaire of Louis Bonaparte*, in Karl Marx and Frederick Engels, *Collected Works*, vol. 21 (London, 1985), 56–8.
63 Baehr notes the linguistic connection and historical allusion in the Latin word "plebs" and the modern term *plebi*scite; "Accounting for Caesarism," 353; Napoleon in fact severely restricted the universal (male) suffrage instituted by the revolution 1789–93.

1790s. The revolution of 1848, by contrast, could only parody this heroism in a cartoon-like way, and it follows therefore that Marx was not inclined to dignify such a caricature with an "ism," either of Caesar or Bonaparte. Rather, he exposed the bourgeois character of the representative democracy of the time in no uncertain terms, and tracked the fateful trajectory of the party of order as it delivered France into the hands of a common conman.[64] It is clear from Marx's account that he regarded Louis Bonaparte as a gangster and his Society of 10 December as paid thugs.[65] Marx should have the last word here, in a passage that shows how little Bonaparte there is in Bonapartism:

> The French bourgeoisie balked at the rule of the working proletariat, so it brought the lumpenproletariat to power, making the chief of the Society of 10 December its head. The bourgeoisie kept France in breathless terror at the prospective horrors of red anarchy; Bonaparte sold it this future cheaply when on 3 and 4 December he had the distinguished citizenry of the Boulevard Montmartre and the Boulevard des Italiens shot through their own windows by the drunken army of order. It deified the sword; now the sword rules over it. It destroyed the revolutionary press; now its own press is destroyed. It put public meetings under police surveillance; now its drawing rooms are spied on by the police. It disbanded the democratic national guard; its own national guard has been disbanded. It imposed a state of siege; now a state of siege has been imposed on it. It replaced juries with military commissions; now its juries have been militarized. It put public education under the influence of the church; now the church subjects it to its own education. It transported people without trial; now it has been transported itself without trial. It suppressed every impulse in society through the use of state power; now every impulse of its society is crushed by state power. It rebelled against its own politicians and intellectuals to line its own pocket; now its politicians and intellectuals have been disposed of; but after its mouth was gagged and its presses smashed, its pocket has been picked.[66]

This is a chilling vision, a testament to Marx's commitment to democracy (even in a bourgeois guise), and a warning. The warning is that the interaction of class politics, as played out by the wealthy within the political

---

64 Marx, *Eighteenth Brumaire*, in *Later Political Writings*, 36.
65 Marx was at his most colorful in commenting on the "secret sections" of this "benevolent association":

> From the aristocracy there were bankrupted roués of doubtful means and dubious provenance, from the bourgeoisie there were degenerate wastrels on the take, vagabonds, demobbed soldiers, discharged convicts, runaway galley slaves, swindlers and cheats, thugs, pickpockets, conjurers, card-sharps, pimps, brothel keepers, porters, day-laborers, organ grinders, scrap dealers, knife grinders, tinkers and beggars, in short, the whole amorphous, jumbled mass of flotsam and jetsam that the French term bohemian.

Marx, *Eighteenth Brumaire*, in *Later Political Writings*, 77–8.
66 Ibid., 111–12.

institutions of representative democracy, involves a flirtation with dictatorship. Democratic institutions are but imperfectly protected from this kind of class struggle, office holders can be corrupted into betraying democratic practice, and the electorate can be fooled about the democratic credentials of its leaders. It does not take a great man (or woman) to be a dictator. *Caveat civis.*

6

Bonapartism as the Progenitor of Democracy

The Paradoxical Case of the French Second Empire

SUDHIR HAZAREESINGH

The proposition that Bonapartist political thought and political practice may have contributed significantly to the emergence of modern French republican democracy may appear to be stretching intellectual provocation to the point of extravagance. The Eighteenth Brumaire, after all, killed off the First Republic and instituted despotic monarchical rule under Napoleon I; and the latter's nephew Louis followed the same pattern in 1851 by his coup d'état, which abolished the Second Republic and restored hereditary rule under the Second Empire. On both occasions, a legally constituted republican political order was overthrown by force; and the "sovereignty of the people" as construed by the republican tradition (a government chosen through freely elected representative institutions and accountable to them) was replaced by a "Caesarist" political system in which ultimate power was exercised by one individual.

Indeed, the antidemocratic properties of the Bonapartist regime that governed France between 1852 and 1870 have long been proclaimed from a variety of sources and ideological perspectives. In his writings, Marx stressed that the overthrow of the "bourgeois" republic of 1848 was the consequence of intense class struggles in France, whose result was the emergence of a tyrannical authority which stood above all social groups: "the struggle seems to have reached the compromise that all classes fall on their knees, equally mute and equally impotent, before the rifle butt."[1] The republicans, the main victims of the 1851 coup, also vehemently attacked Napoleon III's regime as a government which systematically ruled through despotism and arbitrary rule. In their more simplistic writings, such as Victor Hugo's *Napoléon le petit*, all fire was directed at the personality of the imperial

---

1 Karl Marx, "The Eighteenth Brumaire of Louis Bonaparte," in David Fernbach (ed.), *Karl Marx, Political Writings*, vol. II (London, 1977), 236.

ruler, a depraved and egotistical figure who epitomized the evils of the Bonapartist tradition.[2] Later republican writers were somewhat less crude, stressing that behind the Emperor lay a political system which developed subtle mechanisms to override "true" democracy. In 1868, the republican thinker Jules Barni thus defined Caesarism as one of the aberrant forms of modern democracy.[3] The republican leader Léon Gambetta articulated a similar view in a speech at Auxerre in June 1874:

> Who are (the Bonapartists)? They are a forgery (and it is in this respect that they represent, for our rural populations, a definite danger) a forgery of democracy. They speak our language, they parody our ideas; they disfigure our principles. In a certain conception of democracy, which fortunately cannot be confused with the true one, they are the first of democrats, ready to abolish everything which rhymes with institutions, parliaments, constitutions, and laws.[4]

It is worth noting that there was a recognition here of family resemblance between Bonapartism and republicanism. Whatever common intellectual ground was shared by the two movements was transcended by the apparently fundamental chasm over democracy and the rule of law, a split which originated in the 1851 coup and the repression that followed it, which was never forgiven by the republicans.[5] Indeed, this antidemocratic image was reinforced by the particular strand of the movement which represented Bonapartism in French politics after the fall of the Second Empire in 1870. This post–Second Empire Bonapartism was politically authoritarian and socially conservative, and many of its members were directly involved in attempts to overthrow the Republic in the 1870s, 1880s, and 1890s.[6] It therefore comes as no surprise that political historians of modern France have consistently stressed the antidemocratic properties of Bonapartism. Emphasizing the political originality of Bonapartism, René Rémond saw its three main ideological components as the reference to 1789, the principle of authority, and the search for glory. The Bonapartist conception of democracy was viewed as "plebiscitary" and therefore a deviation from the republican norm.[7] The same image of a viscerally antidemocratic Bonapartism appears in standard accounts of the history of democratic institutions in France, where the Second Empire tends to be given short shrift.[8]

---

2 Victor Hugo, *Napoléon le petit: Histoire d'un crime* (Paris, 1907).
3 Jules Barni, *La Morale dans la Démocratie* (Paris, 1885 ed.).
4 Quoted in Pierre Barral, *Les Fondateurs de la Troisième République* (Paris, 1968), 101.
5 Vincent Wright, "The coup d'état of December 1851: repression and the limits to repression," in Roger Price (ed.), *Revolution and Reaction: 1848 and the Second French Republic* (London, 1975), 327–8.
6 See John Rothney, *Bonapartism after Sedan* (New York, 1969).
7 René Rémond, *Les droites en France* (Paris, 1982), 106–7.
8 See for example Pierre Rosanvallon, *Le sacre du citoyen* (Paris, 1992).

The point of this chapter is not to dispute that Bonapartism contained repressive, coercive, and socially exclusionary elements in both its political philosophy and its practice. However, these were not the only or necessarily even the dominant aspects of the movement in nineteenth-century France, especially in the period between 1820 and 1870. Indeed, the ideological and historical complexity of Bonapartism makes it difficult to isolate an "essence" of the movement in nineteenth-century France. The flamboyant but despotic First Empire was radically different from the popular and proto-republican Bonapartism which emerged in the 1820s and 1830s. The Bonapartism of the young Louis Napoleon in the 1840s was in turn different from the official Bonapartism of the Second Empire. There were of course (and this is well recognized by historians of the regime) notable political variations as between the authoritarian early years of Napoleon III's rule and the later "liberal Empire."[9]

Another common misconception that will also be disputed in this chapter is the denial of any theoretical or conceptual elements to Bonapartism. The French Napoleonic tradition, we are too often told, was simply concerned with the glorification of force and the practical exercise of power. Thus, any reference to "democracy" within the Bonapartist tradition was merely instrumental or, even worse, an exercise in cynicism. This again willfully understates the depth of thinking about political institutions in Bonapartist circles after 1848 and, in particular, Napoleon III's commitment to mass democracy. The (justified) French republican indignation over the origins of the Second Empire should not in this respect be allowed to override two simple historical truths. First, it was the Second Republic, paralyzed by the fear of social revolution, that introduced significant restrictions to the "universality" of male suffrage in 1850. Second, it was Napoleon III's regime (born out of violence and illegality, undeniably) that restored male universal suffrage immediately after the 1851 coup d'état.[10]

The argument of this chapter will be that the Bonapartism of the Second Empire took democracy seriously and played an important role in the emergence of modern republican institutions in France. This argument is not entirely new: Theodore Zeldin and others since have rightly underscored the significance of imperial parliamentary institutions between 1852 and 1870, and have suggested that the transition from Second Empire to

---

9 Recent works on nineteenth–century Bonapartism include Frédéric Bluche, *Le bonapartisme* (Paris, 1980); Bernard Ménager, *Les Napoléon du Peuple* (Paris, 1988); Jean Tulard, *Dictionnaire du Second Empire* (Paris, 1995); and Sudhir Hazareesingh, *From Subject to Citizen: The Second Empire and the Emergence of Modern French Democracy* (Princeton, 1998).
10 Louis Girard, *Napoléon III* (Paris, 1986), 168.

Third Republic was marked much more by continuity than by fundamental change.[11] This argument will be made here in a new way by examining the theory and practice of territorial democracy under the Second Empire. At this point will emerge a further surprise: Not only did Bonapartists become increasingly committed to democracy between 1852 and 1870, but many of them also worked (for a variety of reasons) to promote the development of local democracy and decentralization. The elites of the Second Empire did not merely theorize about these matters: They actively changed the territorial structure of the French Jacobin state along more decentralized lines – so much so that by 1870 their republican successors essentially formalized the status quo they inherited from Napoleon III's regime.

THE BONAPARTIST TERRITORIAL SYSTEM

As with all French regimes since the Revolution, the territorial units of the commune, the canton, and the department constituted the principal basis upon which the administrative territorial order of the Second Empire was founded. Distinct to the imperial regime, however, was a particular conception of the vertical relationship between higher and lower administrative bodies. This approach was based largely on the principles of political and administrative centralization, which were directly inherited from the Bonapartist tradition. At a speech delivered at the opening of the Corps Législatif in January 1858, Napoleon III categorically asserted that "the Empire requires a strong state, capable of overcoming the obstacles which might impede its advance, for, let us not forget, the progress of every new regime is a long struggle."[12] The wider ideological justification of centralization was the protection of the general interest. In the lofty words of a Bonapartist Councillor of State:

[W]hat does this word [centralization] mean in its general and summary definition? It means: a government far removed from the men it governs. This distance is necessary so that the law can be fair and impartial; nothing is as odious and unfair as a fragmented government, where particular interests are all-powerful, and where the wounds inflicted by a superior to his subordinate are constantly irritated and even exacerbated by the very presence of the master; man only submits himself and accepts a superior in a more elevated sphere than his own; from this height, he obeys an order because he feels it dictated by a hand which has not been implicated in the miserable passions which surround him.[13]

11 Theodore Zeldin, *The Political System of Napoleon III* (London, 1958).
12 Napoleon III, *Discours, messages, et proclamations de l'Empereur* (Paris, 1860), 373.
13 Edouard Boinvilliers, *Paris souverain de la France* (Paris, 1868), 19.

The local political and administrative arrangements which the Second Empire aspired to maintain centered around the simple precepts of order, harmony, and common interest. The rejection of partisan or factional politics was a consistent theme of Bonapartist ideology: "Let us not be Orléanists, legitimists, republicans, or even Bonapartists; let us only love our country."[14] The commune was part of an elaborate hierarchy whose paternalism offered all the requisite guarantees of order, discipline, and rationality. The local government regime inaugurated by Napoleon III in the laws of July 1852 and May 1855 bore the centralist imprint of the Bonapartist tradition in a number of key respects.[15] The leading figures in local assemblies – the mayor and the assistant mayor – were appointed by the state rather than chosen by their respective councils.[16] The president and executive officers of the General Council were also chosen by the state. In Paris, Lyon, and all the communes of the Seine, the municipal councils and mayors were appointed by the Emperor. Furthermore, the executive powers of the commune and the department were constrained by statutory provisions that severely limited their ability to initiate and execute policies independently of the wishes of central government. Municipal councils lost the powers of nomination that some had fleetingly exercised during earlier regimes.[17] For much of the Second Empire, the General Council enjoyed less power and autonomy than its counterpart under the July Monarchy.[18] In addition, the activities of the municipalities and the General Councils were carried out under the watchful surveillance of the Prefects, the representatives of the central government in each department, and often the dominant figures in local political life.[19] Nominations of mayors were generally made on the recommendation of prefects. Under the terms of the 1855 law, the prefects also had the power to suspend municipal councils and dismiss mayors.[20]

---

14 E. Chérot, *La bourgeoisie et l'Empire* (Paris, 1860), 30.
15 See Edme Simonot, *Le suffrage universel et l'existence communale sous le régime de la loi de 1855* (Paris, 1861); more generally, see Henry Berton, *L'évolution constitutionnelle du Second Empire* (Paris, 1900), 144–5.
16 Mayors of large cities were chosen by the central government, while those of smaller towns and villages (those with less than 10,000 inhabitants) were appointed by prefects. By virtue of the laws of March 21, 1831 and May 5, 1855, the government had the discretionary right to terminate the functions of mayors. After 1855, prefects also appointed assistant mayors.
17 For example, the right to elect the mayor, and to be consulted over the choice of the local schoolteacher.
18 Felix Ponteil, *Les institutions de la France de 1814 à 1870* (Paris, 1966), 372–3.
19 See Bernard le Clère and Vincent Wright, *Les Préfets du Second Empire* (Paris, 1973), which demolishes the myth of prefectoral omnipotence during the Second Empire. Nonetheless the powers of the prefects remained considerable when compared to those wielded by their successors in the Third Republic.
20 Between 1852 and 1870, a total of 323 mayors were sacked, often to the intense fury of the political opposition. But it should be noted that this figure represented less than half the number of mayors

Local and central administrative institutions were also given explicitly political functions of control, surveillance, and repression. These powers were exercised against individuals and groups who engaged in activities deemed hostile to the interests of the Empire. The elimination of political dissent was part of a broader conception of public life in the provinces that particularly stressed the value of nonpartisanship. Representative institutions were presented as administrative rather than political bodies, whose deliberations were not allowed to enter the public domain. As a circular letter from the minister of the interior made clear to all prefects, "the most serious considerations require that municipal discussions should be contained within the sphere of purely administrative interests; they should be prevented from being perverted either by the dangerous provocations of external passions, or by regrettable appeals to a vain popularity."[21] Similar considerations applied to the departmental councils: "Members of the General Councils should be above all wise and prudent men, impervious to party intrigue and devoted to the government."[22] Indeed, mayors and presidents of the General Councils were generally chosen on the basis of technical proficiency and local prestige rather than ideological orthodoxy. Legislation adopted in the early days of the Empire forbade the General Councils from expressing political views.[23] At the same time, local assemblies were presented as performing a useful civic role, notably in educating the citizenry in the virtues of sound administration. This Bonapartist conception of the educative function of departmental administrative councils was delineated in Eugène Rouher's opening speech at the session of the General Council of the Puy-de-Dôme in August 1864:

> These assemblies are in the whole of France a great technical school which facilitates the deeper study of our administrative, economic and financial organization in which the politician prepares or completes his education, and acquires the experience and maturity necessary to face on a greater stage those struggles of a higher order in which more considerable interests are at stake... Politics and its irritant passions are banished from these surroundings so as to preserve a greater purity in the atmosphere.[24]

---

dismissed by the July Monarchy. See Elzéar Lavoie, "La révocation des maires 1830–1875," in *Europe et Etat. Actes du Colloque de Toulouse 11–13 Avril 1991* (1992), 61.

21 *Bulletin Officiel du Ministère de l'Intérieur*, circular of the Minister of the Interior on the publication of the deliberations of the municipal councils, September 16, 1865, 632.
22 Archives Nationales, Paris (hereafter Arch. Nat.) F1c IV 8; circular of the Minister of Interior to all prefects, July 7, 1852.
23 In 1870, 60% of all general councillors were apolitical; only 15% were clearly defined as hostile to the Empire. See Louis Girard et al., *Les conseillers généraux en 1870* (Paris, 1967), 133.
24 Arch. Nat. Papiers Rouher 45 AP 19.

Local public life, in sum, was about fostering a distinct type of citizenship, which was concerned with technical means rather than ideological ends, and thus administration rather than politics (the Saint-Simonian imprint on Bonapartism was very clear here). Bonapartist institutions sought to unite the citizenry behind issues of common interest rather than to appeal to the demons of class, religion, and ideology. Even though every attempt was made to keep political conflict out of the communes and departments, the Empire also sought to legitimize its authority through universal suffrage, an eminently political instrument. Persigny, the ideologue of the Empire, sought to overcome the apparent contradiction:

> [U]niversal suffrage, that is to say the collective will of an entire people, which has constituted public authority in the person of the Emperor, engenders in its turn all liberties: communal liberty in the municipal council alongside the mayor, the representative of authority; departmental liberty in the general council, with the prefect at its side; and national liberty in the legislative corps, beside the sovereign... by ensuring the reciprocal independence of authority and liberty, instead of subordinating the one to the other, napoleonic theory has virtually resolved the problem of liberty in France.[25]

The Bonapartist conception of the relationship between local and central institutions was thus doubly hierarchical.[26] Representative institutions at the center (the Corps Législatif and the Senate) were clearly ranked above their counterparts in the departments and communes, whose functional attributes were considerably more restricted. In this respect, the Second Empire merely reaffirmed a Jacobin commitment to a unitary conception of the state (and a rejection of federalism) common to all regimes since the French revolution, whether monarchical or republican. Furthermore, each of these deliberative bodies exercised its respective mandate under the scrutiny of a higher administrative body: the Council of State (and ultimately the Emperor himself) for the Corps Législatif[27] and the Senate,[28] and the Prefectorate for the departmental assemblies and the municipalities. The Second Empire's local government regime was thus centralist not only in its commitment to functional and territorial unity, but also in its intended subjection of political representation to administrative control.[29]

---

25 From a speech given at a banquet of the Loire General Council, in *Courrier de Saint-Etienne*, August 25, 1864.
26 Auguste Pougnet, *Hiérarchie et décentralisation* (Paris, 1866), 135.
27 On the legislative role of the Council of State, see Vincent Wright, *Le Conseil d'Etat sous le Second Empire* (Paris, 1972), 109–11.
28 On the role of the Senate, see Henri Perceau, *Le Sénat sous le Second Empire* (Paris, 1909).
29 Maurice Pain, "Le Second Empire et ses procédés de gouvernement," in *Revue Politique et Parlementaire* June 1905, 574–7.

It is interesting to note that this approach found favor within all undercurrents of the Bonapartist movement. For authoritarians such as Persigny, Rouher, and Jérôme David, a centralized regime was justified because they believed it delivered political stability, maintained social cohesion, and protected the country from the subversive inclinations of revolutionary socialism. For liberal Bonapartists such as the Prince Napoleon, on the other hand, centralization was an essential means of creating a sense of national identity and unity, and of breaking down the particularist attachments which often tied peasant communities to local social elites. In sum, authoritarian Bonapartists welcomed centralization as a means of preserving order, while their liberal counterparts viewed it as a way of upholding the Napoleonic principles of civil and political equality.

CENTRALIZATION AND ITS DYSFUNCTIONS

The benefits derived from such a centralist regime for local government appeared obvious enough, and during the first decade of the Second Empire the political system generally operated according to the logic prescribed by its authors. The centralization of information enabled the Empire to select its national and local political elites through the system of official candidatures. These figures were chosen by the government on the basis of information provided by prefects, who then attempted to ensure that the full weight of the local administration was thrown behind the candidates.[30] How this system worked in practice is well illustrated in this tirade by a frustrated member of the departmental assembly of the Gard:

> As soon as an official candidate is proclaimed, all the agents of the administration have but one thought, one goal, making his candidature a success; sub-prefects, mayors, justices of the peace, commissioners of police, schoolteachers, tax collectors, employees of state companies, clerks, roadmenders, rural policemen, postmen, tobacconists make this candidature their constant preoccupation.[31]

Despite its obvious advantages to the regime, the centralist system that governed the Second Empire's management of the provinces did not fully serve the political and administrative purposes for which it was established. Indeed a number of serious problems emerged very rapidly, even in the relatively placid political climate of the 1850s. Repression was not always enthusiastically carried out by those – prefects, magistrates, members of the police, and mayors – entrusted with its execution. The relationship between the

---

30 Pierre Rosanvallon, *Le sacre du citoyen*, 311.
31 A. de la Borderie, *Les élections départementales de 1867. Lettres à un électeur* (Rennes, 1867), 14.

administrative and elective bodies did not always proceed smoothly. Prefects and elected notables fought fierce battles for control of local power bases. In 1855, Morny, President of the Corps Législatif, bitterly complained to Minister of Interior Billault that many of his deputies were being "persecuted" by the prefects.[32] Furthermore, despite the apolitical nature of the process of local administration, the regime did not entirely succeed in eliminating political conflict from local public life. For example, prefects who found themselves in legitimist or republican departments often had to negotiate (and indeed compromise) with local opposition forces.[33]

The nominating powers of the regime were also a source of problems. Communes were often bitterly divided into rival factions (almost always on the basis of purely local considerations), and currying favor with one camp could often result in alienating the opposite side from the regime altogether.[34] To compound the problem, the regime did not always find it easy to recruit local elites. This difficulty was acutely manifested in the search for good candidates. At the very worst, the regime's local agents found it hard to find any local figures willing to serve on elective councils. This rather desperate report from the sub-prefect of Ancenis in July 1852 reveals the scale of the problems imperial agents sometimes faced:

> Generally the people to whom I offer municipal positions express the desire to accept them only when the municipal council is formed; they fear being perceived as having been imposed by the imperial authorities, especially if their name did not come out of the electoral urn. In any event, as I had anticipated, I find it very difficult to obtain a frank, clear, and definitive response to my openings... Indifference, pusillanimity, and lack of initiative are the three major flaws of the political fabric of this locality.[35]

Above all, the local government system rested on a central contradiction between the principle of legitimation by universal suffrage and the imposition of imperial control by political and administrative fiat. The uncomfortable relationship between appointed mayors and elected municipal councillors went to the heart of this dilemma. Mayors found it increasingly difficult to establish their authority purely on the basis of their mode of appointment. A growing number of first magistrates accordingly sought to

---

32 Archives Départementales de la Loire-Atlantique (Nantes: hereafter Arch. Dépt. Loire-Atlantique), Papiers Billault, 20 J 20; Morny to Billault, July 14, 1855.
33 Bernard le Clère and Vincent Wright, *Les Préfets du Second Empire*, 131.
34 For an appreciation of the difficulties faced by a Bonapartist Minister of the Interior in striking a balance between central and local interests, see Noël Blayau, *Billault Ministre de Napoléon III* (Paris, 1969), 274–5.
35 Arch. Dépt. Loire-Atlantique, 1 M 188; report of the sous-préfet of Ancenis to the prefect of Loire Inférieure, July 9, 1852.

increase their legitimacy by standing for election after being chosen by the authorities.[36] In the municipal elections of 1855, around 30,000 mayors thus stood for election or re-election.[37] Local politics thus became an increasingly important concern for the Bonapartist regime. The most significant development in this respect was the re-emergence of adversarial politics in the late 1850s and early 1860s. Opposition forces (notably the republicans) began to gain ground in urban areas and by the late 1860s the deterioration of the Empire's position in heavily populated areas was clearly apparent. As a report from the procureur-général of Rouen noted, "oppositional tendencies are enjoying notable and continuous progress... the rebellious and dissatified spirit of the bourgeoisie has awakened with all its inconsistency; a muffled sense of discontentment is spreading in the large centres of population where the bourgeoisie is dominant."[38] His colleague from Lyon (where, as with Paris, the entire municipal council was nominated by the Emperor) underlined the same point: "It must be recognized that in cities, in county towns and even in the smallest industrial centres oppositional tendencies have made considerable progress."[39]

There was also great public dissatifaction with the formalism and obstructivess which came to be seen as the hallmarks of bureaucratic behavior. Of particular significance were the administrative delays suffered by rural communes. In a letter to all prefects in 1863, Behic, the Minister for Agriculture, Commerce, and Public Works, commented, "In the current state of legislation and the regulations which complete it, the processing of business, hampered by numerous formalities, suffers often regrettable delays." He ended with a plea, "that matters in general, and especially those which bear on private interests should be examined, resolved and treated with the greatest promptitude."[40] Some measures were taken to expedite affairs in the ensuing years, most notably the decree of April 1861, which transferred many of the powers exercised by central government to the prefects. This merely compounded the general view of the bureaucracy as an unproductive and excessively rule bound institution.

This perception of growing public opposition to the administration provoked a contradictory response from the Empire. On the one hand, the

---

36 The traditional practice was to appoint the mayors before municipal elections were held, so as to separate clearly the executive and deliberative functions of local councils.
37 Information given by Marquis d'Andelarre during debate on 1867 municipal law; in *Corps Législatif, séance 12 avril 1867* (Paris, 1867), 86.
38 Arch. Nat. BB30–89.   39 Arch. Nat. BB30–89; report of July 10, 1869.
40 Arch. Nat. F1a 49 (circulaires du Ministre de l'Intérieur 1861–9); Behic note to Prefects, July 2, 1863.

regime accepted (and eventually encouraged) a greater degree of mayoral politicization, endorsing the actions of a large number of first magistrates who sought to enhance their legitimacy by standing for election in the municipal elections of 1865. In the words of Rouher, it was "the nature of things which forced mayors to seek a double baptism, that of nomination by the government and of election"; the government had to "leave mayors in the movement so that they could control it."[41] Even some authoritarian Bonapartists recognized that the Second Empire's commitment to universal suffrage made it necessary for mayors to stand for election. Haussmann, while expressing opposition to this custom on grounds of principle, nonetheless conceded that "Mayors and Municipal Councillors have always shown themselves more eager to please their electorate than to satisfy the Government from which they derived their principal attributions. In any case, when there exists the possibility of holding both qualities, the Mayor, if he only holds the one, suffers a certain discredit as long as he is not invested with the other."[42]

This acknowledgment of the necessity and legitimacy of politics was accompanied (somewhat contradictorily) by continuing efforts to depoliticize local elections. From 1864, elections for muncipal and general councils were increasingly conducted without extensive administrative interference, except in cases where known enemies of the Empire were standing for election. As a circular from Minister of Interior la Valette to prefects made clear in March 1864, "Every time an election assumes a political character, you should intervene clearly. But when, in the light of the opinions of the contestants and the good spirit of local populations, the elections present no political significance, you should leave mayors and voters entirely free to choose the candidate which will seem best suited to defend the interests of their locality."[43]

By the 1860s, accordingly, the Empire faced multiple problems in its management of the provinces. The administration, which had helped consolidate the new imperial order in the aftermath of the 1851 coup, was universally decried for its abrasiveness and its inefficiency. The key agents of the Empire in the departments and communes, the prefects and the mayors, found their authority challenged by the re-emergence of electoral politics and by the growing local hostility to administrative authoritarianism. The centralization that the Emperor himself had seen as an unlimited

---

41 Cited by Lucien-Anatole Prévost-Paradol, *Quelques pages d'histoire contemporaine* (Paris, 1866), 279.
42 Baron Haussmann, *Mémoires*, vol. I (Paris, 1890–93), 537–8.
43 Arch. Nat. Papiers Rouher, 45 AP 5; circular to all Prefects, March 15, 1864.

political benefit had become a clear liability, as the public blamed all the failings of their local administration on central government. The political opposition, which had bowed to the force of arms and the repression of the *commissions mixtes*, was challenging the Empire strongly in many areas by the late 1860s as the system of official candidatures proved increasingly ineffective and unpopular. As a report from the procureur-général of Rennes made clear after the 1869 elections, "Public opinion has not concealed its view that the moment had come to give back to the country a greater role in the management of its own affairs."[44] Imperial decentralization was thus not primarily born out of deference to the demands of the constitutional opposition, but through an assessement of the internal failings and contradictions of the Second Empire's local government regime.

THE EMPIRE'S DECENTRALIST RESPONSE

Our system of centralization, despite its advantages, has had the grave inconvenience of creating an excess of regulation ... Formerly the constant control of the Administration over a host of matters could perhaps be justified, but to-day it has become a burden. To make the greatest possible number of citizens participate in the management and responsibility of affairs, while preserving for central authorities those powers necessary to ensure the internal and external security of the State, to strengthen the autonomy of the department and the commune, to seek the new attributions which should be devolved to elected councils, this is the programme which we should pursue.[45]

In a letter to Rouher in June 1863, Napoleon III asked his minister to initiate a wide-ranging review of decentralization, which should include measures to enhance the attributions of elected councils. Despite his commitment to a strong state, Napoleon III was not insensitive to the charms of decentralization, partly as a result of his memories of the English system of local government, partly through the influence of close advisors such as Le Play.[46] His response to the political and administrative difficulties he faced was to accelerate the pace of institutional liberalization, and in particular to promise significant reforms in the field of decentralization. In 1865, the Emperor asked the Council of State to produce a comparative study of decentralization.[47] In 1866 and 1867, there were modest increases in

---

44 Arch. Nat. BB30–89; report dated July 29, 1869.
45 Arch. Nat. Papiers Rouher 45 AP 11; Napoleon III letter to Rouher, June 27, 1863.
46 Luc Gazeau, *L'évolution des libertés locales en France et en Belgique au cours du XIXeme siècle* (Paris, 1905), 247–8.
47 *L'Opinion Nationale*, August 31, 1865.

the competences of municipalities and General Councils, primarily in the budgetary powers of local government institutions; this gesture was offset, however, by an extension of the powers of the prefects. In 1868, laws granting greater press freedom and the right to hold electoral meetings without prior administrative sanction were promulgated, and a step was taken in the direction of greater accountability by instituting the practice of ministerial interpellation in the Corps Législatif.[48]

This general trend toward liberalization was accentuated in 1870 with the establishment of the liberal Empire. The appointment of Emile Ollivier was accompanied by the promise of wide-ranging political and economic reforms. High on Ollivier's list of priorities was decentralization, for by 1870 many Bonapartists and liberals felt that a thorough re-examination of the local government regime was necessary. The liberal Empire established an extra parliamentary commission on decentralization as early as February 1870. The Minister of the Interior Chevandier de Valdrôme recognized, in a letter to the Emperor, that the promotion of further political liberalization had made the institution of greater decentralization all the more necessary: "One cannot, without a fundamental contradiction, give citizens a large and sincere measure of participation in the government of their country, and yet continue to deny them the management of their most direct and intimate matters."[49]

The promise of further local liberties aroused interest and even enthusiasm in the immediate aftermath of the creation of the 1870 commission. In the words of the Procureur-Général of Agen: "The proposed reforms [by Emile Ollivier] which have aroused the greatest interest in our furthest provinces are not those which bear on general political matters... but rather those which are intended to promote greater *communal liberties* and to develop individual initiative."[50]

Speaking in the Corps Législatif in June 1870, Clément Duvernois called for the "broadening of the role of provincial assemblies."[51] In the eyes of many liberal Bonapartists, the promotion of greater decentralism represented an intellectually coherent and politically effective response to the growing political and administrative problems the regime faced in the late 1860s. Presenting the 1867 law on municipalities to the Senate, the liberal Bonapartist Louis-Bernard Bonjean underlined the numerous advantages of

---

48 Alain Plessis, *Nouvelle Histoire de la France contemporaine 1852–1871* (Paris, 1979), 215.
49 *Journal Officiel* February 22, 1870; report of Minister of Interior to Emperor on formation of 1870 Commission of Decentralization.
50 Arch. Nat. BB30–90; report from Procureur-Général of Agen, April 1870; emphasis in text.
51 In *Journal Officiel*, June 4, 1870.

a moderate form of decentralism:

> If indeed, it is indispensable that the government should retain firm control of the direct *management* of all parts of the administration which are concerned with state security and general prosperity, it could not take charge of the collective interests of local communities without getting bogged down in details and multiplying beyond reason the number of its agents: this would be a form of communism, that is to say the most absolute and intolerable form of despotism. It is in the nature of things... to allow local communities to administer those affairs which are of exclusive concern to themselves. This system has, furthermore, considerable advantages: it forms the civic customs of the country, and accustoms the citizenry to the management of public affairs; it lightens the burden of central government; and, just as important, it reduces the budget, by replacing salaried officials with the unremunerated efforts of the citizenry.[52]

However, the promotion of decentralization was not the sole concern of "liberal" Bonapartists. Many of their authoritarian counterparts also actively endorsed the principle. Former Minister of the Interior Ernest Pinard justified greater local freedom by an organic analogy: "In order that a nation be strong and prosperous, there must be overabundance nowhere, and some activity in all parts. The social organism is like the human body, which remains strong and healthy only if blood circulates freely in all its organs."[53] The Bonapartist "conspirator" Jules Amigues, who was strongly hostile to the liberal evolution of the Empire in the late 1860s, nonetheless advocated the adoption of substantive measures of decentralization.[54] His specific proposals included the "decapitalization" of Paris, the reform of universal suffrage, and the "emancipation" of the commune. All these measures were deemed to be entirely compatible with the principles of "authority" which were necessary for the continued health of the French polity.[55]

There were also a number of political justifications for the pursuit of the strategy of administrative decentralism. First, there was a need to provide a political response to the opposition groups' clamours for greater civil and political liberties. For many supporters of the Empire (indeed for many authoritarian Bonapartists), the promotion of greater local liberty offered an ideal opportunity to meet the opposition on its own terrain and demonstrate the ideological superiority of imperialism over its adversaries. Decentralism was in this sense a means of appealing to (and capitalizing on) the instinctive attachment of French society to order and social conservatism.[56] Following

---

52 Bonjean speech, July 12, 1867, in *Bulletin du Ministère de l'Intérieur* 1867, 472–3; emphasis in text.
53 Ernest Pinard, *Mon Journal*, vol. 1 (Paris, 1892), 223.
54 Jules Amigues, "Restaurons les Parlements!" in *La politique d'un honnête homme* (Paris, 1869), 45–9.
55 Jules Amigues, *Les aveux d'un conspirateur bonapartiste* (Paris, 1874), 8.
56 Anonymous, *Le Tiers parti et les libertés intérieures* (Paris, 1866), 13.

directly from the above, the Empire's decentralism was also part of a deliberate strategy of playing rural populations off against urban centers. As noted earlier, the middle and late 1860s saw a steady progression of support for opposition groups, notably republicans, in populated agglomerations. Faced with the prospect of political decline in these parts of the country, the Empire hoped that the offer of greater decentralization might consolidate and even broaden its support in rural France, hence countering the threat to the political base of Bonapartism. The establishment of the 1870 commission on decentralization was thus part of a strategic calculation. In particular, it was believed that freeing local populations from the stifling burden of administrative conservatism would help to regenerate the social and organizational fortunes of Bonapartism by attracting powerful local notables to the movement. In the late 1860s, as the political pressure on the Empire began to mount, administrative decentralism was seen as a valuable opportunity to reinvigorate local Bonapartist elites.

The importance of enhancing the social base of Bonapartism was spelled out in a report of the Procureur-Général of Agen in early 1870. Writing about the local population's insistent demands for greater communal and departmental freedoms, he stressed: "These freedoms would have a no less favourable consequence: They would give back to those intelligent and devoted men, the rich landowners who devote their time and fortune to the public good, the legitimate influence which they lose under the regime of bureaucracy and excessive centralization."[57] Interestingly enough, this opposition to the administrative despotism of local imperial potentates was shared by many authoritarian Bonapartists. These notables were often uncomfortable with the constitutional evolution of the regime in the late 1860s, but sympathized with the idea of promoting greater local liberty to the municipalities and especially the General Councils. There were even Bonapartist suggestions that provincial parliaments should be restored: These measures were seen to have "the double advantage of giving greater satisfaction to liberal demands, and not weakening central authority by directing the pretensions of a single assembly at it."[58]

Decentralism was also deployed as a means of building bridges with other opposition groups, particularly the monarchists. By the late 1860s, as the Empire's political position in urban centers became increasingly precarious, the prospect of rallying provincial royalists and Catholics into "the ranks

---

57 Arch. Nat. BB 30–90; report dated January 1870.
58 Jules Amigues, *Les aveux d'un conspirateur bonapartiste* (Paris, 1874), 8–9.

of the great conservative army" seemed appealing to many Bonapartists.[59] The legitimists were a particularly worthy object of the Empire's attentions for a number of reasons. The conflict over the Roman question had created a sharp antagonism between the regime and the ultramontane clergy, and indeed rekindled the anticlerical component of popular Bonapartism.[60] However, many supporters of the Empire did not lose hope of re-establishing close relations with the legitimists, who were believed to share a number of common interests with the Empire. Like the Bonapartists, they regarded order as a supreme political virtue and firmly believed in hereditary authority. Also like the Bonapartists, they were attached to the principle of equal treatment of citizens by the law, but rejected the revolutionary notion of social equality; similarly, they tended to regard freedom as a civil rather than political attribute.

This attempt to bring closer two of the major forces of French conservatism bore some fruit in 1869–70. In the aftermath of the appointment of the Ollivier administration, there were attempts to effect a rapprochement between Bonapartist and legitimist groups. This was manifested in the formation of the Commission of decentralization, which included a number of leading liberal legitimists such as Claude-Marie Raudot and Charles Garnier. It was also particularly evident in the stronger showing of Bonapartism in Catholic and legitimist heartlands in the elections of 1869, the plebiscite of May 1870, and the subsequent municipal and departmental elections.[61] In the department of the Loir-et-Cher, for example, the legitimist newspaper completely rallied to the Bonapartist cause during the campaign for the 1870 plebiscite, arguing for a common front against the threat of social revolution.[62] Similarly, in Nantes, the municipal elections of August 1870 saw the triumph of the republican list against an alliance of Bonapartists, legitimists, and clericalists.[63]

Finally, the pursuit of decentralism was intended to encourage the emergence of independent forms of associational activity and strengthen the country's sense of social solidarity. The first of these objectives represented an extension of a consistent Bonapartist theme throughout the Second Empire. In a speech given at Limoges in 1858, for example, the Prince Napoleon had

---

59 Fernand Giraudeau, *Nos moeurs politiques* (Paris, 1868), 393.
60 Bernard Ménager, *Les Napoléon du peuple*, 206–7.
61 For the elections of 1869, see Louis Girard, *Les élections de 1869* (Paris, 1960), xv. See also Pierre de La Gorce, *Histoire du Second Empire*, vol. VI (Paris, 1903), 106–7; and Arch. Nat. BB30–90, for the reports of the Procureurs-Généraux of Angers (July 4, 1870), Besancon (July 8, 1870), Bordeaux (July 9, 1870), Caen (July 11, 1870), and Toulouse (July 7, 1870).
62 Georges Dupeux, *Aspects de l'histoire sociale et politique du Loir-et-Cher 1848–1914* (Paris, 1962), 400.
63 *Le Temps*, August 18, 1870.

warned against the dangers of allowing the state to occupy too prominent a position in the nexus of social and economic relations: "What we must fear, indeed, is the absorption of individual forces by collective powers; this would amount to the substitution of the state for the citizen in all matters pertaining to social life, and would entail the weakening of all individual initiative under the tutelage of an excessive administrative centralization."[64] This reconstitution of an autonomous civil society was seen as a necessary condition for the cultivation of a genuine feeling of citizenship. Moreover, decentralization was also necessary to consolidate rural society, one of the key electoral pillars of Bonapartism. Ernest Pinard spelled out the point:

> If we make the province more attractive, there will be more settled families, a greater sense of morality and a higher birth rate, and two of the plagues of our countryside will abate: the absenteeism of the rich, and the migration of the poor. The landowner would remain with his farmers, the manager with his workers, the industrialist among his factories. There would be fewer marginals, and many more men attached to their land. Patriotic sentiment, which is weakening to-day, would keep its deep roots in the native soil, which would no longer be abandoned. One loves one's great motherland only in so far as one remains attached to one's place of origin. Patriotism is the virtue of a sedentary, not nomadic nation. In this population which would work harder as it became more sedentary, some men would rise above others by their personal merits, and by the services rendered to their communities; they would acquire a favourable influence through the healthy education of universal suffrage. They would become a guide for the weak, and the fulcrum of the State.[65]

Decentralism could thus help bring about many of the key objectives of the Bonapartists: the rekindling of patriotism, the strengthening of the family, the defense of a form of social corporatism, the maintenance of its rural interests, and the promotion of social solidarity for conservative purposes.

THE RESISTANCE OF THE ADMINISTRATIVE CENTRALISTS

Although there was broad ideological support for the promotion of greater local liberties in the Bonapartist camp, this project was hindered by the fierce opposition of some authoritarian Bonapartists to any decentralist measures which appeared to threaten the strength and cohesion of the administration. In contrast with liberal Bonapartists such as the Prince Napoleon and

---

64 Prince Jérôme Napoléon, quoted in *Economie politique: discours et rapports du Prince Napoléon* (Paris, n.d.), 100–101. See also *Choix de discours et de publications du Prince Napoléon* (Paris, 1874).
65 Ernest Pinard, *Mon Journal*, vol. 1 (Paris, 1892), 223–4.

Bonjean who sought to provide greater scope for autonomous associational activity in society, and those authoritarian Bonapartists who welcomed decentralization as a means of undermining the role of local administrative agents, many doctrinaire supporters of the Empire were skeptical of the clamor for greater political liberty.[66] Their approach was aptly summarized by a Bonapartist administrator from Dijon, "In all human institutions, as in man himself, independently of the organs which help to carry out the different functions of existence, there is an internal and invisible force, which is the very principle of life; such appears centralization to us."[67]

The mouthpiece for the views of the administrative centralists was the Duc de Persigny, one of Napoleon III's earliest and ablest collaborators. After his replacement at the Ministry of the Interior in June 1863, Persigny joined in the incipient debate over decentralism. In three letters to the Emperor in July and August 1865, Persigny denounced the drift toward greater liberalization in the regime's dealings with local government. He regretted the Empire's increasing willingness to expose mayors to the uncertainties of universal suffrage. As the sole representatives of political authority in the commune, mayors were functionaries, and therefore could not be made accountable to the electorate. Any defeat suffered by a mayor thus constituted an affront to the legitimacy of the administration.[68] Furthermore, Persigny objected to the tactical withdrawal of administrative agents from the local electoral arena, arguing that such a move would compromise the "authority and independence" of mayors, and thereby reduce their ability effectively to discharge their duties as agents of the state.[69] The withdrawal of the administration from local politics could only benefit greedy and unscrupulous provincial elites, who would be allowed to enjoy unfettered control over local affairs. The public interest would thus be subverted, and private concerns would be given a free run.[70]

In Persigny's view, the introduction of greater political autonomy in the departments and communes would weaken the powers of the prefects and thus further compromise the integrity of the administration.[71] Last, but not least, the decision to allow the electorate to express itself through universal

---

66 See, for example, Adolphe Granier de Cassagnac, *Souvenirs du Second Empire*, vol. III (Paris, 1883), 165–8.
67 Virgile Mouline, *Etude sur la centralisation, son origine et ses résultats* (Dijon, 1863), 49.
68 Bibliotheque Nationale (hereafter Bib. Nat.), Papiers Persigny naf 23066; Persigny to Napoleon III, June 29, 1865. In the words of Cormenin: "Every mayor is a functionary; all functionaries have a mandate from the government; all mandatees owe a good and loyal service to their superiors"; in Louis de Cormenin, *Le maire de village* (Paris, 1848), 44.
69 Bib. Nat. Papiers Persigny naf 23066, Persigny to Napoleon III, August 5, 1865.
70 Ibid., July 27, 1865.   71 Ibid.

suffrage without administrative interference in local elections threatened the political base of the Empire. Bereft of the clear guidance traditionally provided by the provincial administration, local populations would become entirely vulnerable to false prophets and demagogues. Never known to understate his case, Persigny conjured up a dramatic vision of a country overcome by anarchy and subversion: "Disorder is being introduced in almost all the communes of France... the very foundations of the Empire, that is to say the foundations of universal suffrage seem shaken."[72]

This fear of the political and administrative consequences of decentralization was widespread among authoritarian Bonapartists. Quentin-Bauchard expressed the typical view that most communes were effectively incapable of self-government:

> Have those who demand that administrative decentralization should extend as far as communal *autonomy* considered the practical consequences of such a regime? To allow communes to govern themselves would be a very good thing, if they did so; but who does not have the sense of the thousands of interests which would suffer at the hands of incompetent municipalities?[73]

In short, the introduction of greater political decentralization would bring nothing but disaster to France. This perspective was summed up in the apocalyptic (and somewhat prophetic) vision of a Bonapartist prefect anticipating the consequences of the collapse of the centralized state: "Destroy this organization, and the first revolutionary tremor will bring all public services to a halt, and suspend the administrative life of France; parties will take advantage of the weakening of authority to divide the country, civil strife will break out in favour of socialism and the Foreigner who will come to exploit our divisions and to try and capture France."[74]

THE BALANCE SHEET OF BONAPARTIST DECENTRALISM

Like the Second Empire as a whole, Bonapartist decentralism was a diverse and often contradictory phenomenon. However, it has been sufficiently analyzed in these pages to dispel the notion that it was merely a tactical or rhetorical device. This is our first general conclusion: Underlying the Bonapartist conception of local liberty was a distinct civic project, which was articulated by imperial ideologues and pamphleteers, and widely discussed among the different branches of the Bonapartist state. Furthermore, the

---

72 Bib. Nat. Papiers Persigny naf 23066, Persigny to Napoleon III, August 5, 1865.
73 Quentin-Bauchard, *Etudes et Souvenirs*, vol. II (Paris, 1902), 362.
74 Boyer de Sainte Suzanne, *La vérité sur la décentralisation* (Amiens, 1861), 29.

Second Empire's proposals for greater local liberty were not merely theoretical. The Empire's record on decentralization can also be judged on the basis of the evolution of the regime's local political and administrative practices. In this respect, the picture in 1870 differed considerably from the early days of the Empire. This was notably the case at the departmental level, where the July 1866 law widened the budgetary attributions of the General Councils, and reduced the role of the prefects to one of a posteriori control in a large number of areas concerned with departmental matters (such as road construction and maintenance). The cause of economic decentralization was thus substantively advanced during the 1860s, and this as a direct result of the Empire's legislation.[75]

More fundamentally, the political and administrative relationship between Paris and its provinces became progressively less centralist during the two decades of imperial government. The centralized control of the prefects over local political and administrative life, which had been intended by the regime in the early days of the Empire, was effectively replaced by a much more fluid and complex set of interactions between center and periphery (as well as within the periphery itself). The prefects' powers were progressively challenged by three (sometimes rival, often collusive) sets of local actors: the mayors, General Councillors, and the elected representatives in the Corps Législatif. Mayors of large towns or cities and leading members of the General Council were almost invariably figures with strong local prestige, many of whom also enjoyed powerful positions in Paris. As one wag noted in 1869, "The race of multiple office-holders has always existed, but it has never been as flourishing as today."[76]

Indeed, throughout the duration of the Empire, it has been estimated that two-thirds of all ministers, three-fifths of the Council of State, and more than four-fifths of all members of the Corps législatif also served on the General Council.[77] The presidency of the latter body was often held by a highly influential figure in the Parisian hierarchy of Bonapartism. These individuals could sidestep the machinations of the local administration with relative ease, and indeed it was often they who set the standards and norms the prefects had to follow. In departments where the presidency of the departmental assembly was held by the likes of Persigny, Morny, Rouher, Baroche, Billault, and Fould, it was clearly these elected notables who held sway over local affairs, not the representatives of the state. The same was

---

75 Pierre Bodineau and Michel Verpeaux, *Histoire de la décentralisation* (Paris, 1993), 53.
76 Aurélien Scholl, in *Le Lorgnon*, December 11, 1869.
77 Bernard le Clère and Vincent Wright, *Les préfets du Second Empire*, 136.

true of a large number of powerful members of the Corps Législatif, whose networks allowed them to circumvent and often subvert the position of the administration in their department.

Already in 1866, Persigny had deplored the political consequences of the drift toward parliamentary government: "the deputy is tending to become a figure of disproportionate importance in his locality, for he is the source of all favours and disposes of the patronage of the State over the whole administration. Moral influence is thus slipping away from the administration into his hands."[78] At a lower level of the administrative hierarchy, Bonapartist bureaucrats watched helplessly as power seeped away from administrative to elective bodies. The sub-prefect of Tournon noted rather plaintively in 1865:

> By a singular anomaly in our administrative organization, [the sub-prefects] witness the arrival, through the Prefects, of precise daily orders which have to be executed within specific times; but when they look around them to ensure that these injunctions have been followed, they come face to face with mayors, whose various and important attributions have given them greater effective powers than their own, and whose failings cannot be remedied by administrative action.[79]

The same remark, incidentally, could have been made by prefects in relation to the role of mayors of big towns. These peripheral forms of power increasingly undermined the centralist thrust of the Empire's political management of its provinces, and forced the government to take local opinions, preferences, and interests into account. A similar change could be noted in the electoral arena. In the early days of the Empire, as noted earlier, the regime spared no effort to line up the administration behind official candidates in legislative and local elections. By 1870, as a result of a number of factors (most notably the parliamentary evolution of the regime, the internal political fragmentation of the administration, the unpopularity of official candidatures, the growing ineffectiveness of the system in many areas, and the social and political entrenchment of local notables) this practice was no longer considered practicable or even desirable in many constituencies.[80] In the Limousin, for example, the 1869 elections were conducted with little prefectoral direction, largely because many local administrative officials politely but firmly refused to rally behind the official candidate.[81]

---

78 Speech in Senate, February 14, 1866; quoted in Farat, *Persigny*, 293.
79 Marquis Tristan de l'Angle-Beaumanoir, *Etude administrative* (Paris, 1865), 12.
80 Louis Girard, *Les élections de 1869*, viii–ix.
81 See Alain Corbin, *Archaïsme et modernité en Limousin au XIXeme siècle* (Paris, 1975), 893–4.

Equally significant was the Second Empire's role in the emergence of modern municipal politics. Local political factors were therefore allowed to play a much more significant role in determining electoral outcomes, as was symbolized by the growing proportion of mayors who stood for election.[82] The re-emergence of adversarial politics and the challenge of opposition groups in electoral contests from the early 1860s rapidly demonstrated the limits of a centralist system which had to operate through universal suffrage. This was brought home most vividly in the government's policy over the appointment of mayors. In the early days of the Empire, the regime made clear that it expected the absolute subordination of the mayor to central government. Mayors who failed to give effective support to official candidates, for example, could expect little sympathy from the government. By the early 1860s, however, the regime was forced to adopt a much more flexible posture. Dismissing a mayor who exhibited sympathies for republican or legitimist candidates was recognized as a counterproductive gesture in areas of local opposition strength.[83] Similarly, it made little sense to appoint a mayor from outside the municipal council if the vast majority of elected councillors were from the opposition.

Thus, while the government retained the power to appoint mayors, and reaffirmed this prerogative in its confrontation with the 1870 commission, the nature of its choices was increasingly influenced by a recognition of local correlations of power. By the late 1860s, accordingly, republican mayors were being appointed by the regime in urban areas with large republican support, and this represented a further recognition of the regime's departure from centralist practices.[84] Even with respect to such a hallowed principle as the appointment of mayors, therefore, the evidence clearly suggests a trend toward what might be termed creeping (or incremental) democratization. As a defender of the Bonapartist record stated, "The choices of mayor made by the Empire were fitting, and based much less on partisan considerations than is generally believed."[85] We would thus conclude that both the debates of the 1860s on centralization and the municipal practices of the Second Empire constituted a turning point in defining a new civic consensus in France about the status and functions of the mayor.[86]

---

82 See Jean Goueffon, "La candidature officielle sous le Second Empire: le rôle des considérations locales," in Albert Mabileau (ed.), *Les facteurs locaux de la vie politique nationale. Colloque* (Paris, 1972), 379.
83 Thus, after the 1863 elections only 31 mayors were dismissed for political reasons. See Bernard le Clère and Vincent Wright, *Les préfets du Second Empire*, 145.
84 See, for example, the reports on the 1870 municipal elections in *Le Temps*, August 24, 1870.
85 Fernand Giraudeau, *Vingt ans de despotisme et quatre ans de liberté* (Paris, 1874), 79.
86 Maurice Agulhon, *Les maires en France du Consulat à nos jours* (Paris, 1986), 14.

CONCLUSION: BONAPARTISM, DEMOCRACY, AND MODERN CITIZENSHIP

The Second Empire attempted to use its local government system to promote a specific type of democratic citizenship, which respected established order, concerned itself with material and technical rather than political matters, and identified with the Bonapartist values of consensus and order. However, this conception of citizenship struggled to emerge from the contradictory objectives of Bonapartist elites: depoliticization and the practice of universal suffrage, administrative omniscience and citizen involvement in local life, the maintenance of social order and preservation of the Revolutionary heritage of civil equality; the cultivation of a traditional and deferential polity and the modernization of political life. There is no doubt that the Second Empire genuinely desired to see greater civic participation in public affairs. However, the imperial regime never really decided on what precise terms this civic involvement should occur, nor indeed what ultimate purpose it might serve. In the end, it was the Republic (the regime which eventually established itself after the collapse of the Second Empire in 1870) that succeeded in reconciling these conflicting imperatives, and creating a stable and durable framework for the operation of national and local democracy in France.

The institutional failure of Napoleon III's regime should not detract from the significant contributions of the Second Empire to modern democratic theory and practice in France. What has emerged in this chapter is that Bonapartists reflected seriously about universal suffrage and its place within their political system. In this sense, their important legacy to the republicans was to stress the socially conservative character of the mass vote, a message that was not lost on the opportunist and radical elites of the Third Republic after 1877. The political dynamics of the local government regime that emerged in the 1860s, also clearly anticipated the republican system of territorial government, most notably in the pre-eminence of powerful elected notables over administrative agents of the state. The democratic and parliamentary evolution of the Second Empire in this sense confirmed (despite the regime's initial contempt for politics) that the political legitimacy which stemmed from direct election through universal suffrage was greater than that conferred by patronage or traditional state offices. By the late 1860s, this "democratic superiority" was manifested at all levels of the representative hierarchy, from the deputy to the mayor (a point which, incidentally, also highlights the major discontinuity between the First and Second Empires).

More generally, between 1852 and 1870 the Bonapartist regime served as a laboratory for the exploration of some of the key questions raised by democratic theory. Within the Bonapartist movement itself, centralizers and decentralists argued about fundamental issues that still engage our attention today. At what point should local democracy be overridden by considerations of general interest? Does the devolution of power to local bodies not unduly expose the ignorant and the vulnerable to the machinations of provincial oligarchies? Is the Bonapartist ideal of a "government far removed from the men it governs" not the best means of guaranteeing civil equality and state impartiality? At a time when modern democracies are increasingly lulled by the sirens of decentralization and "subsidiarity," the years of the Second Empire offer a robust reminder that in the tradition of 1789 (which was, let us not forget, as much republican as Napoleonic) "government of the people" is not merely about formal processes, but more fundamentally about creating institutions to promote a distinct conception of "the good life."

PART II

Bonapartism, Caesarism, Totalitarianism

Twentieth-Century Experiences and Reflections

7

Max Weber and the Avatars of Caesarism

PETER BAEHR

Only nations of masters are called upon to thrust their hands into the spokes of the world's development.

Max Weber, 1918[1]

The study of Caesarism lends itself to at least two distinctive lines of enquiry, and both of them have rather different implications for our understanding of Max Weber. The first approach treats Caesarism as an idea whose value hinges on its historical veracity and conceptual utility. Does Caesarism help illuminate particular chapters of European history, particularly those of the French and German Second Empires? Or is it a largely vacuous idea, overgeneralized and tending toward obfuscation? Historians and political theorists, as we know, disagree fundamentally on these questions,[2] yet all disputants are free in principle to enlist Max Weber to support their cause. They can do this by treating his concept of Caesarism in much the same way as they would his concepts of charisma, rationality, and bureaucracy, either applying it to various political formations or showing its essential limitations and inadequacy. So considered, Weber would be in effect a forerunner of *our* (laudable or misguided, depending on one's standpoint)

---

1 "Parliament and Government in Germany under a New Political Order," (1918) in Peter Lassman and Ronald Speirs (eds.), *Weber: Political Writings* (Cambridge, 1994), 269; hereafter *PW*.
2 The literature on this debate is growing, but a useful place to start is K. Hammer and P. C. Hartmann (eds.), *Der Bonapartismus. Historisches Phänomen und politischer Mythos* (Munich, 1977). For one of the more spirited early clashes see Michael Stürmer, "Caesar's Laurel Crown – The Case for a Comparative Concept," and Allan Mitchell, "Reply," *Journal of Modern History* 49:2 (1977), 203–7, 207–9. Mitchell writes, "The term [Caesarism] strikes me as overloaded with ambiguity, one that is likely to land sooner or later on a heap of platitudes along with the concept of totalitarianism." Stürmer's more elaborated application of the concept can be found in his *Regierung und Reichstag im Bismarckstaat 1871–1880. Cäsarismus oder Parlamentarismus* (Düsseldorf, 1974), esp. 322–33 on Bismarck as a "Caesaristic statesman." Peter Gay lends weight to, while markedly adapting, Stürmer's analysis in chapter 3 of *The Cultivation of Hatred. The Bourgeois Experience, Victoria to Freud*, vol. III (New York/London, 1993); see also 628–9 and the literature cited there.

modern efforts to understand, say, Bismarck's regime or plebiscitary rule more generally.

A second approach to the study of Caesarism, and the one that I will adopt in this chapter, focuses less on the empirical validity of the concept than on its meaning for those who employed it in the vernacular of their time. From this perspective, Caesarism is of interest because of the light it throws on a series of linked nineteenth- and early twentieth-century debates on the tendencies of mass democracy. Here the focus is not on finding concepts adequate to the historian's job of theorizing about the past, but on reconstructing how various agents in that past made sense of their situation; on discerning the lexical significance of Caesarism as a topos, speech act, debating foil, accusation, or discursive token. More concretely: What was a thinker like Max Weber doing with this term – what purpose or purposes was he pursuing – when he invoked it? What were the discursive conventions around Caesarism with which he was in accord or which he sought to overturn?

The distinction that I have just drawn between these two kinds of investigation is, to be sure, somewhat artificial. After all, many modern historians who find profitable work for the concept of Caesarism can claim with justice that they are not imposing an alien vocabulary onto the nineteenth century, but merely extending a term that was then both current and widespread. But if that argument is to be advanced credibly, modern historians are still obliged to show that they understand the mercurial quality of the terms with which they are working. Even for the best historians, this is not always the case. Consider, for instance, the following remark on the nature of German "politics as theatre" between 1848 and 1933:

> The idea that politics, and especially foreign policy, can serve as a drama to distract public attention, is a fairly familiar one. It is also at least as old as the Roman emperors' provision of "bread and circuses." In our period [1848–1933] the key concept is indeed Caesarism, *or Bonapartism* as it is more usually called. The *modern idea* of Caesarism or Bonapartism owes much to Marx, who developed it as a way of describing the regime of Napoleon III that followed the revolution of 1848 in France. Of the many features of Bonapartist rule about which *historians* continue to argue, two are especially relevant here. One is the use of foreign policy success to divert opinion at home, the other the use of plebiscitary techniques to appeal direct to the people over the heads of political opponents. In recent years many German historians have looked at Bismarck's form of rule in this way. [emphasis added][3]

---

3 David Blackbourn, "Politics as Theatre: Metaphors of the Stage in German History, 1848–1933," in *Populists and Patricians: Essays in Modern German History* (London, 1987), 246–64, at 249.

What is wrong with this, on the face of it, quite unexceptional view? To begin with, it involves a double slippage, eliding Caesarism with Bonapartism, and Bonapartism with one theory of it, Marx's. As a result, it leaves little room for those contemporaries who, like Leopold von Gerlach, categorically distinguished between Bonapartism and Caesarism,[4] or who, like Max Weber, described Bismarck as a Caesarist but not as a Bonapartist figure. It is also very unlikely that Marx's theory of Bonapartism had much purchase outside socialist circles in the second half of the nineteenth century, whereas other notions – employed by conservatives, political Catholics, liberals, and republicans – covered a far greater range of popular discussion.[5] So perhaps with "the modern idea" of Caesarism David Blackbourn is referring to the appropriation of the idea by post-1945 historians of Germany and France, an inference that gains in plausibility as we read the rest of the passage. However, if that is the case we have evidently left far behind nineteenth- and early twentieth-century commentators, and are now concerned instead with those among *us* who seek to interpret the former epoch and who are looking for the most appropriate concepts with which to do so. Finally, as Blackbourn later acknowledges, when Weber himself turned to criticize the debacle of German foreign policy[6] – notably, the Krüger telegram (1896), the "Yellow Peril" speech (1905), the Moroccan crises (1905, 1911) – his target was not Bismarck's success in diverting public attention from domestic problems, but the crises engendered by the "personal regime" of Wilhelm II – whom, incidentally, Weber never publicly called either Bonapartist or Caesarist.[7]

I have quoted Blackbourn not to trip up with pedantry a fine historian of the *Kaiserreich*, but to show how easy it is to skate unreflectively over modern and vernacular usages of Caesarism and to assume a kind of vague symmetry between them. But as I now want to demonstrate with the example of Max

---

4 Gerlach, letter to Bismarck, June 5, 1857: in Horst Kohl (ed.), *Briefe des Generals Leopold von Gerlach an Otto von Bismarck* (Stuttgart/Berlin, 1912), 218. While Caesarism, "the arrogation of *imperium* in a lawful republic . . . is justified by an emergency," Bonapartism, Gerlach argues, is revolutionary and illegitimate.
5 Unrivalled discussions of German usage remain; Heinz Gollwitzer, "The Caesarism of Napoleon III as Seen by Public Opinion in Germany," *Economy and Society* 16:3 (1987), transl. Gordon C. Wells, 357–404 (German original 1952); and Dieter Groh, "Cäsarismus, Napoleonismus, Bonapartismus, Führer, Chef, Imperialismus," in Otto Brunner, Werner Conze, and Reinhart Koselleck (eds.), *Geschichtliche Grundbegriffe. Historisches Lexikon zur politisch–sozialen Sprache in Deutschland*, vol. I (Stuttgart, 1972), 726–71.
6 Weber, "Parliament and Government," *PW*, 196–209.
7 In private correspondence to Hermann Baumgarten, Weber did refer to Wilhelm II as Bonapartist and also called him a "Caesar," though Weber is probably punning here on the word "Kaiser." See, respectively, the letters of December 31, 1889 and January 3, 1891, in Max Weber, *Jugendbriefe*, edited with an introduction by Marianne Weber (Tübingen, 1936), 323, 328.

Weber, this is exactly what we cannot assume. More specifically, I will examine how, even in his own epoch, Weber employed the concept of Caesarism in highly unusual and, for the history of the human sciences, fateful ways.

AVATARS OF CAESARISM

When Max Weber first began writing extensively about politics in the 1890s, the public debate about Caesarism in Germany turned primarily on Bismarck rather than on Napoleon III, yet the scent of the Bonapartes still hung heavy in the national air. During roughly the third quarter of the nineteenth century, public opinion in Germany had been divided between those who condemned the Napoleonic system root and branch as oppressive, illegitimate, and "un-German" (the vast majority of commentators) and those who saw some merit in a few of its achievements. Not the least of these, of course, was its containment of red revolution. Moreover, the Empire of Napoleon III offered the literati many other reasons to commend it. From the standpoint of political Catholicism, Napoleon III could be seen, as he was by Philipp Anton von Segesser, as the vehicle through which a Catholic-Romanist zone might be established in Europe. Alternatively, in this age when philosophy of history still walked hand in hand with the analysis of political events, Napoleon's Mexican adventure could be interpreted, as it was by the "democrat" Julius Fröbel, as the "setting up of a pillar of Romanism in America on which Romanism in Europe can climb up, just as undoubtedly Germanism in Europe owes to Germanic America essential, rejuvenating influences."[8]

Napoleon III's crushing defeat at Sedan put paid to such pipe dreams. But had it also destroyed the broader "Napoleonic idea," that unorthodox combination of conservatism and radicalism, popular mobilization and authoritarianism that had intrigued, perplexed, and bewildered so many nineteenth-century observers? Bismarck's actions appeared to suggest otherwise. In particular, his policy of instituting universal manhood suffrage, or, more accurately, extending its compass from the now defunct North German Confederation constitution to its imperial successor, was a "Caesarist" initiative about which many commentators had profound misgivings. Liberals of the stature of Hermann Baumgarten, Heinrich

---

[8] Gollwitzer, "The Caesarism of Napoleon III," 77, on which I am relying more generally for this paragraph.

von Sybel, and the young Max Weber,[9] fervent supporters all of national unification, were convinced that Bismarck's use of the ballot for demagogic and reactionary purposes threatened to nullify the great achievement of 1871. Characteristically, however, Weber's concerns were more complex than this.

In the *German* context, Weber associated Bismarckian Caesarism[10] with two clusters of related debilities. The first was the political immaturity and cowardice[11] of his own bourgeois class, features that impeded its ability to accept responsibility for leading the Reich. Weber remarked, "The bourgeoisie did not create the German state by its own efforts, and when it had been created, there stood at the head of the nation that Caesarist figure made of distinctly un-bourgeois stuff. The nation was set no other great power political tasks again; only much later on, timidly, and half unwillingly, did an overseas 'power policy' [*Machtpolitik*] begin, one which does not even deserve the name." Moreover, the members of the upper bourgeoisie who could have provided a source of leadership for the Reich had split into two reactionary segments. One of these "longs all too clearly for the coming of a new Caesar to protect it, both against the masses of the people rising from below, and against the threat from above, in the socio-political impulses which they suspect the German dynasties of harboring"; while the other segment has sunk "back long ago into that political philistinism from which broad strata of the lower middle classes have never yet awakened."[12] The proletariat was in no better shape. Like the bourgeoisie, it remained politically immature and "philistine," characterized by both an alarming deficit of political education and an awkward defensiveness singularly unable to deal with the great geopolitical tasks that faced the new Reich. In contrast to the English working class, situated in a nation-state that is constantly confronted by the "reverberations" of a "world power," and that, in

---

9 Weber to H. Baumgarten, November 8, 1884, in *Jugendbriefe*, 143.
10 One may conjecture that Weber preferred the designation "Caesarist" to "Bonapartist" (a term he rarely uses) because of the latitudinous applications it allowed. Bonapartism smacked of a regional, Gallic location with various imitators. Caesarism pointed to an occidental genus of which French Bonapartism was but one national species.
11 Cowardice, the ultimate antipolitical and "plebeian" (in Nietzschean terminology) vice, was a charge that Weber often leveled at the bourgeoisie. See, for instance, "Suffrage and Democracy in Germany" (1917), *PW*, 80–129, at 80, where Weber writes of Bismarck's "Caesarist ambitions" and his attempt "to exploit the *cowardice* . . . of the bourgeoisie in the face of 'democracy' and thereby preserve the rule of the bureaucracy." See also 88 on "craven *cowardice in the face of democracy*." For a detailed discussion of Weber's view of "unpolitical" characteristics and the human types that represent them, see Kari Palonen, *Das "Webersche Moment." Zur Kontingenz des Politischen* (Opladen/Wiesbaden, 1998), 64–101.
12 Weber, "The Nation State and Economic Policy ([Freiburg] Inaugural lecture)" (1895), *PW*, 1–28, at 23, 24–5.

consequence, "exposes the individual to 'chronic' political schooling," the German proletariat "receives such training here only when our borders are threatened, that is in 'acute' cases."[13]

For this reason, then, Caesarism is above all a product of, and a contributory factor to, the dismal political credentials of the bourgeoisie. Weber saw the proletariat's contribution to Germany's malaise as secondary and derivative, and this contention distanced him from those voices that so often invoked Caesarism precisely to warn of the danger of "the masses" and of the demagogue at their head.[14] Furthermore, the presence of Caesarism in its Bismarckian manifestation appears to be injurious not only because it arrests the domestic development of the bourgeoisie as a political force, but also, and principally, because of its geopolitical consequences. A nation that lacks political education and maturity, that substitutes Caesarism for responsible direction of power-interests, is almost by definition a nation ill equipped to provide "elbow-room in the world"; yet it is precisely the amount of the world "we conquer and bequeath"[15] on which, Weber adds, the present generation will be judged.

It is true that Weber's imperialistic tone, and a number of the sentiments that accompanied it in the 1890s, mellowed over the years. When he wrote in 1918 that "*Only a politically mature people* is a 'nation of masters' [*Herrenvolk*]," he did not mean a nation that ruthlessly dominated others,[16] but "a people controlling the administration of its affairs itself, and, through its elected representatives, sharing decisively in the selection of its political leaders." Even so, and while widening his attack to encompass conservative and other antidemocratic forces in Germany, Weber continued to insist that an absence of self-mastery at home is related to a chaotic global presence. A nation incompetent at ruling itself, shackled to a "'will to powerlessness' in domestic affairs" is one clearly unable to project "the 'will to power' in the world."[17] Yet Germany, by its very position as one of the European *Machtstaaten*, had an "accursed duty and obligation" to that world to preserve cultural plurality. Should Germany collapse as a continental power,

---

13 "The Nation State and Economic Policy," *PW*, 26.
14 "The danger does *not* lie with the *masses* . . . The deepest core of the *socio*-political problem is not the question of the *economic* situation of the *ruled* but of the *political* qualifications of the *ruling and rising classes*" from "The Nation State and Economic Policy," *PW*, 26.
15 "The Nation State and Economic Policy," *PW*, 16.
16 "By a 'nation of masters' we do not mean that ugly, parvenu face worn by people whose sense of national dignity allows them and their nation to be told by an English turncoat like Mr Houston Stewart Chamberlain what it means to be a 'German'"; "Parliament and Government," *PW*, 269.
17 "Parliament and Government," *PW*, 269–70. Also, "Suffrage and Democracy," *PW*, 129, where a *Herrenvolk* is characterized as a state of "co-rulers." Weber adds that "only" a *Herrenvolk* "can and may engage in 'world politics'."

the vacuum it left behind would be filled by the domination of Russia and England.[18]

What were the structural impediments to Germany's becoming a *Herrenvolk*? Or to put the question in a different way: what were the factors conducive to the cowardice, timidity, immaturity, insecurity, and hysteria – the "purely *defensive* form of politics"[19] – that typified the Reich of Weber's day? Here we come to the second cluster of debilities that Weber associated with Bismarckian Caesarism. Weber was keenly aware that political virtues and vices are themselves strongly conditioned by institutional factors. Optimum political arrangements do not automatically produce great leaders, but they can at least facilitate and help cultivate them. It followed that the vital desideratum for Germany was to organize a state most conducive to the "selection"[20] of leaders and of leadership qualities worthy of a great power. While the day-to-day rule of a modern state is of necessity in the hands of either military or civilian bureaucratic officials, its policy and overall direction must, if the polity is to be vibrant, be under the control of those with different instincts. The official, Weber contended, is most honorable and most effective when he is willing to "sacrifice his own convictions to his duty of obedience." In contrast, the "leading politician must publicly refuse to accept responsibility for political actions if they conflict with his own convictions; his duty is to sacrifice his office to his convictions."[21] The point was not to remove Caesarism from the political process – its absence is unthinkable in a democratic state – but to radically remodel it in such a way that those with a vocation for politics could actually practice their art in a manner that combined conviction with responsibility. However, as matters stood, Germany labored under a legacy of "negative politics": a constitutional structure that offered only the pitiful impotence of complaint, veto, and ideological posturing. The architect of that structure of pseudopolitics had been Bismarck. Through various constitutional provisions (notably

---

18 Weber, "Between Two Laws" (1916), *PW*, 75–9, at 76. The agony Weber endured over the failure of German foreign policy, particularly its abuse by officialdom and the intemperate and public interventions of the Kaiser, comes across forcefully in "Parliament and Government." At one point, he says that it is the issue that matters "most" to him personally (*PW*, 134). He also appears to interpret it as a key cause that "led to the formation of the unnatural world coalition against us" (204).
19 "Parliament and Government," *PW*, 271.
20 The editors of *PW* are right to emphasize the importance of "selection" (*Auslese, Ausleseprozess*) and other quasi-Darwinian concepts to Weber's political thought (2, n. 5). See *PW*, 10, 16, 84, 134, 180, 225, 267, 306, 389. Also, see the section on "Conflict, Competition, Selection," in Max Weber (eds. Guenther Roth and Claus Wittich; various transls.), *Economy and Society* [1922] (Berkeley/Los Angeles, 1978), 38–40.
21 "Parliament and Government," *PW*, 204 (emphasis omitted).

Article 9, which stipulated that no one could be a member of the Bundesrat and the Reichstag simultaneously)[22] or omissions (the absence of the right of cross-examination of the executive under oath, the denial of the parliamentary right of enquiry) parliament had been decapitated by an "authoritarian state" (*Obrigkeitsstaat*) that allowed only "passive democratisation."[23]

While Bismarck was alive, Weber recalled, the leaders of the National Liberal opposition had respected him for his remarkable intellectual qualities and personal dynamism. They had candidly acknowledged "that 'Caesarism,' the governmental form of genius, would be the accepted political arrangement in Germany if there were the slightest chance of some new Bismarck always emerging to fill the highest position."[24] However, the brutal irony of the state Bismarck established was not only that its leader tolerated no independent colleagues so long as he was alive, but that, once he was dead, there was no one of comparable ability to replace him. Bismarck politically unified the nation as a state entity, but the constitution he installed was expressly designed to allow no competitors for power. The challenging task that Germany now faced was to create a political order that enculturated qualities of leadership, while being tied to no *particular* leader. That would only be possible with a vigorous parliament of the English sort.[25]

Thus far Weber's analysis of Caesarism might appear relatively conventional. The use of Caesar's name in a political polemic echoed the general nineteenth-century fascination with Republican Rome's last dictator as a human and political type.[26] The cowardice of the bourgeoisie was a familiar accusation of the right, of the left, and of disaffected liberals.[27] Seeing Bismarck as a Caesarist figure required no great intellectual acuity in an age that still lived in his shadow. However, what was highly unusual about Weber's political theory was its flexibly discriminating attempt to show that Caesarism, typically seen as the gravedigger of parliamentary government

---

22 "Thus, whereas countries with parliamentary government consider it absolutely indispensable for the leading statesmen to be members of parliament, this is legally impossible in Germany"; "Parliament and Government," *PW*, 168.
23 "Parliament and Government," *PW*, 175–6, 222 (emphasis omitted). On constitutional liabilities, see esp. 177–96.
24 "Parliament and Government," *PW*, 138.
25 "The one and only question one can properly ask about the future ordering of the state in Germany is, '*How is parliament to be made capable of assuming power?*' Anything else is a side issue." "Parliament and Government," *PW*, 190.
26 Friedrich Gundolf's *Caesar im neunzehnten Jahrhundert* [1926], in F. Gundolf, *Caesar* (Düsseldorf and Munich, 1968), 278–360, remains indispensable.
27 See Fritz Stern, *The Politics of Cultural Despair: A Study in the Rise of the Germanic Ideology* (1961; reprint New York, 1965); and David Blackbourn and Geoff Eley, *The Peculiarities of German History: Bourgeois Society and Politics in Nineteenth-Century Germany* (Oxford, 1984).

or, more mildly, its antithesis,[28] could function well within a parliamentary system, and that both Caesarism and parliamentary government could be articulated successfully to mass democracy. Such a move required that Weber conceive Caesarism quite differently from its Napoleonic or Bismarckian expressions. Simultaneously, it put him at odds with two common positions of the time.

The first was associated with scholars like Albert Schäffle and Wilhelm Roscher, who envisaged the Bonapartes as the modern exemplars of Caesarism and who considered Caesarism inherently repressive.[29] Whereas for Roscher Caesarism derives from the death-throes of democracy and assumes naturally the form of a "military tyranny," Weber insists that it need not be tied to, or eventuate in, such parlous conditions. On the contrary, Caesarism is capable of being a normal, not a crisis, form of rule; a formation in which the civilian, as distinct from the military, arm of government is dominant; and a type of leadership in which civil liberties (entirely obliterated in Schäffle's and Roscher's versions) are protected by a robust parliament with real power. Breaking free of Schäffle's and Roscher's cyclical (Aristotelian/Polybean) view of history, Weber offered a theory of the modern state in which seemingly opposed phenomena – Caesarism and parliament – were co-present.[30]

Second, Weber's reformulation of Caesarism within a parliamentary context sets him apart from one of his main sources. In *Democracy and the Organization of Political Parties* (1902), Ostrogorski had shown that the "sort of popular Caesarism, with which the great chief of the party has become invested" in England severely eroded the standing of MPs and was making them increasingly redundant as political actors.[31] The advance of mass democracy, and the party system that accompanied it, was a direct threat

---

28 For the classic analysis of the incompatibility of Caesarism and parliamentarism, see Auguste Romieu, *L'ère des Césars* (Paris, 1850), esp. 19–24. Also, F. W. Rüstow, who remarks that "in recent political literature, especially in the daily press, we often encounter the terms 'Caesarism' and 'Parliamentarism' which are always used in a certain opposition to one another." *Der Cäsarismus. Sein Wesen und sein Schaffen* (Zurich, 1879), 3; and Julius Langbehn, *Rembrandt als Erzieher* (1890), as quoted by Stern, *Politics of Cultural Despair*, 191–2. The visceral hatred of mass democracy so evident in writers like Romieu and Langbehn is completely absent in Weber.
29 Albert Schäffle, *Bau und Leben des sozialen Körpers* [1875–6] (2 vols.) (Tübingen, 1896), vol. II, esp. 486–7; Wilhelm Roscher, *Politik. Geschichtliche Naturlehre der Monarchie, Aristokratie und Demokratie* (Stuttgart, 1892), esp. 588–608.
30 Weber, thinking of the English case, also considered Caesarism to be compatible with (despite its tensions with) hereditary monarchy, a position that would have seemed impossible to the older generation. See Weber, "Parliament and Government," *PW*, 221, 227. He did accept, however, that a Caesarist hereditary monarchy was a contradiction in terms.
31 *Democracy and the Organization of Political Parties* (2 Vols.) (New York, 1970), F. Clarke, transl., vol. I, 608.

to the parliamentary order. As we know from his gloss on Ostrogorski in "Politics as a Vocation" (1919), Weber shared much of the latter's analysis of the collapse of the notable system and the rise of leaders with the plebiscitarian touch. What Weber rejected was the contention that parliament had thereby been rendered irrelevant by Caesarism; if anything, its value to the nation had been increased. True, the status of the individual parliamentarian had been degraded by the whip-system and the regimentation this imposed. Nonetheless, the *institution* of a *working* parliament, conceived as the sum of its conventions and political mechanisms, provided the vital forum for the emergence, cultivation, and monitoring of responsible Caesarism: a Caesarism that was not merely emotional or demagogic in the negative sense, but rather equipped to mobilize the masses in an orderly way to secure the nation's power interests. Using England as his model, Weber enumerated a number of roles that a vigorous parliament played "in relation to the (de facto) Caesarist representative of the masses." A working parliament functioned as a proving ground for leaders, disciplining their will to power through the necessity of mastering committee procedure, and ensuring that demagogy was complemented by skill in dealing with officialdom. Such a parliament also imparted a measure of stability to the political process; protected civil liberties against an imperious politician; and provided "a peaceful way of eliminating the Caesarist dictator once he has lost the trust of the masses."[32]

Weber believed that Germany faced a momentous choice: either to continue down the road of authoritarianism that had led Germany to its present desperate plight or to construct a vibrant parliamentary system similar to – though, given German federalism, not identical with – its English rival. To advance such a view in 1918–19 and to praise the political institutions of a country that Germany had just been fighting took enormous personal courage.[33] What was also remarkable, in a different sense, was Weber's resigned acceptance that, either way, one would have Caesarism, a mode of leadership that was simply inevitable under modern democratic conditions.

Up to this point, I have concentrated on two versions of Caesarism, Prussian and English, but this is by no means exhaustive; Weber considers,

---

[32] "Parliament and Government," *PW*, 222 (emphasis omitted), for this and the previous quote. On parliament's functions vis-à-vis Caesarism, see also 227 (on resolving the problem of succession, "the Achilles heel of all purely Caesarist rule") and 229–30 (on the "rich opportunities to satisfy political ambition and the will to power and responsibilty" opened up by a parliamentary career).

[33] On Weber's refusal to capitulate to the "mindless hatred of 'the street'" toward England, see "Parliament and Government," *PW*, 267 (Weber's note).

albeit briefly, a number of others. His starting point is the observation that the "active democratisation of the masses" means the eclipse of the leadership of "notables," dependent above all on parliamentary support, and their replacement by "mass demagogy." In a democracy, only a demagogue can hope to gain "the confidence of the masses," which means "that the selection of the leader has shifted in the direction of *Caesarism*."[34]

What are these other forms of Caesarism? Weber mentions a type of leader whose legitimacy rests on the plebiscite, defined not as a regular election but as "a confession of 'belief' in the vocation for leadership of the person who has laid claim to this acclamation." Prominent examples include Napoleon I (a "military dictator" who "rises by the miliary route" and who "then has his position confirmed by plebiscite") and Napoleon III (who "rises via the civil route, as a non-military politician . . . whose claim on the leadership is confirmed by plebiscite and then accepted by the military"). However, Weber also makes it plain that figures as diverse as Hindenburg, Gladstone, and the occupants of the American presidency are Caesarist figures too, since all of them depend for their political power, durability of rule, and legitimacy "on the trust of the masses rather than that of parliaments," never mind the precise technical means (e.g., plebiscite or election) through which such trust is garnered.[35]

In the background of Weber's various comments on modern political leadership was a perception of the subpolitical body, "the masses," over which such leadership is exercised. Mass democracy, Weber insists, is democratic in name only. Just as control of the state lies in the hands of those who operate it on a day-to-day basis, so control of political parties lies in the hands of the party bosses and election agents who routinely direct the "machine." In turn, the machine must, if its members are to capture state power and thereby satisfy the material and ideal interests that have motivated their efforts, succumb to the leader best able to win the masses' devotion. The role of the masses boils down to proclaiming, endorsing, or rejecting individuals that the parties have groomed. It follows that in a democracy those persons will be demagogues able to fight with words and mobilize the nation. How they do this, with what techniques and with what success, will differ. That "the major decisions in politics, particularly in democracies," are "made by individuals"; that "mass democracy, ever since Pericles, had always had to pay for its positive successes with major concessions to the Caesarist

---

34 "Parliament and Government," *PW*, 220–1.
35 "Parliament and Government," *PW*, 221; "The Profession and Vocation of Politics," *PW*, 309–69, at 342 (on Gladstone).

principle of leadership selection," Weber took as the most elementary of political axioms.[36]

Such views reflect the prevailing social psychology of the time, but again Weber offers a twist on the work of writers like Le Bon. Mass, in Weber's usage, is not a synonym for "mob" or for members of the working class, though it can take on these connotations. Mass typically refers to members of *all* classes insofar as they remain an unorganized, atomized public or an assembled body in a crowd-like situation. Moreover, unlike many analysts of mass psychology, and unlike many conservatives and liberals as well, Weber argues that the rise of the masses as an electoral force is not something to be dreaded. On the contrary, mass democracy provides ample opportunity for gifted politicians to realize their ideas – provided they have the necessary oratorical gifts and personal appeal to do so. The real antitheses of contemporary politics are not Caesarism for or against, or Caesarism versus parliament; they are positive versus authoritarian Caesarism, leader democracy versus leaderless democracy, charismatic rule or the rule of a clique.

OF POLITICS AND SOCIOLOGY: A TALE OF TWO DISCOURSES

Over the past two decades, a series of studies[37] have sought to recover the concealed dimensions of Weber's thought, notably the political or legal writings, and those long forgotten investigations that belong to the tradition of *Nationalökonomie*.[38] To be reminded that there was a "Weber before Weberian sociology"[39] and that sociology was only one of his academic persona, is welcome. It allows us to consider Weber afresh, unhindered by the caricature of his work that is still common in much of the secondary literature. At the same time, it is evident from Weber's scholarly output from 1909 until his death in 1920 that sociological theory and research increasingly absorbed his energies. To deny that fact is to compound, rather than repair, the earlier ahistoricism to which writers like Wilhelm Hennis so trenchantly object, replacing one parody by another. It also misses entirely

---

36 "Parliament and Government," *PW*, 222; "Vocation of Politics," *PW*, 331. See my *Caesar and the Fading of the Roman World: A Study in Republicanism and Caesarism* (New Brunswick, 1998), 236–42, on how Weber's conception of the masses as "irrational" strongly conditions his belief that Caesarism is inescapable.

37 Pioneered by Wilhelm Hennis. See especially his *Max Weber. Essays in Reconstruction* (London, 1988 [1987]), Keith Tribe, transl.; and Wilhelm Hennis, *Max Webers Wissenschaft vom Menschen* (Tübingen, 1996).

38 See Keith Tribe, "Introduction" to *Reading Weber* (London/New York, 1989), 1–14.

39 Lawrence A. Scaff, "Weber before Weberian Sociology," in K. Tribe (ed.), *Reading Weber*, 15–41.

what Weber was doing when he redescribed Caesarism via the categories of sociology.

Weber made heroic attempts to establish a method for sociology that could be of empirical use to all practitioners of the human sciences, irrespective of the other issues that might divide them.[40] Sociology was to be a science, and science presupposes a basic commitment to truth telling, however uncomfortable and disruptive such a commitment might be, a stance of intellectual discipline ("objectivity"), and a recognition that the scientific "life order" contains autonomous principles of validation irreducible to other *Lebensordnungen*.[41] Weber's attempt to distinguish between scientific reasoning and political partisanship remains controversial and cannot be pursued here. Instead, I want to suggest that, despite Weber's claims to the contrary, sociology was the narrative framework within which a number of his *political* concepts were, so to speak, naturalized: taken out of their polemical context – inherently fractious and unstable – and reformulated within a discourse, sociology, that Weber claimed to be free of value judgments. If one examines the various drafts of *Economy and Society*, two developments are apparent. First, one sees that while Caesarism emerges twice in the 1913 draft of the typology of legitimate *Herrschaft* (domination), it has vanished entirely from its 1918 and 1919 counterparts; in those cases, Caesarism as a *term* has become interchangeable with a number of other expressions that have essentially superseded it: *Führer-Demokratie, plebiszitäre Führerdemokratie*, and *plebiszitäre Herrschaft*. The second development in *Economy and Society* is that all of Caesarism's cognates have themselves become absorbed into, and are understood as mere expressions of, Weber's master sociological concept of charisma.[42] The effects of this transformation are important to grasp. Caesarism's various forms are no longer inherently contentious, to be argued about in public debates about the means and goals of politics. Instead they have become part of a typology of legitimacy professing universal application. Whereas Caesarism in Weber's political writings (i.e., his political speeches, pamphlets, and contributions to such newspapers as the *Frankfurter Zeitung*) refer to one kind of rule, born of contingent

---

40 Weber, *Economy and Society*, 3. "The method [employed here] . . . attempts only to formulate what all empirical sociology really means when it deals with the same problems."
41 For an excellent account of Weber's theory of life–orders, see Lawrence A. Scaff, *Fleeing the Iron Cage: Culture, Politics, and Modernity in the Thought of Max Weber* (Berkeley/Los Angeles, 1989), 73–120, esp. 112–20 on the scientific calling.
42 See, for instance, *Economy and Society*, 268: "Plebiscitary democracy – the most important type of leader democracy – is a variant of charismatic authority, which hides behind a legitimacy that is *formally* derived from the will of the governed." Weber includes under this category "the dictatorship of Cromwell, and the leaders of the French Revolution and of the First and Second Empire[s]."

circumstances and capable of a variety of manifestations, in his sociological writings "charisma" is integral to all modern kinds of rule. Caesarism, rendered now as a form of charisma, is simply the democratic corollary of an overarching and inescapable iron law of leadership, and Weber's own value commitments are camouflaged under a scientific rubric. No wonder that most of the elements Weber had earlier described as "Caesarist" now appear as aspects of charisma (leadership as a "gift," the need to provide great proving deeds, the relationship of the leader to a largely credulous, passive, but sometimes explosively irrational "mass," the problem of succession).

But why, in that case, did Weber not simply make Caesarism, rather than charisma, the leadership concept par excellence in the sociological writings? I have already anticipated part of the answer. As a polemical and highly charged term, Caesarism could not serve as a sociological category in Weber's sense. Moreover, Caesarism was largely confined to the political arena, whereas Weber wanted a concept that could embrace all forms of leadership. Finally, a signal feature of the Caesarism debate in Weber's day was the question of legitimacy;[43] Caesarism was seen as challenging regular monarchical government and as seeking, unsuccessfully, to establish itself with dynastic credentials.[44] As such, Caesarism automatically disqualified itself from playing a role in a classification of *legitime Herrschaft*.[45] Weber

---

43 From among many sources (which go back at least to Romieu and, employing somewhat different terminology, Benjamin Constant), suffice it to note: the entry on Caesarism in the thirteenth edition of Brockhaus's *Conversations Lexikon* (Leipzig, 1883), 38: "Caesarism has come into use mainly to characterize the Napoleonic system. In this sense it means a particular kind of monarchy, that is different from the absolute as well as the constitutional ones because of its democratic basis and lack of legitimacy"); Heinrich von Treitschke, *Politics* [1897–8], 2 vols. (New York, 1916), B. Dugdale and T. de Bille, transl., with an introduction by A. J. Balfour, vol. II, 222–3: "Caesarism was never a matter of legitimate inheritance"; and Ferdinand Tönnies, *Der englische Staat und der deutsche Staat* (Berlin, 1917), 210: "Caesarism (after Julius Caesar) is a form of state in which a leader of the people (usually a leader of the army) sets himself up as a sole ruler [*Alleinherrscher*] (Illegitimate or irregular monarchy)." The best analyses of the relationship between Caesarism and illegitimacy are Melvin Richter, "Toward a Concept of Political Illegitimacy: Bonapartist Dictatorship and Democratic Legitimacy," *Political Theory* 10:2 (1982), 185–214; and Richter, "Tocqueville, Napoleon, and Bonapartism," in A. S. Eisenstadt (ed.), *Reconsidering Tocqueville's Democracy in America* (New Brunswick/London, 1988), 110– 45.

The conventional association of Caesarism with an upstart tyrant (i.e., with a monarch devoid of a venerable dynastic lineage) explains why Weber did not, publicly at least, describe Wilhelm II as Caesarist. It also helps explain why Bismarck, de facto ruler of the Reich until his "retirement" in 1890, often did attract that epithet: see Weber's observations on "the reaction of monarchic hereditary legitimism" to Bismarckian "Caesarist forces" ("Parliament and Government," *PW*, 223), which echoes a remark Weber had made over two decades earlier in a letter to Hermann von Baumgarten (January 3, 1891), *Jugendbriefe*, 327–8. Also, *Economy and Society*, 986, where "legitimate" and "Caesarist" political powers are presented as antinomies.

44 For documentation, see Baehr, *Caesar and the Fading of the Roman World*, 165–254.

45 In the process, Weber was also compelled to redescribe the traditional and (for Weber's purposes) claustrophobic concept of legitimacy. Weber's sociological framework swept away the old linkage

wanted to emphasize the inevitability of leader democracy under modern conditions. He wished also to underline the vital importance of individual leadership more generally. Sociology was the discourse within which he could accomplish both tasks, and charisma was the fundamental tool to help him do so. Charisma could borrow liberally from characteristics usually attributed to Caesarism while avoiding the associations with tyranny and illegitimacy that helped make Caesarism such an incendiary term.

THE QUALITIES OF THE CAESARIST POLITICIAN

We have seen that Weber, accepting the inevitability of Caesarism, nonetheless pressed for a variant of it situated within a working parliament. Given that a Caesarist leader operates within a democracy and that democracy involves the periodic intervention of the masses, what kind of qualities should that leader have? Clearly, he should possess the qualities that Weber thought all responsible politicians should possess, but then again, in a somewhat circular way, Weber thought of politics in terms of leadership. This comes across prominently not only in his definition of politics as a mode of life that embraces "every kind of independent *leadership* activity" and, more specifically, "the leadership, or the exercise of influence on the leadership, of a *political* association, which today means a *state*."[46] It is also the case that Weber's essay on politics as a vocation is, as he acknowledges, focused squarely on that modern kind of charisma associated with the democratic Caesarist leader.[47] Accordingly, Weber's discussion of the individual who is called by politics under modern democratic conditions, is, among other

---

between dynastic right and legitimacy by redefining the latter to mean either a report of the nature of people's beliefs about a power relationship, or a series of "legitimations" – traditional, rational-legal, charismatic – projected by those in power. In both cases, the antique strains of legitimacy became sociologically irrelevant. On the one hand, belief in the rightness of an authority claim is now a sufficient ground for its legitimacy irrespective of its content. On the other, legitimacy itself appears to dissolve into the declarations that the powerful make about themselves and about their ability to persuade others of their right to rule.

46 "Vocation of Politics," *PW*, 309–10.
47 "Here we are interested above all in the second of the three types [of legitimate *Herrschaft*]: rule by virtue of devotion to the purely personal 'charisma' of the 'leader' on the part of those who obey him." The main contemporary example is the parliamentary party leader. "Vocation of Politics," *PW*, 312–13. A probing discussion of some of the issues I am raising here, particularly of Weber's close identification of politics with individual leadership, can be found in Peter Breiner, *Max Weber and Democratic Politics* (Ithaca/London, 1996), chaps. 4 and 5. He quotes on 167 Weber's remark from "The Meaning of 'Value-Freedom' in the Social and Economic Sciences" [1917]: "Every type of ordering of social relations whatever its form, must, if one wants to *evaluate* it, be ultimately examined according to the human type to which it affords optimal chances to gain superiority by means of external or inner (motivational) selection procedures."

things, an enquiry into the possibility of responsible Caesarist rule. This point will bear some elaboration.

Weber's leader-centered view of politics can be understood as an attempt to answer three related questions. What must politicians worthy of their vocation do to *be* political? What attracts such persons to politics? And what are the qualities they should possess to live well the political life? To the first question, Weber replies that the politician must first recognize viscerally what politics *is*: "Politics," Weber says, "is *struggle*,"[48] it is the "striving to influence the distribution of power between and within political formations"; and since politics involves "partisanship, fighting, passion – *ira et studium*" it is not a profession for the timid or weak of heart.[49] The essential means of politics everywhere is "power, backed up by the use of *violence*."[50] But in a democratic polity, power involves something else: the ability not only to fight, but to fight with spoken and written words. As Weber puts it, "Nowadays the physical instrument of leadership (both in the political and military spheres) is no longer a blow from a sword but quite prosaic sound waves and drops of ink. . . . What matters is simply that these words – whether in the form of orders or an electioneering speech, diplomatic notes or official declarations in one's own parliament – should be shaped by intellect and knowledge, by strength of will and well-considered experience."[51]

Yet if violence and demagogy are fundamental instruments of politics, what are its purposes? Weber argued that a *Herrenvolk*, and the politicians at its helm, should pursue a number of related objectives, mindful that while conflict can be sublimated (for instance, into "competition"), it can never be eliminated.[52] Chief among the ends of politics is to fight for individuality, a labor that allows no pause. For energy and distinction are threatened everywhere by the human condition itself, which tends toward entropy and

---

[48] "Parliament and Government," *PW*, 154, Weber's footnote. Also, 219: "What is crucially important is the fact that the only persons with the training needed for political leadership are those who have been selected in political *struggle*, because all politics is essentially struggle."

[49] "Vocation of Politics," *PW*, 316, 330. On the latter page Weber goes on to say that this is "the very element in which the politician, and above all the political *leader*, thrives."

[50] "Vocation of Politics," *PW*, 357, 361. Also, 310 on violence as "the means specific to the state," though this is not to say that it is "the normal or sole means used by the state."

[51] "Parliament and Government," *PW*, 181. Their training in verbal battle, together with their economic "dispensability" and "availability," explain why legal advocates play such a prominent role in parliament: see "Suffrage and Democracy," 110; and "Parliament and Government," 191. Also "Vocation of Politics," 343 on "the power of demagogic speech."

[52] E.g., "Nation State and Economic Policy," *PW*, 15: "We do not want to breed well-being in people, but rather those characteristics which we think of as constituting the human greatness and nobility of our nature."

satedness.[53] Moreover, modern economic developments threaten to impose the shell of industrial, bureaucratic capitalism (or socialism) onto every day.[54]

Since politicians committed to individuality and liberty must seize "the spokes of the wheel of history"[55] rather than allow this wheel to rotate on its own accord, their vocation is daunting. Still, Weber argues, politics has its own "inner joy," derived from a feeling of power and the knowledge that the political actor weaves one thread of a tapestry of historically fateful events. This pleasure carries the danger, however, of degenerating into vanity and empty *Realpolitik*: a politics devoid of any purpose other than the urge for power for its own sake. Representatives of this mentality may appear to be strong and confident, but their shallowness becomes evident when, faced with a dramatic reversal of fortunes, they collapse inwardly. Their weakness "stems from a most wretched and superficial lack of concern for the *meaning* of human action . . . that knows nothing of the tragedy in which all action, but quite particularly political action, is in truth enmeshed."[56]

Contending with this tragic quality of political action demands a rare combination of intellectual and emotional attributes on the part of the politician. He must be dedicated to a cause for which he assumes personal responsibility. He needs sound judgment, composure, and a sense of proportion.[57] The political vocation demands stamina and stoicism that together enable the politician to be free of bitterness and, in defeat, to forgo in defeat "a mystical flight from the world."[58]

It is likely that Weber's model of the responsible political leader drew on a number of sources. Traces of Machiavelli, of Burckhardt, of Nietzsche are palpable in the preceding description. Yet for the student of Caesar and Caesarism there is another resonance that is striking. Of all the great works on Caesar that the nineteenth century produced, none was more widely read or admired than Theodor Mommsen's *History of Rome* (1854–6).[59] Weber first perused the work when he was fourteen and, as a boy at least, shared Mommsen's withering disdain for Cicero.[60]

---

53 E.g., "Russia's transition to pseudo-constitutionalism" [1906] in Max Weber, *The Russian Revolutions* (Cambridge, 1995), Gordon C. Wells and Peter Baehr, eds. and transl., 148–240, at 233: ". . . the future for 'sated' nations is bleak."
54 E.g., "Bourgeois Democracy in Russia" [1906], *The Russian Revolutions*, 41–147, at 108.
55 "Vocation of Politics," PW, 352; "Parliament and Government," 269.
56 "Vocation of Politics," PW, 352–5.
57 Ibid., 353. 58 Ibid., 368.
59 Theodor Mommsen, *History of Rome*, 5 Vols. (London, 1996), Thomas Wiedemann, ed., William Purdie Dickson, transl.
60 Marianne Weber, *Max Weber: A Biography* (New Brunswick, 1988 [1926]), Harry Zohn, transl., 52–4.

Mommsen's depiction of Caesar was always more than a reconstruction of the past; it was a cudgel to pummel the politicians of the present. Caesar, for Mommsen, was both the greatest statesman Republican[61] Rome had produced and a template of political greatness more generally against which Germany's dearth of leadership after the collapse of the liberals' hopes of 1848 might lamentably be measured. Employing a terminology that was evidently anachronistic, a price he was willing to pay for political insinuation and instruction, Mommsen described Caesar as a "democrat," but also a monarch, though one who "never played the king" and who "never resorted to outrages such as was that of the eighteenth Brumaire." Caesar was "a statesman in the deepest sense of the term" who stands "aloof from all ideology and everything fanciful." He was "a man of passion . . . but his passion was never stronger than he could control." On the contrary, Caesar was a thorough "realist" and "whatever he undertook and achieved was pervaded and guided by the cool sobriety which constitutes the most marked peculiarity of his genius. To this he owed the power of living energetically in the present, undisturbed either by recollection or by expectation." Caesar, moreover, was a man of "collected vigour," of prudence and "clearness of judgement" never forming "to himself illusions regarding the power of fate and the ability of man." Here was a human type "where the great contrasts of existence meet and balance each other."[62]

Might this depiction of Caesar have influenced Weber's thinking about political greatness? We can only speculate, and, in any case, it would be absurd to reduce Weber's picture of the responsible politician to Mommsen's encomium. We can be more certain, however, that Caesar was also the archetype of greatness, political or otherwise, for Nietzsche[63] and

---

61 Among the emperors, it was Diocletian whom Mommsen appears to have most admired. His discussion of Diocletian has some memorable parallels with his earlier praise of Caesar. See Theodor Mommsen, *A History of Rome Under the Emperors* (London/New York, 1996), 409–36. Based on the lecture notes of Sebastian and Paul Hensel, 1882–6, Clare Krojzl, transl., Thomas Wiedemann, ed. Mommsen remarks that Diocletian's "nature was one of remarkable sobriety and realism about the nature of things, and no one like him has perhaps ever appeared again," 411. On his *clementia*, 413.

62 I have been quoting from Mommsen, *History of Rome*, vol. 5, 305–27. See also Peter Gay, *The Naked Heart. The Bourgeois Experience, Victoria to Freud*, vol. IV (New York/London, 1995), 206: "Mommsen found the core of Caesar's being in the propitious interaction of two, only apparently incompatible, traits: passion and sobriety."

63 For Nietzsche, Caesar is one of the great examples of a man with "powerful and irreconcilable drives" who is also a genius of "self-control, self-outwitting." Such a man is especially rare when he emerges in "an era of dissolution"; for in that epoch of "late cultures and broken lights," a man will typically be weak: "his fundamental desire is that the war which he *is* should come to an end; happiness appears to him, in accord with a sedative (for example Epicurean or Christian) medicine and mode of thought, pre-eminently as the happiness of repose, of tranquillity, of satiety, of unity at last attained,

Burckhardt;[64] and that even Machiavelli's crushing indictment of the Roman dictator in the *Discourses* finds some mitigation in *The Art of War*. It has been said that "Only against the background of Nietzsche – and Jacob Burckhardt – is Weber's 'characteristic' individualism rendered intelligible."[65] If that is true, it is worth adding that in the background of *their* individualism lay the spectre of Caesar.

CONCLUSION

I have sought to show the multidimensional character of Weber's reflections on Caesarism. Negatively, Caesarism stood for all that was wrong with the Bismarckian system and legacy. Positively, it affirmed what political leadership could do if, as in England, it were given the proper parliamentary conditions in which to thrive.[66] However, Weber did more than give Caesarism a political articulation; he also redescribed it in sociological terms under the rubric of charisma, thus stabilizing, and to a degree erasing, a highly contestable idea that now largely disappeared beneath the imposing categories of legitimate *Herrschaft*. This helps to explain why Caesarism as a specific concept has received so little attention from sociologists. Even for historians and theorists of politics, it is easy to overlook the originality Weber brought to the discussion of concept. Unlike Oswald Spengler, who inserted Caesarism, putatively the degenerate phase of "civilization," into a philosophy of history, or Antonio Gramsci, who carefully catalogued Caesarism into a host of subtypes, Weber offered an analysis that was subtle and unobtrusive. Caesarism was so embedded in the vernacular of the time that he rarely paused to define it. Simultaneously, though, Weber himself adapted, stretched, and, through deft and provocative inversions, reshaped the vocabulary of politics and sociology in a way that has become platitudinous for us now that the debates of Weber's day are past.

At the beginning of this chapter I remarked that there are at least two ways to investigate the phenomenon of Caesarism. Other modes of enquiry

---

as a 'Sabbath of Sabbaths,' to quote the holy rhetorician Augustine, who was himself such a man." Friedrich Nietzsche, *Beyond Good and Evil. Prelude to a Philosophy of the Future* (Harmondsworth, 1973 [1886]), R. J. Hollingdale, transl., 103.

64 For whom Caesar is "the greatest of mortals." See Jacob Burckhardt, *Judgements on History and Historians* (London, 1959), Harry Zohn, transl., 34. Burckhardt made the comment in lectures delivered to students at the University of Basel in 1867.

65 Hennis, *Max Weber. Essays in Reconstruction*, 178.

66 Even when, shortly before his death, Weber lost confidence in the short-term ability of German parliamentary institutions to invigorate themselves, he never wanted to see a Caesarism free of parliamentary restraint, "The President of the Reich," *PW*, 304–8.

include analyses of the extent to which French politicians of the twentieth century have followed the example of their nineteenth-century predecessors[67] or studies that chart the relationship between Caesarism (however defined) and those modes of domination – particularly Nazism and Stalinism – that have come to be called "totalitarian."[68] These are not debates to which I can contribute here. Nonetheless, I take it as self-evident that those who do engage in them need to be clear about the checkered career Caesarism has enjoyed as a term, and be aware, too, that there are few political ideas more liable to anachronistic usage than this one.

67 E.g., Philip Thody, *French Caesarism From Napoleon I to Charles de Gaulle* (London, 1989); René Rémond, *La droite en France* (Paris, 1969); Theodore Zeldin, *France 1848–1945: Politics and Anger* (Oxford, 1979).
68 See Gollwitzer, "Caesarism of Napoleon III," 357–61, 394–6; Franz Neumann, "Notes on the theory of dictatorship," in F. Neumann, *The Democratic and the Authoritarian State*, Herbert Marcuse, ed. (Glenco, 1964), 233–56; and Alain Plessis, "Napoleon III, un dictateur?" in Maurice Duverger, ed., *Dictatures et légitimité* (Paris, 1982), 188–215, at 211–14.

8

The Concept of Caesarism in Gramsci

BENEDETTO FONTANA

In Western political thought Caesarism, whether associated with, or subsumed under, its various cognate concepts such as tyranny, dictatorship, and Bonapartism, has had a durable and contradictory history. From the perspective of the history of ideas, the emergence and development of the bundle of ideas described by the term Caesarism is more than an intellectual attempt to formulate categories capable of capturing and characterizing it as a political and historical phenomenon. Theories of dictatorship and tyranny are also ideological constructions with normative and moral content, and thus political.[1]

It is only since the French Revolution and its aftermath, however, that Caesarism and its various interpretations have assumed both political and intellectual importance. It is the emergence of modern forms of politics, and the undermining of traditional norms and institutions, that has fueled debates over the nature and role of Caesarism.[2] Thus, in the nineteenth century, ideological and theoretical battles reflected and expressed political alignments and social conflicts among liberals and conservatives (in the classical European sense), monarchists and Bonapartists, classical Marxists and republicans. In the twentieth century, the political struggle among liberal democrats, socialists, communists, and Fascists was expressed in part by

---

This essay is dedicated to the late Dante Germino, friend and colleague.
1 For an analysis of the history of the concept of despotism and its variants, see Melvin Richter, "Despotism," *Dictionary of the History of Ideas* (New York, 1973), 3:1–18. For a discussion of the relation between political transformation and conceptual innovation, see the essays in Terence Ball, James Farr, and Russell L. Hanson, eds., *Political Innovation and Conceptual Change* (New York, 1989).
2 See the series of essays on modern forms of illegitimacy and domination by Melvin Richter, "Modernity and its Distinctive Threats to Liberty: Montesquieu and Tocqueville on New Forms of Illegitimate Domination," in Michael Hereth and Jutta Höffken, eds., *Alexis de Tocqueville: Zur Politik in der Demokratie* (Baden-Baden, 1981), 61–80; "Toward a Concept of Political Illegitimacy: Bonapartist Dictatorship and Democratic Legitimacy," *Political Theory* 10, 2 (1982), 185–214; and "Tocqueville, Napoleon, and Bonapartism," in Abraham S. Eisenstadt, ed., *Reconsidering Tocqueville's Democracy in America* (New Brunswick and London, 1988), 110–45.

ideological polemics over the nature and meaning of such terms as totalitarian dictatorship and totalitarian democracy.[3]

Marxist theories of Bonapartism and Caesarism emerged within this intellectual and historical context. Beginning with Marx and Engels, Marxists of all stripes have had an ambivalent relationship with Caesarist and Bonapartist forms of dictatorship.[4] Stressing the coercive and violent nature of the state under class rule, and constructing a Hegelian notion of politics understood as *Machtpolitik* and *Realpolitik*, they preached the necessity of violent revolution and dictatorship in order to arrive at a more just order. On the other hand, they realized, Western Marxists especially, that forms of dictatorship presupposed an inert, passive, and essentially backward mass base. Thus, Marx and Engels opposed educational dictatorships of the Buonarroti and Babeuf type, and offered their version of revolutionary dictatorship as essentially a majoritarian (democratic) transitory condition of proletarian rule.[5]

The transformation of the Marxian dictatorship from a transitory revolutionary condition of a democratic majority to the Leninist dictatorship of a minority party as the permanent form of the proletarian state reflected a profound shift in the nature of the ideological and theoretical discussion over the nature of dictatorship. The Bolshevik revolution in Russia ushered in a period in Continental Europe where modern forms of dictatorship both as sociopolitical systems of power and as massive bureaucratic structures of state coercion had become prevalent. Thus, while liberals and conservatives were compelled to ponder the implications of the rise of totalitarian dictatorship, socialists and communists confronted equally the political and ideological significance of the victory of Fascism in the advanced West and the victory of Leninism in the backward East.[6]

This chapter will discuss the idea of Caesarism in Antonio Gramsci. Like all of his concepts, Caesarism developed from his efforts to understand, both

---

3 For some examples, see Renzo de Felice, *Interpretations of Fascism* (Cambridge, Mass., 1977); Hannah Arendt, *The Origins of Totalitarianism* (New York, 1951); Sigmund Neumann, *Permanent Revolution* (New York, 1942); and Carl J. Friedrich and Zbigniew K. Brzezinski, *Totalitarian Dictatorship and Autocracy*, 2[d] rev. ed. (New York, 1965).
4 See Shlomo Avineri, *The Social and Political Thought of Karl Marx* (Cambridge, 1971); George Lichtheim, *Marxism: An Historical and Critical Study*, 2[d] rev. ed. (New York, 1970); and Robert C. Tucker, *The Marxian Revolutionary Idea* (New York, 1969), especially chapter 3, "The Political Theory of Classical Marxism," 54–91.
5 Richard N. Hunt, *The Political Ideas of Marx and Engels*, vol. I, *Marxism and Totalitarian Democracy, 1818–1850* (Pittsburgh, 1974), chapters 7–9; J. L. Talmon, *The Origins of Totalitarian Democracy* (New York, 1960); and Peter Baehr, *Caesar and the Fading of the Roman World: A Study in Republicanism and Caesarism* (New Brunswick and London, 1998), chapter 2.
6 Leopold Labedz, ed., *Revisionism: Essays on the History of Marxist Ideas* ((New York, 1962), provides, in a series of essays, a good overview of the Marxist Left's reaction to twentieth-century political and social transformations and to the rise of Bolshevik dictatorship.

politically and theoretically, the victory of Fascism and the failure not only of the revolutionary left, but also of liberalism and liberal institutions generally. Gramsci isolated this failure in the political weakness and social backwardness of the Italian state, which he traced to the chronic absence within Italian history, especially in the Risorgimento, of a hegemonic relation between the ruling elite and the general population. Gramsci saw both the failure of liberalism and the rise of Fascism in Italy as resulting from the inability of the dominant groups to move from an "economic-corporate" to a hegemonic phase of political development. While there has been much debate about various aspects of Gramsci's political thought – especially about the concepts of hegemony, civil society, and the modern prince – for some reason his treatment of Caesarism as a political form has received comparatively little discussion.[7] This seems a very unusual state of affairs, especially when one considers that Gramsci's concepts are closely interwoven. His method of exposition is "dyadic": One concept is presented in opposition to, or as the antinomy of, another. Thus, hegemony is to be understood in opposition to its opposite, dictatorship; civil society is opposed to political society; and war of position is contrasted to war of movement. Caesarism straddles two overarching sets of antinomies: hegemony/dictatorship, and political society/civil society. What connects them is Gramsci's antithesis between domination and moral-intellectual leadership.

Gramsci, like any Marxist, clearly understands Caesarism as a class phenomenon, and he sees its political forms as products of class and factional

---

[7] The following works deal with Gramsci's Caesarism, either specifically or as part of a larger, more encompassing theme or project: Baehr, *Caesar*, 267–75; Carlo Guarnieri, "Cesarismo," in Norberto Bobbio, Nicola Matteucci, and Gianfranco Pasquino, eds., *Dizionario di politica* (Turin, 1983), 155–7; Luisa Mangoni, "Cesarismo, bonapartismo, fascismo," *Studi storici* 3 (1976), 41–61 (for Gramsci see 54–61), and her "Per una definizione del fascismo: I concetti di bonapartismo e cesarismo," *Italia contemporanea* 135 (1979), 17–52, in which Thalheimer and Trotsky, not to mention Schmitt and Weber, figure more prominently than Gramsci, whose work is mentioned very briefly (24–5); Mario Spinella, "Cesarismo (o bonapartismo) in Antonio Gramsci," *Il calendario del popolo* 419 (1980), 7141–2; and Paolo Cristofolini, "Dal dispotismo al 'moderno Principe,'" in Franco Ferri, ed., *Politica e storia in Gramsci* (Rome, 1979), vol. II, Proceedings of the International Conference on Gramscian Studies, Florence, December 9–11, 1977, 343–50.

Moreover, writers such as Franco de Felice, in "Una chiave di lettura in Americanismo e Fordismo," *Rinascita*, October 27, 1972, and "Rivoluzione passiva, fascismo, americanismo in Gramsci," in Franco Ferri, ed., *Politica e storia in Gramsci*, vol. I; and C. Buci-Glucksmann, in *Gramsci et L'État: pour une théorie matérialiste de la philosophie* (Paris, 1975), look at Gramsci's attempt to link economically Fascism and modern methods of industrial organization. Gramsci sees the Fascist dictatorship as trying to develop in a backward society and economy means of "economic policing" and industrial control that attempt to parallel the methods proposed by Ford and Taylor in the more advanced American economy. For an excellent analysis of the link between Fascism and economic rationalization, see Donatella di Benedetto, "Americanismo e razionalizzazione in Antonio Gramsci dall'*Ordine Nuovo* ai *Quaderni del carcere*," doctoral dissertation, l'Istituto Universitario Orientale di Napoli, 1992.

strife. In the *Prison Notebooks*, he writes:

> Caesarism can be said to express a situation in which the forces in conflict balance each other in a catastrophic manner; that is to say, they balance each other in such a way that a continuation of the conflict can only terminate in their reciprocal destruction. When the progressive force A struggles against the reactionary force B, not only may A defeat B or B defeat A, but it may happen that neither A nor B defeats the other – that they bleed each other mutually and then a third force C intervenes from outside, subjugating what is left of both A and B. In Italy, after the death of Lorenzo il Magnifico this is precisely what occurred.[8]

This passage recalls Marx and Engels's theory of Bonapartism, where it is seen as the outcome of the exhaustion of the bourgeoisie and the working class, and as the political expression of the peasantry and small proprietors.[9] However, the passage is more suggestive. For the third force C, though coming from the outside, and "subjugating what is left of both A and B," nevertheless intervenes not only because of the mutual exhaustion of A and B, but also because A or B invites C's intervention as a second best (or least unfavorable) solution to the conflict. Thus, though the eventual outcome of the intervention might be the subjugation of both groups, the intervention itself is sparked by interests internal to the conflict.

As Gramsci notes, that was the case in Italy after the death of Lorenzo. The struggle for supremacy that underlay the balance of power among the Italian states led to foreign intervention in the affairs of the peninsula. This intervention, though obviously from the "outside," took its specific forms and produced a particular outcome (the eventual subjugation of the Italian states) as a consequence of the internal dynamics of the relations between the Italian states themselves. The fact that no state was able to amass the necessary power to become a hegemonic or imperial force was both the cause and the result of foreign intervention. At the same time, this failure of any one Italian state to achieve supremacy over the others is linked by Gramsci, in his interpretation of Machiavelli, to the failure of the ruling elites to establish a durable and stable hegemony over the subordinate groups within a given principality or republic.

The "third force" was always present, that is, always an active factor in the conflict. The subjugation is the unintended consequence of an intervention

---

[8] Antonio Gramsci, *Selections from the Prison Notebooks*, ed. and trans. Quintin Hoare and Geoffrey Nowell Smith (New York, 1973), 219, hereafter *SPN*.

[9] Karl Marx, *The Civil War in France*, in David Fernbach, ed., *The First International and After* (Harmondsworth, 1974), 208–9. See also his *The Eighteenth Brumaire of Louis Bonaparte*, in D. Fernbach, ed., *Surveys from Exile* (Harmondsworth, 1973); and Friedrich Engels, *The Origin of the Family, Private Property, and the State*, in Marx and Engels, *Selected Works* (Moscow, 1968), 290.

whose purpose is to freeze and to redirect the antagonism, certainly the open, political forms of it, in order to prevent the reciprocal destruction. Thus, Caesarism "always expresses the particular solution in which a great personality is entrusted with the task of 'arbitration' over a historico-political situation characterised by an equilibrium of forces leading towards catastrophe."[10] The dictator (the "great personality," or, as Gramsci writes elsewhere in quasi-Weberian fashion, the "charismatic leader" and "charismatic 'men of destiny'")[11] is "entrusted" with the power to arbitrate between the contending groups. Caesarism is therefore either progressive or reactionary: "Caesarism is progressive when its intervention helps the progressive force to triumph, albeit with its victory tempered by certain compromises and limitations. It is reactionary when its intervention helps the reactionary force to triumph."[12] Gramsci presents Julius Caesar and Napoleon Bonaparte as examples of the former and Louis Napoleon and Bismarck as examples of the latter.

Not only is this definition tautological.[13] It reflects the teleological, and from our perspective in time, somewhat innocent and optimistic faith in the forward march of history, not to mention the ultimate victory of the workers and peasants. Even from Gramsci's own political and theoretical position, the progressive/regressive dichotomy is not very coherent. For the content of the two terms is determined by the ongoing political and ideological struggle, and it can have no meaning or value independent of this struggle, that is, independent of the power of the actors. However, the ideological character of the progressive/regressive dichotomy does not make it valueless. It demonstrates that Caesarism, though a third force in Marx's and Gramsci's sense, is nevertheless a force that can only emerge from the power struggle of antagonistic groups.

What Gramsci means by the progressive/regressive dyad is explained by a second dichotomy, that between "qualitative" and "quantitative." The Caesarism of Julius Caesar and Napoleon Bonaparte was of a qualitative

---

10 Gramsci, *SPN*, 219.   11 Ibid., 210–11.
12 Ibid., 219.
13 Baehr, *Caesar*, 267. Baehr rightly notes the teleological character of progressive Caesarism. However, it might be shorn of its obvious ideological character if it is seen solely as a form of dictatorship that leads to major structural and systemic transformation – something along the lines of Schmitt's "sovereign dictatorship," or Sulla's revisionist *dictatura legibus scribendis et rei publicae constituendae*. In addition to Baehr, see Norberto Bobbio, *Democracy and Dictatorship* (Minneapolis, 1989). Of course, Schmitt would reject Gramsci's dichotomy between regressive and progressive, and replace it with dictatorship which is either "commissary," or limited and preserving of the existing order, and "sovereign," which is unlimited, and may thus be innovating and lead to the institution of a new order. See George Schwab, *The Challenge of the Exception: An Introduction to the Political Ideas of Carl Schmitt Between 1921 and 1926* (Westport, 1989).

character, while that of Louis Napoleon was merely quantitative. The first "represented the historical phase of passage from one type of State to another type, a passage in which the innovations were so numerous, and of such a nature, that they represented a complete revolution," and the second represented a phase in which "there was no passage from one type of State to another, but only 'evolution' of the same type along unbroken lines."[14] In effect, the two dyads, progressive/regressive and qualitative/quantitative, parallel each other, and each may be understood in terms of the other. The second pair of distinctions dilutes the tendentiousness of the first, for it becomes clear that the criteria employed are not moral (though certainly ideological), but rather socio-economic and political: namely, structural transformation and innovation. Since, according to Gramsci, "restorations *in toto* do not exist,"[15] regressive Caesarism, while reactionary, can never establish, or reestablish, outmoded forms of the ancien régime. What they can do is elaborate "marginal possibilities for further development and organisational improvement."[16]

It is in this context that we should understand Gramsci's puzzling and provocative statement regarding the emergence of Caesarism from parliamentary compromises and from coalition government. Here we see a particularly novel and modern reinterpretation of Caesarist dictatorship. It moves away from the specifically "praetorian"[17] and individualistic understanding to a Caesarism more attuned to modern electoral politics based on mass mobilization and mass representation through institutional mechanisms such as political parties and legislatures. In the same way that Gramsci interprets Machiavelli's new prince as the "modern Prince,"[18] he transforms the metaphor of Caesarism into a modern language of organization, bureaucracy, and institutions. He writes:

A Caesarist solution can exist even without a Caesar, without any great . . . and representative personality. The parliamentary system has also provided a mechanism for such compromise solutions. . . . Every coalition government is a first stage of Caesarism, which either may or may not develop to more significant stages (the common opinion of course is that coalition governments, on the contrary, are the most "solid bulwark" against Caesarism).[19]

---

14 Gramsci, *SPN*, 222. 15 Ibid., 220.
16 Ibid., 222.
17 See Karl Marx, "The Rule of the Praetorians," in K. Marx and F. Engels, *Collected Works* (New York, 1986), 15:464–7, and "The Attempt upon the Life of Bonaparte," in ibid., 453–8. In the former essay, Marx writes that "Under the second Empire the interest of the army itself is to predominate. The army is no longer to maintain the rule of one part of the people over another part of the people. The army is to maintain its own rule, personated by its own dynasty, over the French people in general . . . ," 465.
18 Gramsci, *SPN*, 125–33, 147. 19 Ibid., 220.

Gramsci gives Ramsey MacDonald's Labour governments as examples of a Caesarist solution without a representative personality – a "compromise solution" that did not evolve into a more developed, fully mature form of Caesarism. On the other hand, he points out that in Italy from October 1922 to November 1926 "there was a politico-historical movement in which various gradations of Caesarism succeeded each other, culminating in a more pure and permanent form."[20] Presumably because of the great strength and resilience (measured in terms of ideology, degree of consensus, as indicators of regime legitimacy), the crisis in Britain never moved beyond the "gradation" of a coalition government as a compromise solution.[21] In Germany, the deadlock in the Reichstag produced by the opposition of the Communists and Nazis led to a series of compromise solutions imposed on parliament from an extra-parliamentary force, namely the Reich President, in the form of presidential cabinets under Brüning, von Papen, and Schleicher.[22] A decade earlier in Italy, the governments of Giolitti, Bonomi, and Facta were all based on parliamentary coalitions and represented the attempt on the part of the liberals, nationalists, and Catholics to find a nonfascist and nonrevolutionary socialist solution to the crisis of the state.

In Italy and in Germany, various gradations of Caesarist fascism could be identified. Both Mussolini and Hitler came to power constitutionally and legally as heads of government within parliamentary coalitions. Whatever the ideological pretensions regarding the revolutionary nature of fascism, power was achieved through the conventional channels provided by

---

20 Ibid.
21 See Baehr, *Caesar*, 270–72, 275–6. Criticizing Gramsci's assertion that coalition government is a first stage of Caesarism, Baehr makes the important observation that "coalition governments are not necessarily crisis governments, nor are they necessarily heading in any direction whose goal is extrinsic to them" (276). This is a good point. However, as far as Italy and Germany are concerned, Caesarist dictatorship emerged out of coalition governments. Perhaps Gramsci's notes regarding the relation between coalition governments and Caesarism should be understood within the context of observations on what Gramsci calls the "crisis" of authority and hegemony, or the "general crisis of the State." In this context, and though Gramsci may not have had Russia in mind, Lenin's first revolutionary government following the seizure of power in November 1917 was, or at least took the parliamentary/political form of, a coalition government. On the other hand, Baehr is right to point to the implausibility of the "neo-Gramscian theory" of Caesarism, which takes Gramsci's comments regarding compromise and coalition governments and applies them to post-War liberal-democratic systems.
22 The twenties and thirties produced lively debates regarding the nature of dictatorship and Bonapartism, for obvious historical reasons. These theories ranged from the communist, such as those of Thalheimer and Trotsky, to the conservative and nationalist right, such as that of Schmitt. While these three recognized the dictatorial character of the presidential cabinets in Weimar Germany, they disagreed over its meaning and specific aspects. See Luisa Mangoni, "Cesarismo, bonapartismo, fascismo," and "Per una definizione del fascismo: i concetti di bonapartismo e cesarismo."

electoral campaigns and party mobilization. Fascism and National Socialism came to power as movements allied with established forces within the state (military, police, civil service) and civil society (political parties, veterans' associations, business interest groups, etc.). In both instances, the seizure of power occurred within the state, not against the state. It is in this sense that Gramsci understands both Fascism and National Socialism as the products of the ongoing evolution of the bourgeois state as it confronts crises within the economy and within its legitimating institutions.

The reference to the evolutionary character of regressive Caesarism, its inability to move beyond the preexisting social, economic, and political structures, may be seen as a Gramscian critique of Italian Fascism. At one level, Gramsci exposes Mussolini's revolutionary and populist pretensions; the Fascists' claim of constructing an entirely new type of state is derided. At another level, to say that the Fascist regime represents the further evolution of "marginal possibilities" of the state established by the Risorgimento is to launch a devastating and all-encompassing critique of the political and theoretical bases of Italian liberalism and of the state and culture it produced.

Fascism is the logical and natural evolution of the liberal state in Italy for two fundamental reasons. First, the Risorgimento was a form of "revolution from above," what Gramsci calls a "passive revolution"[23] in which the Piedmontese ruling class imposed its supremacy over the rest of the Italian peninsula. The revolution is "passive" because the people or the masses are absent from the process. Unlike the French and American Revolutions, in which the people emerged as an active and conscious force, the Risorgimento in Italy was possible precisely because of the passivity of the people. The people as an active force in Gramsci means the formation of ruling elites able and willing to organize and lead the masses, which, in turn, means the ability to transform the narrow, particular interests of a given group into those of a more general, universal nature. The method and pattern of the establishment of the unified Italian state set the parameters for its future development: a weak, narrow social base and a ruling elite pursuing narrowly defined economic interests.

This leads to the second point regarding Fascism as a regressive form of Caesarism. Gramsci establishes a clear relation between regressive/quantitative Caesarism and the prevalence of hegemonic structures of power within both civil society and the state apparatus. Writing about the radical and innovative character of the bourgeoisie as a new type of ruling

---

23 Gramsci, *SPN*, 58–9, 105–20.

class, Gramsci notes:

> The previous ruling classes were essentially conservative in the sense that they did not tend to construct an organic passage from the other classes into their own, i.e. to enlarge their class sphere "technically" and ideologically: their conception was that of a closed caste. The bourgeois class poses itself as an organism in continuous movement, capable of absorbing the entire society, assimilating it to its own cultural and economic level. The entire function of the State has been transformed; the State has become an "educator", etc.[24]

The ruling elites of the Risorgimento and, later, of the liberal state it spawned did not achieve the political and economic integration of the various social groups of Italian society. The liberal and bourgeois elements of Italian society were isolated politically and socially. The divorce of the state, or rather of the ruling elites, from the mass of the people prevented it from acting as an educator, that is, from exercising moral and intellectual leadership. Lacking widespread consensus and unable to generate mechanisms of legitimation within society, it also lacked the moral and political resilience to withstand what Gramsci calls a "crisis of authority," which is a "crisis of hegemony, or general crisis of the State."[25]

Although hegemony assumes many guises for Gramsci and moves on various levels, it refers to the movement from the economic-corporative to the political, and from the particular to the universal.[26] This Gramsci underlines when he contrasts the *particulare* of the noble *case* (as seen in Guicciardini) and the collective popular will expressed and embodied in Machiavelli's new prince.[27] At the same time, hegemony describes the kaleidoscopic generation of alliances as differing and competing social groups form and reform as they eventually coalesce around a particular preeminent group. A group becomes hegemonic to the extent that it exercises intellectual and moral leadership over the other groups in a manner such that the latter function as allies or associates of the former. Opposed to hegemony is domination, the exercise of coercion over other groups. Gramsci notes, "[T]he supremacy of a social group is manifested in two ways: as 'domination' and as 'intellectual and moral leadership.' A social group is dominant over those antagonistic groups it wants to 'liquidate' or to subdue even with armed force, and is leading with respect to those groups that are associated and allied with it."[28] What Gramsci calls the "integral State" – the social and political order – embodies a hegemonic equilibrium between coercive power and

---

[24] Ibid., 260.
[25] Ibid., 210.
[26] Ibid., 159–61.
[27] Ibid., 125–33, 173–5.
[28] Gramsci, *Quaderni del carcere*, critical edition of the Gramsci Institute, ed. Valentino Gerratana, 4 vols. (Turin, 1975), vol. 3, Notebook 19, 2010, henceforth cited as QC.

moral/cultural mechanisms of persuasion. Moreover, in modern liberal and democratic states, "[t]he 'normal' exercise of hegemony ... is characterized by a combination of force and consent which are balanced in varying proportions, without force prevailing too greatly over consent."[29] Domination and leadership, force and consent, together characterize the political, so that for Gramsci the state is formed by two distinct, and interwoven, spheres: "dictatorship plus hegemony" and "political society plus civil society." The synthesis of the two spheres is what Gramsci means by the "state." [30] This view revises the standard Marxist and Leninist conception of the state as the organized force of the ruling class and the executive committee of the bourgeoisie. Intellectuals, by generating and disseminating beliefs, values, knowledge, and culture within civil society, are the experts in legitimation and function as intermediaries between the rulers and the ruled.

A note in which Gramsci contrasts the socio-political order confronting Lenin's Bolsheviks in Russia and that faced by the communists in the West is revealing. Gramsci says that the differences in social and political structures between the East and the West require different methods and strategy to make successful revolutions. It is also significant in what it implicitly reveals about the different forms of Caesarism. Gramsci writes, "In Russia the State was everything, civil society was primordial and gelatinous; in the West there was a proper relation between the State and civil society, and when the State trembled a sturdy structure of civil society was at once revealed. The State was only an outer ditch, behind which there stood a powerful system of fortresses and earthworks."[31] Civil society is the sphere of liberty where consent and persuasion are generated. It is the sphere of cultural, ideological, and religious conflict where conflict is defined by the contest of voluntary and secondary associations such as trade unions, political parties, sects and churches, schools and universities, civic organizations, and interest groups of various kinds. Gramsci continues: "The massive structures of the modern democracies, both as State organisations, and as complexes of associations in civil society, constitute for the art of politics as it were the 'trenches' and the permanent fortifications of the front in the war of position: they render merely 'partial' the element of movement which before used to be 'the whole' of war."[32] In the West, a direct assault (what Gramsci calls a war of movement) on the state is not possible precisely because of the multiple interwoven layers of complex associations in modern democracy. Only a war of position – that is, ideological, cultural, and intellectual struggle – will

29 Ibid., 3:13, 1638.
31 Gramsci, *SPN*, 238.
30 Ibid., 2:6, 763–4.
32 Ibid., 243.

undermine the established order. A revolutionary transformation of society in the West requires a long and steady process of ideological trench warfare, with the aim of undermining the cultural, intellectual, and moral fortifications of civil society and its state. In the East, the weakness of civil society and the coercive character of the state enabled Lenin to engineer a direct and revolutionary assault on the state apparatus. At the same time, in Western liberal democracies a regressive Caesarist solution to factional conflict is politically feasible when the "proper relation between state and civil society" no longer obtains. In Italy and Germany, the state was never directly attacked. The struggle for power was conducted within the sphere of civil society by opposing and antagonistic private groups, political parties, paramilitary organizations, veterans' organizations, newspapers, and journals. This struggle, it is important to note, was never waged against the state; indeed, in some cases it was waged with the support of the legal organs of the state.

What is decisive in this context is the fact that Lenin and his Bolsheviks were able to organize a coup d'état against the Provisional Government in Russia, whereas three years later in Germany the Kapp Putsch failed miserably. In the former, there was no mobilization of the free forces of civil society; in the latter, those forces were mobilized against the seizure of power. The organization of civil opposition was sufficient to restore the legal order in Germany. In Russia, there was no civil opposition; on the contrary, the Bolshevik coup degenerated into open military conflict. In the West, the strength and density of civil society circumscribed factional conflict and class struggle within civil and institutional channels, a circumstance that necessitated a "war of position" as a strategy for revolution. In the East (Russia), the "gelatinous" nature of civil society made inevitable the civil war between the Whites and the Reds (a "war of movement").

Each type of factional conflict and power struggle appears as a crisis of authority, which is always a crisis of hegemony, a disintegration of the legitimating structures of the state. This means that the state no longer performs its educative role in integrating and assimilating new groups into the prevailing socio-political order. Gramsci writes, "If the ruling class has lost its consensus, i.e. is no longer 'leading' but only 'dominant', exercising coercive force alone, this means precisely that the great masses have become detached from their traditional ideologies . . . The crisis consists precisely in the fact that the old is dying and the new cannot be born; in this interregnum a great variety of morbid symptoms appear."[33]

---

33 Ibid., 275–6.

The exercise of coercive force is thus always a necessary element in Caesarism. In consequence, Gramsci, like others before and after him, sees Caesarism as being related to the military, both as a bureaucracy and as an organization of violence. To Gramsci, the "military influence in national life means not only the influence and weight of the military in the technical sense [such as the officer cadres and the General Staff] but the influence and weight of the social stratum from which the latter (especially the junior officers) mostly derives its origin."[34] Gramsci locates the social and class bases of military power and military interests within the "medium and small rural bourgeoisie" whose material life experience (such as its domination of the peasantry, its rentier income, its hostility to and fear of the urban bourgeoisie, its cultural animus toward urban life) render it receptive to military culture and to military control of civil and political life.[35] Thus, identifying the class nature of military power "is indispensable for any really profound analysis of . . . Caesarism or Bonapartism – to distinguish it from other forms in which the technical military element as such predominates, in conformations perhaps still more visible and exclusive."[36] While military power and organized coercion are necessary elements of Caesarism, they are obviously not sufficient, and one must look elsewhere to identify its essential nature as a political form. For Caesarism is more than a simple military government or a military dictatorship. Caesarism is connected to the social and material base from which it emerges. It must therefore also be linked to a "formally organic, political and social ideology."[37] The relation between military and political power is crucial to Gramsci, and the political generally plays the preeminent role. In his discussion of the progressive/qualitative Caesarism of Julius Caesar, Gramsci notes:

Even in those cases in which the political and military leadership is united in the same person, it is the political moment which must prevail over the military. Caesar's *Commentaries* are a classical example of the exhibition of an intelligent combination of political art and military art: the soldiers saw in Caesar not only a great military leader but especially their political leader, the leader of democracy.[38]

Here the political is connected to the concept of moral and intellectual leadership in that Gramsci sees Caesar as acting as the representative of the common soldiers. The social base of this "democracy" is the landless and unemployed Roman peasantry and urban proletariat whose mobilization and organization form the basis of Caesar's rise to power.

34 Ibid., 214–15.
36 Ibid., 215.
38 Ibid., 88.

35 Ibid., 212.
37 Ibid., 215–16.

Gramsci's use of the term "from outside" in describing Caesarism is significant.[39] It points to the ancient Greek and Roman distinction between power exercised within the polity and power exercised outside it. In Republican Rome, for example, the *imperium* of the magistrates was of two kinds, the *imperium domi*, or power exercised within the *pomerium* of the city, that was limited and circumscribed by various institutional checks, and the *imperium militiae*, or power exercised outside the confines of the city, like that of a general on campaign or a promagistrate within his *provincia*. This latter power is not subject to appeal and to countervailing checks, and it is thus absolute.[40] Both forms of *imperium* are constitutional and legitimate as long as they are exercised within their respective legal and political spheres. The Roman dictatorship was a mechanism by which the *imperium militiae* could be exercised constitutionally and legitimately within the city in times of crisis or emergency. It represented an attempt to subject such an *imperium* to the control of republican institutions. It is with the Marian and Sullan civil wars that the constitutional dictatorship (which by that time had fallen into disuse) was transformed into a type totally novel and innovating, the Sullan *dictatura legibus scribendis et rei publicae constituendae* (dictatorship to rewrite the laws and reconstitute the state).[41] Caesar's dictatorship was of a similar type. Accordingly, Caesarism represents the introduction of the *imperium militiae* into the civil and political space of the polity not as a temporary and emergency measure, but rather as a normal and permanent political/bureaucratic form that dominates and directs the institutions of the polity. The military power of the general, when brought to bear within the city, subordinates the civil authorities of the city to the army and freezes civil and political life by abolishing the customary competition among the various factions and parties. Gramsci recognizes the theoretical importance of this distinction when he writes:

The theory of Caesarism, so prevalent today . . . is expressed in the political language of Napoleon III, who is certainly neither a great historian nor a philosopher nor a political theorist. Certainly in the history of Rome the figure of Caesar is not only or principally characterized by "Caesarism" in this narrow sense. The historical development expressed by Caesar assumes, within the "Italic peninsula" as well as

---

39 Ibid., 219; quoted above.
40 On the *imperium*, see Frank Frost Abbott, *A History and Description of Roman Political Institutions* (Boston, 1902), 149–54, and *Dictionnaire des Antiquités Grecques et Romaines* (Graz, Austria, 1969), 545. See also Norberto Bobbio, *Democracy and Dictatorship*, 158–61; and Benedetto Fontana, "Tacitus on Empire and Republic," *History of Political Thought* 14, 1 (1993), 34–5. See also Baehr's discussion of ancient Roman politics in his *Caesar and the Fading of the Roman World*.
41 On the differences between the constitutional dictatorship and the Caesarist one, see Theodor Mommsen, *The History of Rome*, trans. William P. Dickson (New York, 1888), 4:560–4.

in Rome, a "Caesarist" form. However, it must be inserted within the larger frame of the Empire as a whole, and thus in reality consists of the "denationalization" of Italy and its subordination to the interests of the Empire . . . the Empire's capital was wherever the Emperor resided, who was always on the move . . . Rome became a cosmopolitan city, and all Italy became the center of a cosmopolis. Caesar should be compared to Catiline: Catiline was more "Italian" than Caesar, and his revolution perhaps would have preserved for Italy (with a different class in power) its hegemonic function during the republican period. The revolution represented by Caesar was not a solution to the class struggle in Italy, but rather to that of the Empire as a whole, or at least of those classes having imperial functions (the military, the bureaucracy, bankers, contractors, etc.).[42]

Here Gramsci is drawing a parallel between "Italy" and the "Empire," on the one hand, and on the other, "Rome" and its "provinces." In the same way that the *imperium militiae* represents the subordination of Rome to the power of the general outside in the provinces, so, too, Caesarism and its imperial army and bureaucracy represent the subordination of Italy to the Empire. But what is the Empire but the provinces formerly conquered by Roman and Italian armies? The statement in the above quotation, "the Empire's capital was where the Emperor resided, who was always on the move" is crucial, for it underlines the relation between military and political/civil power.[43] Julius Caesar was perceived by his soldiers as the leader of the democracy mobilized against the Republican oligarchy, in the same way that later the emperors mobilized and organized the armies of the provinces and led them against Rome.

---

42 Gramsci, QC 3:17, 1924. The distinction Gramsci makes between Caesar and Catiline – the former representing the cosmopolitan classes of the Empire, the latter the "Italic" and national groups of Italy – is tendentious and ideological. He wants to contrast the cosmopolitan intellectual (defined as lacking ties to the people-nation), a type dominant throughout Italian history (found in the cosmopolitan Catholic Church, the humanists of the Italian Renaissance, and in modern Italian intellectuals such as Croce), with the national-popular intellectual (who is closely linked to the people or the masses), a type absent in Italian history and culture. The absence of the latter, and the dominance of the former, are a major factor in the weakness of the Italian state and of the backwardness of Italian politics and culture in general. To Gramsci such political, social, and cultural weakness may lead to Caesarism as a response to war and other crises. For the civil wars and factional strife in late Republican Rome, see Lily Ross Taylor, *Party Politics in the Age of Caesar* (Berkeley, 1961). See also H. H. Scullard, *From the Gracchi to Nero: A History of Rome 133 BC to AD 68* (London and New York, 1992).

43 There is a remarkable affinity between Gramsci's statement and Tacitus's observation about the infamous year of the four emperors. Discussing the factional strife and the rebellion of the provincial armies that accompanied the fall of Nero and the ascension of Galba, Tacitus notes that the secret of empire is now revealed – an emperor can be made elsewhere than in Rome: "evulgato imperii arcano, posse principem alibi quam Romae fieri." *Historiae*, I:4, 2. In effect, the *arcanum imperii* is that there is no longer any distinction between the *imperium domi* and the *imperium militiae*. What was once a secret veiled by the republican facade established by Caesar Augustus has now become known to all, namely, that the *imperium militiae* exercised in the provinces, by invading the public space of the polity, had destroyed liberty and constitutional government.

In the modern world, the supremacy of the political moment is much more obvious and decisive. In the twentieth century, military power and the mere exercise of coercion are not sufficient to sustain a durable and stable form of Caesarism. Social and economic changes, as well as parallel transformations in the means of mass communication, mass mobilization, and mass organization, have made the military element of Caesarism less significant and have correspondingly given greater weight and force to "economic-trade-union and party-political coalitions."[44] This means that ideological and cultural factors have become critical. A coup d'état is not enough to acquire and maintain power, as the Kapp Putsch in 1920 demonstrated. At the same time, while the explicitly military element may have decreased in importance, the fundamentally irreconcilable struggle between capital and labor, between the dominant social bloc and the subordinate groups, compels the former increasingly to resort to police and security measures. Therefore, "modern Caesarism is more a police than a military system."[45] This observation is quite revealing, but unfortunately is not explored. It suggests a structural contradiction within the political structures of modern Caesarism (such as Fascism and Nazism): the opposition between the military and the police/state security organs and the paramilitary organizations. The "variety of morbid symptoms" the crisis brings to the social foreground is an aspect of this opposition.

On one level, Caesarism to Gramsci is a form of rule in which the relation between rulers and ruled becomes attenuated and in which the ruling group is no longer able to generate ideological and cultural systems of legitimation.

---

44 Gramsci, *SPN*, 220.
45 Ibid., 222. Gramsci's analysis of modern Caesarism bears a close resemblance to the post-1945 discussions of the essential characteristics of totalitarianism and totalitarian dictatorships. These theories share six basic elements: (1) an "official" ideology or world view actively disseminated throughout the population; (2) monopoly over the technology and mechanisms of mass communication and mass dissemination; (3) a centralized party superior to the state apparatus; (4) party control over the military; (5) prevalence of police and security organs as means of control; (6) state domination over civil society; specifically, autonomous secondary and voluntary associations, such as unions, churches, parties, etc., which together constitute civil society, no longer exist. On the other hand, Friedrich's (and others') stress on the "unique" nature of the form, as well as on the importance of an eschatological ideology, is absent in Gramsci's Caesarism. While Gramsci saw the novelty of the mass party in modern politics, he did not recognize until much later a point that Mussolini quickly grasped: the potential for turning the mass party into a vehicle of modern dictatorship. See, for example, the essay by Carl J. Friedrich, "The Unique Character of Totalitarian Society," in Carl J. Friedrich, ed., *Totalitarianism*; Karl D. Bracher, "Totalitarianism," *Dictionary of the History of Ideas* 4:406–11; and Franz Neumann, "Notes on the Theory of Dictatorship," in his *The Democratic and the Authoritarian State: Essays in Political and Legal Theory* (Glencoe, Ill., 1964).

Neumann, of course, identifies three forms of dictatorship: simple, Caesaristic, and totalitarian. Gramsci's Caesarism encompasses the latter two, but distinguishes between modern and nonmodern forms. What they have in common (except for Neumann's simple form) is the necessity of addressing the people or the "mass" as a variable in the power equation.

Caesarism is the result of a breakdown of hegemony and civil society, of an imbalance in the relation between civil society and political society. In other words, what Gramsci calls the organization of permanent consent – the beliefs, ideas, and ideals of a society that, when embodied as habits and "norms of conduct," provide the conventional underpinning to social and political power[46] – has become fragile, and is disintegrating. Gramsci's notes on Caesarism are not merely the most sophisticated writings on the subject within the Marxist tradition, but they also express a more subtle and sophisticated political theory of domination and subordination than that presented by classical Marxist thought.

The link that Gramsci establishes between regressive Caesarism and the crises of authority and of hegemony enables him to formulate a critique of Fascism based on the historical and political weakness of the state and society established by the Italian Risorgimento. It was possible to establish a political and cultural connection between Fascism and Italian liberalism, not in the typical reductionist manner of Leninists and Stalinists, but through a subtle and ironic analysis of the underlying social and cultural bases of Italian liberalism. The critique, in effect, asserts that Fascism evolved from liberalism in Italy because the Italian ruling class was not liberal and capitalist in the same manner as the ruling classes in Britain, France, and the United States. Paradoxically, Gramsci's critique is closer in substance to Anglo-American criticisms of Fascism than it is to those of his Marxist contemporaries. Gramsci's critique of Italian liberalism is basically a lament that it was not liberal enough: It could not construct a modern state capable of further liberal development and broadly democratic expansion.

The "crisis of the modern state" takes place when the ruling groups are shorn of their "spiritual prestige and power" so that their rule is reduced to maintaining their "economic-corporate" interests, which, in turn, reveals the narrow, particularistic character of the state.[47] A major crisis may thus occur when the "ruling class has failed in some major political undertaking for which it has requested, or forcibly extracted, the consent of the broad masses (war, for example), or because huge masses . . . have passed suddenly from a state of political passivity to a certain activity, and put forward demands which taken together . . . add up to revolution."[48] Such a political state of affairs, where the sequence of factors and the interaction of the opposing forces are contingent and unpredictable, is precisely what defines a revolutionary situation.

---

46 Gramsci, *SPN*, 344.   47 Ibid., 270.
48 Ibid., 210.

Gramsci goes on to say that the outcome is neither determined nor inevitable: the crisis of the state may lead to revolution, or it may lead to Caesarism.[49] What determines the ultimate result is the relative balance of power (or "relations of force") of the contending forces as well as the level of organization and consciousness of the opposing groups (the nature of the relation between leaders and led). The subordinate groups, given their political, organizational, and technical skills and experience, are generally less prepared than the ruling classes to respond effectively and decisively to the contingencies of events. At the same time, Gramsci notes that every ruling social group is an alliance or bloc of competing and unequal interests, each with different ideologies and beliefs, and during a crisis of authority the dominant bloc may become unstable. One interest may see Caesarism as the solution to the crisis, thus leading to a struggle for power within the ruling social-political bloc. In this case, the emergence of Caesarism is not so much the result of the activity of the subordinate groups, but rather of the opposition of groups within the dominant bloc. Gramsci cites the Dreyfus affair as an example of such a conflict within the dominant bloc of alliances.[50]

Whether the solution to the hegemonic crisis of the state is Caesarist or revolutionary, it is evident that Gramsci's analysis of such a crisis contradicts his original formulation of Caesarism as expressing a "situation in which the forces in conflict balance each other in a catastrophic manner" in such a way that "their reciprocal destruction" leads to the emergence of a "third force" from outside. In both cases, progressive Caesarism and revolution, a crisis of hegemony sets up a structural situation in which the outcome of the struggle among the various social forces is a fundamental transformation of the entire society, an innovating movement from one structure to another. Yet, in progressive Caesarism, structural change occurs through the mutual exhaustion of pre-existing forces and the consequent intervention of an external third force, while in revolution it issues from the victory of the subordinate group over its once dominant antagonist.

It is difficult to distinguish revolution conceived as the overthrow of an established ruling class or social bloc by a newly hegemonic and dominant group from Caesarism of the progressive/qualitative type. Moreover, it is also difficult to distinguish the new order established by the victorious revolution from that established by a progressive Caesarist dictatorship.

The difficulty arises out of Gramsci's revision of the classical Marxist conception of the state. The state is no longer simple coercion, no longer

---

49 Ibid.   50 Ibid., 223.

the organized force of the ruling class used to maintain its supremacy over the subordinate groups. As Gramsci notes, no state can maintain its stability and permanence without establishing mechanisms to generate legitimating institutions by which the consent of the population is mobilized. Thus, his conception of the state is basically Hegelian: The "integral State" is a synthesis of dictatorship and hegemony, political society and civil society, in which the first element of each pair represents the moment of force and the second the moment of consent. Consequently, this concept of rule is the synthesis of domination (organized coercion) and moral and intellectual leadership.

Revolutionary or Caesarist solutions to crises of authority within the state are obviously conditioned by the nature of the relation between dictatorship and hegemony, and between political society and civil society. What now becomes crucial is the structure of civil society, its differentiation and articulation into relatively complex associations and institutions, and its consequent level of interwoven layers of structures and functions. The more complex the articulation of structure within civil society, the stronger the legitimating institutions, the more the state appears as ethical and cultural, and the less it appears as the organization of coercion. Hegemony, therefore, is precisely the structural and institutional dissemination of cultural, ideological, and moral ways of thinking and believing throughout state and civil society.

These distinctions together describe a movement from Marx's and Lenin's dictatorship of the proletariat to Gramsci's hegemony and his concept of moral and intellectual leadership. In the works of Marx and Lenin, rule is seen as the dictatorship of a particular class. Thus, formally speaking, there is little difference between a bourgeois and a proletarian dictatorship. The major difference resides in the class content or nature of the dictatorship: one is of the minority (or oligarchic), the other is of the majority (or democratic). However, both constitute the organized and coercive power of the ruling class.

Although Gramsci's formulations retain the fundamentally Marxist class character of the state and of rule generally, they nevertheless constitute a major formal and methodological break with both Marx and Lenin. To a Marxist, as with the ancient Greeks, politics is always class politics, that is, a politics of friend/enemy. In the famous discussion in the first book of Plato's *Republic*, where Polemarchus and Thrasymachus see politics and justice as arising out of the conflict between friend and foe, the polis is always a divided and contested space, not one but two cities. It is within the battle line drawn between the forces of oligarchy and democracy that tyranny is generated. Machiavelli's new prince is a brilliant reformulation of the Platonic and Aristotelian critique of tyranny. For Aristotle, Machiavelli, and Marx, no less than for Gramsci, state and society (or the "integral State") are always fields of battle and conflict, sometimes violent and brutal, most often ideological and cultural. Gramsci's conceptual move from dictatorship to hegemony, and from domination to hegemony, tries to modernize Marx (and westernize Lenin) in order to account and allow for the sophisticated structures of economic and political power in the modern, especially Western, world.

Gramsci's distinction between domination and moral and intellectual leadership, cited above, bears repeating. Gramsci asserts, "A social group is dominant over those antagonistic groups it wants to 'liquidate' or to subdue even with armed force, and is leading with respect to those groups that are associated and allied with it."[51] Such a distinction, at a theoretical level, is quite conventional, not to say traditional. Witness Plato's linking of power to reason, Cicero's relation between rhetoric and politics, and Machiavelli's metaphor of the centaur: Every state combines elements of force and consent, violence and persuasion.

Gramsci is not merely defining power in general or identifying the theoretical bases of rule. Nor is he referring to conflict and competition that occur within an already established socio-political structure. Conflict takes place not within the structure, but over the structure, or rather, the conflict is to determine the nature of structural transformation itself. Thus, power is exercised both over and against opponents who are also enemies, and it takes the form of domination or dictatorship; power is also exercised over opponents who are not enemies, but (possible and potential) allies and associates, and it takes the form of leadership. These two ways of exercising power, one arbitrary and despotic, the other hegemonic and "moral and intellectual," correspond to Plato's two cities, to Machiavelli's *umori*, and to Marx's classes. The movement from one structure to another is characterized by uncertainty, instability, unpredictability, and violence (what Machiavelli would subsume under the category of *fortuna*).

Gramsci's Caesarism combines two major schools or traditions. First, like Marx and Engels's Bonapartism, Gramsci's Caesarism is class-based, and it is thus inserted within the general struggle of the classes and is the product of their immaturity and mutual exhaustion. Second, Gramsci's distinctions between hegemony and dictatorship, and between domination and moral and intellectual leadership constitute a more textured and complex notion

---

51 Gramsci, QC, 3:19, 2010.

of politics and state. In fact, these dichotomies describe a conceptual turn away from dictatorship as the defining characteristic of class rule and as class despotism *tout court*. The pivot of this turn is the concept of hegemony, rule understood as the generation and organization of consent by the transformation of narrow economic interests into interests general and universal enough to attract the adherence of multiple groups. Hegemonic rule, in other words, is defined not simply by the class or group that exercises power, but also by the method employed in the exercise of power. The class content is no longer sufficient to determine the nature of rule; the form of rule has now become crucial. Thus, Gramsci has moved from the merely social or economic to the political. Gramsci's thought recalls, though obliquely, the classical concerns of traditional liberal and republican thought: the problem of legitimate power and the differences between constitutional and tyrannical regimes, questions which bring to mind the ancient contrast between despotic and political forms of rule. The concept of hegemony harks back to the Aristotelian and Ciceronian ideas of the polis and the *civitas* as well as to the factional strife and class struggles that, by introducing the "third force" of tyranny and dictatorship, destroyed the polity.

It is in these senses that Gramsci's Caesarism is a political form that arises out of a "crisis of authority" or a "crisis of hegemony." Moreover, it is not a static form. It has various gradations, beginning with a compromise or coalition government that may or may not, depending on the resilience of the hegemonic class and its state institutions, eventuate into a "more permanent and purer" form of Caesarism. That form of Caesarism combines elements of the coercive and administrative organs of the state (the military, police, and security bureaucracies) with its ideological and cultural apparatus (mass media, mass communication, and mass mobilization). The coercive power of the state is expressed preeminently by the police and security organs, although the military (in the form of the officer corps) is never absent.

There is no question about the class nature of Gramsci's Caesarism. It is located within the struggle of the classes for domination and control over the state and the economy. However, unlike traditional Marxist theorists, Gramsci is more attuned to modern forms of mass electoral politics and representative government, and also to modern bureaucratic organizations. To point to the class nature of Gramsci's Caesarism is also to point to its fundamentally republican underlying character.

Caesarism is a political form that acquires force and meaning only within the context of a republican politics defined by the contest of opposing factions within an open and public space constituted by a formally free citizenry. Republican institutions establish a protective and insulating buttress which surrounds the organized violence and coercive power that form the core of public and state power. As such, the rise of Caesarism signals a degeneration and corruption of a free and republican politics, that is, a crisis of hegemony and authority.

9

From Constitutional Technique to Caesarist Ploy

Carl Schmitt on Dictatorship, Liberalism, and Emergency Powers

JOHN P. MCCORMICK

Carl Schmitt begins *Dictatorship*,[1] his classic work of 1921, by distinguishing the political institution of the title from Bonapartism and Caesarism. However, Schmitt himself eventually conflates dictatorship with Caesarism, somewhat cryptically by the end of the book, more directly in his next book, and unequivocally over the course of his Weimar career. This chapter explicates Schmitt's theory of dictatorship, especially his distinction between "commissarial" and "sovereign" dictatorship, and his diagnosis of the abuse or desuetude of the concept in the twentieth century; examines the extent to which, and attempts to explain the reasons why, Schmitt's doctrine of dictatorship eventually collapses into Caesarism; and evaluates the validity of Schmitt's charge that liberal constitutionalism is incapable of dealing with the kind of political circumstances that call for dictatorship.

DICTATORSHIP BETWEEN MARXISM AND LIBERALISM

Schmitt's argument in *Dictatorship* hinges on the theoretical-historical distinction between the traditional concept of "commissarial" dictatorship and the modern one of "sovereign" dictatorship. The two are separated by a conceptual distinction, on the one hand, but, on the other, joined by the historical transformation of one into the other in modernity. Commissarial dictatorship, as practiced in the Roman Republic and championed by Machiavelli,[2] was limited in its exercise during emergency circumstances by

---

This essay is an extensively revised and considerably expanded elaboration of Chapter 3 of my *Carl Schmitt's Critique of Liberalism: Against Politics as Technology* (Cambridge, 1997).

1 Schmitt, *Die Diktatur: Von den Anfängen des modernen Souveränitätsgedankens bis zum proletarischen Klassenkampf* (Berlin, 1989), hereafter *D*.
2 Niccolò Machiavelli, *The Discourses on Livy*, trans. Harvey C. Mansfield and Nathan Tarcov, I, 34 (Chicago, 1996), 73–5.

allotted time, specified task, and the fact that the dictator had to restore the previously standing political-legal order that had authorized the dictatorship. Sovereign dictatorship, as encouraged by both modern absolutist and revolutionary political practices, is unlimited in its parameters and may, and likely will, proceed to establish a completely new order as a result of its exercise.[3]

Schmitt identifies the Roman dictatorships of Caesar and Sulla as "sovereign," because they used emergency powers to change the constitutional order of Rome for their own personal political agendas. However, it was not until the development of the modern notion of sovereignty that individuals like Cromwell and Bonaparte or political bodies like those of revolutionary France could use military force and claims to represent the whole or the "real" people to abrogate an old order and institute a new one. As unlimited as the means available to a Roman dictator *within* his commission to address an emergency such as a rebellion, war, or famine were, there was a strict boundary in his requirement to return the polity to a situation of *status quo ante*. In other words, commissarial dictatorship must seek to "make itself superfluous."[4] Sovereign dictatorship, on the other hand, seeks to perpetuate itself, even if it uses its power under the pretense of merely "temporary" circumstances.

I will not recapitulate the details of Schmitt's account of how commissarial dictatorship gives way to sovereign dictatorship, or even transmutes into it. What is more pertinent here is Schmitt's understanding of why he takes up such a project at this point in the early twentieth century. There are obvious reasons of historical context: In the new political order of the Weimar Republic, first Reichspräsident Friedrich Ebert made extensive use of emergency powers at the time of the composition of *Dictatorship* to address right-wing and communist rebellion as well as an overwhelming economic crisis.[5] However, there are broader world historical motivations at issue for Schmitt as well.

According to Schmitt, liberals, to the extent that they pay attention to the concept at all, completely misapprehend dictatorship. What Schmitt

---

[3] On Schmitt's appropriation of the etymological-theoretical distinction of "commissarial" and "sovereign" from Jean Bodin, and a general discussion of the thesis, see George Schwab, *The Challenge of The Exception: An Introduction to the Political Ideas of Carl Schmitt between 1921 and 1936* (Westport, 1989), 30–1.

[4] *D*, xvi.

[5] See Frederick Mundell Watkins, *The Failure of Constitutional Emergency Powers under the German Republic* (Cambridge, 1939); Clinton Rossiter, *Constitutional Dictatorship: Crisis Government in Modern Democracies* (Princeton, 1948); and Hans Boldt, "Article 48 of the Weimar Constitution, Its Historical and Political Implications," in Anthony Nicholls and Erich Matthias, eds., *German Democracy and the Triumph of Hitler* (London, 1971), 42–63.

calls the "bourgeois political literature" either ignores the concept of dictatorship altogether or treats it as a slogan to be used against its opponents.[6] Liberals have completely forgotten its classical meaning and associate the idea and institution solely with "sovereign" dictatorship: "a distinction is no longer maintained between dictatorship and Caesarism, and the essential determination of the concept is marginalized... dictatorship's commissarial character."[7] Liberals deem a dictator to be any single individual, often democratically acclaimed, ruling through a centralized administration with little political constraint, and they equate dictatorship unreflectively with authoritarianism, Caesarism, Bonapartism, military government, and even the Papacy.[8] This inattention and misapprehension rules out an important resource for constitutionalists, liberal or conservative, in the present time of crisis and allows dictatorship to be misused by those who would put it to less than "classical" ends.

Schmitt is alarmed that the concept of dictatorship seems to be taken seriously only by the communists with their doctrine of the "dictatorship of the proletariat."[9] The communists have the concept partially right in classical terms, according to Schmitt, for they recognize its purely technical and temporary characteristics: The dictatorship of the proletariat is "the means for the implementation of the transition to the communists' final goal."[10] The revolutionary seizure of the state by the proletariat is not "definitive" for the communists, according to their ideology, but rather "transitional."[11] Schmitt notes that one might then see the communist theory of dictatorship as simply a modern incarnation of the classical institution. But this obscures the truly fundamental transformation of the essence of the classical concept: The communist institution employs temporary means to create a new situation, the classical institution employed them to restore a previously existing one.[12]

This difference has important ramifications for the question of just how limited a dictatorship can be if it is legitimated and bound by a *future* situation as opposed to being legitimated by a *previously existing* one. The communist dictatorship represents for Schmitt the culmination of the modern historical trend toward totally unrestrained political action: The radical orientation of modern politics is driven by a fervor to bring about some future good, whose qualities are so vague as to justify unbounded means in the achievement

---

6 *D*, xi–xii.
7 Ibid., xiii.
8 Ibid.
9 Ibid.
10 Ibid., xiv.
11 Ibid.
12 For an excellent analysis of dictatorship in Marx and Engels, see Peter Baehr, *Caesar and the Fading of the Roman World: A Study in Republicanism and Caesarism* (London, 1998), 131ff.

of the end. Schmitt distrusts the general historical development by which the concepts of sovereignty, increasingly popular sovereignty, and emergency action are merged, culminating in the theorists of the French Revolution, such as Mably and Sieyès. In Schmitt's view, they advocate a sovereign dictatorship that destroys an old order and creates a new one *not* on the authority of a specific constitutional arrangement or legal charge, but rather as the agent of a vague entity such as the "people."[13]

In the conclusion of *Dictatorship*, Schmitt returns to the communist use of the term dictatorship, for he clearly sees the communists as the heirs of the French Revolution: a radical elite that (a) will use violent means, (b) in step with supposedly world-historical processes, (c) according to the sanction of an anointed populace to which it can never really be held accountable. Schmitt writes,

> The concept of dictatorship ... as taken up in the presentations of Marx and Engels was realized at first as only a generally requisite political slogan ... But the succeeding tradition ... infused a clear conception of 1793 into the year 1848, and indeed not only as the sum of political experience and methods. As the concept developed in systematic relationship to the philosophy of the nineteenth century and in political relationship with the experience of world war a particular impression must remain. ... Viewed from a general state theory, dictatorship by a proletariat identified with the people as the overcoming of an economic condition, in which the state "dies out," presupposes a sovereign dictatorship, as it underlies the theory and practice of the National Convention. Engels, in his speech to the Communist Union in March 1850 demanded that its practice be the same as that of "France 1793." That is also valid for the theory of the state which posits the transition to statelessness.[14]

In other words, the dangerous spirit of France in 1793, a spirit of sovereign dictatorship in the name of a newly sovereign people, a spirit that culminates for Schmitt only in domestic terror and continental war, was radicalized in the revolutions of 1848. Now it is embodied by the new Soviet power to Germany's east and by the German revolutionary organizations that, at the very moment that Schmitt wrote *Dictatorship*, were attempting to seize the German state.

The tone of Schmitt's conclusion differs significantly enough from that of the preface and the body of the work such that we can detect a subtle yet distinct change in his strategy. Schmitt's preface seemed to suggest that his goal was: (1) to make up for the scholarly deficiency in the "bourgeois literature" on the subject of dictatorship; (2) to render it possible to deem the communist use of the term dictatorship "sovereign" in

---

13 *D*, 145.   14 Ibid., 205.

essence, and hence somehow illegitimate; and (3) to offer a more legitimate, constitutional, "commissarial" alternative with which the new republic might tackle the barrage of emergencies with which it was assaulted. Again, the communists understand the classical notion of dictatorship but tamper with it so as to *eliminate* the kinds of legal constitutional orders that require such an institution for their preservation. Liberals ignore or mischaracterize it and thus aid and abet the communists and their designs. However, Schmitt intimates toward the close of *Dictatorship* that perhaps what should confront the sovereign notion of dictatorship, touted by domestic and foreign revolutionaries, is not a notion of commissarial dictatorship at all, but perhaps a counter-theory of sovereign dictatorship. Since both absolutism and mass democracy arise out of the same historical movement, Schmitt suggests, gently and furtively, that perhaps a radicalized notion of sovereignty derived from absolute monarchy should meet the radicalized notion of sovereignty derived from the French Revolution.[15]

Schmitt intimates that, due to the trajectory of modern history, the conjunction of emergency powers and mass socio-political movements as embodied in the revolutionary/counterrevolutionary moments of 1832 and 1848 ought not to be severed. A revival of the notion of commissarial emergency powers would enact such a divorce. Additionally, the return of powerful social groups threatening the state in the form of working-class movements ought to be met by a political response new and yet akin to the way that the absolute monarchs had earlier neutralized or destroyed aristocratic and religious groups. Finally, the populist Soviet state that can be directed to do almost anything by an all-powerful, unaccountable, historically legitimated elite should be engaged by a similarly defined German state directed by a charismatically, and plebiscitarily, legitimated president. These are conclusions implicitly suggested, not explicitly argued, in the closing pages of *Dictatorship*.

Thus, Schmitt grapples with the dilemma that the concept of dictatorship is being pulled radically leftward by the success of Bolshevism and the vacuum that liberals have created with respect to constitutional dictatorship on their side of the spectrum. Liberals, those who are most concerned with constitutionalism in the contemporary world, have forsaken

---

15 On the relationship between the theory of sovereignty during the French Revolution and Schmitt's own (*D*, 203–4), see Stefan Breuer, "Nationalstaat und pouvoir constituant bei Sieyès und Carl Schmitt," *Archiv für Rechts- und Sozialphilosophie* LXX (1984), 175–96; and Pasquale Pasquino, "Die Lehre vom pouvoir constituant bei Abbe Sieyès und Carl Schmitt: Ein Beitrag zur Untersuchung der Grundlagen der modernen Demokratietheorie," in Helmut Quaritsch, ed., *Complexio Oppositorum: Über Carl Schmitt* (Berlin, 1988), 48–62. I would argue that Schmitt is trying to re-absolutize the revolutionary concept of popular sovereignty as much as appropriate it.

this constitutionally crucial institution and allowed it to be abducted and reprogrammed by their enemies on the left. Communists are pressing for emergency, populist constitutional change with various versions of the dictatorship of the proletariat. Liberals are neither able nor willing to defend a viable theory and practice of dictatorship in its classical sense even in the midst of such crisis-ridden times. They refuse to resort to the time- and task-specific temporary measures necessitated by the same economic and political crises that the left uses as occasion and justification to overhaul centuries-old dynasties and new republican constitutional systems.[16]

As we examine Schmitt's developing theory of dictatorship in the next section, I argue that Schmitt seeks to push liberal constitutionalism definitively aside as politically ineffectual and obstructionist in the face of the leftist appropriation of dictatorship. To do so, he develops a right-wing Caesarism to combat the vitality of what he sees as the left-wing Caesarism of Bolshevism, a counternotion of dictatorship that is as substantive, all-encompassing, misleadingly "temporary" yet just as constitutionally abrogating as that of the communists. Schmitt effectively argues that since the liberal imagination can do no more than conflate dictatorship with Caesarism, this conflation is exactly what the liberals deserve, and Schmitt will be the one to give it to them.

In his next book, *Political Theology*, Schmitt espouses a notion of sovereignty embodied in the *Reichspräsident*, who is not encumbered by constitutional restraints but only the demands of a political exception. The president, as the personal embodiment of the popular will that can not be procedurally ascertained in a time of crisis, has the democratically charismatic authority to act – unconstitutionally or even anticonstitutionally, with all the force and legitimacy of that originary popular will.[17] Schmitt advances the very fusing of popular sovereignty and emergency powers that he showed to be potentially abusive in *Dictatorship*.

---

16 Schmitt protests too much. He makes it sound as if his case for dictatorship against liberalism is more difficult than it actually is, as his prescriptions conform with a powerful sociological reality: Schmitt's call for Caesarism was likely to be received warmly by a Weimar bourgeoisie that was no longer so readily inclined toward liberalism. See the devastating analysis of Schmitt, his intellectual circle, and the German bourgeoisie by Siegfried Kracauer: "Revolt of the Middle Classes" (1931), in Kracauer, *The Mass Ornament: Weimar Essays*, trans. and ed. Thomas Y. Levin (Cambridge, 1995), 107–28.

17 Space constraints do not permit a discussion of the significance of Schmitt's continued engagement with Max Weber's political and legal sociology on this topic. The most extensive and incisive discussion of Caesarism and charisma in Weber is Baehr, *Caesar and the Fading of the Roman World*, chap. 4.

COMMISSARIAL OR CAESARIST DICTATORSHIP?

One of the central aims of Schmitt's Weimar work is to justify sovereign dictatorial powers for the *Reichspräsident* of the Republic. Does Schmitt's formulation of presidential sovereign dictatorship conform with Caesarism? If the latter concept can be understood in terms of a single leader who claims to represent an entire people as a result of plebiscite, who maintains his authority through powerful military authority and extensive bureaucratic machinery, then the answer is, as this section demonstrates, yes.[18]

The first sentence of *Political Theology*, published the year after *Dictatorship*, signals Schmitt's endorsement of something much closer to sovereign than commissarial dictatorship: "Sovereign is he who decides on the exception" (*Souverän ist, wer über den Ausnahmezustand entscheidet*).[19] Schmitt celebrates the very merging of the normal and exceptional moments that in *Dictatorship* he analyzed as a politically pathological element of sovereign dictatorship. He even encourages it with the ambiguous use of the preposition "on" (*über*), which belies the distinction that he himself acknowledges in the earlier book between, on the one hand, the body that decides that an exceptional situation exists (in the Roman case, the Senate through the consuls) and, on the other, the person appointed by that body to decide what to do in the concrete particulars of the emergency, the dictator himself. The two separate decisions, one taking place in the moment of normalcy, the other in the moment of exception, are lumped together and then hidden behind the ostensible directness of Schmitt's opening statement in *Political Theology*. Indeed, further on in the work Schmitt explicitly and deliberately conflates the two decisions: The sovereign "decides whether there is an extreme emergency *as well as* what must be done to eliminate it."[20]

There is also no attempt in *Political Theology* to prescribe what fundamental time- (or task-) related limits might be imposed on a sovereign's action in the exceptional situation; Schmitt suggests that this is, in fact, impossible because an exception "cannot be circumscribed factually and made to conform to a preformed law... The preconditions as well as the content of a jurisdictional competence in such a case must necessarily be unlimited."[21] Rather than restoring a previous order in an emergency, the emergency

---

18 I draw somewhat loosely on the more refined tracing of Bonapartism and Caesarism to fascism by Luisa Mangoni, "Per una definizione del fascismo: I concetti di bonapartismo e cesarismo," *Italia Contemporanea* 31 (1979), 17–52.
19 *Political Theology: Four Chapters on the Theory of Sovereignty* (1922), trans. George Schwab (Cambridge, 1986), 5, hereafter *PT*; German references correspond to *Politische Theologie: Vier Kapitel zur Lehre von der Souveränität* (München, 1934), here 11.
20 *PT*, 7 (emphasis added). 21 Ibid., 6–7.

actor *is* the order itself made dramatically manifest by a crisis: "It is precisely the exception that makes relevant the subject of sovereignty, that is, the whole question of sovereignty."[22] According to the commissarial notion of dictatorship, the dictator was free to do whatever was necessary in the particular exceptional moment to address an unforeseen crisis that is identified by a different and regular institution. And the dictator was bound as a "precondition" to return the government to that law within a specific period of time. Schmitt occludes these crucial distinctions in the second more famous work and expands the unlimitedness of dictatorship by renouncing the very characteristics of the classical model he only recently admired as well as those of the liberal constitutionalism he now consistently derides: "If measures undertaken in an exception could be circumscribed by mutual control, by imposing a time limit, or finally, as in the liberal constitutional procedure governing a state of siege, by enumerating extraordinary powers, the question of sovereignty would then be considered less significant."[23] Indeed, his use of the term "sovereign" implies some kind of lawmaking or lawgiving power that could change the previous order or even create a new one.

The conclusion that one is compelled to draw from *Political Theology* is that a regime with institutional diversity, with a constitutionally enumerated "division and mutual control of competences"[24] – or what is more generally known as separation of powers – inevitably paralyzes a state in the face of an exception because it obscures who is sovereign, who must decide and act at that moment.[25] According to Schmitt's formulation, in all cases of emergency it would seem necessary to have recourse to a unitary institution with a monopoly on decisions so that no such confusion or conflict occurs. Thus, in violation of the main principles of classical dictatorship, normalcy and exception are collapsed, and ordinary rule of law and constitutional structure are dangerously encroached upon by exceptional absolutism.

---

22 Ibid.
23 In *Dictatorship* Schmitt observes that the military state of siege is the closest thing to commissarial dictatorship allowed by liberal theory, but even this is conflated with sovereign dictatorship (*D*, xiv). Schmitt distinguishes between dictatorship and a military state of siege most extensively in "Diktatur und Belagerungszustand: Eine staatsrechtliche Studie," *Zeitschrift für die gesamte Strafrechtswissenschaft* 38 (1917), 138–61. For an excellent discussion of the essay, see Peter C. Caldwell, *Popular Sovereignty and the Crisis of German Constitutional Law: The Theory and Practice of Weimar Constitutionalism* (Durham, 1997), 54–8. Caldwell's interpretation of this essay suggests that Schmitt turned to the notion of commissarial dictatorship after it became clear that the state of siege had been irrevocably linked with dictatorship in a sovereign sense. As I argue above, Schmitt abandons commissarial dictatorship as well once he realizes that it too can no longer be extricated from "sovereign" connotations. Schmitt's own capitulation to sovereign dictatorship hence serves to radicalize his theory from conservatism to fascism. Also, *PT*, 12.
24 *PT*, 11. 25 Ibid., 7.

In later practical political treatises that deal with emergency powers written during Weimar, such as "The Dictatorship of the *Reichspräsident* According to Article 48 of the Weimar Constitution" (1924), *The Guardian of the Constitution* (1931), and *Legality and Legitimacy* (1932), Schmitt continues to argue that only the *Reichspräsident* can defend the Weimar constitutional regime during a crisis.[26] The "Article 48" piece of 1924 is not so obviously an endorsement of sovereign dictatorship.[27] Schmitt declares that according to Article 48 "dictatorial authority" is only "lent" to the president, and he seemingly argues that the scope of that authority should remain within a commissarial rubric.[28] However, after that commissarial gesture, Schmitt makes it clear that he does not want *too* extensive and explicit limitations on the emergency powers of the president because "it is a dangerous abuse to use the constitution to delineate all possible affairs of the heart as basic law and quasi-basic law."[29] Moreover, Schmitt's descriptions of the source of the president's legitimacy in preserving the constitution in "Article 48" increasingly sound as though they were mandated *not* by the constitutional order itself, but by something like a sovereign will that is itself *prior* to that order: "The dictatorship of the *Reichspräsident* ... is necessarily commissarial as a result of specific circumstances ... In as much as it is allowed to act so broadly, it operates (in fact, not in its legal establishment) as the residue of the sovereign dictatorship of the National Assembly [which created the constitution]."[30]

At the conclusion of the essay, Schmitt recalls the framing of Article 48 at the Republic's constitutional founding: "In the Summer of 1919 when

---

26 Respectively, "Die Diktatur des Reichspräsident nach Art. 48 der Weimarer Verfassung" (1924), appended to subsequent editions of *Dictatorship*, 213–59, and thus hereafter *DII*; *Der Hüter der Verfassung* (Tübingen, 1931), hereafter *HV*; and *Legalität und Legitimität* (1932), hereafter *LL*, from the reprint in Schmitt, *Verfassungsrechtliche Aufsätze aus den Jahren 1924–1954: Materialien zu einer Verfassungslehre* (Berlin, 1958), 263–350. An English translation of *Legalität und Legitimität* by Jeffrey Seitze will be published in 2004.

27 In general, there is little scholarly consensus on the exact moment of Schmitt's conversion to sovereign dictatorship: Renato Cristi, for instance, locates it already in the 1921 main text of *Dictatorship*, while Stanley L. Paulson dates it even after the 1924 "Article 48" essay: see Cristi, "Carl Schmitt on Sovereignty and Constituent Power," in David Dyzenhaus, ed., *Law as Politics* (Durham, 1998), 179–95; and Paulson, "The Reich President and Weimar Constitutional Politics: Aspects of the Schmitt-Kelsen Dispute on the 'Guardian of the Constitution'" (paper presented at the Annual Meeting of the American Political Science Association, Chicago, Aug. 31–Sept. 3, 1995). Compare also Gabriel Negretto and Jose Antonio Aguilar, "Schmitt, Liberalism and Emergency Powers in Latin America," and Oren Gross, "Rethinking the Myth of Schmitt's 'Norm-Exception' Dichotomy," in *Cardozo Law Review* 21, no. 5 (2000); 1825.68. I must emphasize that my interpretation of *Dictatorship* does *not* rule out the presence of a sovereign-dictatorial element in Schmitt's 1921 book. In other words, I do *not* conclude that the entire thrust of *Dictatorship*, as Cristi charges (194), promotes only "functional" and "temporary" dictatorship. See my discussion in the previous section and *Carl Schmitt's Critique of Liberalism*, 137–9.

28 *DII*, 255.   29 Ibid., 243.
30 Ibid., 241.

Article 48 came to be, one thing was clear: Germany found itself in a wholly abnormal crisis and therefore for the moment a one-time authority was necessary which made possible decisive action."[31] Schmitt calls for similar "abnormal" and "decisive" action, but attempts to allay the fears of those who might be concerned with the constitutional status of such action with his final sentence: "That would be no constitutional alteration."[32] In other words, he is not calling for constitution-abrogating action characteristic of sovereign dictatorship on the part of the president, but rather commissarial, constitutionally preserving action. Of course, his harkening back to the crisis in which the constitution was founded and to the preconstitutional constituting decision and *not* to the body of the constitution itself implies a repetition of a sovereign act of founding to save the constitution. This "rescue" may in fact entail changing the constitution as long as the preconstitutional will is not changed. Of course, Schmitt gives us no way of evaluating how a people might change their original will or demonstrate that they would prefer it not be altered at all. This strategy of justifying presidential dictatorial action on the basis of the preconstitutional sovereign will of the people and not the principles embodied within the constitution itself becomes more pronounced in his books *The Guardian of the Constitution* and *Legality and Legitimacy*, published in the wake of a second devastating economic depression and renewed widespread political unrest in the early 1930s.

Schmitt begins *Guardian* of 1931 in much the same way that he began his book on dictatorship exactly ten years earlier. He blames nineteenth-century liberalism for bringing a crucial constitutional institution into ill repute and he draws upon examples from classical Sparta and Rome to demonstrate the historical legitimacy of such a concept and authority. But whereas in *Dictatorship* the example that Schmitt is attempting to revive is commissarial dictatorship, in *Guardian* it is the notion of a defender of the constitution.[33] Indeed, the merging of the two phenomena (emergency powers and the question of in what institution sovereignty lies) is, again, just his strategy.[34]

The socio-economic fracturing of society that Schmitt attributes to an uncontrolled pluralism has rendered parliament superfluous and was threatening the very existence of the state: "The development toward an economic state was encountered by a simultaneous development of parliament into a stage for the pluralist system. In that lies the cause of the constitutional entanglement as well as the necessity for establishing a remedy and

---

31 Ibid., 258–9.   32 Ibid., 259.
33 *HV*, 7–9.
34 For a detailed account of this strategy, see Ingeborg Maus, *Bürgerliche Rechtstheorie und Faschismus: Zur sozialen Funktion und aktuellen Wirkung der Theorie Carl Schmitts* (München, 1980), 127–31.

countermovement."[35] However, this particular socio-economic situation that the president must address necessarily calls for activity that is substantially beyond commissarial action and restitution. In fact, it entails the wholesale redirecting of structural historical transformation on a macro-economic, social, and political scale; a redirecting that could never be met in the time- (and task-) bound fashion of commissarial dictatorship, but that must rather be met by the constitution amending of sovereign dictatorship.[36] Does Schmitt expect that he can address the wholesale reconstruction of the state society relationship that he describes in *Guardian* and not be perceived as simultaneously calling for the wholesale reconstruction of the Weimar constitution? No. Schmitt does not rely on the earlier example of President Ebert's temporary economic measures in the new republic, but rather speaks in terms of much more comprehensive change.

Thus, given the scale of the necessary state control of the economy, the presupposed doling out of social transfers through military service benefits rather than universal welfare provisions, the promotion of nationalism through mass media, and the achievement of cultural conformity through bureaucratic administration, Schmitt can be said to theorize the socially transformative aspects of Caesarism to another level. The redistributive/military projects of Julius Caesar, the Jacobins, and the Bonapartes are smaller scale and qualitatively less intrusive politically than Schmitt's reformulation of the state/society divide in his works of the early thirties. Schmitt disapproves of socially generated state intervention, whether liberal, social democratic, or Bolshevistic, but encourages state self-generated intervention characteristic of Mussolini's Fascism.[37]

In specific constitutional terms, this socio-economic agenda is to be achieved by dismantling or neutralizing the separation of powers. By marginalizing the other branches of government in *Guardian*, Schmitt cleverly removes any checks that could limit or shape the president's dictatorial actions in such a way as to give them any semblance of commissarial character. Schmitt admits that a working Reichstag would be an appropriate check on presidential emergency powers.[38] Since such a situation of parliamentary efficacy does not obtain in the socially tumultuous conditions of

---

35 *HV*, 117.
36 On the radically dynamic as opposed to statically conservative character of Schmitt's socio-economic proposals, see Maus, *Bürgerliche Rechtstheorie und Faschismus*, 109, 126; on the constitutionally abrogating ramifications of his political economy, see Jean Cohen and Andrew Arato, *Civil Society and Political Theory* (Cambridge, 1992), 231–41.
37 See McCormick, *Carl Schmitt's Critique of Liberalism*, 194, 229–44, 279–80.
38 *HV*, 130–1.

Weimar, he makes no effort to search for an alternative check. In fact, precisely because the president is plebiscitarily elected by the people there is no need for checks because the unity of the people's sovereign will is charismatically embodied within him and his emergency action is thus necessarily legitimate.[39] By the conclusion of *Guardian*, Schmitt has formulated a popularly legitimated sovereign dictatorship of the nation in the person of a purportedly charismatic German president that in essence mirrors the popularly legitimated sovereign dictatorship of the Soviet communist party. Schmitt counters the "dictatorship of the proletariat" with a "dictatorship of the nation." Presumably it is against the external enemy and its domestic partisans who champion the former dictatorship that Schmitt's national dictatorship is ready to take "action." The Weimar Constitution, concludes Schmitt,

> presupposes the entire German people as a unity which is immediately ready for action and not first mediated through social-group organization. It can express its will and at the decisive moment find its way back to unity and bring its influence to bear over and beyond pluralistic divisions. The constitution seeks especially to give the authority of the *Reichspräsident* the possibility of binding itself immediately with the political total will of the German people and precisely thereby to act as guardian and protector of the unity and totality of the German people.[40]

Schmitt emphasizes the partial, that is, democratically illegitimate quality of the de facto party dictatorship of Bolshevism. He hides the elitist, and hence equally partial and illegitimate, quality of his own formulation of a dictatorship of the president, which means in actuality, government of the aristocrats and corporate barons that surround *Reichspräsident* Hindenburg.

In 1932, just as the crisis of the Weimar Republic was reaching its climax, and just before Schmitt would endorse a more radical form of fascism as the ultimate solution to that crisis, Schmitt published the book-length essay, *Legality and Legitimacy*. Schmitt caps off the line of thought that he had been developing over the last decade such that it is almost completely impossible to identify in the book when he is talking about normal constitutional operations and when he is talking about emergency ones. The tension that Schmitt sees inherent in the Weimar constitution and that serves as the source for the book's title ("plebiscitary *legitimacy*" versus "statutory *legality*")[41] is definitively resolved in favor of the former. Schmitt resolves it on the basis of the historical necessity of a mass democratic moment, what Schmitt calls "the plebiscitary immediacy of the deciding people as

---

39 Ibid., 116, 156–7.   40 Ibid., 159.
41 *LL*, 312.

legislator."[42] The president, as conduit for such "immediacy," takes on authority similar to that of the traditional "extra-ordinary legislator" who may act "against the law."[43] The possibility of a commissarial dictatorship is no longer mentioned either as it was for substantive purposes in 1921 or as it was for cosmetic purposes in the mid-twenties. The unlimited extent of power that was previously reserved for extraordinary moments is now invoked as the ordinary competence of an executive answerable only to the acclamation of plebiscitary moments. In May 1933, Schmitt joined the National Socialist party.

For the purposes of this volume, Schmitt's theory is clearly important for better understanding the continuity and ruptures within the legacy of modern authoritarianism. However, Schmitt's writings pose something of a puzzle for those who wish to see the historical specificity of fascism within this legacy. After all, at the most abstract level, at the level of textual analysis alone, it is difficult to pinpoint what makes Schmitt's thought fascist, as opposed to absolutist or Bonapartist. His writings call for the rule of one person who embodies the popular will to maintain social order and to defend against external enemies. His persistent rhetoric insists on the state's separation from society so as to better maintain order within it. These arguments can be read in passive as opposed to aggressive terms. Students of Schmitt with *and* without neoconservative political agendas have read him in this way.

I would submit that were it not for our historical knowledge of Schmitt's complicity with the political strategies of, successively, Prussian military elites, Catholic aristocrats, and, finally, National Socialism, it would be difficult to decipher the specificities of Schmitt's practical program from his work alone. The case of Schmitt highlights the necessity of using sociological and historical methods along with those of textual political theory. Once we take into account Schmitt's political affiliations and practical engagements, we can begin to make some provisional comparisons. What is interesting about Schmitt's own brand of fascism is its combination of absolutist and Bonapartist/Caesarist elements. Schmitt's theory differs from Caesarism in its fundamentally reactionary quality. Caesar and Napoleon could claim to solve political crises while at the same time advancing the populist spirit of the regimes they overthrew. The more or less genuinely egalitarian social policies of the first Caesar and Bonaparte (notwithstanding the stultifying effects of those policies on the populace) do not exist in Schmitt's scheme.

Unlike theorists of absolutism, Schmitt celebrates popular sovereignty, even democracy. However, the authentic equality of "all before the one" in

---

42 Ibid., 314.   43 Ibid., 320.

Caesarism and Bonapartism is appropriated only rhetorically by Schmitt. The programs that he endorses serve cliques ruling through the presidency and policies that reinforce social hierarchy. Like absolutism then, Schmitt's position is far more tolerant in practice than it is in the theory of "intermediary bodies" that serve, rather than threaten, the state. Thus, while Caesarism and Bonapartism might be pathologically democratic, Schmitt's political theory and practice remind us that fascism is bogusly democratic.

LIBERALISM, EXCEPTIONS, AND THE SOVEREIGN DICTATORSHIP OF PROCEDURES

If we examine Schmitt's critique of liberalism with respect to dictatorship at its most abstract, we observe these two prongs of his assault: (1) liberals have no conception of the political exception because of scientistic delusion, a delusion that will lead to the collapse of constitutional regimes; and (2) if liberals concede that they do indeed have such a conception, they will necessarily resort to measures that are antiliberal to address such circumstances, thereby also endangering constitutional regimes. In this section, I evaluate these two aspects of Schmitt's critique of liberalism and political crisis. I conclude the section with Schmitt-informed reflections on Bruce Ackerman's liberal theory of crisis and constitutional change.

The first component of Schmitt's critique is grounded in his understanding of modernity: As Enlightenment political thought falls increasingly under the thrall of modern natural science, it comes to regard nature, and hence political nature, as a more regular phenomenon. Consequently, there is deemed less need for the discretionary and prudential powers, long conferred upon judges and executives by traditional political theories, including Aristotelianism and Scholasticism – discretion and prudence that found its extreme example in the case of classical dictatorship. As the functional necessity of such discretion apparently subsides in the Enlightenment, the normative assessment of it becomes increasingly negative, and such prudence becomes associated with arbitrariness and abuse of state power.

Schmitt compares the exception in constitutional theory to the miracle in theology: The latter is the direct intervention of God into the normal course of nature's activity, and the former is the occasion for the intervention of the sovereign into the normal legal order.[44] However, the "rationalism of the Enlightenment rejected the exception in every form."[45] Deism, with its

---

44 *PT*, 36–7.   45 Ibid., 37.

watchmaker God, who never interacts with the world after its creation, banished the miracle from religious thought; and liberalism, with its strict enumeration of governmental powers, rejected any political possibilities outside of those set forth within the parameters of its constitutions.[46] Schmitt's view of modern constitutionalism undergirded by the separation of powers is best reflected in his rather chilling remark, "The machine now runs by itself."[47]

The second prong of Schmitt's strategy becomes clearer in his discussion of John Locke: Schmitt remarks that the exception was "incommensurable" with Locke's theory of constitutionalism.[48] Locke's famous "prerogative" power is perhaps the best example of the notion of political prudence within liberalism:

'tis fit that the laws themselves should in some cases give way to the executive power... that as much as may be, all the members of the society are to be preserved... since many accidents may happen, wherein a strict and rigid observation of the law may do harm... [I]t is impossible to foresee, and so by laws provide for, all accidents and necessities, that may concern the public... therefore there is a latitude left to the executive power, to do many things of choice, which the laws do not prescribe.[49]

Contra Schmitt's account of the disappearance of the exception in modernity, Locke clearly does have an explicit notion of acting above or against the law in times of unforeseen occurrences. However, does this notion compromise his constitutionalism? The question of "commensurability," as Schmitt puts it, is important. Liberals may in fact admit the existence of exceptional situations, but the particular sharpness of Schmitt's point is whether they can address them without undermining constitutional principles.

The first and more historical part of Schmitt's critique has real merit, notwithstanding the prominence of the example of Locke. The post-Lockean theory of the separation of powers, particularly in the form that Montesquieu made so influential, is, as Schmitt suggested, unequivocally culpable in a somewhat mechanistic de-discretionizing of politics.[50] As Bernard Manin observes, "One of Montesquieu's most important

---

46 Ibid.
47 Ibid., 48.
48 Ibid., 13.
49 John Locke, "The Second Treatise on Government," XIV, 159, 15–19, in Locke, *Two Treatises on Government*, ed. Peter Laslett (Cambridge, 1988), 375 (spelling updated). Or as he defines it more succinctly later in the text: "Prerogative being nothing, but a power in the hands of the prince to provide for the public good, in such cases, which depending upon unforeseen and uncertain occurrences, certain and unalterable laws could not safely direct, whatsoever shall be done manifestly for the good of the people" (XIII, 158, 15–20, 373).
50 See Baron de Charles de Secondat Montesquieu, *The Spirit of the Laws*, ed. and trans. A. M. Cohler, B. C. Miller, and H. S. Stone, XI (Cambridge, 1989), 6.

innovations was precisely to do away with any notion of a discretionary power in his definition of the three governmental functions."[51] The pinnacle of Enlightenment constitutional engineering, the U.S. Constitution, is both the exemplar of sophisticated separation of powers and the most famous constitution not to have clearly enumerated provisions for emergency situations.[52] This is a powerful testament to liberalism's neglect of the political exception. It is this liberalism that Schmitt was most concerned to criticize for attempting to systematize all of political phenomena. In the essays defending the U.S. Constitution collected as *The Federalist Papers*,[53] it is interesting to observe the contrast between the papers written by principal framer, James Madison, the liberal technician who seeks to account for all possibilities by enumerating them or building them into the constitutional mechanism, and Alexander Hamilton, the proponent of political prerogative who seeks to keep open the possibility of exceptional circumstances. Schmitt, not surprisingly, criticizes the Madisonian *Federalist Papers* and praises the Hamiltonian ones.[54]

Liberalism's denial of the exception and avoidance of the discretionary activity that was traditionally sanctioned to deal with it not only makes liberal regimes susceptible to emergencies but also leaves them vulnerable to the more profound criticism leveled by Schmitt. As Manin formulates the problem, "Once the notion of prerogative power was abandoned, no possibility of legitimately acting beside or against the law was left."[55] Hence, the first aspect of Schmitt's critique coerces liberalism into entertaining the possibility of the second: that the only apparent recourse available to political actors confronted with a political exception is to act *illegitimately* and hope to pass off such action as legitimate. This is an outcome that would seriously

---

51 Bernard Manin, "Checks, Balances, and Boundaries: The Separation of Powers in the Constitutional Debate of 1787," in Biancamaria Fontana, ed., *The Invention of the Modern Republic* (Cambridge: Cambridge University Press, 1994), 41, n. 51. See also Manin, "Drawing a Veil over Liberty: The Language of Public Safety during the French Revolution." Paper presented at the Colloquium on Political and Social Thought, Columbia University, Sept. 1997.
52 I continue to focus on the U.S. context in what follows for these reasons, as well as the fact that the two other most prominent extant written constitutions, the French and German, include emergency powers provisions. Besides the fact that these constitutions are not "Enlightenment products," i.e., they were written after the eighteenth century, Schmitt and others would argue that they exhibit emergency power provisions to some extent *due to* the influence of Schmitt himself.
53 Alexander Hamilton, John Jay, and James Madison, *The Federalist Papers* (New York, 1961).
54 See Schmitt, *The Crisis of Parliamentary Democracy* (1923), trans. Ellen Kennedy (Cambridge, 1985), 40, 45.
55 Manin, "Checks, Balances, and Boundaries," 41. Albert Dicey even went as far as to define the rule of law exclusively as the opposite, not only of "arbitrariness," but also "of prerogative, or even of wide discretionary authority on the part of the government." See A. C. Dicey, *Introduction to the Study of the Law of the Constitution* ([1915] Indianapolis, 1982), 120.

undermine the overall legitimacy of liberal constitutionalism, an outcome clearly "incommensurable" with its principles.

For instance, here is one way to view the crisis of full-scale political rebellion in the American Civil War: Without recourse to specifically enumerated, constitutionally legitimated emergency provisions, President Abraham Lincoln was forced to stretch the traditional means of suspending habeas corpus far beyond reasonable limits, putting himself in the position of being called a tyrant in his sincere attempt to preserve the republic.[56] Constitutional enabling provisions would prevent a legitimately acting executive from running the risk of compromising his or her legitimacy at a time when it is most important. Further applying the Schmittian critique to the supposedly most de-discretionized constitutional model: U.S. President Franklin Roosevelt's well-known and perhaps overextended appeal to the "general welfare" clause of the preamble of the U.S. Constitution served as justification for dealing with the economic emergency of the Great Depression. Such a potentially far-fetched justification for emergency measures may in some respect compromise a constitution at the very moment when it is most threatened, should the appeal be successfully challenged as illegal and in fact illegitimate.

The "successes" of the emergency actors in these two crises in U.S. constitutional history should not be taken at face value as proof of the efficacy of *not* having constitutional emergency provisions. The political proficiency of a Lincoln or an FDR and the "prudence" allegedly characteristic of the American populace surely cannot be counted upon in all circumstances of crisis. Blind faith in the inevitable emergence of true "statesmen" and the acquiescence to them by an understanding "people" in times of crisis is as unreasonable and naive as is complete trust in purely constitutional means of addressing political emergencies consistently and rightfully derided by *Realpolitiker*. This is the perspective on liberal constitutionalism with which one is left after encountering Schmitt's critique, but one might disagree with it. Should this be the last word on the topic?

Recently, Bruce Ackerman has developed an ambitious theory of political crisis and constitutional change that confirms some, but challenges and repudiates many of Schmitt's charges against liberal constitutionalism.[57] Some critics have remarked upon certain ecstatic qualities of Ackerman's account that might be reminiscent of Schmitt. The fundamental differences

---

56 See R. J. Sharpe, *The Law of Habeas Corpus* (Oxford, 1991) and Mark E. Neely, Jr., *The Fate of Liberty* (Oxford, 1991).
57 Bruce Ackerman, *We the People 1: Foundations* (Cambridge, 1991); and *We the People 2: Transformations* (Cambridge, 1998), hereafter *WTP1* or *WTP2*.

between the two are manifested in: (1) Ackerman's reclaiming for liberalism from Schmitt's critique the separation of powers as an indispensable means for constitutional change; (2) his reassertion, contra Schmitt, of the transformative flexibility of the U.S. Constitution; and (3) his argument that the constitutional responses to the crises surrounding the Civil War and the New Deal conform fully with the spirit of constitutionalism and do not violate it as Schmitt's arguments would suggest.

There are certainly surface similarities between Ackerman and Schmitt. Both refer to political populaces in quasi-mystical ways: Ackerman has a propensity to capitalize "the People" in a reifying manner and even refers to them in "I am who am" fashion as "We the People." Ackerman, like Schmitt, concedes the illegality of constitutional foundings; a decision that creates a constitutional order is logically prior to, and can not be legally authorized by, that order. Also, Ackerman's distinction between normal and constitutional politics has certain Schmittian overtones. However, the differences between the two will show these similarities to be superficial and actual distractions from the way in which U.S. constitutional experience defies Schmitt's arguments in fundamental ways.[58]

Ackerman may confirm Schmitt's charge that liberals do not grasp the *immediate* quality of exceptions. Crises, as Ackerman understands them, develop over time and may be dealt with over extended periods of time as well. An emergency or an exception defined in a narrow sense that could be best addressed by commissarial dictatorship in classical terms, presumably may be dealt with in Ackerman's scheme by the enumerated and acquired prerogative powers of the president or even legislative measures. But Ackerman's model explicitly addresses the kind of large-scale social change that Schmitt's model only surreptitiously sought to address under the guise of attention to an immediately pressing situation. An exception, as Schmitt later develops the concept, means a changed socio-political landscape that the constitutional structure was not designed to address, but one that the "constitutional will" does, in fact, want addressed. Ackerman interprets the U.S. Constitution as being able to confront these changes through elaborate procedural means. Schmitt conflates the constitution to the one institution within its structure that could claim recent legitimation by the widest part of the population through the most direct means, the presidency.

---

58 Ackerman never mentions Schmitt in either volume of *WTP*, but sharply distinguishes his conceptions of democratic will and constitutional change from Schmitt's in "The Political Case for Constitutional Courts," in Bernard Yack, ed., *Liberalism Without Illusions: Essays on Liberal Theory and the Political Vision of Judith N. Shklar* (Chicago, 1996), 205–19.

Thus if Schmitt *conflates* immediately pressing emergency exceptions with long-term structurally transformative exceptions, Ackerman focuses exclusively on the latter. In so doing, Ackerman defies the Schmittian charge that liberalism is incapable of any kind of constitutional adaptation or transformation. Schmitt certainly would have claimed that Ackerman's liberal transformative constitutionalism was not sufficiently dynamic to counter, for instance, Bolshevism's exploitation of immediate crises. Since Bolshevism no longer poses a threat to constitutional regimes, however, Ackerman's project may be understood as demonstrating the flexibility of liberal constitutions in adapting to large-scale and more gradual social change.

Ackerman's description of constitutional change as "revolutionary reform," as repudiation of the past, as refounding[59] may sound like Schmitt to some extent. For Ackerman, however, change must take place over a duration of time measured in years, not months or days, and by channels not normally open to lawmaking. It is not enacted through the momentary lightning bolt of a quasi-divine executive authority. Moreover, all the branches of government are involved in the transformation process, not just one. This is, of course, the very opposite of Schmitt's instantaneous response, which is justified only by the most recent presidential election (supposedly re-confirming the preconstitutional sovereign will) and the active discrediting and neutralizing of other governmental branches. Emergency powers as envisioned by Schmitt, in short, amount to an intra-institutional coup that hides behind the sham of constitutionality.

Schmitt's distinction between normal and constitutional politics effectively places the latter outside the reach of popular participation even though it is invoked in the people's name. For Ackerman, on the contrary, it is the constitutional moment that is *more* popularly participatory than normal moments. After all, even Schmitt pays lip service to the possibility of conventional electoral politics in ordinary time.[60] As Ackerman describes the distinction, constitutional moments are those "rare moments when transformative movements earn broad and deep support for their initiatives"; they are "moments of mobilized popular renewal."[61] On the other hand, normal politics is identified with the routine political participation that competes with the activities of people's private lives for their attention. Constitutional moments are fundamentally different because in them,

> politics can take center stage with compelling force. The events catalyzing a rise in political consciousness have been as various as the country's history – war, economic

---

59 *WTP1*, 19.
60 See Schmitt, *The Crisis of Parliamentary Democracy*.
61 *WTP2*, 4–5.

catastrophe, or urgent appeals to the national conscience. For whatever reason, political talk and action begin to take on an urgency and breadth lacking most of the time. Normally passive citizens become more active – arguing, mobilizing, and sacrificing their other interests to a degree that seems to them extraordinary.[62]

Inherent in Ackerman's conception of crises is an intensified engagement by the people with politics, not, as in Schmitt's, their stupefaction by politics.

What separates Ackerman from Schmitt then is, first, a longer time frame for the resolution of crisis; as much as a whole generation of political foment and a decade devoted to change itself. Second, and related, is an emphasis on the discursive, as opposed to acclamatory, quality of popular participation at these times. As Ackerman puts it, the U.S. constitutional system "encourages an engaged citizenry to focus on fundamental issues and determine whether any proposed solution deserves its considered support."[63] There is, in his own words, a "plebiscitary" quality to Ackerman's model, but constitutional change is never legitimated on the basis of any *one* plebiscite but rather a "series" of House, Senate, and presidential elections.[64] Ultimately, Ackerman is most un-Schmittian institutionally in his understanding of the separation of powers as the enabling "central engine" of – not the obstacle to – the resolution of a constitutional crisis. The structural rivalry among branches intensifies deliberation and competition for popular support which clarifies issues, and eventually initiates definitive preference declarations by the people.[65] Schmitt's Reichspräsident can have no clear idea of the substantive preferences of the people derived from one election, regardless of how recent it is. Issues can not be clarified for anyone in this framework except to the extent that the political and economic elites around the president deign to do so for him and the people. Schmitt unashamedly calls such a scenario "democratic." The schema shown in Table 9.1 compares and contrasts Schmitt and Ackerman on these points.

Ackerman partly confirms and partly repudiates Schmitt's first criticism of liberalism's response to unforeseen circumstances: Ackerman's kind of liberalism will take too long and be too deliberative to address an immediate crisis. But this is not what Ackerman's framework is designed to resolve. However, his framework *is* open to the kind of dramatic constitutional change that Schmitt was doubtful liberalism could successfully undertake. Is Ackerman nevertheless susceptible to Schmitt's second criticism that liberal attempts to address constitutional crises will be illiberal? Ackerman resorts to arguments that surely make more conventional liberal constitutionalists

62 Ibid., 6.
63 Ibid.
64 Ibid., 21.
65 Ibid., 21, 23.

Table 9.1.

	Schmitt	Ackerman
Exceptional moment	emergency/transformation	transformation
Political response	sovereign dictatorship by president	constitutional emendation led by president or legislature
Popular will	people acclaiming through plebiscite	people "deliberating" through presidential and congressional elections, judicial decisions, and state ratification process
Time frame	immediate	extended

uncomfortable.[66] Ackerman champions the, shall we say, legally creative way in which political actors at times avoided established modes of U.S. constitutional revision. For instance, Ackerman argues that it is a mistake to characterize the history of American constitutional change as a faithful adherence to the "rules of the game."[67] The Constitution itself was illegal given the lack of authorization from the Articles of Confederation government to refound the regime; and the post–Civil War Republicans circumvented prescribed methods to ratify the Fourteenth Amendment. In general, Ackerman may perhaps dwell too long for some liberals' taste on the fact that Article 5 of the U.S. Constitution is the described, but not necessarily *exclusive* means of revising the Constitution.[68] He leaves open the possibility that there might in fact be a variety of such other means.

Ackerman certainly avoids Schmittian Caesarism by taking the very constitutional mechanisms that Schmitt claimed would be incapable of addressing extraordinary moments and interpreting them as in fact being better at facilitating such redress and having more substantive popular legitimacy. Yet the Ackerman model still retains certain Caesarist traces. For one, it unapologetically acknowledges the importance of "wartime triumphs" in both the Federalist founding and the Republican refounding after the Civil War.[69] It emphasizes the use of "old institutions in new ways"[70] that, according to

---

[66] In fact, Ackerman's understanding of how extraordinary crises may be actually absorbed into the regime itself through constitutional adaptation over time is closer to Machiavelli's republican theory than anything in the liberal or Enlightenment tradition. For Machiavelli, crises were absorbed directly into the institutions of republican regimes rather than via procedures as in Ackerman's theory. On this aspect of Machiavelli, see John P. McCormick, "Addressing the Political Exception: Machiavelli's 'Accidents' and the Mixed Regime," *American Political Science Review* 87, no. 4 (December 1993), 888–900.
[67] *WTP2*, 11.
[68] Ibid., 15.
[69] Ibid., 22.
[70] Ibid., 9.

cynical readings, is precisely what both Caesars and both Bonapartes did with respect to the republican orders they supplanted but pretended to maintain. The repeated emphasis on "unconventional adaptation"[71] may not need to be stretched too far to be understood as a euphemism for extra-legal action. The observation that each transformation in U.S. constitutional history further nationalized the federal government at the expense of state power will not endear Ackerman to Tocquevillian critics of the administrative state. Each of these is an element of traditional Caesarism. Yet, Ackerman puts them in the service of a deliberating populace rather than a demagogic individual or group of elites. In contrast to the bogus populism of the Caesarist case, the people themselves advance their claim to power through procedures that if followed can allow and facilitate "sovereign" change. Ackerman is comfortable with the fact that the people of the United States could reach any social goal desired, so long as they do so through the time-extended and institutionally arduous procedures of constitutional change. It is precisely the elements of time and procedure that separate liberal sovereign dictatorship, if that is what we should call it, and Jacobin or Bonapartist sovereign dictatorship.[72]

CONCLUSION

Schmitt's theory of dictatorship fulfills his own prophecy that the merging of sovereign will and emergency circumstances would serve as the occasion for Caesarist coups against constitutional orders. When an individual like a Caesar or a Bonaparte can claim *both* (1) to bring stability to a republican order that has become ungovernable *and* (2) to represent the whole people when so doing, constitutional government is finished. Schmitt comes to the conclusion that history has decreed that increasingly economically egalitarian forces will make such moves in times of crisis to enact sovereign dictatorships that liberals would make no effort to counter with commissarial emergency measures. Thus, he takes it upon himself to formulate a right-wing version of sovereign dictatorship. It emphasizes nationalism over egalitarianism and attempts to buy off populaces, not with straightforward social welfare measures, but those mediated through military service. To exclude any alternative other than his fascist theory of sovereign dictatorship

---

71 Ibid., 22.
72 These qualities are what separates Ackerman's version of what Andrew Arato calls "constitutional dictatorship" from the more pathological ones that arise from easy access to the apparatus of constitutional emendation. See Andrew Arato, "Elections, Coalitions and Constitutionalism in Hungary," *East European Constitutional Review* 3, nos. 3 and 4 (Summer/Fall 1994), 72–83.

and its Bolshevist adversary, Schmitt fashions a narrative about liberalism and political exceptions that insures that liberals will be unable to intercede in the debate and that if they do, they will further jeopardize their politics and principles.

Two challenges to Schmitt on these points: First, left-wing Caesarism did not have a monopoly on the practice of dictatorship in the years just preceding and following the turn of the century, as shown by the official regime of the second Bonaparte in France and the de facto one of General Erich Ludendorff in Germany during World War I. Consequently, there was *not* the dire need for the conceptually brilliant and historically cunning alternative theory of dictatorship outlined by Schmitt. Second, the liberal tradition, from Locke to Ackerman, while obviously not as preoccupied with constitutional crisis management as Schmitt, certainly has more to offer on the matter than Schmitt and his historical logic suggest.

Through both diagnosis and demonstration, Schmitt's writings on dictatorship confirm the socio-political continuity from Caesarism to fascism in the twentieth century. Indeed it serves to remind us of the necessity of further theoretical analysis of the legacy of modern authoritarianism from absolutism to fascism.[73] There continues to be a need for scholarship that challenges the comforting narratives which posit an overcoming of organized domination since the end of the Middle Ages, as a result of the wave of revolutions that succeeded the overthrow of the ancien regime in France, or the subsequent emergence of liberal and social democracy. Any account of modern political history and political philosophy that views authoritarian movements and regimes as "exceptions" in the "age of reason" must be dispelled, lest we let down our collective guard permanently. Moreover, work on authoritarianism should resist the temptation to support the equally inaccurate and harmful counter-narrative (one that combines a particular reading of Tocqueville with neoconservatism) which asserts an inherent and unavoidable authoritarian strain in modern politics and expanding forms of mass democracy. Schmitt is a crucial figure for this kind of analysis precisely because his writings point out the dangers of authoritarianism in mass democracy and, more importantly, also serve as a model for how *not* to respond to such supposed pathologies: specifically, by concluding that some supposedly less evil form of sham mass democracy is an appropriate solution to such dangers.

---

73 See the pioneering work of Melvin Richter, "Toward a Concept of Political Illegitimacy: Bonapartist Dictatorship and Democratic Legitimacy," *Political Theory* 10, no. 2 (1982), 185– 214, and Baehr, *Caesar and the Fading of the Roman World*.

10

Bonapartist and Gaullist Heroic Leadership

Comparing Crisis Appeals to an Impersonated People

JACK HAYWARD

Attempts to simplify by dichotomizing the complexity of French political traditions, either in an attempt to achieve intellectual clarity or from a polemical urge to promote guilt or virtue by repulsion and association, have been numerous since the French Revolution. There have been more historically sensitive efforts to respect the variety within each component of the left/right duality. In particular, René Rémond's distinction between three French rights – ultra-racist legitimist, Orléanist, liberal and Bonapartist nationalist – had much to commend it when first formulated in 1954. However, in later editions he sought to force Gaullism into this tripartite straightjacket while warning that "Historical rapprochements are normally only the most subtle form of anachronism."[1] A presupposition of this chapter's deliberate use of hindsight to see nineteenth-century Bonapartism through the twentieth-century phenomenon of Gaullism is that it allows us to offer a retrospective corrective to ill-considered attributions of either ignominious or glorious ancestry.

While acknowledging that the Bonapartist nationalist right incorporated minority left-wing elements, Rémond argued that dependence upon its predominantly right-wing support pushed it rightward under Napoleon, Louis Napoleon, Boulanger, and de Gaulle. He was prepared to accept that in theory Bonapartism "lent itself to many interpretations. Political Janus, its ambiguity allowed within limits some scope for adaptation. In 1849 it could, almost equally and with equal likelihood, have given birth to a left-wing or right-wing Bonapartism."[2] In practice, the votes of the peasantry, with the support of the Church, the new business notables, and administrative

---

[1] René Rémond, *La Droite en France, de la Première Restauration à la Ve République*, 3rd ed. (Paris, 1968), 304.
[2] René Rémond, *La Droite en France, de la Première Restauration à la Ve République*, 1st ed. (Paris, 1954), 99; cf. 100–117.

elite inexorably pulled the Second Empire to the right, despite the belated Liberal Empire Orleanist turn toward the center.

In a more fair-minded way than either the communist and noncommunist left polemicists who engaged in a crude assimilation of Gaullism and Bonapartism, Rémond, as a scrupulous historian with strong Social Catholic affiliations, nevertheless emphasized those features that they shared. These were the control of the media of mass communications; reassuring property owners and business accompanied by "social concerns"; Saint-Simonian technocratic reformism; an assertive foreign and military policy and an authoritarian, monocratic political regime, supported by a centralized administrative elite, notably through the partisan activities of the prefects.[3] The problem is that all these features are not confined to Bonapartism, even if they were given especially strong expression by it. Leaving to others the discussion of whether Bonapartism is itself incontrovertibly of the right, why did the Gaullist synthesis based upon the founding myth of popular sovereignty succeed in institutionalizing itself when Bonapartism conspicuously failed? Is it not because Gaullism was not merely able to live up to the claim that "Everyone has been, is or will be Gaullist" but that the "republican monarch" did rise above monarchy and republic, legitimism, Jacobinism, Bonapartism, and Orleanism and could not simply be reduced to one of its constituents?

As far as the attempt to equate Bonapartism with nationalism and Gaullism is concerned, Sudhir Hazareesingh has usefully distinguished the two faces of French nationalism. "The aggressive and backward-looking nationalism of the anti-Dreyfusards was overcome by the democratic and progressive nationalism of the republicans; the despondent and penitent nationalism which culminated in the *Etat Français* was swept away by the optimistic patriotism of the resistance, and the retreating and cramped chauvinism of the extreme right over the Algerian question was defeated by the realistic nationalism of Charles de Gaulle."[4] While borrowing from the royalists their preoccupation with legitimate authority, from the republicans' primacy of the led over the leader, and from the Bonapartists their concern to lead from the front rather than from behind, de Gaulle infused state power with a democratic legitimacy in a personalized but accountable authority: the directly elected president of the republic.

From Karl Marx to François Mitterrand, the left has been addicted to portraying Bonapartism as the dictatorship of the bourgeoisie and monopoly

---

3 René Rémond, *La Droite en France, de la Première Restauration à la Ve République*, 3rd ed., 302–4. Also summarized by Olivier Duhamel, *La Gauche et la Ve République* (Paris, 1980), 106.
4 Sudhir Hazareesingh, *Political Traditions in Modern France* (Oxford, 1994), 148.

capitalism, as relying upon coup d'état to attain power and upon plebiscites and repression to sustain its control of the state. Olivier Duhamel has thoroughly documented the attempt by the French communist and noncommunist left to discredit Gaullism by assimilating it to Bonapartism. Duhamel has convincingly shown how reluctant the communists were to use Marx's *The Eighteenth Brumaire of Louis Bonaparte* for their crude purpose of pillorying "personal power" in the service of financial speculators and thereby demystifying de Gaulle's status as a national hero.[5] Despite the desire to stress General de Gaulle's dependence on the military in retrieving power in 1958, it is significant that it was the less glorious Louis-Napoleon, lacking his uncle's place in the pantheon of French heroes, who was the peg on which the left hung their attacks.

Another way of linking Bonapartism and Gaullism has been to regard them as sharing a desire to subordinate society to the state. In his 1977 study of the aspiration of the French state to political autonomy, Pierre Birnbaum concluded that "From bonapartism to gaullism, this ephemeral pretension of the state to independence is a constant feature of French history."[6] By showing that in *The Eighteenth Brumaire* and *The Civil War in France* Marx had acknowledged the partial autonomy of the state from society, which Tocqueville had discussed in relation to bureaucratic centralization, Birnbaum not only exposes why French communist criticisms of the Fifth Republic found it difficult to draw on Marxist analysis. He goes on to argue that de Gaulle's 1945 creation of the Ecole Nationale d'Administration reflected the Bonapartist urge to build a supra-partisan state power capable of sovereignty by deciding in the national interest.[7] We shall return later to the way in which heroic Gaullism had to routinize its charismatic character by a process of partisanization and bureaucratization that was profoundly repugnant to its progenitor and his most faithful disciples. For the present, let us note in passing that while Napoleon established and Louis-Napoleon utilized a centralized state bureaucracy and the Council of State to exert despotic power, de Gaulle was always suspicious that the bureaucracy would pursue its own agenda rather than his. He was also impatient with the Council of State's independence, seeing it as a herald of the Constitutional Council's increasing inclination to

---

5 Duhamel, *La Gauche*, 107–17. See especially Jacques Duclos, *De Napoleon III à de Gaulle* (Paris, 1964) and Pierre Juquin, "De Gaulle et le myth du 'heros'," *Cahiers du Communisme* July–August 1961, 1133–69. More generally, see Alain Rouquié, "L'hypothèse bonapartiste et l'emergence des systèmes politiques semi-compétitifs," *Revue Française de Science Politique*, XXV, Dec. 6, 1975, 2077–111 and Georges Conchon, *Nous, la gauche, devant Louis Napoléon* (Paris, 1969).
6 Pierre Birnbaum, *Les sommets de l'état. Essai sur l'élite du pouvoir en France* (Paris, 1977), 185.
7 Ibid., 14–26.

review judicially not merely the administrative but the legislative acts of government.

While the Socialist Section Francaise de l'Internationale Ouvrière (SFIO) had helped de Gaulle to power in 1958, it was particularly opposed to the subsequent direct election of the president, its constant desire being to "'parlementarise' Bonapartism," reducing the new institutions to a constitutional parenthesis.[8] However, it was Mitterrand, the future leader of the new Socialist Party – who as president of the republic exploited to the full the power of the Fifth Republic president – who launched the most vitriolic attack on de Gaulle's regime in 1964. "There is in our country a solid permanence of Bonapartism in which converge the monarchic traditional vocation of national grandeur and the Jacobin passion for national unity. In 1958 Gaullism had no difficulty in bringing together the scattered components and reviving the synthesis sought by the protagonists of personal power," assisted by the "tried and tested recipe of Napoleonic plebiscite."[9] Mitterrand attacked the "second style Gaullism (as one says Second Empire)," with May 13, 1958, being de Gaulle's December 2, 1851.[10] "Between de Gaulle and the republicans there is first and always the *coup d'état*."[11] However, Mitterrand traced the problem back to de Gaulle's use of "illegal action to base his legitimacy on the higher necessity of saving the country over written laws," asserting that "The match between legality and legitimacy summarizes the history of Gaullism since 1940."[12] Mitterrand put his finger on the contrast between the heroic leader's exceptional "personal legitimacy, independent of the political context, mystical alliance, indissoluble between the people and him"[13] and the conventional representative leader relying upon routine legality. So, it is to Max Weber that we must turn for guidance, before moving on to Stanley Hoffmann's elucidation of de Gaulle's heroic style of leadership.

THE HEROIC VARIANT OF CHARISMATIC AUTHORITY

The Napoleons and de Gaulle are classic examples of Weber's charismatic type of authority that challenges an existing institutional order and then

---

8 Duhamel, *La Gauche*, 145, 230, quoting among others the first President of the Fourth Republic Vincent Auriol's *Hier... demain* (Paris, 1945), 237–9.
9 François Mitterrand, *Le coup d'état permanent* (Paris, 1964) quoting from F. Mitterrand, *Politique. Textes et discours, 1938–1981* (Paris, 1984), 110.
10 Ibid., 111.
11 Ibid., 104, 106: "the Fifth Republic is a *coup d état* régime."
12 Ibid., 106–7.
13 Ibid., 109. For an analysis of Mitterrand's changing post-1964 constitutional interpretation of the Fifth Republic, see Duhamel, *La Gauche*, 252 and ff.

seeks to found a new order. They could not have done so without changing their character by invoking traditional and legal legitimacy to perpetuate an otherwise ephemeral and exceptional achievement. However, they are its heroic variant, relying initially on the use of force or military prowess, either directly in the case of Napoleon or indirectly for Louis-Napoleon, who traded on the name of his uncle, thereby demonstrating that the response to the question "What's in a name?" is "Sometimes, a great deal." The fact that Louis-Napoleon could rely upon familial borrowed finery to gain election as president in 1848 suggests that a dynastic element of traditional authority had been successfully absorbed by French public opinion. There may also be a prophetic aspect, reflected in the memoirs of both Napoleons, but the heroic aspect predominates, specific cases never fully replicating Weber's pure types. So, it is by reference to their heroic achievements in war and as saviors from defeat and disorder that charismatic military leaders evoke deferential "hero worship."[14]

Max Weber emphasizes the importance of the plebiscite as "the specific means of establishing the legitimacy of authority on the basis of the free confidence of those subject to authority, even though it be only formal or possibly a fiction."[15] Once the transmutation of charismatic authority by infusions of legal and/or traditional leadership is under way, "instead of recognition being treated as a consequence of legitimacy, it is treated as the basis of legitimacy" by those subject to it.[16] Weber also explains the centralization of prefectural power in the two Empires as being "derived from the charismatic administration of the revolutionary democratic dictatorship," which demonstrates that "It is not impossible, as in the case of Napoleon, for the strictest bureaucracy to issue directly from a charismatic movement."[17]

I have followed Stanley Hoffmann in preferring the term heroic to either charismatic or crisis leadership. The appellation "heroic" is less diffuse and less encumbered with controversial conceptual mystique than is "charisma," and it is also more clearly related to empirically identifiable activities. "Crisis" leaders do not always act heroically or challenge the traditional or legal norms of authority. Hoffmann's model of heroic leadership is based on normative collapse resulting in "a blank check given to a superior no longer bound by restraints and bullied by resistance," a reassertion of personal authority seen as a "heroic exercise of self-expression, a holiday

---

14 Max Weber, *The Theory of Social and Economic Organisation*, ed. Talcott Parsons (New York, 1947), 359; cf. 328.
15 Ibid., 387; cf. 362.   16 Ibid., 386.
17 Ibid., 389, 383.

from rules and routine, an exalting spectacle."[18] This is necessary because of the "fragility of routine authority" and "its tendency towards paralysis."[19] Yet Hoffmann goes on to point out that "the resilience of routine political authority explains why resort to a different kind of leadership is postponed until a situation breeds something like a national sense of emergency, a conviction that there is no alternative."[20] Two rival heroic military-cum-political leaders were produced in 1940 in Pétain and de Gaulle, outsiders who offered to clean up the mess left by a discredited and defeated Third Republic.

Hoffmann's analysis was influenced by Michel Crozier's study of *The Bureaucratic Phenomenon*, which showed the need for agents of change to mobilize mass support to break the stranglehold of the traditional elites, political parties, and sectional interests. As Crozier put it in the early 1960s, no doubt with de Gaulle in mind, "During crises, individual initiative prevails and people eventually come to depend on some strategic individual's arbitrary whim."[21] De Gaulle in 1932 had described the "divine game of the hero" who rises to the challenge: When the hour of "crisis comes, he is the one followed"; "to him naturally falls the difficult task, the main effort, the decisive mission ... all he requests is accepted."[22] How can such an outsider create the routine legitimacy to perpetuate innovation in post-crisis circumstances?

Hoffmann picks up the Weber theme of how difficult it is to institutionalize the savior and draws an analogy between the attempts by both Napoleons and de Gaulle to rekindle legitimacy by constitutional plebiscites. De Gaulle's suicide by plebiscite in 1969 showed how "heroic leadership in France is connected too clearly with a cataclysmic sense of emergency and with the notion of 'total' transformation to handle a process of gradual evolution easily and well. Napoleon III tried – by a gliding descent into

---

18 Stanley Hoffmann, "The Rulers: Heroic Leadership in Modern France," first published in Lewis J. Edinger, ed., *Political Leadership in Industrialized Societies* (New York, 1967), 127 ff., but quoted as reprinted in Stanley Hoffmann, *Decline or Renewal? France since the 1930s* (New York, 1974), 71–2; cf. 68.
19 Ibid., 74–5. 20 Ibid., 77.
21 Michel Crozier, *The Bureaucratic Phenomenon* (London, 1964), 196.
22 Charles de Gaulle, *Le Fil de l'épée* (Paris, 1932, 1962 ed.), 54–7. The interpretation of Gaullism in terms of charisma was challenged by Jean Charlot in Chapter 2 of his *The Gaullist Phenomenon* (1970: English ed., London, 1971). He did so by emphasizing the variations over time of its popularity in relation to the political context to sustain his argument focusing on the increasing importance of the Gaullist party, which I would argue betokened the routinization of de Gaulle's heroic authority, especially in matters of domestic policy. The Hoffmann conception of heroic leadership was referred to by Philip Cerny specifically in relation to foreign policy in *The Politics of Grandeur. Ideological Aspects of de Gaulle's Foreign Policy* (Cambridge, 1980), 247–8, but he subscribes to the Charlot thesis, 249–54.

parliamentarism – and failed."[23] De Gaulle's Fifth Republic managed the transition more effectively but remains bedeviled by the awkward problem of periodically filling the post of presidential semi-heroic leader with someone of adequate stature.

"Routine authority is legitimate because of what it *is*, the heroic leader is legitimate because of what he *does*."[24] He does not allow himself to be confined by established procedures and prefers spectacular unilateral initiatives characteristic of military tactics to patient and pedestrian negotiation. Ambitious undertakings as part of an assertive striving for national greatness punctuate the domestic and diplomatic arenas of political action, "which drives heroic leaders into an endless and often reckless gamble for legitimacy" owing to their excessive activism.[25] Yet it is necessary periodically to save the routine system from paralysis. Then it is time to return to routine authority. In 1969, the democratic rejection of de Gaulle's leadership meant that he departed as a decision of the electorate rather then being compelled to do so by the 1968 rioters, giving the Fifth Republic "a decisive seal of legitimacy."[26] By not having been defeated in battle in 1969 (as were Napoleon in 1815 and Louis Napoleon in 1870) but by verdict of the voter, de Gaulle demonstrated acceptance of the subordination of his personal sovereignty to national popular sovereignty. A majority of the people having assumed that a hostile vote would not lead to chaos, de Gaulle drew the conclusion that they wanted to return to routine representative government and that his mission of destiny's agent to rescue France had come to an end. The transition from heroic to humdrum leadership which Georges Pompidou, his prime minister from 1962–8, had surreptitiously prepared, could now proceed more smoothly.

CONSTITUTIONALIZING THE HEROIC LEADER

Since 1789, France has had some twenty-one constitutions (the precise number depending on those you include) of which only fourteen have actually operated – in the case of the *"Benjamine,"* Benjamin Constant's *Acte Additionnel aux Constitutions de l'Empire* of 1815, for only the two months

---

23 Hoffmann, *Decline or Renewal*, 81; cf. 79–80. See also Jack E. S. Hayward, "Presidential Suicide by Plebiscite: De Gaulle's Exit, April 1969," *Parliamentary Affairs* 22/4 (Autumn 1969), 289–319, which makes clear that de Gaulle's threat to resign if defeated was like making a threat to commit suicide to change the behavior of others, rather than an intention to take one's own life which went wrong.
24 Hoffmann, *Decline or Renewal*, 86.   25 Ibid., 109.
26 Ibid., 104; cf. 103.

before Waterloo.[27] Of these attempts to stabilize and thereby "end the revolution," both Napoleons changed the constitution several times, which was an indication of the difficulties they encountered in routinizing the basis in heroic legitimacy of their regime. However, the Caesarist subordination of the legislature to the political executive was based on the bland principle that "authority comes from above and confidence from below." The lapidary phrase was cynically elaborated by Pierre Cabanis with all the dogmatic arrogance of a positivist *Idéologue* scientist. "Choices must be made not at the bottom, where they are necessarily made badly, but at the top where they are necessarily made well." The Sieyès-Bonaparte 18 Brumaire coup had purged democracy of "all its disadvantages . . . the ignorant class no longer exercises any influence either on the legislature or on the government; consequently no more demagogues. All is done for the people and in the name of the people; nothing is done by it under its unthinking guidance."[28]

However, Sieyès's intention of using "the most civil of the military men"[29] to set up a senatorial republic failed, as did the Second Republic Orleanist oligarches who placed their hopes on Louis-Napoleon and the Fourth Republic politicians who helped de Gaulle to power in the belief that they could dispense with his services once the Algerian crisis was settled. The illusory Jacobin aspiration to imitate the Roman Republic degenerated under Napoleon into what Tocqueville, during the democratic despotism of Louis-Napoleon, resentfully dubbed "a minor copy of the gigantic and despicable Roman Empire" with "the despotism of a single person resting on a democratic basis."[30]

In 1799, Napoleon secured popular approval of a conclusive violation of constitutional legality, a violation that followed several earlier violations during the Directory for regime and self-preservation against challenges from the Royalist right and the Jacobin left. The argument of popular sovereignty was invoked to justify executive supremacy. On December 2, 1851, the anniversary of his uncle's overwhelming victory at Austerlitz, Louis-Napoleon presented himself in his appeal to the people as the defender of the republic and of universal suffrage (abrogated by the 1850 law instigated by the

---

27 Claude Emeri and Christian Bidegaray, *La Constitution en France de 1789 à nos jours* (Paris, 1997), 13–14. Constant's prediction was: "The intentions are liberal; the practice will be despotic." *Oeuvres*, Pléiade ed. (Paris, 1957), 778.
28 Pierre J. G. Cabanis, *Oeuvres Philosophiques*, II (Paris, 1956), 474–5.
29 Testimony of Joseph Bonaparte, *Mémoires et Correspondance*, I (Paris, 1853), 77.
30 Alexis de Tocqueville, *The European Revolution and Correspondence with Gobineau* (New York, 1959), 58, 154–5.

Orleanist oligarches) replacing party strife by popular sovereignty. Having secured a massive majority in the December 21–2, 1851, plebiscite asking for the people's confidence, he notoriously proclaimed on December 31 that the voters had shown they understood that "I only went outside legality to return to the law. More than seven million votes have absolved me."[31] The rigidity of constitutions that had perpetuated misgovernment by Assembly in the First Republic and the denial of re-eligibility of the president in the Second Republic had led to their displacement, with popular approval, by the First and Second Empires. Both Napoleons characteristically hastened to make and remake new constitutions to suit changing circumstances as a respite from violating them.

Was de Gaulle's return to power in May–June 1958 his "Seventeenth Brumaire," as his biographer Jean Lacouture has tentatively suggested? The mixture of dupery and duplicity that accompanied it unfortunately makes it difficult to offer a clear-cut or objective answer, de Gaulle having acted with calculated ambiguity during the decisive days. In 1985, an opinion survey showed that the French people shared this perplexity: 33% of those polled thought that de Gaulle had returned to office because of a conspiracy, 25% rejected this explanation, and 42% gave no reply.[32] He clearly did not initiate the army coup in Algeria, although his supporters were involved in it. In subsequent negotiations to avoid an invasion of France by its own army and possible civil war, de Gaulle presented himself as willing to save France but insisted as a precondition upon a free hand to reform its political institutions. Having "white mailed" most of the Fourth Republic politicians into accepting his terms, he secured a legal handover of power, becoming the last prime minister of the Fourth Republic before a new constitution enabled him to assume office as first president of the Fifth Republic.[33]

Was the September 28, 1958, referendum asking the French people to ratify de Gaulle's new constitution a coup d'état?[34] That it is more accurately described as a plebiscite rather than a referendum can be justified, first, because the initiative came from above not from below, from the leader not the led. Rather than an exercise in direct democracy, it was, second, a personalized request for passive political support, to confirm the popular

---

31 "Je n'étais sorti de la légalité que pour rentrer dans le droit. Plus de sept millions de suffrages viennent de m'absoudre..." Quoted in French, to retain its full sophistical flavor with a hint of guilt, from Emeri and Bidegaray, *La Constitution*, 44.
32 Jean Lacouture, *De Gaulle*, II (Paris, 1985), 487–9 and chapter 20 passim.
33 See the summary of events in Emeri and Bidegaray, *La Constitution*, 46–9.
34 The question posed by Emeri and Bidegaray is pertinent, but I do not fully agree with their answer to it. *La Constitution*, 69–76.

legitimacy of his authority, not to resolve a specific issue. While not seeking ex post facto approval for the coup, it could be described as securing support for de Gaulle's peaceful resolution of the crisis in a context of a forced choice, "me or chaos." He was asking the people to place their trust in him, not merely for a specific crisis resolution but as lawgiver to solve institutional problems and thereby prevent the recurrence of such crises.

The contrast with the October 21, 1945, referendum is instructive because it asked two questions. The first allowed the voters to reject a restoration of the Third Republic without simultaneously approving the outline of the Fourth Republic constitution that would replace it. This procedure separated the choice concerning the past from the future. In 1958, de Gaulle insisted on a package deal which conflated rejection of the Fourth Republic and approval of his Fifth Republic. His four subsequent referendums always included an implicit personal vote of confidence, so that when he was defeated in 1969 he immediately resigned even though not constitutionally required to do so. Such an outcome would not have been envisaged under either of the Napoleons. To avoid the resulting destabilization of the presidency that copying de Gaulle's behavior would have involved, subsequent referendums have not carried the threat of presidential resignation, a mark of the post-Gaullist move away from heroic toward humdrum leadership under the Fifth Republic.

De Gaulle shared something of the cavalier attitude of both the Bonapartes toward their constitutions. Napoleon activated the 1799 constitution even before it had been approved by plebiscite, and Louis-Napoleon asked in advance for popular approval in December 1851 of the January 14, 1852, constitution. The latter Napoleon proclaimed: "Since France for the last fifty years has only functioned thanks to the administrative, judicial, military, religious and financial organization of the Consulate and Empire, why should we not also adopt the political institutions of that period?"[35] Like Louis-Napoleon, de Gaulle relied on a group of experts, not a constituent assembly, to prepare the 1958 constitution, having also committed himself in advance to five general principles set out in his 1946 Bayeux model. He subsequently asserted his right as lawgiver to interpret the constitution as he chose, without being bound by his own rules. Thus, when he was challenged by Paul Reynaud for violating the constitution by using a

---

35 Quoted by Emeri and Bidegaray, *La Constitution*, 113; cf. 112, 128. On Louis Napoleon's reaffirmation of his uncle's legacy, see his *Des idées Napoléoniennes* of 1839 which had sold over half a million copies by 1848. Reprinted in *Life and Works of Louis Napoleon Bonaparte*, Vol. 1 (London, 1852), and T.A.B. Corley, *Democratic Despot. A Life of Napoleon III* (London, 1961), 38–9, 110–11.

referendum (Article 11) rather than a constitutional amendment (Article 89) to secure direct election of the president, he replied in barrack room manner: "Come, come! One does not rape one's wife," adding in his memoirs, "I am myself the main inspirer of the new institutions and it is beyond the limit to contradict me on what they mean."[36]

De Gaulle was also skeptical that his heroic leadership could be institutionalized, believing as he did that he had neither predecessors nor successors, but it was in a determined effort to overcome this problem that he forced through the 1962 reform by referendum. In April 1961, he confided to a staff member his anxiety about his succession, knowing his life to be threatened by assassination. "I re-established monarchy in my favour, but after me there will be no one who will impose his authority on the country. I was elected without the need for a referendum but after me this will no longer be true. So it will be necessary to establish a presidential system to avoid returning to the struggles of the past. The president of the republic must be elected by universal suffrage. Elected in this way, whatever his personal qualities, he will nevertheless have some semblance of authority and power."[37] In his memoirs, he claimed that despite favoring direct election of the president he had "to avoid prejudicing the almost unanimous national support, decided to take account of the impassioned hostility since Louis Napoleon to the idea of a 'plebiscite' in many sectors of public opinion."[38] However, despite Prime Minister Pompidou's assurance in cabinet that "Twenty-two years of Gaullism have wiped out the stain of Bonapartism,"[39] his government was censured in the Assembly and only vindicated by massive popular votes in the referendum and legislative election following de Gaulle's dissolution of the Assembly. Popular sovereignty once again trumped constitutional legality and established direct presidential election, which has continued to enjoy a high level of public support, including during periods of "cohabitation" ("cohabitension" would be more accurate) when the president's supporters have not had a majority in the National Assembly.

Like de Gaulle, both Bonapartes became dissatisfied with their initial constitutions and found a method of circumventing the problem, Napoleon by increasing his arbitrary power, his nephew by liberalizing the Second Empire. Charles de Talleyrand is credited with inventing the flexible device

---

36 Reply to Paul Reynaud quoted in Pierre Viansson-Ponté, *Histoire de la République Gaullienne*, II (Paris, 1971), 42 and *Mémoires d'Espoir* (Paris, 1970), 335; cf. 334–6.
37 François Flohic, *Souvenirs d'outre – Gaulle* (Paris, 1979), 58.
38 De Gaulle, *Mémoires d'Espoir*, 327.
39 Viansson-Ponté, *Histoire*, 39.

of the *senatus-consulte* for amending the constitution of which the Senate was supposed to be the guardian. Given juridical form by the Conseil d'Etat, this procedure allowed the head of state and Senate to decide whether or not the constitutional amendment should be submitted to a plebiscite.[40] De Gaulle did not dispose of this convenient device, although he benefited from the refusal of the Constitutional Council in 1962 to declare the use of Article 11 to bypass a hostile Senate as unconstitutional. However, since the defeat of the 1969 referendum, none of de Gaulle's unheroic successors have dared to misuse Article 11 to revise the constitution. As a French constitutional lawyer has sardonically remarked: "It is paradoxical that in a Cartesian country we cannot say with certainty what are the constitutional means for amending the constitution."[41]

THE INTERDEPENDENCE BETWEEN PERSONAL AND POPULAR SOVEREIGNTY

Having earlier accepted the anachronistic character of using most historical analogies, however tempting they may be, to judge the Bonapartes or de Gaulle as leadership reincarnations of either Julius Caesar at one extreme or George Washington at the other, or as lawgivers like Solon or Rousseau's legislator, it is clear that they have certain affinities with these illustrious predecessors or prototypes. It would take us too far afield to explore these affinities, so let us focus particularly upon the contrast between Napoleon's utilization of popular sovereignty for essentially personal ambitions and de Gaulle's sublimation of his personal ambition to an elevated conception of national ambition. As Napoleon himself put it: "My ambition is so intimately allied to my whole being that it cannot be separated from it."[42] The impetuous Corsican never fully identified himself with more complex French traditions in which de Gaulle was steeped.

De Gaulle shunned the *fuite en avant* which led Napoleon to lust after absolute, unlimited arbitrary power. "He rendered France mad with ambition... He conceived his destiny, even at Saint-Helena, as that of an extraordinary individual. Yet an individual is of little consequence

---

40 Emeri and Bidegaray, *La Constitution*, 74–5, 139–41.
41 G. Conac quoted in ibid., 144; cf. 142–3.
42 Quoted in Pieter Geyl, *Napoleon: For and Against* (London, 1965), 377; cf. 368. François-René de Chateaubriand contrasted George Washington, the democratic "hero of a new type," with the anachronistic Caesarism of Napoleon. See the anthology of Chateaubriand's political writings, selected by Jean-Paul Clément, *De l'Ancien Régime au Nouveau Monde. Ecrits Politiques* (Paris, 1987), 96.

compared to a people."[43] De Gaulle saw his power as supreme but restricted. As Hoffmann put it, "the limits to this power were not spelled out in texts but stemmed partly from outside, so to speak, from the people's right to repudiate it; and partly from within, from the obligation laid on de Gaulle... to be guided only by the national interest, which includes respect for liberal traditions and the rejection of dictatorship."[44] Both Napoleon and de Gaulle had a romantic conception of legitimate authority but in the former it was individualist and in the latter an outgrowth of the unity and continuity of the French nation, not of a cult of personality.

Yet personal and popular sovereignty, while distinct, could not be separated in practice. This was especially true if one was determined to be "as ambitious, universal, and inventive an actor as world politics in general and the national power base in particular allowed," a determination coupled with "subordination of domestic politics to the primacy of international affairs,"[45] a stance that Napoleon and de Gaulle shared in their pursuit of grandeur. Although they both acted as supra-partisan Shakespearean sovereigns, Napoleon's prime concern was securing despotic unity for waging war, whereas de Gaulle's prime task was restoring France's past glory by guiding it to accept the modernization that would allow it to act independently but not belligerently toward other states. De Gaulle's less world-domineering ambition was to steer international relations in a nonhegemonic direction, provided it did not require the sacrifice of either France's sovereignty or her vital interests. Whereas in the first decade of the nineteenth century Napoleonic aggression provoked a German nationalism whose triumph Louis Napoleon inadvertently completed in 1870, de Gaulle fostered Franco-German rapprochement and collaboration inside the European community. Again, while Napoleon extravagantly sought to emulate the Roman Empire and reimposed slavery in the French colonies, de Gaulle, however reluctantly, dismantled the French Empire and

---

43 Quoted in André Malraux, *Les Chênes qu'on abat* (Paris, 1971), 111–12; cf. 107 and Charles de Gaulle, *La France et son Armée* (Paris, 1939), 115–16, 147, 154–5. Despite de Gaulle's admiration for Maurice Barrès, he did not share his unbounded admiration for Napoleon, famously reflected in *Les déracinés*, Vol. I of his trilogy entitled *Le Roman de l'Energie Nationale* (Paris, 1897). When in 1944 Georges Bidault said in Moscow that war leaders like Napoleon never knew when to stop, de Gaulle replied that Bismarck did in 1871. Quoted in Jean-Raymond Tournoux, *Jamais dit* (Paris, 1971), 143. However, in January 1958, when his return to power still seemed unlikely, de Gaulle said to Tournoux: "The thing which spurs a people on is ambition and France cannot do without a great national ambition." Previous French régimes had such ambitions – Napoleon to dominate Europe and Louis Napoleon to reverse the 1815 treaties – and his desire was to restore a grandiose sense of ambition to France. Tournoux, *La tragédie du Général* (Paris, 1967), 267–8.
44 Hoffmann, *Decline and Renewal*, 262, from his conflated reviews of de Gaulle's *Memoirs of Hope*.
45 Hoffmann, *Decline and Renewal*, 191, from his review of de Gaulle's *War Memoirs*, first published in *World Politics*, 13/I, October, 1960.

condescendingly assisted the ex-colonies militarily and financially, as required of the heroic leader of an ex-superpower.

If de Gaulle, unlike Napoleon, placed his inordinate self-esteem at the intransigent service of his idealized, personified France, it was because he did not impersonate the nation whose destiny he provisionally controlled and always respected. Yet, he sometimes expressed a view of authority that sounded perilously close to the enlightened despotism attributed to Napoleon, notably by historians as diverse as François Mignet, Jacques Bainville, and Georges Lefebvre.[46] Thus, in a notorious press conference of January 31, 1964, de Gaulle roundly asserted that all ministers including the prime minister were subordinate to him. "So it should clearly be understood that the indivisible authority of the state is confided in its entirety to the president by the people who elected him, that there is no other be it ministerial, civil, military or judicial authority besides what is conferred and maintained by him, finally that it is up to him to decide between his supreme domain and what he asks others to manage, including the distinction between the function and activities of the head of state and those of the prime minister."[47] While the government should concern itself with the day-to-day concerns of the French, only the president could be entrusted with protecting and promoting the interests of France. It was this claim that laid de Gaulle open to the criticism that he equated the general will with the will of the General, that the commander in chief reduced his prime minister to a chief of staff.

However, in a perceptive essay on "De Gaulle as Political Artist: The Will to Grandeur," Stanley and Inge Hoffmann underline his pride in being the self-confident servant of France, not its master. "France was the entity that provided de Gaulle with the transcendence he needed and also the limits he craved. To be 'France's champion' meant depending on no one yet being oneself completed; but the need to preserve France's personality and the subordination of self to her service imposed prudence, harmony, and moderation, and protected the nation and the missionary from the excesses of men (like Napoleon and Hitler) who used their nation as instruments for personal glory or to work out their ideological or psychological obsessions."[48] Napoleon's correspondence with his vassal king brothers contained "ceaselessly repeated admonitions, as if the entire art of government

---

46 Geyl, *Napoleon*, 33, 338, 379.
47 Appendix 4 of Dominique Chagnollaud and Jean-Louis Quermonne, *Le Gouvernment de la France sous la Ve République* (Paris, 1996), 845.
48 Hoffmann, *Decline and Renewal*, 220; cf. 215, 234. This essay was first published in *Daedalus*, Summer 1968.

consisted of the giving of orders and the application of force."[49] De Gaulle regarded repression not as a substitute for consent but as an occasional adjunct of national consensus. For the will of the General plausibly to embody the general will, the nation had to accept the leader's personal dependence upon the higher norm of national sovereignty, elevated almost to God-like status.

HEROIC LEGENDS AND INSTITUTIONAL LEGACIES

As a devout Roman Catholic, de Gaulle could not succumb, like Napoleon, to the absolutist temptations of Caesaropapism. Napoleon, who abolished the Holy Roman Empire and took the Pope hostage, treated religion as an instrument of social control. "I have seen Godless man at work since 1793. One cannot govern such a man, one can only shoot him." Referring to bishops as his "purple prefects" and priests as his "sacred gendarmes," he justified his pragmatic accommodation with the Church with the words: "I do not see in religion the mystery of Incarnation but of social order."[50] The concordat with the papacy was intended to convert the Church into an ecclesiastical agent of a state power that Napoleon personified: an instrument to ensure subjection to his will, the better to mobilize all France's resources to serve his warlike ambitions. The Pope having been summoned to Paris for his coronation, Napoleon chose symbolically to place the crown on his own head. He ensured that the seventh lesson of the new catechism inter alia extended the traditional Gallican duty of obedience to rulers. "What must one think of those who should fail in their duty to our Emperor? According to the apostle Paul, they would resist the established order of God himself, and would render themselves worthy of eternal damnation."[51] Coupled with the state monopoly of education, the Church was to be a powerful instrument of socializing the French into post-Revolutionary subjection after a prolonged period of insubordination. Their joint effectiveness is evident in the French people becoming in the Dutch historian Pieter Geyl's words, "a most willing tool in the hands of Napoleon, and after his death a credulous dupe of the legend."[52]

The Napoleonic legend was exploited to the full by his nephew, just as the reaction against it was later promoted by hostility to the Second Empire.

---

49 Geyl, *Napoleon*, 63; cf. 62–4.
50 Quoted in Pierre Haubtmann, *P-J Proudhon: Genèse d'un Antithéiste* (Paris, 1969), 161.
51 Ibid., 113; cf. 108–23.
52 Ibid., 335. See also P. Gonnard, *Les Origines de la Légende Napoléonienne. L'oeuvre historique de Napoléon à Sainte-Hélène* (Paris, 1906).

In a prescient speech of October 1848 on the Second Republic constitution, Jules Grévy argued that the proposed directly elected president was either useless or more probably dangerous because he would have more power than Louis-Philippe. Reminding the Assembly of the Bonapartist precedent, Grévy contended that the proposal amounted to an elected restoration of royalty. "Such a power, attributed to a single person, however named, king or president, is a monarchical power; and the one you are creating is greater then the one you have overthrown." He went on to warn that if the elected president "had been able to make himself popular, if he is a victorious general garlanded with the prestige of military glory which the French find irresistible; if he is the offspring of one of the families that have reigned in France and if he has never expressly renounced what he calls his rights; if trade is slack and the people is suffering, during one of those crises when poverty and disappointment place them in the hands of those who conceal designs against their liberty behind promises, can you be sure that such an ambitious person will not succeed in overthrowing the Republic?"[53]

The Assembly instead allowed itself to be persuaded by the poet/politician Lamartine that it should trust the people. If the voters made a bad decision, it was "so much the worse for the people," and in any case "the disappearance of the Republic will not be our fault!"[54] Grévy's failure to overcome such lamentable rhetoric was to be rewarded thirty years later by his election as president of the Third Republic. In reaction against the Second Empire, it established government by assembly, which proved ineffective in the twentieth century. It was left to de Gaulle to wind up both the Third and Fourth Republics and replace them by a reconciliation between a directly representative president and parliament in the Fifth Republic, synthesizing by modifying the Revolutionary and Bonapartist legacies.

Proudhon, who regarded France as unready for democracy in 1848, responded to Louis-Napoleon winning three-quarters of the vote for president with the words: "The people have spoken like a drunk." He went on to declare that democracy had disgraced itself. "Universal and direct suffrage, consulted on three consecutive occasions, has produced the most counterrevolutionary and antirepublican results.... The eruption of the masses, suddenly summoned, has made of society an incomprehensible monster."[55] Democracy had unleashed an "anti-liberal and persecuting Church" placated by the French suppression of the Roman Republic and by establishment

---

53 Quoted at length in Emeri and Bidegaray, *La Constitution*, 262; cf. 260–3.
54 Ibid., 263; cf. 262.
55 Pierre-Joseph Proudhon, *Confessions d'un Révolutionaire* (Paris, 1849, Rivière ed. 1929), 364.

of an unprecedently arbitrary state power. His warnings against the coming coup landed him in jail and following the plebiscite approving it, Proudhon exclaimed: "On Second December the last of the Gods died, the People... We woke up citizens and we shall go to bed as subjects."[56]

Louis-Napoleon, in seizing power, had not needed an Article 16 such as de Gaulle insisted on including in the 1958 constitution to deal with crisis situations, much to the hostility of traditional republicans who feared another 1851 or 1830, when Charles X invoked Article 14 of the constitutional charter. De Gaulle wanted to give the president the power to defend the country in circumstances such as confronted Presidents Albert Lebrun in 1940 and René Coty in 1958. "In 99 cases out of 100, in such circumstances, the man at the head of state would not be inclined by his age, temperament or the circumstances to take such initiatives. The constitution must oblige him to do so. The constitution must give him the duty and then he will carry it out."[57] This remark suggests de Gaulle had a touching faith in the power of constitutions, an uncharacteristic triumph of hope over French experience.

This is not the place to explore the view, argued most recently by Sudhir Hazareesingh, that "despite the claims of orthodox republican historiography, the Second Empire was the period in which universal suffrage acquired a pre-eminent position in the French political system."[58] Despite systematic electoral pressure and manipulation, Louis-Napoleon had restored universal suffrage, and it was never again abandoned in France. The catchall nature of his appeal is reflected in his jocular remark: "The Empress is Legitimist, my cousin (Prince Jerome) is Republican, Morny is Orleanist, I am a Socialist. The only Bonapartist is Persigny, and he is mad."[59] There was undoubtedly a minority left-wing Bonapartism, sometimes confused by Louis-Napoleon among others with Louis-Napoleon's Saint-Simonism, which had much more to do with a materialistic plutocracy and technocracy than with

---

56 Quoted in Pierre Haubtmann, *Proudhon, 1849–55*, I (Paris, 1988), 338–9.
57 See Consultative Constitutional Committee discussion of August 8, 1958 in *Documents pour servir à l'histoire de l'elaboration de la Constitution*, I (Paris, 1987), 301; cf. 68, 74, 302; and Jean-Louis Debré, *Les Idées Constitutionnels du Général de Gaulle* (Paris, 1974), 207–9.
58 Sudhir Hazareesingh, *From Subject to Citizen. The Second Empire and the Emergence of Modern French Democracy* (Princeton, 1998), 26. He notes that this argument had been advanced earlier by Marcel Blanchard, *Le Second Empire* (Paris, 1956), 211–12; Theodore Zeldin, *The Political System of Napoleon III* (London, 1958), 98; and Raymond Huard, *Le suffrage universal en France, 1848–1946* (Paris, 1985), 142.
59 Quoted in Corley, *Democratic Despot*, 373, note 9. The Duke de Morny, Louis-Napoleon's half-brother, became minister of the interior (1851–2) and president of the Legislative Assembly (1854–65). The Duke de Persigny was Minister of the Interior (1852–4, 1860–3) and the Second Empire's principal ideologist. See Joseph Delaroa, ed., *Le Duc de Persigny et les doctrines de l'Empire* (Paris, 1856).

socialism. He did ask Charles Robert to investigate worker profit-sharing, which anticipated schemes favored by left-wing Gaullists a century later. However, although a Gaullist leader such as Philippe Séguin wrote a book to explain his joint admiration for Louis-Napoleon and de Gaulle,[60] this linkage did not commend itself to his Rassemblement Pour la République (RPR) members or, more generally, to the French people.

To assess the enduring standing of Bonapartism and Gaullism in contemporary France, comparison must be made between Napoleon and de Gaulle. In a public opinion poll conducted in 1990 to coincide with an international conference on "De Gaulle en son Siècle," respondents were asked to name the most important people in French history. Among those named in first place, de Gaulle (18%) came second to Charlemagne (20%), with Napoleon a close third (17%). Taking the respondents' top three choices together, de Gaulle came first (51%), with Napoleon second (46%), and Charlemagne third (37%).[61] Another poll of lycée students in 1988 showed that setting aside primarily nonpolitical figures like Victor Hugo and Louis Pasteur, de Gaulle outclassed Napoleon, whose support significantly is much greater on the right and extreme right of the political spectrum of support.[62]

De Gaulle did not achieve his goal of becoming a supra-partisan leader, but he came closer than Napoleon had.[63] As a heroic leader, de Gaulle was able to survive his role as crisis leader to become the founding father of an enduring regime that combined assured republican authority and relative constitutional stability with dirigiste economic modernization. None of these achievements is immune to the impact of persisting internal dissension and external competitive pressures that make it more difficult for France to preserve its treasured identity despite its habitual inclination to inertia. The increasing tendency toward "cohabitension" suggests that the French preference for parliamentary rather than presidential government

---

60 Philippe Séguin, *Louis Napoléon le Grand* (Paris, 1990), a title chosen to play off Victor Hugo's *Napoléon le Petit* of 1852. In the third of his letters on the French coup d'état of 1851 published by the *Inquirer* and dated from Paris, January 15, 1852, Walter Bagehot drew the contrast between "Napoleon the Great" and "Napoleon the Little." See Bagehot's *Historical Essays*, ed. N. St John-Stevas (London, 1971), 398.
61 Institut Charles de Gaulle, *De Gaulle en son siècle. Sondages et enquêtes d'opinion* (Paris, 1992), 33, poll of 1,500 interviews conducted by SOFRES.
62 Annick Percheron, "Le général de Gaulle vu par les lycéens: un personnage entre mémoire et histoire" in Institut Charles de Gaulle, *De Gaulle en son siècle*, I (Paris, 1992), 382–90. A sample of 2,641 lycéens were interviewed.
63 Tony Judt in his review of the abridged English edition of Pierre Nora, ed., *Realms of Memory* (New York, 1998) criticized the absence of any entries for Napoleon Bonaparte, Louis-Napoleon, or Bonapartism, asserting that "France is suffused with the legacy of Bonapartism" and "the spirit of Napoleon is still with us." "A la Recherche du Temps Perdu," *New York Review of Books*, December 3, 1998, 54.

is reasserting itself. The scope for assertive leadership capable of imparting impetus is being reduced as the administration of things increasingly supersedes the government of men. France has returned to a humdrum era in which the electors do not wish to be disturbed by the heroics of a de Gaulle, still less of a Napoleon. They can be safely lodged in the pantheon of dead heroes, without confusing the man of Eighteenth Brumaire with the man of Eighteenth June.

11

The Leader and the Masses

Hannah Arendt on Totalitarianism and Dictatorship

MARGARET CANOVAN

Everything we know of totalitarianism demonstrates a horrible originality which no farfetched historical parallels can alleviate.[1]

Totalitarian government is different from dictatorships and tyrannies; the ability to distinguish between them is by no means an academic issue which could be safely left to the "theoreticians," for total domination is the only form of government with which coexistence is not possible.[2]

Hannah Arendt claimed that the regimes of Hitler and Stalin represented varieties of a single type[3] that was as unprecedented as it was appalling. Struggling against the universal human impulse to categorize the new in terms of what is familiar, she reflected at length on the difficulties of trying to understand phenomena that had "exploded our categories of political thought and our standards for moral judgement."[4] She was herself well aware, however, that some political commentators ever since the time of the French Revolution had been exclaiming over the novelty of modern forms of oppression, while others had found remote historical precedents for the apparently new. Edmund Burke had been first in the field with his warning that the Jacobin dictatorship represented a new and particularly dangerous kind of tyranny,[5] but the phenomenon that had set off most rethinking among political theorists was the Revolution's culmination in the

---

I am grateful for Peter Baehr's helpful comments on a previous draft of this chapter.
1 Hannah Arendt, "Understanding and Politics," in H. Arendt, *Essays in Understanding, 1930–1954*, ed. Jerome Kohn (New York, 1994), 309.
2 Hannah Arendt, *The Origins of Totalitarianism* (London, 1967), xi–xii.
3 "Totalitarianism" as described by Arendt owes most of its features to the Nazi regime, but also incorporates some more characteristic of Stalinism, notably the purges.
4 Arendt, "Understanding and Politics," 310.
5 "It is with an *armed doctrine* that we are at war." "First Letter on a Regicide Peace" (1796), *The Works of the Right Hon. Edmund Burke*, Vol. II (London, 1834), 280.

regime of Napoleon Bonaparte.[6] His explosively powerful combination of personal dictatorship and popular mobilization led many to draw parallels with the rule of Julius Caesar, apparently implying that there was nothing really novel here. Developments later in the nineteenth century, particularly the establishment by Louis Bonaparte of the second Bonapartist regime, prompted commentators not only to draw parallels with the end of the Roman Republic but to speculate on new features of European society. For it seemed that modern politics harbored the potential for an unfamiliar form of repressive rule, one that was no more acceptable to conservative monarchists than it was to progressive liberals. As Peter Baehr has shown,[7] accounts and diagnoses of the new "Caesars" varied a good deal, but key themes recur. Napoleon and his imitators exercised centralized, autocratic rule that lacked constitutional foundation and showed scant respect for legality, but that claimed the legitimacy of popular consent. Established and sustained by force, devoted to military aggrandizement, it was confirmed by the acclamation of a populace dazzled by the vision of national glory. By way of explanation, analysts of "Caesarist" dictatorship regularly pointed to the new influence in European politics of "the masses": ignorant, irrational, and easily manipulated.

These nineteenth-century traditions of political experience and analysis seemed to some to offer a framework in which to place the widespread establishment of dictatorships in Europe after the First World War. In so far as the Russian Revolution echoed the French, its culmination in personal dictatorship was only to be expected. Further west, wider popular participation in politics was in many cases followed by militaristic dictatorships of a more or less Caesarist kind. From Bonaparte to Mussolini, and from Mussolini to Hitler, was perhaps not a very big step. It was of course true that both Bolsheviks and Fascists insisted on their own novelty, the latter coining the term "totalitarian" to describe their own regime.[8] Widespread adoption of the term in both academic and popular use by the mid–twentieth century implied a perception that there was indeed something novel about twentieth-century dictatorships; nevertheless, the novelty was often thought of as an intensification of previous efforts

---

6 Melvin Richter, "Toward a Concept of Political Illegitimacy: Bonapartist Dictatorship and Democratic Legitimacy," *Political Theory* 10 (1982), 185–214.
7 Peter Baehr, *Caesar and the Fading of the Roman World: a Study in Republicanism and Caesarism* (New Brunswick, 1998).
8 "For the Fascist all is in the state and nothing human or spiritual exists, or much less has value, outside the state. In this sense fascism is totalitarian." *The Doctrine of Fascism*, written by Giovanni Gentile and published under Mussolini's name in 1932, quoted in A. James Gregor, *The Ideology of Fascism: the Rationale of Totalitarianism* (New York, 1969), 223.

at control rather than as something wholly without precedent. Franz Neumann suggested, for example, that whereas a "caesaristic" dictator combined "monopolized coercion and popular backing," a "totalitarian" dictatorship goes one step further than that, finding it necessary to control education, communication, and the economy in order "to gear the whole of society and the private life of the citizen to the system of political domination."[9] "Total" control of all aspects of life is achieved by organizing the masses into a single party held together by an official ideology. On this view, the mass participation in modern politics that makes democracy possible also provides the conditions for the most intensive form of dictatorship yet achieved.[10]

This tradition of analysis makes it hard to see at first glance why Arendt put so much stress on the qualitative novelty of totalitarianism, and it is easy to miss the distinctiveness of her own account of it. Many familiar features seem to be present in her book: the personal dictatorship of a leader who has no constitutional legitimacy but enjoys mass support; repression within the state's borders and aggression without; a mass movement with an ideology. One signal that should warn readers to take note, however, is the care Arendt takes to restrict her use of the term "totalitarian" to two cases only, the regimes of Hitler and Stalin.[11] Most of the dictatorships counted as examples of totalitarianism by other writers are in Arendt's view nothing of the sort. All the post-Stalinist communist regimes of the USSR and Eastern Europe, for example, often regarded as classic examples, fall outside her category. Reviewing the situation after Stalin's death, she observed that totalitarianism had ceased. "The people of the Soviet Union have emerged from the nightmare of totalitarian rule to the manifold hardships, dangers and injustices of one-party dictatorship."[12] All the apparatus of total control was still there: the party, the ideology, the secret police, and the lack of rights, but the system was no longer totalitarian. It is perhaps even more telling that Arendt denied the label to the regime that first proclaimed itself "totalitarian," Mussolini's Fascism. In its prime, before Mussolini fell under Hitler's influence, his regime was in her view "not totalitarian but just an

---

9 "Notes on the Theory of Dictatorship," in Franz Neumann, *The Democratic and the Authoritarian State: Essays in Political and Legal Theory*, ed. Herbert Marcuse (Glencoe, 1957), 236.
10 According to the classic theory of Friedrich and Brzezinski, totalitarianism is the type of autocracy that fits modern societies, just as absolute monarchy was characteristic of traditional societies. Carl J. Friedrich amd Zbigniew Brzezinski, *Totalitarian Dictatorship and Autocracy* (New York, 1967).
11 "Lenin's was a revolutionary one-party dictatorship." Arendt dated the beginning of totalitarianism in the USSR from 1930, and in Germany from 1938. "On the Nature of Totalitarianism: An Essay in Understanding," in *Essays in Understanding*, 347–8.
12 Arendt, *Origins*, xxi.

ordinary nationalist dictatorship,"[13] with a leader at the head of a single party in possession of the state.

What is it, then, that is special about totalitarianism in Arendt's unusual sense? The essay in which she confronted this question directly, trying to provide a general characterization of this "novel form of government" to add to Montesquieu's characterizations of "monarchy," "republic," and "despotism," is entitled "Ideology and Terror." This title seems only to add to the mystery, since ideology and terror in the ordinary senses of the words certainly existed in Mussolini's Fascism and Brezhnev's Soviet Union. Nor was it the sheer scale of terror that was decisive. "Suffering...is not the issue, nor is the number of victims."[14] She insists that totalitarianism is not just more extreme than other forms of political oppression, but that it is essentially different, with special characteristics that show up regardless of the particular national traditions of the country in which it appears or the specific source of its ideology.[15] Elsewhere she observes that the Nazi leaders were well aware of this distinctiveness, despising Mussolini's Fascism but recognizing that Stalin's regime was akin to their own. In his diary, Goebbels recorded disparaging comments on the superficiality of Fascism compared with Nazi radicalism. Mussolini, he said, "is not a revolutionary like the Führer or Stalin. He is so bound to his own Italian people that he lacks the broad qualities of a world-wide revolutionary and insurrectionist."[16] Together with respectful references by Hitler and other Nazis to the genuinely ideological character of Stalin's regime (quoted on the same page of *The Origins of Totalitarianism*), this makes it even harder to see why Arendt thought totalitarianism was such a novelty. For the stress on ideological revolution seems reminiscent of the Jacobin "armed doctrine" so much feared by Burke at the time of the French Revolution and makes totalitarianism sound like a kind of quasi-religious ideological crusade. Yet Arendt continues to insist on the complete lack of precedents for the phenomenon she is concerned with. Totalitarian regimes "operate according to a system of values so radically different from all others, that none of our traditional legal, moral, or common sense categories could any

---

13 Ibid., 257.
14 Ibid., 459. The quotation continues, "Human nature as such is at stake." Cf. Arendt's essays, "Mankind and Terror," and "On the Nature of Totalitarianism," both in *Essays in Understanding*. On the distinctiveness of totalitarianism, see also Margaret Canovan, *Hannah Arendt: A Reinterpretation of her Political Thought* (Cambridge, 1992), Chap. 2, and "Arendt's Theory of Totalitarianism: a Reassessment," in *The Cambridge Companion to Hannah Arendt*, ed. Dana Villa (Cambridge, 2000).
15 "Ideology and Terror: A Novel Form of Government" (1953), included in Arendt, *Origins*, 460.
16 Arendt, *Origins*, 309.

longer help us to come to terms with, or judge, or predict their course of action."[17]

Arendt's account of what it is that is distinctive about totalitarianism is in fact quite difficult to grasp, for the good reason (she would have said) that she was struggling to articulate phenomena that were themselves well nigh incomprehensible.[18] Despite apparent similarities in the use of violence, totalitarianism as she understands it is in some ways the direct opposite of normal repressive regimes, which are characterized by ruthless Machiavellianism. Instead, it is a purposeless, senseless, gigantic mobilization for destruction, in which "terror is no longer a means to frighten and suppress opponents, but, on the contrary, increases with the decrease of opposition."[19] The key point is that totalitarianism is a mass *movement*: a movement without end, a perpetual motion of destruction.

> The totalitarian form of government depends entirely upon the fact that a movement, and not a party, has taken power... so that instead of the tyrant's brutal determination and the dictator's demagogic ability to keep himself in power at all costs, we find the totalitarian leader's single-minded attention directed to the acceleration of the movement itself.[20]

My aim in this chapter is to make use of comparisons with "normal" forms of dictatorship to help fix this elusive phenomenon, focusing attention especially on the peculiarities of totalitarian leadership and its relation to the masses.

THE LEADER

From Machiavelli's "prince" to Weber's "charismatic" individual, post-classical theories of dictatorship have been constructed around the figure of the leader: the larger than life man who embodies dominance in his person. Within the nineteenth-century tradition of thinking about Caesarism, the illegitimacy of the dictator's rule itself testifies to his stature: He is a man who has made himself lord by sheer force of personality, without being able to rely on traditional or institutional support. The figure of Napoleon is paradigmatic. Here is the man of destiny, able to seize the moment, to master his rivals, to dazzle the masses, to dare great enterprises and to crush opposition with an iron hand. Even those who hated him did not deny

---

17 "Ideology and Terror," 460.
18 "Understanding and Politics," *passim*. Cf. Margaret Canovan, "Beyond Understanding? Arendt's Account of Totalitarianism," *Hannah Arendt Newsletter* No. 1 (April 1999), 25–30.
19 Arendt, "Authority in the Twentieth Century," *Review of Politics* 18 (1956), 408.
20 Ibid., 408.

his exceptional qualities. In the twentieth century, Fascism transformed this grudging recognition of personal dominance into an ideological justification of dictatorial rule by *il Duce*, the man who had given practical proof of his ability to lead. If Mussolini showed the way, Hitler and his followers went further, explicitly personalizing his regime so that everything revolved around the *Führer*, whose will had the force of law.

It is therefore very striking (and puzzling for readers of *Origins*) that Arendt pays so little attention in her account of totalitarianism to the individual leaders, Hitler and Stalin. It is no part of her thesis to deny their importance – as we have seen, she stresses that it was only under Stalin's rule that the Soviet Union was totalitarian – but nothing in her treatment of them hints at the Caesarist tradition of world historical individuals or charismatic leaders setting their personal stamp on their times. They are at the center of totalitarianism, but it is a peculiar kind of centrality. Not for nothing does she adopt the metaphorical figure of the onion to describe the totalitarian movement, with the leader inside its enclosed layers, in the space at its center.[21] Elsewhere, in a revealing footnote, she comments on the incongruity of treating Hitler and Stalin ("these non-persons") to "the undeserved honor of definitive biographies" simply "because of their importance for contemporary history."[22] This is not a moral judgment but a comment on the total disproportion between their personal stature and the havoc they wreaked.[23] While admitting Hitler's renowned charisma, she offers a demystifying and un-Weberian explanation of the phenomenon. Reviewing an edition of his table-talk, she notes his dominance over those around him, but maintains that:

> The problem of Hitler's charisma is relatively easy to solve . . . it rested on the well-known experiential fact that Hitler must have realized early in his life, namely, that modern society in its desperate inability to form judgments will take every individual for what he considers himself and professes himself to be . . . Extraordinary self-confidence and displays of self-confidence therefore inspire confidence in others; pretensions to genius waken the conviction in others that they are indeed dealing with a genius.

She adds that "Hitler's real superiority consisted in the fact that under any and all circumstances he had an opinion," not because he was better informed or had special insight, but simply because of his fanatical consistency.[24] Among

---

21 Ibid. Arendt's metaphor is discussed below.
22 Arendt, *Men in Dark Times* (London, 1970), 33–4.
23 Cf. Arendt's comments on Adolf Eichmann in her *Eichmann in Jerusalem: A Report on the Banality of Evil* (London, 1963), 49 and 253.
24 Arendt, "At Table with Hitler," in *Essays in Understanding*, 291 and 293. Cf. *Origins*, 305.

people with no firm grasp on reality (which in her view is characteristic of "masses," as we shall see), sheer certainty is itself convincing, especially when wedded to an ideology, however mad, that provides an instant answer to every question.

Charisma understood in this way bears no relation to the creative genius Weber attributed to those supermen who were able to inspire and dominate the masses. In Arendt's view, the totalitarian leader is not a towering figure of that kind, nor even "a power-hungry individual imposing a tyrannical and arbitrary will upon his subjects."[25] Rather, his role is to be the center and personification of a mass movement. According to the "leader principle," everything done within the movement is supposed to emanate from the will of the leader, who claims total responsibility for all its actions.[26] Yet Arendt insists that "the totalitarian leader is nothing more nor less than the functionary of the masses he leads." Leader and masses are mutually dependent: "without him they would lack external representation and remain an amorphous horde; without the masses the leader is a nonentity."[27] Both are caught up and carried along in the momentum of the movement, whose perpetual motion is the essence of totalitarianism.

Aware of the difficulty of grasping and communicating so outlandish a phenomenon, Arendt tries to dislodge from her readers' minds the familiar image of the tyrant who dominates his subjects and rules by arbitrary decree. In her view, the model of a commander issuing orders to his troops is misleadingly institutional in this context. The source of authority in the Nazi regime was not any specific "order," but the fluid, perpetually mobile "will" of the Führer.[28] Even more bafflingly, however, we should not interpret this will as the arbitrary lawlessness of the traditional tyrant. In her essay on "Ideology and Terror," Arendt argued that totalitarianism is the reverse of lawlessness, being conceived as obedience to supposed laws of nature or history that are revealed by the movement's ideology. According to those supposed laws, human beings are swept along in a perpetual motion of struggle and destruction over which the ruler himself has no power, except that his insight into the laws enables him to speed up their execution.[29] Neither he nor anyone else benefits from this hurricane of destruction. As Arendt continually insists, to look for utilitarian motives (even of the

---

25 Arendt, *Origins*, 325.   26 Ibid., 374.
27 Both quotations are from Arendt, *Origins*, 325.
28 Arendt, "Authority in the Twentieth Century," 409. Cf. Ian Kershaw, "Working Towards the Führer: Reflections on the Nature of the Hitler Dictatorship," in *Stalinism and Nazism: Dictatorships in Comparison*, eds. I. Kershaw and Moshe Lewin (Cambridge, 1997), 88–106.
29 Arendt, *Origins*, 465.

most ruthless kind) is a waste of time, and it is the combination of gigantic destructive energy with utter senselessness that makes totalitarianism so hard to understand.

It will help us to clarify what she means if we return for a moment to the example of Mussolini's self-proclaimed "totalitarian" state and consider just why it was in her view not a genuine case, but something more old fashioned and less dangerous. The crucial difference from Nazism was that although Mussolini was brought to power by a mass movement, the movement did not remain in motion. It had a destination and an end point, and "was frozen into a party after the seizure of power."[30] Like other dictators, Mussolini saw mobilization as a means to the end of exercising power within an established state structure. Despite its aggressive foreign policy, the aims of the Fascist regime were defined and limited by the structure of the state and the interests of the nation with which it identified itself: It had a settled worldly home and worldly, utilitarian interests. A movement of that sort was revolutionary only temporarily, during the seizure of power. Totalitarianism, by contrast, means *permanent* revolution, which does not exhaust its momentum in the conquest of a particular state, but goes on attacking all institutional structures and all territorial boundaries.

"Movement" is crucial, and Arendt insists on the difference between a movement on the one hand, and a party (however dictatorial and monopolistic) on the other. Some of these differences (but not all) are captured in the everyday terminology that contrasts parties (professional political organizations seeking power within an established political system) with movements (more amorphous and more idealistic organizations aiming to change the system from without). Ordinary terminology assumes, however, that a movement is moving toward some definite goal: toward a better state and society, or, at the very least, toward capturing the state and its powers. The distinctive feature of totalitarian mass movements in Arendt's account is that they have no goal except to keep moving and no motive except hatred of all stable institutions. In particular, she insists, "There are no movements without hatred of the state."[31] Whereas the Italian Fascist regime put the cult of the state and its interests at the center of their official ideology, all true movements recognize that the stable institutions and defined territorial boundaries that constitute any state are obstacles in the way of perpetual revolutionary motion. Having no settled goal or end, movements can adopt and discard programs at will, "for the only thing that counts in a movement

---

30 Arendt, "Authority in the Twentieth Century," 407.
31 Arendt, *Origins*, 259.

is precisely that it keeps itself in constant movement."[32] In so far as there is any practical objective, it is simply to extend the movement's range and to set more people in motion. Arendt states, "A political goal that would constitute the end of the movement simply does not exist."[33] Observers assumed that Hitler's accession to power would domesticate Nazism and turn it into an ordinary party concerned with the interests of the state it controlled. Arendt claims that, like Stalin's regime, Nazism never did settle down into bureaucratic stability.[34] Organizationally it remained shapeless and chaotic, while its actions became ever more radical and less and less in tune with raison d'état. Rather than being a means to capture or create stable political institutions of some kind, a movement is a substitute for such institutions, a way of organizing people without institutional stability.

As we have seen, the leader personifies the movement and has a crucial role in it. Since the movement has no purpose and is not going anywhere in particular, his function is quite unlike those claimed by nontotalitarian dictators, whose rationale is either the salvation of existing institutions or the creation of new ones. The most common justification for dictatorship is that a strong leader (usually a military man) has taken power for the sake of the nation, in order to save a weak state from corrupt politicians and squabbling factions. Dictatorship promises the restoration of order and stability through the strengthening of institutions. More radical justifications, theorized by Machiavelli and Weber and personified by Napoleon, add to these the need for a strong leader to make a new beginning and to found new institutions. Despite their assault on legality and on the institutions of civil society, conventional dictators provide a stable framework within which normal life can be carried on by those who keep their heads down. By contrast, totalitarianism as described by Arendt allows no such tranquility. Totalitarian movements destroy old institutions without being interested in creating new ones, and draw everyone they can reach into a whirlwind of perpetual destructive motion.[35]

Our bewilderment about the anti-utilitarian character of the totalitarian state structure springs from the mistaken notion that we are dealing with a normal state after all — a bureaucracy, a tyranny, a dictatorship — from our overlooking the emphatic assertions by totalitarian rulers that they consider the country where they happened

---

32 Ibid., 260. 33 Arendt, *Origins*, 326.
34 Ibid., 389.
35 It may be argued that this is what Napoleon's career of conquest amounted to. (See the chapters by Blanning and Hayward in this volume.) But Napoleon did establish many lasting institutions in France. Arendt explicitly repudiated the notion that he was comparable to Hitler. *Essays in Understanding*, 108.

to seize power only the temporary headquarters of the international movement on the road to world conquest, that they reckon victories and defeats in terms of centuries or millennia, and that the global interests always overrule the local interests of their own territory.[36]

The only new "institutions" established by totalitarian regimes are the concentration camps and the secret police empire at the center of which they lie, and the peculiarities of police and camps underline the peculiarity of the whole phenomenon. For one thing, stress on the police rather than the army is an expression of the point just made, that totalitarian regimes regard all territories as actually or potentially conquered and already subject to police power.[37] Even more crucially, the role of the police in a totalitarian regime is not the ordinary function, carried out under all conventional dictatorships, of ferreting out and crushing opposition to the regime. Instead, as Arendt repeatedly stressed, their characteristic task starts only after all opposition has been silenced and the population is already too frightened to plot against their masters. At that point the police can get down to the truly totalitarian business of feeding the process of perpetual destruction by rounding up the next batch of innocents to be declared "objective enemies" who are doomed to die by the laws of nature or history.

Dictatorships have often been seen as manifestations of a will to power that rejects all moral limits and asserts amorally that "everything is permitted." However, that image implies the conscious and ruthless pursuit of goals that are intelligible, however cruel and predatory. Arendt claims that the maxim of totalitarian rule, exemplified in the concentration camps in which the secret police practice on their innocent victims, is not just "everything is permitted" but "everything is possible." This takes them into an insane realm beyond utilitarian calculation, where the only purpose is destruction in accordance with ideological "laws" and where killing alone is not enough: where all human individuality and capacity for action are deliberately eliminated, and the victim is reduced to a subhuman "bundle of reactions" before being killed.[38]

Looking back on the experience of the Nazi and Stalinist regimes at the end of the first edition of her book, Arendt emphasized the senselessness and futility of it all, observing that "Until now the totalitarian belief that everything is possible seems to have proved only that everything can be destroyed."[39] It was a mistake to class total domination with the kind of

---

36 Arendt, *Origins*, 411. 37 Ibid., 420.
38 Ibid., 440–1.
39 H. Arendt, *The Burden of Our Time* (first edition of *Origins*) (London, 1951), 433.

hubristic ambition that treats men and nature as material for some new construction, still more to assimilate it to the familiar spectacle of predatory rulers helping themselves to "the time-honored joys of tyrannical rule."[40] Although the regimes did provide themselves with rationales for destruction in the form of ideologies, Arendt maintains that the way in which they developed and interpreted those ideologies rendered them as meaningless as everything else about the whole business. Inheriting all embracing theories that purported to explain human history and predict the future (by reference either to biological or to economic causes), both Hitler and Stalin stripped away the intellectual content of their respective ideologies until nothing was left except belief in an inevitable process of lethal struggle between races or classes, carrying the logical deduction that a race that is unfit or a class that is reactionary is destined for extermination. Both leaders prided themselves on their merciless consistency in carrying out the sentences of execution supposedly delivered by the iron laws of nature or history, Hitler preening himself on his "ice cold reasoning" and Stalin on the "mercilessness of his dialectics."[41] This was a form of ideology that eliminated thought and sense in favor of the compulsive deduction that led inexorably to the next step in the process of extermination. The process is everything: It has no purpose, no final goal, except to continue without end.[42]

THE MASSES

We have seen that Arendt's account of the role of the leader in totalitarian movements and regimes differs very considerably from conventional accounts of dictatorship. Here there is no dominant individual inspiring or manipulating the masses to achieve his own personal ends; instead, the leader is simply at the center of a whirlwind of destruction. Unlike dictatorship, totalitarianism cannot be understood in utilitarian terms, making it impossible for nontotalitarian political actors to anticipate the actions and reactions of such regimes.

How, then, is such a phenomenon to be comprehended at all? Arendt's contention is that although no explanation could make it other than senseless, the key to totalitarianism lies in the masses, on whose support for Hitler and Stalin she lays great stress.[43] As with so many features of her theory, this point about mass support seems at first sight quite conventional, echoing

---

40 Arendt, "On the Nature of Totalitarianism," 346.
41 Arendt, "Ideology and Terror," 471. 42 Arendt, "Mankind and Terror," 306.
43 Arendt, *Origins*, 306.

familiar theories of Caesarist dictatorship that linked it with the ignorance and irrationality of the masses. Such theories were quite various, some of them (notably Max Weber's) assuming that where politics is concerned, most of the human race always has been and always will be nothing but an inert mass that relies on dominant leaders to inspire and shape it. Others were somewhat less pessimistic, attributing "mass" symptoms to particular circumstances of modernity, such as the emergence of a concentrated industrial proletariat, the sudden grant of the suffrage to millions of men previously excluded from politics, or the atomization caused by specific social and economic conditions.[44] Arendt's theory might perhaps be seen as an unusual and particularly complex variant of the diagnosis last mentioned. She claims that "Totalitarian movements are mass organizations of atomized, isolated individuals,"[45] and that the atomization of these "masses" is not the normal condition of humanity but a pathological condition that is widespread in the twentieth century. People are turned into masses through loss of their common human "world," a loss that undermines their grasp of reality and sense of self-interest. Left with nothing except the "negative solidarity"[46] provided by a shared hatred of all the existing institutions, they are only too willing to merge themselves into a nihilistic movement to which they can give undiscriminating loyalty.

"Masses" are a special category, not to be confused either with "the people" or "the mob." Arendt did not accept the pessimistic Caesarist diagnosis that bringing the people into politics was in itself a recipe for populist dictatorship. Admittedly, she did have her own rather different worries about the implications for political freedom of the materialistic priorities of poor people in pre-modern societies and of consumers in modern ones.[47] Furthermore, she agreed that there were circumstances in which the replacement of weak multiparty rule by one-party dictatorship might be hailed by the majority of the population as something of a relief, for reasons that were quite intelligible and nonpathological.[48] However, she denied that dictatorship had an inherent appeal to the people as such, maintaining instead that two separate categories of its potential supporters needed to be distinguished. One, "the mob," to whom demagogic leaders appeal, had long been a familiar feature of politics: the other, "the masses," provided the basis for totalitarianism and were a new phenomenon characteristic of the twentieth century.

44 Baehr, *Caesar and the Fading of the Roman World*, 120–6 and passim.
45 Arendt, *Origins*, 323. 46 Ibid., 315.
47 Arendt, *On Revolution* (London, 1963), Chaps. 2–3.
48 Arendt, *Origins*, 257.

"The mob" features prominently in the first two parts of *Origins*, which are concerned with anti-Semitism and imperialism. These are people on the fringes of society, hanging about the streets of great cities or exported to the frontiers of European empires. Arendt speaks of them as "human debris" and as "the refuse of all classes,"[49] people displaced by the economic dynamism of capitalism and living by their wits. Desperate, amoral, and easily recruited for violence, people of this kind carried out the anti-Semitic pogroms that accompanied the Dreyfus Affair in France at the end of the nineteenth century.[50] Being attracted to violence and criminality, the mob does indeed have the affinity with dictatorship long noticed by theorists of Caesarism, as in the rise to power of Louis Bonaparte.[51] Arendt claims that racist doctrines had a particular appeal to outsiders of this kind because they offered the mob the opportunity to improve their own position through sheer violence, by forcing another group into subordination.[52] In her view, Hitler and others prominent in the initiation of totalitarian movements came from this stratum.[53] However, if nothing more than the mob had been involved, the catastrophes of totalitarianism could never have taken place. The key feature of these movements and regimes was that they managed to harness much wider support, from a large section of the population who were in most respects quite unlike the mob, and whom Arendt calls "the masses."

"The masses share with the mob only one characteristic, namely, that both stand outside all social ramifications and normal political representation."[54] Unlike the mob, which is composed of individuals who have fallen out of a functioning social structure for one reason or another, masses are what results when the social structure itself breaks down. Capitalism had already uprooted people, severing old ties of community and gathering people into broad classes, and when the upheavals of war, revolution, or economic crisis undermined the class structure, vast numbers of people found themselves suddenly deprived of the world in which they had known who they were and how to conduct themselves. Arendt's analysis here draws on one of the most persistent themes of her work, the theme of "world" and "worldlessness." Animals live on the natural earth, and so of course do we. However, to be truly human beings we need also to inhabit a man-made "world" of stable structures. We need this not only to hedge us about with laws and to bestow rights upon us, but also to share a common, many-sided experience of reality with others, for this is the only way in which we can develop common

49 Ibid., 150 and 155.
51 Ibid., 262.
53 Ibid., 317.

50 Ibid., 107–13.
52 Ibid., 206.
54 Ibid., 314.

sense.[55] Without this worldly experience, we are each thrown back upon our own private experience, with no reliable way of distinguishing truth from fiction, and according to Arendt this is the condition of the masses. Therefore, the masses are not equivalent simply to the population at large, or to the poor: They are people in a specific pathological condition shared by large numbers of modern individuals – especially in post–First World War Germany, in the wake of defeat, revolution, inflation, and unemployment, and in Russia, after revolution and civil war.[56] The crucial characteristics of the masses, all of them consequent on loss of the world, are isolation, loss of common sense, and what Arendt calls "selflessness": a weird disregard for ordinary utilitarian self-interest that comes from the experience of being entirely expendable. In contrast to more familiar dictatorships based on mobilization of the mob, these characteristics make possible the organization of a totalitarian movement to which its members are devoted to the point of self-sacrifice; which is informed by a mad ideology and has no rational goals; and which, once set in motion, will just keep moving. The weird senselessness and lack of utilitarian purpose that make totalitarianism so hard to understand, along with its robotic, sleepwalking destructiveness, are on this account traceable to the dehumanized condition of the masses whom it mobilizes and represents.[57]

Arendt argues that the totalitarian movement provides a surrogate not only for the sense of self and the social ties that the masses have lost, but for their lost world of reality. What she calls a "fictitious world" is constructed through a combination of propaganda and organization. The propaganda may be false and absurd, but its consumers have lost the ability to make such judgments; instead, what attracts them is that the message explains everything:

> Totalitarian movements conjure up a lying world of consistency which is more adequate to the needs of the human mind than reality itself; in which, through sheer imagination, uprooted masses can feel at home and are spared the never-ending shocks which real life and real experiences deal to human beings and their expectations.[58]

However, the movement has more than propaganda to offer. Arendt stresses that its particular strength lies in providing an alternative world that is

---

55 H. Arendt, *The Human Condition* (Chicago, 1958), 52–8; Canovan, *Hannah Arendt*, 105–10.
56 Note, though, that according to Arendt, Stalin deliberately created "masses" by destroying structures that had begun to settle down after the revolution. Arendt, *Origins*, 319.
57 Arendt does not attempt to provide empirical evidence in support of her vivid picture of those who were mobilized in totalitarian movements.
58 Arendt, *Origins*, 353.

organized in accordance with the ideology, inside which its followers can live. The movement does of course have to deal with a normal world outside, but it does so by adopting a peculiar onion-like structure. On the outside of the onion are front organizations of sympathizers and fellow travelers with the movement. These provide a link with the ordinary world but also a "protective wall,"[59] behind which members of the movement can avoid direct confrontation with reality. Members are reassured by the knowledge that their ideological beliefs are shared by large numbers of ordinary people, albeit in a less consistent way. Meanwhile people outside are also reassured and deceived about the true nature of the movement, since the fellow travelers they mostly encounter seem relatively normal and unfanatical. Inside the movement itself the same layering process continues, with elite formations separated from ordinary members and committed to more radical versions of the ideological fiction, but reassured by the spurious normality of the members who surround them. This layering process can be repeated indefinitely, enabling those in the inner layers of the onion to inhabit a virtual reality of mad beliefs and projects that has been turned into "a fool's paradise of normalcy."[60] Arendt states, "The movement provides for each of its layers ... the fiction of a normal world along with a consciousness of being different from and more radical than it ... The onion structure makes the system organizationally shock-proof against the factuality of the real world."[61] At the center, though also representing the movement to the outside world, is the leader.

This onion-shaped totalitarian movement, providing its members with a fictitious world in place of the real one, sounds more like a religious cult than a political party[62] and might seem ill-fitted to assume power, since power surely implies having to deal with the outside world as it really is. Arendt's point is precisely that totalitarian regimes do not make that adjustment to reality, but instead devote their organizational energies to remaking reality to fit their ideological fiction. This of course entails all the Orwellian apparatus of information control, systematic lying, rewriting of history and so forth. More ominously, it entails making their fictions come true by force: Non-Aryans are turned into an inferior caste under Nazi rule and the "dying classes" were indeed wiped out in Stalin's Soviet Union. Because all human

---

59 Ibid., 366.   60 Ibid., 368.
61 Arendt, "Authority in the Twentieth Century," 412.
62 Arendt does not herself use this parallel, and has harsh words for those who blur the distinctiveness of phenomena by "functionalizing" all concepts. "What is Authority?" in Arendt, *Between Past and Future: Six Exercises in Political Thought* (London, 1961), 102. But the parallel she herself drew was between totalitarian movements and the organizational features of secret societies, drawing extensively on Georg Simmel's work on the latter. *Origins*, 376–82.

activity that is not under totalitarian control poses a threat to the fictitious world, there are no limits, territorial or otherwise, to totalitarian ambition. The aspiration to global rule is part and parcel of the same process as the destruction of all human spontaneity in the concentration camps.[63]

Theories of dictatorship often point to some partially justifying function which the institution fulfills, if only for some parts of the population: providing order and stability after a period of chaos, for example, or making possible the foundation of new institutions. Even totalitarianism does have a function of a sort, according to Arendt, though only in an unexpected and alarming sense. As we have seen, the main emphasis of her account is on the *futility* of the phenomenon. Totalitarian regimes have so far been failures even on their own terms, and this is scarcely surprising, for their perpetual terror and aspiration to global rule tend to unite the rest of the world against them. Arendt even claims that "The futility of totalitarianism in the long run is as essential an aspect of the phenomenon as the offensive ludicrousness of the tenets for which it is prepared to commit its monstrosities." The fact that sheer destructive nihilism could gain so much support and be carried out on such a scale does indicate, she suggests, that "Totalitarianism became this century's curse only because it so terrifyingly took care of its problems." Foremost among those problems was "the experience of modern masses of their superfluity on an overcrowded earth."[64] Political, economic, and social events generate more and more people who have been uprooted from their communities, have lost a stable world, and are regarded by themselves and others as surplus to requirements. Totalitarian movements can provide such people with an alternative world, and totalitarian terror can dispose of them. These are the only "functions" that totalitarian rule can perform: It is incapable either of restoring a political order or of creating a new one.

CONCLUSION

It is clear that Arendt's account of totalitarian rule distinguishes it sharply from all the conventional forms of dictatorship, but two questions remain to be asked. The first is, does her account help to illuminate twentieth-century history? The second, how do its implications for politics in general compare with the implications of more conventional theories? The first, historical, question cannot be given an unequivocal answer. Vivid as it is, Arendt's account is difficult to measure against the ordinary criteria of historical

---

63 Arendt, *Origins*, 392.
64 All three quotations from Arendt, *Burden of Our Time*, 430.

research because of its exceptionally high proportion of imaginative interpretation to empirical data. Furthermore, battles continue to rage among historians over the interpretation of Stalinism and, especially, of Nazism. Nevertheless Arendt's insistence on the novelty of these regimes and on the parallels between them does in retrospect seem reasonable enough, as does her claim that both regimes defy ordinary utilitarian explanations. Indeed, the features of her account best corroborated by recent historical research are often those that seem most bizarre, especially where Nazism is concerned. Despite being highly critical of many aspects of her book, including its recourse to a controversial and unsubstantiated account of the "masses," Ian Kershaw confirms, for example, that "Her emphasis on the radicalizing, dynamic, and structure-destroying inbuilt characteristics of Nazism has been amply borne out by later research."[65] Similarly, Hans Mommsen observes that "Nazi politics unleashed an unbridled political, economic and military dynamic with unprecedented destructive energy, while proving incapable of creating lasting political structures."[66] For Michael Mann, Nazism and Stalinism alike offer two of the rare examples of "regimes of continuous revolution," characterized by extraordinary levels of terror and a "persistent rejection of institutional compromise."[67] Therefore, there is weighty support for Arendt's view that these regimes really did represent something appallingly original, not to be classed with normal versions of dictatorship. Whether she manages to shed light on this baffling phenomenon in the sense of making it intelligible is a separate issue. Readers coming to the end of her book may indeed feel that the mystery is intensified rather than dispelled by her account of totalitarianism.[68] What remains is incomprehension at the madness of destruction and the willing participation in it of so many people.

More can usefully be said about the second question raised above concerning the political implications of Arendt's account, and particularly about the ways in which they differ from the lessons often drawn by theorists of dictatorship. For there is an interesting paradox here, one highly characteristic of Arendt. "Caesarist" theories tend to carry gloomy messages for lovers of political freedom by tracing dictatorship to the political incorporation of mass populations, a process that is inexorable in modern societies. Since Arendt links totalitarianism directly with the worldlessness of modern

---

[65] Ian Kershaw, *The Nazi Dictatorship: Problems and Perspectives of Interpretation*, 3rd ed. (London, 1993), 21.
[66] Hans Mommsen, "Cumulative Radicalization and Progressive Self-Destruction as Structural Determinants of the Nazi Dictatorship," in Kershaw and Lewin, *Stalinism and Nazism*, 86.
[67] M. Mann, "The Contradictions of Continuous Revolution," in Kershaw and Lewin, *Stalinism and Nazism*, 136 and 144.
[68] Cf. Canovan, "Beyond Understanding?"

"masses" and claims that this condition is spreading, one might expect from her an even more depressing assessment of political prospects. This is indeed provided by some aspects of her later work. One of the main strands of her argument in *The Human Condition*, published seven years after *Origins*, traces a link between loss of a stable human world and the advent in modern times of a society devoted to "labor" (the cycle of production and consumption) rather than to the more specifically human activities, "work," which creates lasting artifacts, and "action" in public.[69] Elsewhere she makes clear her view that even without the new threat of totalitarianism, political freedom would not be easy to achieve or to maintain. Revolutions in traditional societies, like France in 1789, saw it fall victim to the urgent social concerns of the poor, while in modern societies freedom takes second place to consumerism.[70]

If one reads Arendt selectively, therefore, one can find in her work a diagnosis of political prospects quite as dark as the predictions of Caesarism and with the extra downward twist that the totalitarianism threatened by modern mass society is immeasurably worse than anything imagined by those who feared nineteenth-century masses. Crucially, however, this is not the only nor the predominant message of her political thought. Even in the first edition of *Origins*, written at a time when Nazism was very near and Stalinism still at its height, the dark story she tells is framed by warnings against despair. Fighting against predictions of inevitable ruin, she proclaims in her "Preface" that "Progress and Doom are two sides of the same medal; that both are articles of superstition."[71] That first edition ended with the reassuring reminder that human beings are not dependent simply on the meager resources of each lonely individual, offering an alternative to nihilism in the form of "gratitude... that we are not alone in the world."[72] Subsequent writings added emphasis on the human capacity to "begin," to start something new.[73] Arendt's mature political thought is largely an exploration of the implications of these insights – insights into the plural existence of unique beings who have a capacity for initiative – for "action," as she puts it. Not that all these implications are reassuring: Many initiatives have disastrous results, while the plurality of actors often means that each frustrates the others' efforts. Arendt nevertheless emerged from the horrors

---

69 Arendt, *Human Condition*, especially Chap. VI. In her essay on "Ideology and Terror" she explicitly links totalitarianism with the worldless "loneliness" characteristic of a society of "laborers." *Origins*, 474–8.
70 Arendt, *On Revolution* (London, 1963), 105–10 and 135–7.
71 Arendt, *Origins*, xxix.   72 Arendt, *Burden of Our Time*, 438.
73 Arendt, *Origins*, 479.

of the mid–twentieth century insisting that because human beings are capable of freely initiating action, the future is not predictable and cannot be inexorably doomed to totalitarianism or to anything else. Furthermore, because we are plural as well as capable of initiative, we can on occasion act freely "in concert," uniting to generate power and to establish a stable world of lasting institutions. Within such a world we can enjoy political freedom and bestow rights upon one another; within such a world, furthermore, we can share a common experience seen from multiple perspectives and develop the common sense so woefully lacking in the masses who followed totalitarian movements.

Twelve years after publishing the first edition of *Origins*, Arendt offered a long meditation on the foundation of political institutions in *On Revolution*, and it is here that the distinctiveness of Arendt's thought is particularly marked. For those political thinkers who have seen a positive role for dictatorship have usually pointed to exceptional situations, times of hiatus in which a new order can be created only by the exceptional individual who conjures up his own legitimacy and who is absolved from ordinary legal and moral restraints. From Machiavelli to Weber and Schmitt, the message is that only the concentration of power in the hands of one outstanding man can overcome such crises. Without explicitly taking issue with that position,[74] Arendt draws on the activities of the Founding Fathers of the American Republic to offer an alternative account that does not rely on dictatorship and its accompanying violence. Foundation is, she stresses, a matter of *action*, of initiative: But this does not imply the dominance of a single "man of action." As she had indicated in *The Human Condition*, action is in principle a capacity belonging to all human beings, not just to charismatic individuals; furthermore, even the most outstanding leader cannot monopolize action, since he is quite impotent without coadjutors.[75] The successful foundation of free institutions is an outcome of the human capacity not only to act but to "act in concert," to generate power amongst ourselves, and to institutionalize that power by undertaking commitments to one another.[76] In the American case,

> The principle which came to light during those fateful years when the foundations were laid – not by the strength of one architect but by the combined power of

---

[74] Though for references to Machiavelli, see *On Revolution*, 31–2 and 208. Peter Baehr points out Arendt's "studied reticence" toward Weber, despite the fact that many aspects of her political thought seem to be directed against his model. Weber was the idol of Arendt's friend and mentor Karl Jaspers. Baehr, *Caesar and the Fading of the Roman World*, 9 and 14–15.

[75] Arendt, *Human Condition*, 177 and 188–9.   [76] Ibid., 244–5; *On Revolution*, 172–6 and 195–6.

the many – was the interconnected principle of mutual promise and common deliberation.[77]

Free institutions are unpredictable and fragile, but they can on occasion be powerful and enduring, like the American Republic. That republic itself was in Arendt's eyes very far from perfect, and she never had much expectation that even this flawed example would be followed elsewhere. She seems to have assumed that most states would remain autocracies or more or less representative oligarchies, some more civilized than others. If totalitarianism was an unprecedented disaster, political freedom was in her view an exceptional achievement. However, what both had in common was that, in defiance of attempts to reduce politics to a science, both in their different ways testified to the range of human possibilities and to the awe-inspiring unpredictability of human affairs.

77 Arendt, *On Revolution*, 215.

PART III

Ancient Resonances

12

Dictatorship in Rome

CLAUDE NICOLET

The word "dictatorship," a simple nativized version of a Roman term, has had two quite distinct senses in European history, at least since Cromwell. On the one hand, paralleling what one might call the "classical" or original Roman dictatorship, it refers to an exceptional but regular and quasi-constitutional power conferred according to precisely defined procedures upon a magistrate (or in modern Europe, a government or assembly) under critical circumstances, in order to confront an external or internal state of emergency in the name of the common good. In brief, this is what Theodor Mommsen called "an exceptional power, roughly equivalent to what today is called suspension of civilian jurisdiction and the declaration of a state of siege" (*Le Droit public*, III, 187). On the other hand, since the eighteenth century, and most particularly, of course, since the French Revolution, the same term has served to refer to despotisms or tyrannies – in other words, essentially powers which are far from having been regularly conferred, and instead have been usurped through force or deceit, most often by one man, but sometimes by an assembly, sect, or party. The "tyrannical" nature of a dictatorship as understood in this second sense is most often accompanied by the idea of an arbitrary, abusive power, which overthrows political or individual rights, governs by terror, and does not recoil from the most extreme violence. It is not just in recent times that the term's ambiguity has afforded a way of manipulating hearers' sensibilities in political or polemical discourse. Used by itself or in a context that specifies an allusion to Roman "precedent," the term emerges with remarkable frequency as early as 1789, for example in Marat. And it reappears

---

This chapter was originally published under the title "La dictature à Rome" in the volume *Dictatures et Légitimité* edited by Maurice Duverger (Paris, 1982). The editors thank the Presses Universitaires de France for permission to publish this translation.

periodically, especially in France, with reference successively to the Convention, Bonaparte, General Cavaignac in 1848, Louis Napoléon, Gambetta, and of course Boulanger – not to mention the famous "dictatorship of the proletariat" proclaimed in 1847, or the term's extensive use in the 1930s by John Bainville and Elie Halévy, as precursors of Hannah Arendt. The historiographic study of this word and concept in the modern and contemporary period is relatively advanced, thanks to the already old work of J. Gagé and A. Mathiez, and the far more recent work of S. Mastellone and P. Catalano. However, its use among the French positivists, well known in its day, has been generally ignored by recent criticism. I shall return to this point later. I would have avoided bringing up this historical or semantic problem, which lies outside my sphere of competence, had it not in fact originated in the actual historical reality it invokes – namely, the fate of the dictatorship in Rome from its origins to Caesar, or even to the constituent Triumvirs of 43 B.C. (Octavius, Lepidus, and Antonius). Indeed, it has been remarked (at least since Mommsen) that in Rome two entirely different political realities apparently went by the same name: first, a magistracy, exceptional to be sure, but legal and in some sense constitutional, which was invoked on a more or less regular footing between 501 and 202 B.C.; second, after a remarkable interruption of 120 years, the revival of this magistracy – at least in name – but in a form and under circumstances which were utterly different, already bringing it in the most formal terms quite close to the "modern" dictatorship of common parlance, as contemporary accounts themselves attest. By this reading, the semantic slippage cannot be blamed solely on the moderns; it is rooted in Roman history itself, where on the political level it already enabled Sulla, Caesar, and the Triumvirs to maintain a profitable equivocation around the reality of their powers.

It is this historical problem that I propose to address here. I shall attempt to show that this interpretation, while possible and perhaps accurate, nevertheless calls for many corrections of detail and a few serious doubts (excellently expressed by U. Wilcken in 1940). The two principal reasons for this situation are as follows: First, what we know (or believe we know) about the primitive, regular "dictatorship" is essentially founded on evidence dating no farther back than the first century B.C. – in other words, sources contemporary with the dictatorship of the second type which, knowingly or not, run the risk of the sin of anachronism. Second, it is certainly not inconsequential that men like Sulla or Caesar chose the term dictatorship, alone or in combination with others, to refer to their powers. It forces us to wonder about their reasons, most importantly as a function of what public opinion they were trying to counteract – or to utilize. But in order to understand these reservations properly, it is worthwhile first to review schematically what I shall call the "dichotomous" (or Mommsenian) conception of Roman dictatorship.

I. "CLASSICAL" OR "REGULAR" DICTATORSHIP

Apart from certain exceptions which we shall discuss later, the roughly seventy-six dictatorships that occurred between 501 (the traditional date of the creation of this magistracy) and 202 appear to present common characteristics by which we can define them. By one formula, following Mommsen, we might say that these dictatorships are a temporary and exceptional revival of the kingship in all its power, invoked in a regular manner according to strict forms; or, in other cases, for the accomplishment of certain specific ritual or procedural duties that for some reason the ordinary powers of the city were unable to carry out properly.

As such, dictatorship in this period fits in normally among the regular institutions of the State (the names of the dictators appear in the *Fasti*, dictatorship heads the hierarchical list of magistracies in official documents, sacral law deals with its attributes as public law does with its authorities, etc.). But at the same time, through a certain number of rather clearly defined features, it differs spectacularly from the norms for a city's magistracies – so much so that it may look like the result of a temporary suspension or even negation of general law:

A. As to the *circumstances* which call for its invocation: on the one hand, a series of precisely defined but uncommon duties (presiding over the Comitia in the absence of competent magistrates, performing the ancient propitiatory ritual of the *clavus annalis*, presiding over certain festivals, exceptional recruitment of the Senate, etc.); and on the other hand, according to the formula attested in 51 (Cic., *De leg.*, III, 3, 9) and by the Emperor Claudius (ILS, 212, l. 28), "if a war or very substantial civil unrest arises," that is, in the event of a crisis of the "the common good."

Moreover, let us note that assessing such needs, in compliance with quite specific criteria (an absence of magistrates, for example), is the duty of the regular powers of the State – the magistrates, the Senate, and/or the people.

B. As to *nomination*: During this period, those powers who judged that there was reason to resort to a dictatorship are in no case permitted to invest themselves with this office. There are forms to be observed. The dictator (and the ancients sometimes believed this was the etymology of the word) must be *nominated* by one or both of the consuls. With one exception, there is no *election* by the people, and even if the Senate approves or suggests recourse to a dictatorship, the ritual of nomination, with its religious forms – at daybreak, in Rome itself, etc. – remains indispensable.

C. As to *collegiality*: The dictator is by definition unique. One of the purposes of nominating him is precisely to establish unity of military command. Hence he has no colleague (in the Roman system, the colleges of magistrates were not required to act jointly, thus implying that each had the potential to oppose the others successfully). The dictator himself nominated – or more likely someone nominated for him – an adjunct who was nevertheless a subordinate, the Master of the Horse. (The only exception was 217 B.C.: cf. below.)

D. As to *duration* or *term*: The dictator is in fact nominated for a specific task. He must "abdicate" (this is a formal obligation) as soon as his task has been accomplished. At an uncertain date, a maximum duration of six months was introduced (Cic., *De leg.*, III, 3, 9). In any case, the dictator cannot remain in power beyond the expiration of the term of office of the magistrate who nominated him. The one-year dictatorships included in the *Fasti* for the early period are highly suspect. The temporary, circumstantial nature of this magistracy was vital – until it ceased to be so with Caesar.

E. Finally, as to *powers* and *competence*: Being "a provisional revival of the kingship" (Mommsen), the dictatorship did not suppress other magistracies (as, curiously, all the Greek historians of Rome believed, Polybius at their head). Quite the contrary. But all magistracies submitted to its command. Of course, dictators nominated for a ritual or procedural task never in fact ranged beyond this limited purpose.

Those nominated for reasons of "the common good" had an essentially military brief, which might in some cases also be judicial (this precisely is one of the controversial problems). Moreover, unanimous tradition insists that originally (perhaps), a dictator was a magistrate (in fact the only one) whose *total* power of coercion was immune from the *provocatio*, i.e., from the right of appeal to the people, which more or less represented a type of habeas corpus that any citizen might invoke. But this is a much debated question.

Thus summarized, the principal characteristics of the "classical" dictatorship call for a certain number of remarks, without which the semantic slippage mentioned previously would be incomprehensible.

a. The most ancient dictatorships mentioned in the *Fasti* and in tradition are eminently suspect (possibly all of them up to 320 B.C.). Now, it is among these that we find five out of the six attested dictatorships created to "put down sedition" (the sixth and last was that of 287, and appears authentic).

We may therefore legitimately wonder whether this reason for nominating a dictator really existed in the earlier period. And yet this reason is politically the most interesting. The dictatorship of L. Quinctius Cincinnatus in 439, with C. Servilius Ahala as Master of the Horse, is particularly doubtful, owing to the variations in our tradition, the unquestionable exploitation of the episode in the period of the Gracchi, etc.

b. As to the procedures for *nomination*: A group of nine well-attested dictatorships occurred between 217 and 202, during the Second Punic War. Now, notwithstanding the curious redaction of the *Fasti Capitolini* (*interregni causa*, for 217), it appears certain that the people intervened for the first time to nominate Q. Fabius Maximus and his Master of the Horse, M. Minucius Rufus. By a subsequent law, the latter even had his power set equal to that of the dictator (as attested by an inscription).

In 211, on the advice of the Senate, the people were asked to elect a dictator to some degree directly (admittedly, only so as to preside over the *Comitia*, Liv. XXVII, 5). The resistance of one of the consuls shows that this intervention by the people in a procedure which until then had been alien to it was already a cause of divided opinion.

c. As to *powers*: One legal tradition (Festus, 216 L) appears to attest that though operating at first beyond the sphere of protection conferred by the right of *provocatio*, ultimately the dictatorship, like the consulate, became subject to this right. Yet at the end of the second century, during the Gracchian crisis, another tradition claimed that the dictatorship was precisely the *only* magistracy immune from the right of appeal. Moreover, it was not this characteristic which was faulted and kept it from being invoked against Caius Gracchus, because in 121 the consul Opimius was specifically granted coercive powers immune to *provocatio*.

It is necessary to set forth these few irregularities in the tradition handed down to us, which are still a matter of debate among specialists, if we are to understand an incontestable matter of fact: that the dictatorship vanished between 202 and 82 B.C., including in the years 133–121, during the Gracchian crisis, and 101–100 B.C., during the revolutionary agitation of Saturninus and Glaucia. This interruption itself helps explain the nature of the dictatorship of Sulla in 82. Here again, I shall content myself with a few remarks.

1. If we examine the six dictatorships "to put down sedition" listed in our tradition, we note that with one exception (that of 439, mentioned above), these all pertain not to blood-soaked repressive measures taken by the dictator against the authors of a sedition, but either to a vigorous foreign military action (mobilization) which in some way put an end to the trouble,

or to an action of *arbitration* that sometimes clearly favored the plebeians, as is plainly the case in 287 (the *lex Hortensia*, which made plebiscites obligatory for the entire people). In these five cases, the dictatorship looks like a procedure for conciliation, not a power for repression. The only exception is the episode of 439. But ever since Mommsen (*Hermes*, 1871), we have been aware how suspect this episode is; it was presumably embellished to justify the repression against the Gracchi, which rested on highly suspect legal grounds. Nevertheless, it is probable that this tradition, even if it is *not historical*, had already arisen by the end of the third century, and in any case by the time of the Gracchi. This was how dictatorship was viewed, and thus certain persons believed it was a remedy invented entirely to resist reforming tribunes.

2. Nevertheless, despite the existence of what was thought to be a precedent, the fact is that no recourse was taken to a dictatorship at that moment. Why? The reason is presumably that one aspect of this magistracy, which for two centuries had seemed not merely innocuous but advantageous, had by now become insupportable: And by this I mean its *personal* and noncollegial nature. Diverse traditions, perhaps not very reliable, but significant, in fact indicate to us that proposals or desires for a "dictatorship" or monarchical power were voiced by the adherents of the two Scipios, Africanus Major and Minor (Liv. XXXVIII, 56, 12; Cic., *De Rep.*, VI, 12). The people were said to have offered the former a perpetual consulate and dictatorship. The friends of the latter were said to have urged him in 129 to obtain the grant of a "constituent dictatorship" to restore order in the State after the attempted coup and death of Tiberius Gracchus. This, as we can see, is no longer a dictatorship of a traditional type, but something very different: the candidacy of a "providential man," enveloped in the aureole of his victories, for a vague and quite general quasi-monarchical mission to bring factions to heel. This comes so close to the climate of the first-century dictatorships, those of Sulla and Caesar, that the value of these sources has been doubted. Yet the question remains: If this tradition is false, why did the Romans refrain from invoking the "classical" type of dictatorship when faced with a true "sedition"?

3. Albeit distantly, dictatorship is present in the background of the history of the Gracchi. The solution adopted in 121 by the enemies of Caius Gracchus – namely, granting the consul L. Opimius a power of coercion without appeal, by a *senatus consultum ultimum* – is specifically called an imitation of dictatorship by Plutarch (CG, 18, 1). Nevertheless there is one essential difference: Opimius was not in charge alone – he had a colleague; and his powers were required to expire at a normal date.

II. DICTATORSHIP REVIVED: SULLA AND CAESAR

By the end of the year 82, when Sulla revived the term dictatorship after 120 years of almost complete oblivion, the situation was entirely different. We must say a few words about it here to understand the impact of this decision on public opinion. For seven years, Italy had been ravaged by two intermingled wars: First, the war known as "social," waged against the Italian Allies who had despaired of gaining the rights of citizenship and therefore finally revolted. Second, a civil war, begun specifically in 88 by Sulla himself, who refused to give up an important military command, marched on Rome at the head of his troops and, after a brief massacre and a first attempt at a constitutional "restoration," actually left for Greece and Asia to fight Mithridates – a *mortal* enemy of Rome, we must note. At Rome itself, this was followed by a return to power of the faction led by Marius and Cinna, which governed between 87 and 84 and did not fail to dismiss Sulla, in principle, from his command. (The dismissal did not prevent him from liberating Greece, making peace with Mithridates, and reorganizing Asia.) Sulla's return had been expected from 84 onward. He landed in Brindisi in 83, at the head of a victorious, grateful, and devoted army. He overthrew the consular armies, defeated Marius the Younger and Carbo in 82, took Rome (where massacres began), triumphed at the battle of the Colline Gate over the last army (partly Italian) that opposed him, and through terror or persuasion came to be seen as the de facto sole holder of power. We must emphasize the terror aspect: On the mere excuse of imitating his adversaries, but on a far vaster scale than they, Sulla methodically and in cold blood organized the physical elimination of his enemies (the proscriptions). But questions of the forms of power arose, because the two consuls were dead. As one source clearly says (Appian, *BC*, I, 456), de facto absolute power was not sufficient – a basis in law was necessary.

The solution Sulla adopted was to revive the dictatorship. Formally, to solve the problem of nomination posed by the absence of consuls, he invoked the normal procedure for designating an interrex – who would "name" him dictator, but by virtue of a law. There was a double advantage in this move: it gave the appearance of including the people,[1] while at the same time solving the problem of when the term of office would expire. This dictatorship would be provisional, but have as its only limit the accomplishment of the assigned mission, which was to "draw up laws and restore a constitution to the State" – a formula that is of interest for more than one reason,

---

[1] Essential evidence: Sisenna, Fgt. 132 Peter; cf. Appian, B.C. I, 461: "A phantom of liberty."

reminiscent both of the famous Decemvirs of the fifth century and perhaps of the precedent manqué of Scipio Emilianus in 129 (cf. above).

The *lex Valeria* also retroactively covered Sulla's actions prior to his nomination as dictator (very end of 82), accorded him a personal guard, and so on. The dictatorship did not put an end to the proscriptions, "an afflictive penalty imposed by name on citizens without trial" (Cic., *De Domo*, 45); moreover, Sulla frequently exercised his right of extreme coercion, having recalcitrant individuals executed on the spot.

The Problems of Sullan Dictatorship

A. *Authority and scope of powers*. The very title he adopted shows that the powers he appropriated were without limit, and that the "constituent" competence might be exercised in all areas. This looks to be well outside the scope of the traditional dictatorship. Yet the latter also had an *imperium maius*, greater than that of all the other magistrates. In fact the only new feature is the unlimited "constituent" power.

B. *Formal characteristics*. Mommsen insisted very strongly on the differences from "classical" dictatorship, that is, an unspecified duration and unlimited powers. Wilcken, on the other hand, argued that the Sullan dictatorship had much in common with "the most ancient dictatorship, that of the fifth and fourth centuries, prior to its placement within reach of the *provocatio* and tribunician intercession." To accept this thesis, we would need to be sure of a thorough understanding of this older dictatorship. For the dictatorship of Sulla was really entirely different from the relatively well-understood examples dating from the end of the third century.

C. We must not confuse the *Sullan dictatorship* with the *Sullan regime*. We now know (Badian) that in fact Sulla exercised the dictatorship for only a year, or at most eighteen months (end of 82–end of 81). He abdicated from it normally, contenting himself (in 80) with the consulate, after which he returned to being a "private man" – and effectively retired from Roman public life. That is to say that the fiction of a Sullan "quasi-monarchy" would be dismissed. The motivations (individual, spontaneous or not, etc.) matter little against the fact that the exceptional period lasted only a short time; a regular, constitutional situation was restored in 79.

On the other hand, the legislative and constituent mission was taken seriously. Here again, the real inspirations or afterthoughts matter little. What is absolutely certain is that the regime modeled by Sulla in 81–80, as regards public law, was *in no way* a monarchy.

Although this is not my topic, let us recall that this was an oligarchic regime that first of all tended to abolish most of the "popular" initiatives instituted since the Gracchi, particularly through an almost complete dismantling of the tribunician power. The Senate as a body was strengthened in number and influence. But furthermore, by reorganizing the exercise of magistracies, as well as the provincial governments, Sulla attempted to channel ambitions and provide, not only civil peace, but also a certain regularity in the competitions pertaining to the senatorial oligarchy.

The Meaning of the Sullan Dictatorship: Interpretations and Reality

Sulla had his partisans. During his lifetime, even though he had returned to being a "private man," he remained a redoubtable power owing to the number of clients he had and the presence of his former soldiers. And even at the time of his death, and indeed still a generation later, we know that many aspired to imitate him (Pompey, for example), and met with the approval of some. But the rest, on the contrary, viewed him chiefly as a de facto "monarch" – the first Rome had ever suffered – and moreover as the very embodiment of the "bloody, grasping and voluptuous" tyrant (Cic., *De Fin.*, III, 75). Yet even the latter group also regarded him as a legislator, a "new" though cruel Romulus (Sall. *Hist.*, 55, 5) who restored the State. In this sense, the Sullan dictatorship of course bears a relationship with the temporary and exceptional "mission for the common good" evoked by the old word. And it is certainly for this reason that the word was used. Nevertheless the purely circumstantial aspects that made it something quite new, and far more unsettling, ultimately prevailed in the political "myth" (Umberto Laffi) and in historiography. Let us briefly review them:

a. This dictatorship comes only after a bloody civil war, itself the consequence of rivalries among *military* commanders over rich commands. It was preceded by victories and massacres which in reality had bestowed a *de facto power* upon the rebellious and victorious general. Thus, for the first time, the army becomes the instrument for the seizure of power. Hence this dictatorship is founded, as its precondition, on the new nature of the Roman army, the result of profound changes in the *social* and *ethnic* recruitment of soldiers across two decades. Even after Sulla's abdication, the army (the veterans settled in the Italian colonies) would remain the skeleton of a sort of "Sullan" party.

b. By contrast with the always limited and specific missions of the dictatorships of the fifth and third centuries, this one involved the complete placement of all powers – military, judiciary, coercitive, but also legislative, administrative, even religious – in the hands of *a single man*, to do whatever he wished, however he wished.

c. Finally, and above all, it was imposed by the systematic use of terror, executions without trial (the proscriptions), collective punishments inflicted on entire communities, and the physical crushing of the adversarial party even into the next generation (the *lex Cornelia* against the children of proscripts). This way of settling conflicts, if we may call it that, now became part of the interplay of Roman institutions for two generations: each party would in turn brandish it as a threat or denounce it as imminent.

The Dictatorship of Caesar

The regime Sulla intended to establish was supposed to avoid the very possibility of a return of personal power. Yet hardly was Sulla dead, and the battle of ambitions resumed at higher pitch than ever. External and internal crises conspired to prove, it seemed, that regular institutions were unable to cope. At that point two interlinked questions arose: Is it possible to accomplish or obtain anything whatever in the State without resorting to the personal power of a man strong enough and prestigious enough to impose his will? But on the other hand, can one reign innocently, is one not forced to "Sullanize," will it be necessary to resort to civil war, executions, proscriptions? All these questions raised by the Sullan precedent explain the protagonists' reactions in episodes such as those of Lepidus (78), the restoration of tribunician power in 70 (Pompey and Crassus), the pirate war (67) and the Mithridatic war (66), the Catilinian conspiracy (63), the exile of Cicero (58), the "war of the bands" (53–52) – each of them an occasion on which the dictatorship was mentioned, while recourse to it was avoided if possible (Cicero and the *senatus consultum ultimum* in 63; Pompey as consul without a colleague in 52). The specter of Sulla survived.

Caesar had been one of the probable candidates for personal power, among three or four others, since perhaps the very start of his career (Suetonius, *Div. Iul.*, 9, 2). But he had to contend with his rivals, with his own family tradition that made him the political heir of Marius, and with the "Sullan constitution." That his ambition resulted in another civil war at the end of his great command in Gaul was probably not his doing: sincerely or not, he did attempt to negotiate. In any case, his career was far more "regular" than that of Pompey until at least 59 (his first consulate). After that date, two facts are important: (a) During his year in office, Caesar demonstrated a considerable and exceptional *political* activity, establishing friendships and a "party," but also legislating in various areas with an obvious concern for public opinion and as a man of the State; (b) His renewed agreements with Crassus and Pompey make it clear that the game was now in the hands of men who had considerable armies, financial resources independent of the Treasury, and provincial territories which brought about something akin to an explosion of the traditional State. Moreover, through interposed "friends," they controlled a fragmented, disordered, and increasingly impotent "civil" power in Rome itself. If there was to be a civil war, it would be a *world* war, opposing two men or two factions, to be sure, but also entire masses of the Roman world. Public opinion, though frightened (cf. the success of Curio, who thought he had averted the blow, in 50), was resigned. Thus one can easily predict the *renewal of the excesses* of the Sullan period.

1. Caesar would always have a special talent for throwing the blame for the war back upon his adversaries, along with the *suspicion of wanting to remake Sulla* (Caesar, in *Cic. Att.*, IX, 7, C). Neither Pompey nor his friends in the Senate were able to escape the trap. Caesar constantly presented himself, by contrast, as the antithesis of Sulla, promoting the message – more or less justified – of his *clemency*. He did not avoid either civil wars or personal power (quite the contrary), but he did attempt to dissociate them from the memory of the proscriptions. With terror ruled out at least in its paroxysmal form (at any rate once the battles were over), he would have to imagine and find new models to furnish the basis and the legal and political form for the sovereign power he intended to exercise.

Nevertheless, it was dictatorship that came into play once again, but accompanied with many other powers, and in a prudent and gradual manner. It must be noted that for several months after the start of hostilities, Caesar's constitutional position was all the more uncertain as he still hoped to negotiate with Pompey, or at least to rally enough senators and magistrates to get as much legality as possible on his side. It was for this reason that, at the time of the conquest of Italy and his first entry into Rome (49 B.C.), he contented himself with the proconsular *imperium* – and, of course, his de facto power. Not until December of 49, and in his own absence, did he arrange to be appointed dictator by a praetor (but the nomination was presumably confirmed by the people); and not until after the siege of Marseille did he return to exercise this magistracy in Rome, for just eleven days – time to get himself regularly and legally elected consul for 48.

As we know, the civil wars, from one end of the world to the other, lasted for four years, until 46. Caesar was almost constantly in the breach, and the outcome doubtful, although Italy remained firmly in his hands. Under these conditions, it is only from the end of 48 onward (after Pharsalus) that he was named dictator a second time (for one year) while he was simultaneously consul. In April 46 (presumably), he was again appointed dictator, for ten years, an office that was renewable each year – which explains why it was reckoned into the *Fasti*. Finally, in January 44, he accepted the title of dictator for life (Dion, 44, 8, 4; Josephus, *AJ*, 14, 211). These dictatorships were quite in general – "*rei gerundae*" – and even if this was not formally specified, they also entailed a "constituent" power.

2. *These dictatorships present several problems.*

a. First of all: *Why a dictatorship?* Especially since Caesar concurrently arrogated, or had himself assigned, a considerable number of other powers or honors. This is not the place to list them exhaustively, but they were of a political and religious nature: the tribunician power, the office of consul, the right to make peace and war, to make laws, to command all the armies, to appoint magistrates directly or not, to use the Treasury, etc. Great attention must be paid to the *honors*, both triumphal (*imperator* for life, crowns, the right of presiding over festivals, triumphal costume, etc.) and religious, which the dominant ideology of the day held to be essential, especially where the plebs was concerned. The result was a veritable kingship, virtually without limit other than that of a human lifetime. Hence it is essentially as a dictator – *perpetuus*, then for life – that Caesar wished to be seen, and was in fact seen by posterity. And it is definitely for this reason that a few days after the Ides of March, at the same time as they harshly repressed the spontaneous emergence of a cult of Caesar, the consuls enacted a law banning the name of dictatorship from Rome forever, on pain of death.

It is probable that Caesar used the dictatorship at Rome as a kind of smoke screen for the kingship that he certainly desired, but that public opinion could not accept, or rather whose name it could not accept. For the thing existed – provided that one indefinitely extended the temporal duration of what would from now on be the "supreme magistracy" needed to found the State anew. So Caesar was reduced to this, despite Sulla's precedent, which is why he applied himself so vigorously to saying and proving that he would not be a new Sulla: According to his own words at Piacenza (Dion, 4, 32, 5), he would reconcile force with justice. The dictatorship was necessary in order to unify and bind together all his powers, on the condition that clemency was added.

b. But these considerations do not exhaust the meaning of what is quite justifiably called "Caesarism." Caesar had only a very brief time to sketch out the form and foundations of the new regime that he intended to impose on the entire world. But certain characteristics are quite clear:

1. It once again was a *military power*, obtained thanks to a faithful and effective army. Caesar, a new Alexander, had conquered the world. A new

Sulla, he had vanquished his "private enemies" in civil wars. He was "imperator." And he created for himself, and utilized, a military clientele (cf. the role of the army even after his death).

2. It was a power based on many "friends" from broader social or geographical origins than those of traditional political leaders. These "friends" filled the Senate and magistracies, military commands or new "offices." But they were in no way a "party" in the modern sense, even if Caesarism was understood to fit into the tradition of Marius and, in certain regards, of the Gracchi.

3. Surely more original is the aspect of Caesarism that we might call (in the modern sense of the word) *"plebiscitarian"* – seeking "popularity," the support of Italian public opinion, but also that of the urban plebs, through conduct, through largesse (distributions, games, etc.), through an elevation of the network of his clientele almost to the world scale. But notwithstanding Napoleon III, behind these practices and words we must not seek any doctrine of "national representation" analogous to what was invoked by the two Bonapartes. It is at the level of the religious ideologies that were widespread among the urban masses of the day – in terms of public sentiment or indeed instinct, rather than public law – that we must understand this aspect of Caesarism. In Caesar's time we find no formula of a "plebiscitarian" nature (of the type of the *consensus omnium*) analogous to those that would, by contrast, be used by his successor Augustus, who took them from the arsenal of the highly legalistic Cicero. Augustus, having learned the lessons of thirteen more years of civil war, realized that one must go masked, neither saying nor permitting to be said the word "king" or "dictator"; and he was able to reign and even found a monarchy (making everyone forget he had been a new Sulla in his youth) by affecting to be a plain citizen.

It was not my intent to offer an analysis of the forms of absolute power in the history of Rome. It is not for the era of the Republic – the only period in which the word "dictatorship" was used – that this should be attempted, but for the Imperial age. We would have to ask how the change came about from a sort of veiled monarchy (the Principate, which in principle assumed the permanence of a *Res publica* in which the Prince was only a cog in the machine) to the establishment of an autocratic power in which the monarch was the law incarnate. We would have to assume that religious aspects, whether pagan or Christian, had much to do with this. We would also have to investigate the exercise of personal power even in the time of the "Principate" – its tyrannical or bureaucratic deviations, its relationships with what remained of civil, intellectual, or moral "freedom." This is not my purpose. On the contrary, I have attempted to show how, quite aside from extralegal causes such as the consequences of having conquered the world or the changes in the nature and importance of the army, two attempts at taking personal power – one very brief, the other by contrast destined to endure – arose under cover of an official procedure that seemed to fit normally within the institutions of a city. A city: that is to say, an organism founded upon the rule of law and a certain balance of powers. Whatever the original nature of the Roman magistracy, at the end of the Republic it was contained and limited, and the Romans viewed these restraints as the most precious token of their liberty. By contrast, dictatorship, even if innocent, was like it or not the legal negation of this balance, because it implied the suspension of these rules of law, even if only provisionally. The Roman experience proved that the law is a formidable protection, provided that one does not permit the least exception to it, even in the name of the common good. By failing to recognize this principle, the Romans had no choice, as Tacitus says, but to "rush into servitude." We will have to wait for the nineteenth century before the perception sets in, as Jules Ferry said in 1866 (*Discours et opinions*, Robiquet, I, 102), that the "doctrine of the common good is . . . the last refuge of despotism."

BIBLIOGRAPHICAL NOTES

François Hinard and Claude Nicolet

On the origins of dictatorship considered as a magistracy integrated into the republican "system," see Theodor Mommsen, *Le droit public* (French translation by P.-F. Girard), III, Paris, 1893, 161–207. Today this thesis has been rather generally abandoned in favor of the one that views dictatorship as an intermediate stage between kingship and republic. See notably Wilhelm Soltau, "Ursprung der Diktatur," *Hermes*, 49, 1914, 352–68; Arnaldo Momigliano, "Ricerche sulle magistrature romane," *Buletino della Commissione Archeologica*, 58, 1930, 29–55; Aurelio Bernardi, "Dagli ausiliari del Rex ai magistrati della Respublica," *Athenaeum*, 30, 1952, 1–58; D. Cohen, "The Origins of the Roman Dictatorship," *Mnemosyne*, 1957, 303–20.

Concerning the problems posed by this magistracy, notably in regard to constitutional law, one might consult, in addition to Mommsen, Clifton Walker Keyes, "The Constitutional Position of the Roman Dictatorship," *Studies in Philology*, 14, 1917, 298–305; G. I. Luzzatto, "Appunti sulle dittature 'imminuto iure'; spunti critici e ricostruttivi," *Studi de Francisci*, III, Milan, 1956, 405–59; and as more specifically concerns the limitation on duration: Ugo Coli, "Sui limiti di durata delle magistrature romane," *Studi Arangio-Ruiz*, IV, Naples, 1953, 395–418; M. Sordi, "Sulla cronologia liviana del IV secolo," *Helikon*, V, 1965, 3–44; A. Drummond, "The Dictator Years," *Historia*, 27, 1978, 550–72. The problem of dictatorships *comitiorum habendorum causa* is addressed by Joachim Jahn, *Interregnum und Wahldiktatur*, Kallmünz, 1970, 195, and A. Guarino, "Il vuoto di potere nella libera respublica," *Atti dell'Academia de Scienze Morali e Politiche de Napoli*, 82, 1971, 288–312.

Lists of dictatorships have been furnished by Friedrich Bandel, *Die römischen Diktaturen*, Diss., Breslau, 1910 (with indication of principal sources); Arthur Kaplan, "Religious Dictators of the Roman Republic," *The Classical World*, 67, 1973, 172–5; and J. Jahn, *Interregnum* (*interregna* and dictatorships *comitiorum habendorum causa*).

For a political analysis of the dictatorships of the last two centuries, one can notably consult Claude Nicolet, *Rome et la conquête du monde méditerranéen: 1) Les structures de l'Italie romaine*, Paris, 1977 (particularly chapters XI and XII, pp. 393–455) and, for dictatorships discussed without being conferred, Nicolet, "Le *De Republica*, VI, 16, et la dictature de Scipion," *Revue des études latine*, 1964, 212–30, and J.-P. Borle, "Pompée et la dictature," *Les Etudes classiques*, 20, 1952, 168–80.

Sulla and Caesar (and, accessorily, the Triumvirs) have been the topic of many studies. More particularly one may consult Mommsen, *Le droit public*, IV (Paris, 1984), 424–70; Ulrich Wilcken, "Zur Entwicklung der römischen Diktatur," *Abhandlungen der Preussischen Akademie der Wissenschaften zu Berlin*, 1940, 3–32; Vinenzo Giuffrè, *Aspetti costituzionali del potere dei militari nella tarda "respublica,"* Naples, 1973. Regarding Sulla, we will content ourselves here with mentioning, after C. Lanzani (*Lucio Cornelio Silla dittatore*, Milan, 1936), E. Badian, "Additional Notes on Roman Magistrates," *Athenaeum*, 48, 1970, 3–14, followed by Briggs L. Twyman, "The Date of Sulla's Abdication and the Chronology of the First Book of Appian Civil Wars," *Athenaeum*, 54, 1976, 77–97, for the duration of his magistracy. As concerns his image, see Umberto Laffi, "Il mito di Silla," *Athenaeum*, 45, 1967, 177–213 and 255–77, and Settimio Lanciotti, "Silla e la tipologia del tiranno nella letteratura latina repubblicana," *Quaderni di Storia*, 3, 1977, 129–43 and 144, 1978, 191–225. For the dictatorships of Caesar, we will refer solely to a few important studies – in addition to those of Wilcken and Giuffrè cited above: Matthias Gelzer, *Caesar, Politician and Statesman* (transl. P. Needham), Oxford, 1968, for an overall view. On the second dictatorship, Paul Schnabel, "Die zweite Diktatur Caesars," *Klio*, 19, 1925, 354–5; on the third one, D. Felber, "Caesars

Streben nach der Königswürde," in *Untersuchungen zur römischen Geschichte* (ed. Franz Altheim), I, Frankfurt, 1961. The two trends in the interpretation of the Caesarian regime are represented by Eduard Meyer, *Caesars Monarchie und das Prinzipat des Pompeius*, 3rd ed., Stuttgart, 1922 (reprint Darmstadt, 1974), who believes Caesar drew on Hellenistic models, and Konrad Kraft, "Der goldene Kranz Caesars und der Kampf um die Entlarvung des Tyrannen," *Jahrbuch für Numismatik und Geldgeschichte*, 3–4, 1952–1953, 7–97, who interprets Caesar's intent as a return to the sources to model his powers on those on the ancient kings of Rome.

A number of studies provide a historiographic perspective, notably those of Albert Mathiez, "La Révolution française et la théorie de la dictature," *Revue historique*, 1929, 304–15; Jean Gagé, "La dictature romaine," *Bulletin de la Faculté des Lettres de Strasbourg*, 15, 1937, 126–30; Giuseppe Sartori, "Dittatura. Dalla dittatura antica alle dittature contemporanee," *Enciclopedia del diritto*, 13, 1964, 356–60; Salvo Mastellone, "Il problema della dittatura in Francia nella prima metà dell'ottocento," *Il pensiero politico*, 1, 1968, 386–407; "Dittatura 'giacobina,' dittatura 'bonapartista' et dittatura del proletario," ibid., 8, 1975; Pirangelo Catalano, "A proposito dei concetti di 'rivoluzione' nella dottrina romanistica contemporanea (tra 'rivoluzione della plebe' et dittature rivoluzionarie)," *Studia et Documenta Historia et Iuris*, 43, 1977, 440–55; and "Consolato e dittatura: l'esperimento romano della repubblica del Paraguay (1813–1844)," *Studi Romani*, 26, 1978, 178–96. For "dictatorship" among the French positivists, cf. my book *L'idée republicaine en France, 1789–1924: essai d' histoire critique*, Paris, 1982.

13

From the Historical Caesar to the Spectre of Caesarism

The Imperial Administrator as Internal Threat

ARTHUR M. ECKSTEIN

In January of 49 B.C., the army of C. Julius Caesar stood on the banks of the Rubicon River, the boundary between Caesar's legally assigned province and Italy proper. Caesar faced a decision. The Senate in Rome had demanded that he step down from his governorship of Gaul after nine years and had, indeed, already named a successor; when nothing happened, it had then passed the *senatus consultum ultimum*: "the last decree" of political emergency, essentially declaring Caesar a public enemy. We are told that the recalled governor of Gaul hesitated at the Rubicon before responding to the Senate's actions. Not to cross the river (i.e., to submit to "the last decree") meant disaster for himself; but to cross the river meant disaster for the entire world, the beginning of a civil war. Caesar pondered these two fatal alternatives, but not (our sources say) for long. Within a day, he launched his forces down the Italian peninsula toward Rome.[1]

Whatever else Caesar's decision at the Rubicon was, it was an act of monumental egotism. This egotism stands out starkly in a statement made by Caesar a year and a half later, as he surveyed the decisive battlefield at Pharsalus, littered with thousands of Roman dead. According to an eyewitness (C. Asinius Pollio), Caesar remarked: "*This* is what they wanted [*Hoc voluerunt*]. I, Gaius Caesar, after so many great deeds, would have been condemned in the courts, if I had not turned to my army for help."[2] Thus, speaking to his friends, Caesar adduces no great issues behind the civil war, only the outrageous possibility that he, the conqueror of so many Gallic peoples, might have to undergo a civic procedure that ordinary Romans

---

[1] Caesar at the Rubicon: see Suet. *Jul.*, 29–30; Plut. *Caes.*, 32; App. *BC*, 2.35. The central modern study remains H. Strasburger, "Caesar im Urteil der Zeitgenossen," *Historische. Zeitschrift* 175 (1953), 225ff. See also Z. Yavetz, *Julius Caesar and His Public Image* (Ithaca, 1983), Chapter I.
[2] Suet. *Jul.*, 30.

confronted every day. *Hoc voluerunt*: Another translation might be, "They asked for it."

The purposes of this chapter are twofold. First, I want to suggest what experiences as a long-term ruler out in Rome's provinces might have led Caesar toward overthrowing Rome's republic in the name merely of his *sacro egoismo*. Second, I will trace some examples of how the fear that imperial administrators might become internal threats to established political order manifested itself later, both within the Roman Empire and in later empires as well. My thesis is that the experience of governing a large province on one's own, the experience of exercising sole responsibility over large regions and great numbers of people, the experience of independence and power and control, the taste for it (and in some cases the great wealth that could be derived from it), all this sometimes created what one might call an "imperial counterculture" to the law-ruled state existing at the center. The contrast between the conduct of politics at the imperial metropole and the situation prevailing on the imperial peripheries could be very sharp. In the center, politicians had to deal with many foci of power, and they had to cooperate at least minimally with one another, to be dependent upon one another to some extent. Out in the provinces, however, it was different: Often one person, one superior person, made all major decisions. Additionally, out of this difference conflict could develop.

Let me cite one minor example from a modern empire to illustrate my point. In 1919, the wife of the British imperial administrator Joyce Carey demanded that he come home to Britain. Carey, the sole ruler of 100,000 Nigerians, loved his wife, but he refused because he had too much to do and he was enjoying it too much. Carey went everywhere accompanied by 130 porters and guards; a bourgeois life back in some London suburb would be so *reduced* in comparison with this. Joyce Carey is an example, in little, of the addictiveness of the habit of power.[3] Caesar lived on a much grander scale, but like Caesar, Carey found it very difficult to make the transition from the elemental egotism of life on the imperial periphery to the complexities and limits of life at the center. Carey eventually, with great regret, did give up his imperial command (and was unhappy for the next ten years). Caesar, of course, never gave up his command at all: He had to be murdered.

The fears which we find so frequently expressed in various later empires about the corrupting impact on governors of the experience of total control over imperial provinces seem in retrospect somewhat exaggerated. None of

---

[3] On Joyce Carey, see conveniently V. Packenham, *The Noonday Sun: Edwardians in the Tropics* (London, 1985), 57–66.

the later fears I will discuss ever materialized into the imposition of tyranny at the center. However, the existence of those fears is a historical fact, called forth by the recognition of a general reality of imperial political life: the counterculture of personal power on the imperial periphery. Caesar was the prime historical example of it, and these fears existed under his shadow.

What then was the cause of the conflict between Caesar and the Senate that eventually led to civil war? At the simplest level, it was a dispute over the termination date of Caesar's special provincial command in Gaul. This vast command, encompassing Cisalpine Gaul (Northern Italy), Illyricum (the northern coasts of the Adriatic Sea), and Transalpine Gaul (modern France), had been gained by Caesar as consul in 59 B.C., as his payoff in a complicated deal with the politicians M. Licinius Crassus and Cn. Pompeius Magnus. For his part, Caesar had helped Crassus and Pompey push through the Roman assemblies various legislative measures they wished, illegally circumventing the attempts of his consular colleague to block them. Now, Roman public officials could not be prosecuted in court while holding office; but Caesar's actions in 59, as well as some of his actions as proconsul in Gaul in 58–50, left him theoretically vulnerable to prosecution once his term of office ended. Note that I say *theoretically* vulnerable: For if Caesar finished his term as commander in Gaul and returned to Rome with the political support of Pompey, the likelihood of any successful prosecution was nil. Pompey's own attitude toward Roman civil legal procedure (he himself had been a great conqueror in the eastern Mediterranean in the 60s) is shown by the fact that in 52 he ensured the conviction of one of his political enemies by ringing the court with troops. He could certainly ensure acquittal the same way.

That would require Caesar having to cooperate politically with Pompey, to be to some extent *dependent* upon him for political survival. Such dependence might have been acceptable to Caesar as long as Pompey was married to Caesar's beloved daughter (and only child) Julia. This marriage had helped seal the pact between the two men back in 59 B.C., and it had turned out well: Pompey loved Julia as much as Caesar did, and the personal link between the two men was strong. However, Julia died in childbirth in 54 (as did her baby, Pompey's son, Caesar's only grandson). In the following years, the personal connection that might have eased tensions between Caesar and Pompey, and might have eased the psychological strain of cooperation and interdependence, was therefore missing. The polarization of Roman politics between the two men was increased by the death in 53 of the third member of the original coalition of 59, Crassus, while battling against the Parthians on the Syrian frontier.

In 52, there is no evidence yet of a break between Caesar and Pompey. In that year, Pompey used all his great political influence, against much opposition, to pass a special measure through the assembly on Caesar's behalf, giving Caesar the right to run for the consulship again *in absentia*. In this way, Caesar could win the prize of a second consulship, as a reward for his conquests in Gaul, while avoiding any prosecution in the courts for his actions as consul in 59 and in Gaul later. Candidates running for office in Rome had to campaign personally in the city; but no governor returning from a province could enter the city at all without giving up his *imperium*, the legal right he obtained, via high office, to compel obedience to himself as representative of the state. He had to run as a "civilian." Magistrates with *imperium* were, as I noted, not subject to prosecution in court; but if Caesar were forced to lay down his *imperium* in order to run for election to a second consulship, he would at that point be vulnerable to the courts. Giving Caesar the right to run for a second consulship *in absentia* avoided this danger and acknowledged Caesar's special merits. In addition, there were rumors that his second consulship would be followed by a specially assigned command against the Parthians in the East, to avenge Crassus, thereby postponing any possible prosecution years into the future.

This is all rather complex, but my point is that Caesar was receiving very special and favorable treatment as he looked ahead to stepping down from his long command in Gaul and returning to Rome. Yet it was not enough for him. The year 51 turned into 50, late 50, and still there was no sign of his giving up his Gallic armies. This in turn made Pompey, in command of relatively small forces in Italy by special assignment, suspicious. Cato the Younger, and the leaders of other senatorial factions opposed to Caesar, worked on those suspicions. The knowledge that Pompey was associating more and more with his enemies in the Senate in turn alienated Caesar. Pompey's new friendships were symbolized by a new marriage: Replacing Julia was the daughter of a great enemy of Caesar's, Q. Caecilius Metellus Pius Scipio Nasica. It is not necessarily the case that Caesar's enemies consciously sought a civil war; more likely, their aim was to split the coalition of Caesar and Pompey, and thereby establish more traditional freedom of political movement.[4] Their intervention in the relations between Pompey and Caesar turned out to be a disaster, of course. The ultimate cause of this cleavage lay not with them, however, but with Caesar, his reluctance to lay down the Gallic command and come home, even under special conditions.

---

4 See the comments of E. S. Gruen, *The Last Generation of the Roman Republic* (Berkeley/Los Angeles, 1974), 496–7.

Where did that reluctance come from? The issue can hardly have been merely a legal one: Caesar desired more time to settle affairs in Gaul, while Pompey stuck firmly to the legal time limit established as the termination date of Caesar's governorship. This is the so-called *Rechtsfrage*. Leaving aside the likelihood that Caesar's special assignment in Gaul *had* no exact day and month termination date, if the issue between Caesar and Pompey had been this simple, it is hard to believe that some sort of political compromise could not have been reached. It was certainly taking Caesar a very long time to set up his peace settlement among the Gallic tribes, now that his conquests were complete; but there had been fighting well into 52. The peace settlement involved all of Transalpine Gaul up to the Rhine, and the Gallic political situation was complicated. In similar circumstances 150 years earlier (206 B.C.), it had taken Scipio Africanus only a few weeks of decision-making to create the intricate arrangements among tribes and polities that established Roman Spain.[5] However, if Caesar felt he needed even another full year beyond 50 to make stable arrangements among the Gallic tribes, arrangements whose stability could only be in Rome's interest, why not give him that year? Workable political compromises such as this were a Roman specialty: The Romans were the ancient world's greatest diplomats, and not least among themselves. That was the way the Republic had always worked.

So the problem here goes deeper than the *Rechtsfrage*. In fact, it is the judgment of the ancients themselves. Caesar's biographer Suetonius, in explaining how the civil war originated, underlines Caesar's "habit of command" (*imperii consuetudo*), which had given him over time a love of power for its own sake; and Suetonius shows that Cicero was of this same opinion.[6] Appian is similar: Caesar simply did not wish to give up his command, period (*Bellum Civile* 2.28). So is Lucan: Caesar in Gaul could no longer bear the idea of a superior, just as Pompey could not bear the idea of an equal.

Imperii consuetudo: The deep point which I think these ancient writers were making was this. To stand successfully for a second consulship *in absentia*, to have that second consulship carried though with honor and dignity (preceded by a senatorially approved magnificent triumphal procession for the victories in Gaul), to avoid prosecution (or at least conviction) for his actions in 59, and, later, to proceed thenceforth to an honored and secure place in the Senate, or perhaps to another great command, this time against the Parthians: All this would require Pompey's *cooperation* – in other words,

---

5 For discussion of the evolution of Scipio Africanus's peace settlement among the Spanish tribes in 206 B.C., see A. M. Eckstein, *Senate and General: Individual Decision-Making and Roman Foreign Relations, 264–194 B.C.* (Berkeley/Los Angeles, 1987), 209–28.
6 Suet. *Jul.*, 30.

Caesar's *dependence* upon another man. Such cooperation and dependence was the stuff of which normal high politics in the Roman Republic was made. Caesar, it is true, had come to distrust Pompey after 51; but the ancient writers indicate that this, though serious, was not the basic problem. Caesar disliked the general situation, not just the specific man. Explicitly, he disliked any situation where his independent will would not automatically reign supreme. In October of 51, for instance, Pompey was asked in the Senate: What if Caesar wishes to be consul again and simultaneously retain his army and province? The question shows how some key senators were already gauging Caesar's ambitions. Pompey at this Senate session helped engineer the delay even of debate over the reassigning of Caesar's Gallic province until March of 50; but he also said, in answer to the above question: "What if my own son should wish to raise his stick against me?"[7] Whatever Pompey meant by this remark, and perhaps it was that he and Caesar had in fact reached an agreement about the issue, the remark showed that limits were being set to Caesar's conduct and that it was Pompey (as the "father") who was setting those limits. The remark may have been friendly (or perhaps not); but it was, literally, patronizing and perhaps had an undertone of threat.

In the end, Caesar preferred to plunge the world into civil war rather than accept limits to his conduct set by Pompey or anybody else. Indeed, the extraordinary fact is that except for a brief period in the year 60, Caesar had already never been without possession of *imperium* since his praetorship in 62 B.C., that is, for twelve full years. First, he was praetor in 62; then governor of the province of Further Spain in 61–60; then immediately consul in 59; and then immediately governor of the huge special province in the north from 58 to 50. Part of the time in Spain and Gaul would have been spent as an assizes judge whose rulings could not be appealed. Most of his time in Spain and Gaul was spent in absolute command of an army, in an army camp where everyone had to obey his orders instantly.

Caesar had always been self-willed, and he had always been willing to take enormous risks for the sake of his ego: That is shown by his running for the prestigious post of Pontifex Maximus in 63 B.C., at an extraordinarily young age, and winning. Tenure in absolute command of half of Spain did nothing to smooth his rough edges. On the contrary, upon his return to Rome his violent impatience with traditional political maneuvering, as far as the imposition of his own will was concerned, was amply evident in his consulship in 59. He famously ignored his colleague's irritating but

---

7 Cicero. *Ad Fam.*, 8.8.9.

constitutionally legitimate attempts to block his actions and legislation; he jailed those who spoke too long against him in the Senate. The consulship was immediately followed by almost a decade of unprecedented military glory and essentially monarchical power in Gaul. There he created his own policies, always highly aggressive and warlike, without consulting the Senate. He dictated the fates of entire peoples by his own will; he had experiences we can only dimly imagine: What was it *like* to sell 53,000 people into slavery at a single crack and boast about it?[8] Roman commanders traditionally enjoyed enormous freedom of action in their provinces (this was partly a function of distance from the center, and primitive communications; partly, in the Middle Republic, it was an aspect of the existing mutual aristocratic trust). But no one in the history of the Republic had ever ruled such a vast territory for such a long period of time as Caesar. The best parallel is Scipio Africanus, who conquered the wilds of eastern Spain for Rome in 210–206 B.C., and it is significant that not only was Scipio saluted as a king by the Spanish tribes for his victories and his power, but that the Greek historian Polybius, who details Scipio's conquests, thought that Scipio could have become a king except that he was loyal to the Republic (10.40). Pompey's command in the eastern Mediterranean between 67 and 62 B.C. is another parallel: And once again, it is significant that by the end Pompey was accepting honors in the East which had traditionally gone to kings (such as having cities named after him and being worshiped as a god). Ancient writers expressed surprise that he did not establish a military monarchy when he landed his returning army in Italy in early 61. Luckily for Rome, Pompey at that time wished only to receive extraordinary honors and then to settle down to a politically dominant place in the Senate.

Caesar was different. The power and above all the independence that went with his huge command might well become addictive (especially considering his willfulness and sense of superiority). By the beginning of 49 B.C., Caesar had spent close to a fifth of his life as absolute monarch of Gaul. Could he ever become an ordinary (albeit very senior) senator again, even if he had wished it? Here we may note his actions in 45–44. The civil war with Pompey and his supporters which Caesar started in 49 B.C. lasted more than four years, with fighting on a massive scale all over the Mediterranean. Caesar was always in the thick of it: in Italy, Spain, Greece, Egypt, Asia Minor, North Africa, and then in Spain again. What is striking is that upon his return to Rome in autumn 45 he did not settle down to life in the city, even as supreme ruler. He did enact an energetic and confused hodge-podge

---

8 Caes. *BG*, 2.33.

of administrative reforms, but his eyes immediately turned to *more* warfare: This time a campaign of conquest, grandiose in size, against the Parthians, a campaign that would take at least three years in the field. He was about to set off on this campaign when he was assassinated by sixty senators in March of 44.

Caesar's plans here have struck many modern scholars as irresponsible. It is hard, from a modern perspective, to disagree: Caesar was well into middle age now; he had many capable generals to deal with the Parthian question (for instance, Mark Antony); his place was at Rome, attempting to construct a system to replace the republican one he had destroyed. But evidently he found the work of systematic imperial administration a bore; and his dealings even with an overawed Senate were obviously complicated and tense. Better the provinces and the camp. Caesar had many virtues, but patience was not one of them. War promised excitement, even exaltation. In the camp, he would be surrounded by adulation, and everyone would obey him instantly. He essentially made his home there for the last fifteen years of his life.[9]

Caesar, according to Roman estimates, was a man who initiated wars that cost the lives of 1,192,000 human beings, many of them Romans;[10] and at the end, he was happily planning for more of the same. How could such a man, not a modern man at all, but a classic Schumpeterian war machine, habituated to absolute power after nine years in Gaul, ever have returned to normal Republican politics in 49? It could be done, I suppose, but it would require an enormous adjustment and a willingness on Caesar's part to run at least a few normal political risks. Pompey, for his part, seems to have sensed by the spring of 50 Caesar's deep reluctance to return to city politics. Pompey's consequent estrangement from Caesar, and his suspicions of him, made negotiations for a political compromise ever more difficult. Conversely, the growing estrangement from Pompey made Caesar ever less eager to return to the city without ironclad guarantees, although in the autumn of 50 he offered a variety of ways in which such ironclad guarantees could be managed.

Caesar, of course, will ever remain subject to differing interpretations. However, one thing that I would suggest from the above is fairly certain. The transition of Caesar from long-term absolute ruler of Gaul back into

---

9 The parallel would be with the isolated, arrogant, archaic "Titanic" figure of Alexander the Great as presented by F. Schachermeyr: see, e.g., *Alexander der Grosse: Ingenium und Macht* (Vienna, 1949), with the comments of E. Badian, "Some Recent Interpretations of Alexander," *Entretiens Hardt* 22 (1976), 282–5.

10 Plin. *NH*, 7.91–2.

a city politician even of great stature raised enormous difficulties, and it was a transition which Caesar made increasingly clear he would undertake only on very specific conditions. When those conditions were not met, the result was war. Thus, when later writers, intellectuals, and statesmen worried about "Caesarism" in the sense of an imperial administrator who had developed a habit of command in the provinces dangerous to the central state (*imperil consuetudo*), they were looking back at a real phenomenon.

There is a long history of fears of this particular type of Caesarism, and I can only provide a few sketches of it in the space remaining. First, let us look at some stories from the Roman Empire itself, as it developed under the early Emperors. One of the most famous concerns Cn. Cornelius Lentulus Gaetulicus, consul in A.D. 26 and ruler of the great military province of Upper Germany (the Rhineland) for thirteen years, from A.D. 26 to 39. Descended from a great noble family, Gaetulicus – handsome and rich – was popular with his troops and evidently quite happy commanding on the Rhine frontier. Gaetulicus's grip on his province was made easier by the fact that his father-in-law, L. Apronius, was governor of the neighboring great military province of Lower Germany, and we are told that Gaetulicus had made himself popular not only with his own troops, but with those of his father-in-law as well. However, in 34 A.D., various charges were brought against Gaetulicus in the Roman Senate. Allegedly, he then wrote to the Emperor Tiberius, asserting his innocence, but asserting also that if found guilty in the Senate, he would take this as an act of hostility, and finally proposing "a kind of treaty"(*velut foedus*) between himself and the Emperor, whereby Gaetulicus would keep possession of his province and Tiberius would keep possession of the Empire. The historian Tacitus finds the story of Gaetulicus's threatening letter reasonable even if apocryphal, a verdict which in itself tells us much about the potential powers, and the habit of power, of long-term provincial governors.[11] What is certain is that under the next Emperor, Caligula, Gaetulicus was removed from his province – by assassination.[12]

Perhaps Tacitus accepted the story of Gaetulicus's "treaty" with Tiberius because something similar had happened in his own family. Tacitus's father-in-law, Cn. Julius Agricola, was a famous general, conqueror of northern and western Britain during his long governorship there of 77–84 A.D. Tacitus says that the Emperor Domitian became worried about Agricola's brilliant military reputation, far better than the Emperor's own, and by the fact that

---

11 Tac. *Ann.*, 6.30.
12 On Gaetulicus and the Emperor Tiberius, see B. Levick, *Tiberius the Politician* (London, 1976), 205–6.

Agricola had now been in command of the large Roman army in Britain for seven years. The Emperor decided he had to be removed. The question was: how to do it? The answer: very delicately. An imperial envoy was sent to Britain with orders to offer Agricola the prestigious imperial province of Syria in exchange for his leaving Britain at his already allotted time, but this "treaty" was to be made only if the envoy found Agricola still in command of the powerful British army.[13] The way Tacitus tells it, Agricola, out of patriotism, had already given up his command when the envoy arrived, so he never received another.[14] The historian later draws a very painful contrast between Agricola's previous life of glory and personal independence in Britain, and the utterly quiet life the government forced him to live once back in Rome.[15] Yet Tacitus's final judgment is that Agricola acted honorably in surrendering precisely his condition of independence in Britain (his *libertas*) in exchange for the obedience (*obsequium ac modestia*) necessary to preserve the peace of the Empire as a whole.[16] In the long history of the Roman Empire, of course, there were many commanders of military provinces who chose differently, who chose the ultimate independence of becoming emperors themselves, rather than facing the difficult transition to *obsequium ac modestia*. They preferred to *imitate* Caesar rather than obey him, and they marched on Rome.[17]

So to repeat: When intellectuals, writers, and statesmen of later ages worried about "Caesarism" in the particular sense of the danger which imperial administrators might pose to a central government, they were basing their fears on a real historical phenomenon. Of course, many of the people I now turn to discuss were themselves the beneficiaries of thorough Classical educations, and so they knew their Roman history very well indeed, which, in turn, perhaps helps explain their fears. This is important, because their fears in fact turned out to be exaggerated.

Here are two examples of fear from the British Empire. It is a fact that the creation of what were essentially imperial provinces ruled by tyrants – the classic examples being Bengal after 1757 and British Africa after the 1880s – caused a continual cultural and political concern in important circles within Britain itself. The concern was twofold: first, the blatant contradiction of the British, a people with a tradition of political freedom, tolerating despotism exercised in their name overseas; second (and more important here), the possibly harmful impact of returning imperial administrators on British political

---

13 Tac. *Aqr.*, 39–40.
14 Ibid., 40.
15 Ibid., 40, end.
16 Ibid., 42.
17 On Agricola and the Emperor Domitian, see R. Syme, *Tacitus* (Oxford, 1958), 122–4.

life. For it was feared that out in the Empire, they had developed a despotic political counterculture harmful to Britain's freedom-loving traditions.

The first crisis over this phenomenon of empire occurred in the 1770s and 1780s, when men who had made huge fortunes in the new East India Company province of Bengal, primarily by violence, chicanery, and outright theft exercised on the indigenous population, began returning home to Britain. They arrived with unprecedented fortunes in hard cash and, it was feared, with very bad habits. Popular plays such as Samuel Foote's *The Nabob* presented the returning imperial administrators as highwaymen, that is, men who had become accustomed to living by armed robbery. Moreover, they were men corrupted both by the sexual lasciviousness and political ruthlessness endemic to India. Thus Sir Matthew Mite, *The Nabob*'s protagonist (modeled on Sir Robert Clive, founder of British Bengal) has brought home to Dublin with him an actual harem of Indian women, whom he keeps imprisoned by eunuchs. Even worse, however, is that he has learned the habits of bribery in India and ruthlessly spreads his money to undermine the traditional political system, so that he can bribe his way to a seat in Parliament. He acts, we are told, in ways unacceptable "in a country of freedom." As the character Lady Oldham remarks, "With the wealth of the East, we have imported the worst of its vices."[18]

Part of Caesar's power, too, and his arrogance, had rested on vast wealth amassed in Gaul by utterly ruthless means. Moreover, the anxieties described above appeared not only in the theater, but in Parliamentary action. By 1772–3, Parliament itself was investigating the conduct of the East India Company men in Bengal, yet East India money was simultaneously corrupting that very investigation. It was in this context that Horace Walpole could declare: "What is England now? A sink of Indian wealth, filled by nabobs... A senate [Parliament] sold and despised." A pamphleteer of this time depicts the returning Bengal administrators as men carrying sacks of diamonds stolen from Indians they have tortured – the beneficiaries of villages, towns, and entire provinces ransacked and destroyed. The author warns that if the Company is not bridled, it will become "subversive of the liberties of Englishmen, and creative of a set of tyrants."[19] Twenty years later, we find Edmund Burke warning Parliament of the same spectre during his impeachment of the powerful, violent, and corrupt Bengal governor Warren Hastings. Not to condemn Hastings would undermine Parliament as

---

18 On the cultural and political significance of Samuel Foote's play *The Nabob* (1773), see now L. James, *Raj: The Making and Unmaking of British India* (New York, 1997), 45–7.
19 Ibid., 49.

an upright institution (privately, Burke wrote: "They are all bribed"), and it was upon Parliament that the liberties of Englishmen in good part depended. In addition, tyrannical behavior condoned in India would soon be imported into England, "so let you stand for the ancient laws and liberties of this kingdom; ... Let you stand the terror of tyrants!"[20]

No doubt some of this is merely the anxiety of an established landed class in the face of ruthlessly pushy nouveaux riches who had made it big in the overseas provinces. It is fear of loss of traditional place and political influence, as well as sheer snobbery (Horace Walpole is a particular example of the *beau monde*), disguised as fear for liberty at the hands of "tyrannical" nabobs. Even so, there was a striking practical impact. Hastings himself, it is true, was wrongly acquitted (after an impeachment process lasting nine years). But by means of the cultural and political campaign of the 1770s and 1780s, the East India Company's administrative methods, and the Company itself, were brought partially under direct government control. Moreover, a new administrative ethic, stressing stern and incorruptible uprightness and self-restraint as well as firm rejection of all "Indian" ways, was imposed on the old freebooters. The culture of the metropole, in other words, reached out and reasserted itself on its faraway imperial governors, who would no longer be allowed to develop bad habits and a subversive imperial counterculture. Many of the ways in which the British had conducted themselves in India now disappeared – or were actually reversed; it was an enormous cultural revolution, imposed from home. In time, the British administrative class in India, it was said, had become ineffably stodgy and bourgeois, and they were "more British than the British."[21]

But not quite all of them. Even as the cultural revolution from home was accelerating, British India produced one last proconsul in the mold of Caesar: Sir Richard Wellesley, Lord Mornington. Starting from the British base in Bengal, Wellesley (the Duke of Wellington's older brother) masterminded the British military conquest of most of India during his long Governor–Generalship of 1798–1805. He did it mostly against the wishes of the government in London as well as against the wishes of the Board of Directors of the British East India Company. Headstrong, ruthless, and brutal, a man who did not suffer fools gladly, he made vastly important decisions on his own, always in the direction of expansion ("If you do not like it, recall me," he wrote). He brooked no opposition from his subordinates, and none from the British community in India, upon whom he

---

20 See, e.g., R. Kirk, *Edmund Burke: A Genius Reconsidered* (Wilmington, 1997), 116–17.
21 On the cultural revolution: imposed on imperial administrators in India after 1780, see now James, *Raj*, 58–60 and 151–72.

imposed total press censorship. The only justification for his conduct was his deep intelligence and total success. Yet Wellesley's violent methods and character, and even the enormous scale of his success, worked against him once he returned to Britain. People in government distrusted him (for a variety of good reasons), and instead of becoming prime minister, which he expected and felt he deserved, he was plunged into immediate political obscurity.[22]

Even after the cultural revolution in British style in India, the old political fears about the tyrannical impact of the Indian experience remained. Thus in 1860 Richard Cobden worried that the basic problem had not altered: The habit of total command, necessary to rule in India, was still politically corrupting. "Is it not possible that we may be corrupted at home by the reaction of arbitrary political maxims in the East upon our domestic politics, just as Greece and Rome were demoralized by their contact with Asia?" He meant Asian autocracy. Cobden was quoted with approval in 1902 by the great theorist of imperialism John Hobson, who, however, went much further: The "reflux of this poison" of autocracy from the Empire back into England was not merely possible but inevitable. In the eighteenth century, Hobson said, the danger had taken the form of the threatening returning nabob, coming home with "the gains of corrupt and extortionate officialdom, a domineering demeanor, vulgarly ostentatious, and spreading his corrupting largess to ... degrade the life of our people." At the dawn of the twentieth century, it was the more austere but still despotic imperial administrator who was the danger:

> As the despotic portion of our Empire has grown in area, a larger and larger number of men, trained in the temper and methods of autocracy ... whose lives have been those of a superior caste living an artificial life removed from all the healthy restraints of ordinary European society, have returned to our country, bringing back the characters, sentiments, and ideas of this foreign environment. The South and South-west of England is richly sprinkled with these men, many of them wealthy, men openly contemptuous of democracy ... Everywhere they stand for coercion, and resistance to reform ... It is a nemesis of Imperialism that the arts and crafts of tyranny, acquired in the unfree empire, should be turned against our liberties at home. [These men] are hostile to the institutions of popular self-government, favoring forms of political tyranny and social authority which are the deadly enemies of liberty and equality.[23]

---

22 On Richard Wellesley and his career, see the instructive account in E. Ingram, *Commitment to Empire* (Oxford, 1981), Chapters IV and V. As Ingram says (118), Wellesley succeeded in doing what Bonaparte failed to do – he created a permanent empire for his country. They had similar personalities.

23 J. A. Hobson, *Imperialism: A Study* (London, 1902), 150–1.

Cobden and Hobson, however, might be dismissed as mere intellectuals and cranks. What are we to think, though, of the concerns expressed by John Morley, a high government official, Secretary of State for India from 1906 to 1910? A reformer of Indian administration and a biographer of Edmund Burke, Morley distrusted the British men on the spot in India, whom he suspected, as one writer says, "were Caesarian in instinct" and prone to regard coercion as the only solution to any political problem. An official once explained to him that the great Indian executive officers did not like or trust lawyers. "I tell you why," Morley snapped in reply: "*It is because they don't like or trust law*: they in their hearts believe before all else in the virtues of will and arbitrary power."[24] In other words, they had been corrupted by *imperii consuetudo*. The bitter emotion with which these remarks were expressed strongly suggests that Morley was not merely using the accusation of love of tyranny as a political bludgeon here against those who opposed his plan for somewhat increased Indian self-government. He knew his men and believed that the imperial experience was conducive to love of arbitrary command. It was so *un-British* not to trust in the law; but Morley said his countrymen succumbed to "the virus of authoritarianism" within mere weeks of landing in India. He came to believe that it would have been better for the British soul if Clive had lost at Plassy in 1757.[25]

Of course, to a great extent the fears of Cobden and Hobson and Morley turned out to be misplaced. Returning imperialists may not have been easily integrated into increasingly democratic Britain. There were eventually organizations such as the Imperial Fascist League of the 1920s headed by Arnold Spencer Leese, a renowned expert on camel diseases, but it never had more than several dozen members. More serious was that one significant social element in Oswald Mosley's British Union of Fascists in the 1930s was retired Imperial Civil Service officers and general Empire types of all sorts (including, it seems, T. E. Lawrence); Mosley himself was fascinated by Caesar. Retired ICS-types were always a reliable constituency for the right wing of the Conservative Party well into the 1960s. All in all, though, the imperial "internal threat" which seemed so vivid in intellectual and even high administrative circles in 1900–1910 never did develop very far.[26]

---

24 On Morley's severe distrust of the British men on the spot in India because of their addiction to unrestrained power, see James, *Raj*, 418–19.
25 Ibid., 419.
26 On the Imperial Fascist League, see R. Skidelsky, *Oswald Mosley* (New York, 1975), 291. The large number of retired ICS officers in Mosley's British Union of Fascists in the 1930s: Skidelsky, 320–1. T. E. Lawrence's links to Mosley: 350 (Lawrence was on his way to meet with a high BUF personality when he suffered his famous fatal motorcycle accident in 1935).

But what if the man returning from long service in the provinces and long disconnection from the home culture was an outstanding military leader with an awe-inspiring reputation and an egotistic, instinctively authoritarian personality? I am speaking now of General of the U.S. Army Douglas MacArthur. There is no doubt that in April 1951, when President Harry Truman finally found the courage to relieve him of his vast command in the Far East, MacArthur represented to many people the classic figure of the returning, threatening Caesarian proconsul; it was fourteen years since he had even set foot on the soil of the United States. Jokes – detailed jokes – circulated privately within the White House that MacArthur would now stage a coup d'état. Only jokes, of course, but jokes like that betray an underlying unease.

There was some reason for it. A much decorated frontline war hero in World War I (he rose from major to general in eighteen months of continuous fighting), MacArthur's amazing insubordination to civilian authority was already apparent in 1932, when, as Chief of Staff of the U.S. Army, he violently attacked and removed the Bonus March veterans from their campsite east of Washington, D.C., acting, extraordinarily, against the *direct* orders of President Herbert Hoover, twice repeated to him. He never apologized for it. The bold stroke, the imposition of his will, never looking back, were characteristic of MacArthur's personality and military philosophy: quite Caesarian (or Napoleonic: MacArthur did not mind being seen copying Bonaparte's most famous physical gesture as he stood commandingly on the bridges of ships). The president who succeeded Hoover, Franklin D. Roosevelt, put it bluntly: MacArthur was one of the two most dangerous men in America. The other, significantly, was the popular radio fascist Father Charles Coughlin. The combination of authoritarianism and demagoguery is, of course, the meaning of the term "Caesarism" as it has come to be used by most political scientists (though I am employing a more specialized meaning in this chapter). Moreover, FDR's judgment on the danger MacArthur posed to constitutional government was made in 1933: That is, a full decade before MacArthur's brilliant and spectacular victories in the Pacific in World War II had made him one of the most famous generals in American history.[27]

MacArthur's long years away from the United States in uninterrupted high military command – first as Field Marshal of the Philippine Army, then as Supreme Commander, Southwest Pacific, and finally as Supreme

---

27 On Franklin Roosevelt's judgment of the danger MacArthur posed to the Constitution, see W. Manchester, *American Caesar: Douglas MacArthur, 1880–1964* (Boston, 1978), 151–2.

Commander for Allied Powers (SCAP) – did nothing to lessen the fears within the Democratic Party caused by MacArthur's actions and attitudes. Typical of his disturbing egotism was his proclamation to the Philippine people upon landing in the Philippines in October 1944: "I have returned," he announced in lordly fashion; "Rally to me!" Not, one notices, to the United States. As governor of Japan between 1945 and 1951, he enjoyed a combination of total military and civilian powers unprecedented for any American Army officer. He used those powers forcefully to reconstruct traditional Japanese society according to his own sense of what was proper and just (including, as it happens, women's rights, as well as unions for workers): The impact of MacArthur's reforms, which overthrew centuries of tradition in a matter of months, including what is still called "the MacArthur Constitution," remains enormous even a half century later. The proconsul intentionally chose to put his headquarters right next to the palace of the Japanese Emperor, Hirohito, and it soon was called *Dai Ichi* ("Number One"). When the Supreme Commander rode in his huge limousine down to *Dai Ichi*, he was preceded by a corps of motorcycle outriders, a praetorian guard of six-foot tall black soldiers wearing special uniforms with yellow cravats. "I thought he was a king," one young girl (an American girl) said. It was a pardonable mistake. MacArthur's young son Arthur MacArthur was treated literally as a prince. A famous photograph popular in Japan showed him standing next to young Crown Prince Akihito, the Emperor's son; when he took up horseback riding, his mount was a thoroughbred from the Imperial family's personal stable; when he took up tennis, he was tutored by a Japanese Davis Cup winner; Japanese policemen saluted him wherever he went. I repeat, this was MacArthur's *son*, then aged ten. As for MacArthur himself, his naturally authoritarian style combined with his socially progressive reforms to make him both a comfortable and an immensely popular figure with the Japanese people. "You have the feeling," C. L. Sulzburger wrote in his diary, "that people almost bow down when they mention his name." This sounds uncomfortably like Caesarism as the term is indeed traditionally used: the sort of thing FDR had feared about MacArthur back in 1933. Charles Willoughby, one of MacArthur's two major aides, was an open admirer of Franco. Compared to this, MacArthur's subtle manipulation of the 1946 Philippine presidential elections so that the candidate he personally favored won, well, that was small potatoes.[28]

---

28 On MacArthur's proconsulship in Japan, and the autocratic mood there, see Manchester, *American Caesar*, 459–94. This is not to say that MacArthur did not have to work via broad guidelines set down in Washington; but the fact is that he was given a tremendous amount of free rein. On Willoughby's

All this immense power, all these startling trappings of royalty (which MacArthur immensely enjoyed), all of these things which were, again, unprecedented for an American Army officer, were perhaps tolerable as long as there was no division between the proconsul in Tokyo and the central government in Washington regarding policy. After all, people understood MacArthur's personal style. However, there came a time when such a division over policy occurred; the division was sharp, with contempt and fear soon being expressed on both sides; and it involved the brutally dangerous political issue of anticommunism.

MacArthur was appalled by the fall of China to the Communists in October 1949. He was appalled by the North Korean invasion of South Korea the next summer (June 1950). He viewed the State Department as at best incompetent, believed that Japan itself was now in peril, and thought that the crisis of the Cold War had come. Five years as absolute ruler of Japan had not lessened MacArthur's willfulness and self-confidence. Soon he was making his own foreign policy independent of Washington.

The events that followed were complex, but may be summarized as follows. In July and August 1950, without any authorization, MacArthur extended American military protection to Chiang Kai-Shek and the remnants of his Nationalist army on Taiwan, confronting President Truman (who had opposed this) with a fait accompli. MacArthur also indicated the possible "unleashing" of Chiang's forces against the Chinese mainland, without presidential authorization. We are still living with the consequences of these actions, which infuriated Secretary of State Dean Acheson, but which the proconsul of Japan got away with. After MacArthur's brilliant victory over the North Koreans at Inchon in September, he decided on his own to send American forces forward to the Korean-Chinese border, disregarding advice to be cautious both from the State Department and from the Joint Chiefs of Staff. The Chinese, of course, struck back with devastating effect in November–December. The administration's response was to seek some sort of negotiated peace. MacArthur's response was to advocate, publicly, the opposite: massive escalation, including the use of thirty-four Hiroshima-style atomic bombs on Chinese "sanctuaries" in Manchuria. In February–March 1951, the administration sent out careful peace-feelers for compromise. However, MacArthur wrecked this operation by publicly announcing his *own* "MacArthur" peace terms, which amounted to the unconditional surrender of the Chinese forces in Korea. Reprimanded privately for this,

---

admiration of Franco, see Manchester, *American Caesar*, 506. For MacArthur's manipulation of the 1946 Philippine election, 525–6.

within two weeks he had sent his famous "There is no substitute for victory" letter to President Truman's Republican enemies. The violent tone of that letter finally forced Truman to remove MacArthur from his vast Far Eastern command, since it was now clear that he was not obeying the central government.[29]

The great general dismissed from an unprecedentedly large and long provincial command by a government he despised: MacArthur was now in the position of Caesar in 49 B.C. In August 1950, after interviewing MacArthur, Averill Harriman had assured Truman that the Supreme Commander "was loyal to constitutional authority," an amazing assurance to have to give concerning an American Army officer. By April 1951, however, the Joint Chiefs of Staff had their doubts: General Omar Bradley wrote to Truman that MacArthur's conduct was on the verge of destroying civilian control over the military. The president's political situation was further weakened by charges, backed by MacArthur, that the State Department was filled with appeasers and communists. Truman's worst fears were realized when the removal of MacArthur set off a firestorm of protest across the country. Truman was burned in effigy and condemned by state legislatures; powerful newspapers called for his impeachment (or claimed he was being drugged by communist spies); the New York Veterans of Foreign Wars passed a resolution to march on Washington. As MacArthur's plane landed in San Francisco, he was greeted by massive, ecstatic crowds, "the clamor, the outrage against Truman grew greater and greater... Nothing had so stirred the political passions of the country since the Civil War."[30]

It was a true crisis of legitimacy, the crisis which Roosevelt eighteen years before had predicted MacArthur would eventually cause. The following internal memo from the White House, detailing MacArthur's arrival in Washington, demonstrates the mood there:

12:30: General MacArthur wades ashore from submarine
12:40: Parade to the Capitol, with General MacArthur riding an elephant
12:47: Beheading of President Truman's personal military representative (General Vaughn) in the Capitol rotunda
[Note the implications here that MacArthur's long sojourn in the Far East had turned him into an "Oriental Despot."]
1:00: MacArthur addresses Congress

---

29 Detailed narratives of these events can be found both in Manchester, *American Caesar*, 549–647, and in Michael Schaller, *Douglas MacArthur: The Far-Eastern General* (Oxford, 1989), 181–240.
30 On the explosion of public anger against the Truman government for the dismissal of MacArthur, see Manchester, *American Caesar*, 647–52; Schaller, *Douglas MacArthur*, 241–2. The quote is from David McCullough, *Truman* (New York, 1992), 647.

1:30: Congressional storm of applause begins
1:50: Burning of the Constitution
1:55: Lynching of Secretary of State Acheson
2:00: 21 atomic-bomb salute

This vision of a violent military coup is merely gallows humor. But as Michael Schaller (one of the major MacArthur biographers) says, it represents the actual depth of anxieties of destruction at MacArthur's hands running in the White House.[31]

Of course, nothing of the sort actually happened. MacArthur came to Washington and gave his speech before Congress, and it was successful, but in part because he ended it with the famous refrain, "Old soldiers . . . just fade away," which is exactly what Truman wanted MacArthur to do. MacArthur's testimony before the Senate in May 1952, which Truman feared would destroy his government, was actually a dud. MacArthur's keynote address to the Republican National Convention in July 1952, which MacArthur hoped would win him the Republican presidential nomination by acclamation, was another dud. Then the General disappears from politics.

"I could see him in his toga, imperiously mounting his chariot," said his adjutant when MacArthur was Commandant of West Point in the 1920s. However, MacArthur in 1951 was no Caesar and no Franco. Perhaps it was because he was old, seventy-one; Caesar had been twenty years younger when he crossed the Rubicon. Perhaps it was because he had only influence and little personal power or wealth; one should not confuse the New York VFW with Caesar's armed and trained veterans, and Caesar's personal wealth by 49 B.C. was about equal to the Roman State Treasury. Perhaps MacArthur's self-confidence had also been somewhat impaired by the fact that the Chinese had beaten him to a standstill, whereas Caesar had never been defeated in Gaul (or any place else). In other words, MacArthur in 1951, even after all his extraordinary experience of independent decision-making in the Far East, still had a sense of *limits*; Caesar in 49 B.C. had none. Thus, it turned out that MacArthur's real parallel in Roman history was not Caesar but Scipio Africanus, who, after heroic military successes for Rome in Spain, then against Hannibal, and then in the eastern Mediterranean, was forced into political retirement almost immediately upon returning to Rome.

My point is that important figures in the American government in 1950 and 1951 feared that things might turn out differently. Perhaps they had been reading too much Roman history or reading in the wrong *century* of

---

31 For the White House memo, interpreted as revealing actual deep anxieties, see Schaller, *Douglas MacArthur*, 242.

Roman history. But such is the power of Caesar's image – an image based, I have argued, on hard facts – that their fear is understandable. I end by noting that no American Army officer has ever again been given the combination of powers that MacArthur enjoyed in the Far East after 1945; none has ever again been allowed to develop a taste for such totally autonomous, imperial action. None has ever again been allowed to develop *imperii consuetudo*.

Index

1984 (Orwell), 98
absolutism, 10, 67, 70–1, 75, 81, 99, 201, 204, 209–10, 219
Académie Française, 94–5
Acheson, Dean, 295, 297
Ackerman, Bruce, 18, 210, 213–19
Agricola, 287–88
Ahala, C. Servilius, 267
Akihito, Japanese Crown Prince, 294
Albisson, Jean, 43–4
Alexander I, Tsar of Russia, 56
Alexander II, Tsar of Russia, 62–4
Altenstein, Karl Sigmund, 58
Alvensleben, General von, 64
American Revolution, 182
Amigues, Jules, 142
Ampere, J.J., 100
Ancien Régime, Le (Tocqueville), 84–5, 87, 99
anti-Semitism, 253
Antonius, 264
Appian, 269, 283
Arendt, Hannah, 20–1, 26, 241, 243, 244–60, 264
aristocracy, 77, 89, 125
Aristotle, 6, 88, 193
Arndt, Ernst Moritz, 60–1
Arnould, A.-H., 43
Art of War, The (Machiavelli), 173
Auerstedt, battle of, 55

Augustus, 2, 6, 88, 100, 275
authoritarianism, 79, 114, 139, 158, 164, 199, 209, 219, 292–3

Babeuf, François Noël, 176
Baehr, Peter, 155, 244
Bagehot, Walter, 5
Bainville, Jacques, 234
Bainville, John, 264
Barni, Jules, 130
Baroche, Jules, 148
Baumgarten, Hermann, 158
Berdahl, Robert, 70
Bergeron, Louis, 5, 300
Berlier, Théophile, 8, 32–4, 37–41
Berliner Politisches Wochenblatt (newspaper), 70
Berthier, Alexandre, 8, 45–7, 51
Billault, Adam, 137, 148
Birnbaum, Pierre, 223
Bismarck, Otto von, 5, 9–10, 25, 53, 62–5, 68, 72, 77, 79–80, 156–9, 161–2, 179
Blackbourn, David, 157
Blanquism, 107
Bluche, Frédéric, 5, 300
Bodin, Jean, 43
Bolshevik Revolution, 176
Bolshevism, 18, 20, 201–2, 208, 215
Bonaparte, Jérôme, 56

Bonaparte, Joseph, 29, 35, 48, 56
Bonaparte, Josephine, 30, 35–6
Bonaparte, Charles Louis Napoleon, 1, 5–6, 11–14, 24–5, 35, 56, 62, 68, 83–6, 92, 98, 100, 103, 105, 110–12, 116–18, 120, 122, 124–6, 129, 131, 180, 221, 223, 225, 227–8, 230–1, 233, 236–8, 242, 253, 264. *See also* Napoleon III
Bonaparte, Lucien, 31–3, 35, 56
Bonaparte, Napoleon, 1, 5–6, 8–11, 24, 29, 32, 35–6, 39–42, 45–8, 50–1, 53, 55–61, 67, 69, 74, 78–80, 83–5, 87–8, 90–1, 93–8, 101–2, 110, 112–14, 125, 129, 158, 179, 198, 209, 221, 223, 225, 228, 230, 232–5, 238, 240, 242, 245, 249. *See also* Napoleon I
Bonapartism, 2, 4–5, 7–11, 14, 16, 18–21, 25–6, 29, 67–8, 70–1, 73, 75, 79–81, 86–7, 98–9, 102, 104–5, 121–2, 126, 129–31, 135, 143–5, 148, 151, 156–7, 175–6, 178, 186, 193, 197, 199, 210, 221–4, 231, 237–8, 300
Bonjean, Louis-Bernard, 141, 146
Bonomi, Joseph, 181
Boulanger, Georges Ernest Jean Marie, 221, 264
Boulay de la Meurthe, Antoine Jacques Claude Joseph, 8, 33, 40
Bourbon dynasty, 43–4, 50, 56
Bourbon Restoration, 85
bourgeoisie, 79, 107, 110–12, 114, 116–17, 126, 138, 159–60, 162, 178, 182, 184, 186
Bradley, Omar, 296
Brezhnev, Leonid Ilyich, 244
British Union of Fascists, 292
Brüning, Heinrich, 16, 181
Brunswick Manifesto, 54
Brunswick, Duke of, 54
Bundesrat (Germany), 162

Buonarroti, Filippo, 176
Burckhardt, Jacob, 5, 171, 173
Bureaucratic Phenomenon, The (Crozier), 227
bürgerliche Gesellschaft, Die (Riehl), 77
Bürgertum, 77
Burke, Edmund, 241, 244, 289–90, 292

Cabanis, Pierre, 228
Cadoudal, Georges, 36, 45
Cadoudal-Pichegru plot, 45
Caesar, Julius, 2, 6, 22–4, 88, 100, 114, 124–6, 159, 162, 171–3, 179–80, 186–8, 198, 207, 209, 218, 232, 242, 264, 266, 272, 273–5, 279–90, 292, 296–8, 300
Caesarism, 2–4, 6, 11, 16–20, 22–6, 86–8, 91, 100, 105, 122, 124–5, 130, 155–69, 171, 173–82, 184, 186–91, 193–5, 197, 199, 202–3, 207, 209–10, 217–19, 245, 253, 258, 274–5, 279, 287–8, 293–4, 300
Caesaropapism, 235
Caligula, 287
Cambacérès, Jean-Jacques-Regis de, 31–2, 35–8
capitalism, 171, 223, 253
Carey, Joyce, 280
Carnot, Lazare Nicolas Margurite, 35, 41–4, 47–8
Catalano, P., 264
Catholic Center party (Germany), 80
Catholicism, 158
Catiline, Lucius Sergius, 188
Catilinian Conspiracy, the, 272
Cato the Younger, 282
Cavaignac, General Louis-Eugènel, 122, 264
Cessac, Comte de, 94. *See also* Lacuée, Jean-Gérard
Chaptal, Jean-Antoine, 30

Charlemagne, 46, 238
Charles X, of France, 237
Chateaubriand, François-René, 6, 13, 90, 300
Chiang Kai-Shek, 24, 295
Christian universalism, 70
Cicero, 171, 193, 272, 275, 283
Cincinnatus, Lucius Quinctius, 267
Cinna, 269
civil code (France), 42
civil society, 77, 111, 145, 177, 182, 184–5, 190, 192, 249
Civil War (United States), 213–14, 296
Civil War in France, The (Marx), 111, 223
Class Struggles in France, The (Marx), 103
Claudius, Emperor of Rome, 265
Clive, Sir Robert, 289, 292
Cobden, Richard, 291–2
Cold War, 295
Collard, Royer, 94
Commentaries (Caesar), 186
Committee of Public Safety (France), 7, 35, 42–3, 84
Communist Manifesto, The (Marx and Engels), 103, 107
Communist Party, 108
Communist Union, 200
concentration camps, 250, 256
Congress of Vienna, 62, 106
Conseil d'Etat (France), 232
Conseil des Prises (France), 39
conservatism, 67–9, 76, 81, 142–4, 158
Conservative Party (Great Britain), 292
Constant, Benjamin, 7, 88, 92, 102, 227
Constitution of the Year VIII (France), 33

Constitution, American, 212–14, 217
Constitutional Council (France), 223, 232
constitutionalism, 75, 197, 201–2, 204, 211, 213–15
Consulate, 1, 8, 12, 29–30, 32–3, 38, 40, 42–3, 45, 47, 101
consumerism, 258
Contribution to the Critique of Political Economy, A (Marx), 104
Cornwallis, Charles, 29
Corps Législatif (France), 48–9, 132, 135, 137, 141, 148–9
Cortes, Donoso, 5, 89
Costas, Louis, 43–4
Coty, René, 239
Coughlin, Father Charles, 293
Council of State (France), 8, 29–32, 36–8, 40–1, 44, 47–8, 51, 135, 140, 148, 223
Crassus, M. Licinius, 272–3, 281–2
Crimean War (1854–6), 62, 79
Cromwell, Oliver, 198, 263
Crozier, Michel, 226
Curée, Jean-François, 41, 45, 47

Danton, Georges-Jacques, 90
David, Jérôme, 136
De Gaulle as Political Artist: The Will to Grandeur (Hoffmann, Stanley and Inge), 234
De l'esprit de conquête et de l'usurpation (Constant), 92
De Staël, Anne Louise Germaine, 7
Decemvirs, 270
Deism, 210
Democracy and the Organization of Political Parties (Ostrogorski), 163
Démocratie en Amérique, De la (Tocqueville), 83, 90–1, 93–5, 98–100, 102
Democratic Party (United States), 294

Desaix de Veygoux, Louis Charles Antoine, 34
despotism, 42–3, 48, 71, 79, 83, 88–90, 92, 96–100, 129, 142–3, 194, 244, 276, 288
dictatorship, 2, 4, 6, 17–20, 22–3, 25–6, 71, 98, 101, 103–5, 109–10, 113–14, 116–17, 121–3, 125, 127, 175–7, 180, 184, 186–7, 191–4, 197–210, 214, 218–19, 241–5, 251–3, 256–7, 259, 263–6, 300
Dictatorship (Schmitt), 197, 200–3, 206
Dictatorship of the Reichspräsident According to Article 48 of the Weimar Constitution, The (Schmitt), 205
Diet of the German Confederation, 79
Directorial constitution (1795), 33
Directory (France), 42–3, 45, 110
Discourses (Machiavelli), 166, 173
Dittmer, Lothar, 69
Doumergue, Gaston, 16
Dreyfus Affair, 191, 253
Duhamel, Olivier, 223
Dupont, General, 47
Duvernois, Clément, 141

East India Company, 289–90
Ebert, Friedrich, 198, 207
Economy and Society (Weber), 167
Eighteenth Brumaire of Louis Bonaparte, The (Marx), 6, 13–14, 88, 103, 104, 108–10, 112, 114, 118–19, 121, 123, 223
Engels, Friedrich, 2, 5, 13, 103–4, 108–9, 118, 123, 176, 178, 193, 200
Enghien, Duke de, 52
Enlightenment, the, 58, 210, 212
Ense, Karl August Varnhagen von, 78
Épisode napoléonien, L' (Bergeron), 5, 300
Epstein, Klaus, 81

Ere des Césars, Le (Romieu), 87
Erweckungsbewegung, 69
European community, 233

Facta, Luigi, 181
Fascism, 16, 19, 20, 26, 176–7, 181–2, 189–90, 207–10, 219, 243–4, 246, 248
federalism, 135, 164
Federalist Papers, The (Madison, Hamilton, Jay), 212
Ferry, Jules, 276
Fichte, Johann Gottlieb, 58
Fifth Republic (France), 21, 223–24, 227, 229–30, 236
First Empire (France), 1, 5–7, 11–12, 14, 84, 88, 92, 94–8, 101, 131, 151
First Republic (France), 1, 229
Flocon, Ferdinand, 106
Foote, Samuel, 289
Fould, Achille, 148
Fourth Republic (France), 21, 228–30, 236
Francis Joseph, of Austria, 75
Franco, Francisco, 294–7
Frankfurter Zeitung (newspaper), 167
Frantz, Constantin, 77, 89
Frederick II, of Prussia, 53–4, 65, 72, 78
Frederick William II, of Prussia, 54
Frederick William III, of Prussia, 9, 56, 60, 69, 71
Frederick William IV, of Prussia, 10, 67, 70–5, 78, 80
French Revolution (1789), 2, 7–8, 11, 29–33, 37–40, 44, 47–50, 54–5, 57–8, 70, 72–3, 83–5, 87, 89–90, 94–5, 97, 101–3, 110, 132, 175, 182, 200–1, 221, 241–2, 244, 259, 263
French Revolution (1848), 2, 11, 83
Freslon, Pierre, 100

Index

Friedrich Wilhelm von Brandenburg, 74
Fröbel, Julius, 158

Gaetulicus, Cornelius Lentulus, 287
Gagé, J., 264
Gaius, 99
Gall, Lothar, 65
Gambetta, Léon, 130, 264
Garat, Dominique-Joseph, 31
Garnier, Charles, 144
Gaulle, Charles de, 21–2, 25, 221–4, 226–39
Gaullism, 21, 221–2, 223–4, 231, 238
Gerlach, Leopold von, 10, 67, 69, 71–2, 75, 80, 157
Gerlach, Ludwig von, 10, 67–71, 75–6, 78, 80
German Confederation, 62, 79
German Reich, 159, 161, 181
Germanism, 158
Geyl, Pieter, 235
Giolitti, Giovanni, 16, 181
Gladstone, William Ewart, 17, 165
Gobineau, Arthur de, 100
Goebbels, (Paul) Joseph, 244
Gorchakov, Prince, 63
Gracchi, Caius and Tiberius, 267–8, 271, 275
Gracchian crisis, 267
Gramsci, Antonio, 16–17, 19, 173, 175–94
Great Depression (United States), 213
Grévy, Jules, 236
Grünthal, Günther, 75, 77
Guardian of the Constitution, The (Schmitt), 205–8
Guicciardini, Francesco, 183

habeas corpus, 213, 266
Habsburg dynasty, 55, 73
Haffner, Sebastian, 74
Halévy, Elie, 264
Haller, Carl Ludwig von, 70
Hamilton, Alexander, 212
Hannibal, 297
Hardenberg, Karl August von, 54, 57, 69, 71
Harriman, Averill, 296
Hastings, Warren, 24, 289–90
Haussmann, Baron Georges-Eugène, 78–9, 139
Hegel, Georg Wilhelm Friedrich, 58, 192
Heine, Heinrich, 11, 300
Hennis, Wilhelm, 166
hereditary empire, 29, 37, 41, 48
Herman the German, 61
Herman's Battle (von Kleist), 61
Herrenvolk, 160–1, 170
High Conservatism (*Altkonservatismus*), 68
High Conservatives (Prussia), 10, 68–81
Hinckeldey, Carl Ludwig von, 10, 76, 78–9
Hindenburg, Paul von, 165, 208
Hirohito, Japanese Emperor, 294
History of Rome (Mommsen), 171
Hitler, Adolf, 4, 16, 20, 26, 181, 234, 241–4, 246, 249, 251, 253, 300
Hobson, John, 291–2
Hoffmann, Inge, 234
Hoffmann, Stanley, 224–6, 233–4
Hohenzollern dynasty, 53, 65
Holy Roman Empire, 53, 55, 236
Hoover, Herbert, 293
House of Lords (Great Britain), 51
Huber, Ernst Rudolf, 81
Hugo, Victor, 124, 129, 238
Human Condition, The (Arendt), 258–9
Humboldt, Wilhelm von, 58

Ibbeken, Rudolf, 59
Imperial Fascist League (Great Britain), 292

imperialism, 2, 11, 14, 16, 86, 142, 253, 291

Jacobin constitution (1793), 33
Jacobinism, 75, 222
Jacobins (France), 49, 102, 207
Jarcke, Carl Ernst, 69
Jard-Panvillier, 8, 44
Jena, battle of (1806), 55
Josephus, 274
Julia (daughter of Julius Caesar), 281–2
July Monarchy (France), 85, 93, 115, 133

Kant, Immanuel, 57–8
Kapp Putsch (Germany), 185, 189
Kergorlay, Louis de, 91–2
Kershaw, Ian, 5, 257, 300
Kissinger, Henry, 70, 79
Kleist, Heinrich von, 61
Koselleck, Reinhart, 58
Kraus, Hans-Christof, 70
Kreuzzeitung (newspaper), 67, 70, 75, 78, 80
Kroll, Frank-Lothar, 70
Krüger telegram (1896), 157

Lacépède, Bernard-Germain-Etienne de
Lacouture, Jean, 229
Lacuée, Jean-Gérard, 94
Lamartine, Alphonse Marie Louis de Prat de, 236
Langlois, Claude, 33
Lanjuinais, Jean Denis, 31
Lawrence, T. E., 292
Le Bon, Gustave, 166
Le Play, Pierre Guillaume Frederic, 140
Lebrun, Albert, 237
Lebrun, Charles François, 31
Leese, Arnold Spencer, 292
Lefebvre, Georges, 234

Legality and Legitimacy (Schmitt), 205–6, 208
Legion of Honor (France), 42
Legislative Assembly (France), 94
Lenin, Vladimir Ilich Ulyanov, 26, 184–5, 192–3
Leninism, 87, 176
Leo, Heinrich, 69
Leon, Daniel de, 104, 119
Lepidus, 264, 272
Lewin, Moshe, 5, 300
liberal democrats, 175
liberalism, 39, 65, 67, 87, 177, 182, 190, 197, 206, 210–12, 214–16, 219
Lincoln, Abraham, 213
Lloyd George, David, 17
Locke, John, 211, 219
Locré, Jean-Guillaume, 36
Louis Philippe, of France, 74, 106, 111
Louis XV, of France, 54
Lucan, 283
Ludendorff, Erich, 219
Ludwig II, of Bavaria, 53
Luise of Prussia, 60, 74
Lukács, Georg, 109
Lützen, battle of (1813), 57

Mably, Gabriel Bonnet de, 200
MacArthur, Douglas, 24, 293–8
MacDonald, Ramsey, 181
Machiavelli, Niccolo, 171, 173, 178, 180, 183, 193, 197, 245, 249, 259
Machiavellianism, 245
Machtpolitik, 159, 176
Madison, James, 212
Maistre, Joseph de, 70, 72
Manin, Bernard, 211–12
Mann, Michael, 257
Mannheim, Karl, 81
Manteuffel, Otto von, 10, 76–80
Maoism, 16, 20
Marat, Jean Paul, 263

Marius, 269, 272, 275
Mark Antony, 286
Marwitz, Friedrich August Ludwig von der, 69
Marx, Karl, 2–3, 5–7, 11, 13–14, 24, 88, 103–26, 129, 156–7, 176, 178–9, 192–3, 200, 222–3
Marxism, 103–4, 108–9, 114–15, 121, 197
mass democracy, 131, 156, 163, 165–6, 201, 219
mass media, 194, 207
mass society, 258
Mastellone, S., 264
Mathiez, A., 264
Maximus, Q. Fabius, 267
Medici, Lorenzo de' (il Magnifico), 178
Meinecke, Friedrich, 58
Metternich, Clemens Wenzel Nepomuk Lothar, 71
Mignet, François, 234
Mithridates, 269
Mithridatic War, 272
Mitterrand, François, 222, 224
Moltke, Helmuth von, 53, 64, 66
Mommsen, Hans, 257
Mommsen, Theodor, 171–2, 263–6, 268, 270
monarchy, 29, 30, 33, 37, 41–3, 47, 66, 70, 74, 76–7, 83, 87, 107, 110, 114, 116, 201, 244, 270, 275, 285
Moniteur (journal), 41
Montesquieu, Charles de, 6, 48, 88, 211, 244
Moreau, Jean-Victor, 35
Morley, John, 292
Mornington, Lord, 290. *See also* Wellesley, Sir Richard
Morny, Charles Auguste Louis Joseph, 137, 148, 237
Moroccan crises (1905, 1911), 157
Mosley, Oswald, 292

Münchow-Pohl, Bernd von, 59
Murat, Joachim, 56
Mussolini, Benito, 16, 181–2, 207, 242–4, 246, 248

Nabob, The (Foote), 289
Napoleon I, of France, 9, 12, 165
Napoleon III, of France, 9–10, 12, 14, 16, 62–5, 67, 102–3, 111, 129, 131–3, 140, 146, 151, 156, 158, 165, 187, 226, 275
Napoléon le petit (Hugo), 129
Narbonne, Count of, 54
Narochnitskaya, L.I., 63
Nasica, Q. Caecilius Metellus Pius Scipio, 282
National Assembly (France), 31, 37, 48, 54, 116, 117, 120, 231
National Assembly (Germany), 205
National Socialism, 20, 182, 209
National Socialist Party (Germany), 18, 209
nationalism, 65, 207, 218
Nationalökonomie, 166
Nazism, 5, 16, 20, 26, 174, 189, 248–9, 257–8, 300
neoconservatism, 219
Neufchâteau, François de, 41, 49, 50–1
Neumann, Franz, 243
Neumann, Sigmund, 81
New Deal (United States), 214
Niebuhr, Marcus, 69
Nietzsche, Friedrich Wilhelm, 171–3
nihilism, 256, 258
North German Confederation, 158

Octavius, 264
oligarchy, 50, 188, 192, 271
Ollivier, Emile, 141, 144
Opimius, 267–8
Origins of Totalitarianism, The (Arendt), 244, 246, 253, 258–9
Orwell, George, 98

Papen, Franz von, 181
parliamentarism, 75
Pasteur, Louis, 238
Peace of Paris (1856), 64
peasantry, 77, 109, 111–13, 118, 124, 178, 186
Pericles, 165
Persigny, Jean-Gilbert-Victor, 135–6, 237
Persigny, Jean Gilbert Victor Fialin, 146–9
Pétain, Henri Philippe, 16
Pfordten, Baron von der, 53
Pharsalus, 273, 279
Phillips, George P., 71
Pinard, Ernest, 142, 145
Pirate War, 272
Plato, 192–3
Plutarch, 268
Polemarchus, 192
Political Theology (Schmitt), 202–4
Politics as a Vocation (Weber), 164
Pollio, C. Asinius, 279
Polybius, 6, 88, 266, 285
Pompey, 271–3, 281–6
Pompidou, Georges, 22, 227, 231
popular sovereignty, 65, 72, 84, 95–6, 101, 117, 121–2, 200, 202, 209
Principate (Rome), 6, 23, 86, 275
Prison Notebooks (Gramsci), 19, 178
proletariat, 110–11, 126, 159–60, 186, 192, 199–200, 202, 208, 252, 264
Proudhon, Pierre Joseph, 5, 125, 236–7
Provisional Government (Russia), 106, 185
Prussian Reform Movement, 9, 56, 58

Quentin-Bauchard, 147

radicalism, 158, 244
Radowitz, Joseph Maria von, 69, 73
Ranke, Leopold von, 58
Rassemblement Pour la République (RPR), 238
Raudot, Claude-Marie, 144
Realpolitik, 79, 171, 176
Regnaud de Saint-Jean d'Angély, 8, 31, 37–8, 44
Reichstag (Germany), 162, 181, 207
Rémond, René, 21, 130, 221–2
Republic, American, 259–60
Republic, French, 37–8, 41–2, 52, 62, 85, 98, 103, 105–6, 111, 115, 117, 129–32, 151, 203
Republic, The (Plato), 192
republicanism, 130
Restauration der Staatswissenschaft (von Haller), 70
Reynaud, Paul, 230
Rheinische Zeitung (newspaper), 106
Richter, Melvin, 83, 121
Riehl, Wilhelm Heinrich, 77
Riga Memorandum (Hardenberg), 57
Risorgimento (Italy), 19, 177, 182, 183, 190
Robert, Charles, 238
Robespierre, Maximilien, 90
Roederer, Pierre Louis, 8, 31–2, 35, 48, 50–1
Romanism, 158
Rome (Empire), 93, 99–100, 280, 287–8
Rome (Republic), 2, 6, 22–3, 86, 88, 100, 102, 125, 162, 172, 187, 197, 228, 236, 242, 275–6, 283–5
Romieu, Auguste, 87, 89
Roosevelt, Franklin Delano, 213, 293–4, 296
Roscher, Wilhelm, 163
Rouher, Eugène, 134, 136, 139–40, 148
Rousseau, Jean-Jacques, 58, 232
royalists (France), 49, 51, 118, 143
Rufus, M. Minucius, 267

Saegert, Carl Wilhelm, 76
Sans-culottes, 84
Savigny, Friedrich Karl von, 69
Schäffle, Albert, 163
Schaller, Michael, 297
Scharnhorst, Gerhard Johann von, 59
Schinkel, Karl Friedrich, 60
Schleicher, Kurt von, 16, 181
Schmitt, Carl, 17–19, 197–219, 259
Scipio Africanus Major, 268, 283, 285, 297
Scipio Africanus Minor, 268
Scipio Emilianus, 270
Second Empire (France), 7, 11–15, 25, 67–8, 80, 84–5, 89, 93, 98, 100–3, 111–12, 129–33, 135–6, 139–40, 144, 147–8, 150–2, 155, 222, 224, 231, 235–7, 300
Second Empire (Germany), 155
Second Punic War (218–201 BC), 267
Second Republic (France), 1, 14, 228–9, 236
Sedan, battle of (1870), 65, 158
Segesser, Philipp Anton von, 158
Séguin, Philippe, 238
seigneurialism, 30
Senate (France), 29–33, 35, 37, 40–2, 47–51, 135, 141, 232, 273, 285, 287
Senate (Rome), 23, 99, 125, 203, 265–7, 271, 275, 279, 281–6
Senate (United States), 216, 297
Sieyès, Emmanuel Joseph, 30, 58, 200, 228
Smith, Adam, 9, 58
socialism, 102, 136, 147, 171
Socialist Party (France), 224
Socialist Section Francaise de l'Internationale Orvrière (SFIO), 224
Society of 10 December (France), 121, 126
sociology, Weberian, 87, 166–7, 169, 173

Solon, 232
Soviet Communist Party, 208
Spengler, Oswald, 173
St.Jean d'Angély, Regnaud de, 37
Stahl, Friedrich Julius, 10, 69, 75
Stalin, Joseph, 241, 243–4, 246, 249, 251, 255
Stalinism, 5, 16, 20, 87, 174, 257–8, 300
Stein, Freiherr Karl vom, 9, 57–8
Stein, Lorenz von, 5
Strauss, David Friedrich, 72
Stuart dynasty, 43
Suetonius, 272, 283
suffrage, 33, 84, 85, 117, 121–2, 124, 131, 135, 137, 139, 142, 145–7, 150–1, 158, 252
Sulla, Lucius Cornelius, 22–3, 198, 264, 267–75
Sulzburger, C. L., 294
Sybel, Heinrich von, 72, 159

Tacitus, 276, 287–8
Talleyrand Perigord, Charles Maurice de, 8, 31, 35, 231
Taylor, A.J.P., 60
Thibaudeau, Antoine, 30–4, 37–8
Third International, 25–6
Third Republic (France), 15, 226, 230, 236
Thirty Years War, 55
Thody, Philip, 122
Thucydides, 105
Tiberius, 99, 287
Tilsit, treaty of (1807), 56, 60, 74
Tocqueville, Alexis de, 5, 11–14, 24, 83–102, 219, 223, 228
Tombs, Robert, 66
Totalitarian Dictatorship and Autocracy (Friedrich, Brezinski), 26
totalitarianism, 4–5, 16, 20, 26, 87, 241, 243–9, 251–4, 256–60
Treaty of Amiens (1802), 29–30

Treitschke, Heinrich von, 72
Tribunate (France), 8, 29–30, 37, 40–2, 44–6, 48
Triumvirs, 264
Tronchet, François-Denis, 31
Trotsky, Leon, 16
Truman, Harry, 24, 293, 295–7

Ulpian, 99

Valdrôme, Chevandier de, 141
Vergniaud, Pierre Victurnien, 54
Vogel, Barbara, 69
Voss-Buch, Carl von, 69

Wagener, Hermann, 10, 69
Walpole, Horace, 289–90
Washington, George, 11, 232, 293, 295–7, 300
Waterloo, battle of (1815), 228
Wealth of Nations, The (Smith), 58
Weber, Max, 5, 16–17, 19, 155–73, 224–6, 245, 247, 249, 252, 259

Wehler, Hans-Ulrich, 81
Weimar Republic, 17–18, 198, 205, 208
Wellesley, Sir Richard, 24, 290–1
Werner, Anton von, 53, 65
What is Enlightenment? (Kant), 58
Wilcken, U., 264, 270
Wilhelm II, emperor of Germany and king of Prussia, 72, 157
William I, of Germany, 53
William of Prussia, 62
Willoughby, Charles, 294
Wittelsbach dynasty, 53
Wittgenstein, Prince, 71
Woloch, Isser, 29, 94
working class, 107, 122, 159, 166, 178, 201
World War I, 17, 25, 219, 242, 254, 293
World War II, 4, 16, 20, 293

Yellow Peril speech (1905), 157

Zeldin, Theodore, 131